RACE AGAINST EMPIRE

RACE AGAINST

EMPIRE BLACK AMERICANS AND

ANTICOLONIALISM

1937–1957

Penny M. Von Eschen

CORNELL UNIVERSITY PRESS

ITHACA AND LONDON

First published 1997 by Cornell University Press
First printing, Cornell Paperbacks, 1997

Printed in the United States of America

"Rum and Coca-Cola," music by Jeri Sullavan and Paul Baron, lyric by Morey Amsterdam, additional lyric by Al Stillman. © 1944 (Renewed) EMI Feist Catalog Inc. All rights reserved. Used by permission of Warner Bros. Publications U.S. Inc., Miami, Fla. 33014.

Library of Congress Cataloging-in-Publication Data

Von Eschen, Penny M. (Penny Marie)
  Race against empire : Black Americans and anticolonialism,
1937–1957 / Penny M. Von Eschen.
      p.   cm.
  Includes bibliographical references and index.
  ISBN 0-8014-3197-2 (cloth : alk. paper).—ISBN 0-8014-8292-5
(pbk. : alk. paper)
  1. Afro-Americans—Politics and government. 2. Afro-Americans—
Race identity. 3. Anti-imperialist movements—United States—History—
20th century. 4. African diaspora. 5. Pan-Africanism—History—20th
century. I. Title
  E185.615.V66   1996
  325'.3'08996073—dc20
                                                            96-22283

Paperback printing   10   9   8   7   6   5   4

FOR MY FRIEND GERALD HUDSON

CONTENTS

PREFACE

THE IDEA FOR THIS BOOK began to take shape at a time when the end of the Cold War, accompanied by frequent announcements of "the end of history," also witnessed continuing U.S. intervention abroad, assaults on working people worldwide, and a rapid acceleration of global economic inequality. With the untrammeled nature of U.S. power ever more apparent, I was drawn to the story of a group of men and women who had confronted this global reach at its genesis. The title, *Race against Empire*, speaks in part to their sense of urgency as U.S. political, economic, and military dominance crystallized in the aftermath of World War II. It also points to the compassionate, expansive racial solidarity that animated their global democratic vision. The Cold War era's "end of ideology" blithely celebrated the superiority of America when the United States was still a Jim Crow nation, and while millions of Africans and other colonized peoples not only struggled for political independence but fought the economic exploitation that had characterized colonialism and was further solidifying under new forms of U.S. domination. Against the grain of cynicism about democratic and internationalist projects that has deepened with the more recent assertion of "the end of history," and against the racism that continues to render invisible black political initiatives, we would do well to remember the ways in which African American anticolonial activists of the 1940s demanded a genuine transformation of global power relations.

Over the years, the international nature of this project has necessitated an exceptional dependence on the advice, generosity, and kindness of teachers, friends, and strangers. Marika Sherwood and Hakim Adi introduced me to sources in London, and Marika generously shared her home, her ideas, and her extensive international research on anticolonial projects. In Johannesburg, Keith Breckenridge, Cathy Burns, Clive Glaser, Tom Lodge, and Lumkile Mondi guided me around archives and South African historiography. I also thank Keith Breckenridge, Cathy Burns, Tom Lodge, and Karin Shapiro for valuable advice on early portions of the manuscript. In Cape Town, Alan Hirsch and Pippa Green shared their home, set up interviews, and directed me to important sources. Numerous librarians and archivists have provided invaluable assistance. I particularly thank Anna Cunningham of the Historical Papers Library at the University of the Witwatersrand in Johannesburg.

A generous grant from the MacArthur Committee on Peace and International Security of the Social Science Research Council allowed me to travel to South Africa for interviews and research, and to meet Sam Nolutshungu, whose insights on international politics and South Africa in particular have helped shape this project. Critical to the development of the project were interviews with activists in South Africa; A. M. Kathrada, Govan Mbeki, Henry Mohothe, Ray Simons, and Walter Sisulu not only generously shared their memories and perceptions of the late 1940s and early 1950s but also pointed me to valuable newspaper and archival sources. Conversations with Palo Jordan helped clarify my sense of the 1950s and the impact of the Cold War on international solidarity movements. A special thanks to Rica Hodgson for helping me set up interviews. On this side of the Atlantic, many thanks to Lloyd Brown and the late Doxey Wilkerson for sharing their memories and insights.

I owe an enormous debt to Eric Foner. His work inspired me to study history and continues to set an endlessly challenging example of committed scholarship and teaching. From the time when this book was a series of questions and hunches, he has been an immensely supportive and encouraging guide, as well as my most perceptive and exacting critic. I am profoundly grateful. This book has also benefited from the generous criticism and advice of Alan Brinkley. I thank Manning Marable for conversations about George Padmore and C. L. R. James, and Joshua Freeman for wise and generous counsel at crucial moments. Elizabeth Blackmar offered astute criticism, wise advice, and support at every point.

Special thanks to colleagues Leah Arroyo, Martha Biondi, and Sarah Henry for reading and commenting on drafts of the manuscript. Conversation with Martha Biondi about the 1940s and 1950s has been one of the pleasures of this project, and I am grateful for her invaluable criticism and constant support. I also thank Mark Higbee, Lynette Jackson, Anne Kornhauser, Melinda

Lawson, Sumit Mandal, Manisha Sinha, Jotsne Uppal, Michael West, and Wang Xi.

This study owes much to a community of friends and scholars. My greatest intellectual debt is to my friend Gerald Hudson. I thank him not only for years of conversation and love but for the outrageous imagination, uncontrollable spirit, and deep commitment to democracy as a philosopher and trade unionist that have inspired and shaped my work. Conversations over the years with Jerry Watts, along with his penchant for showing up with the right book at the right time, have been vital. A very special thanks goes to Robin D. G. Kelley, first as a fellow historian with an exceptional commitment to getting it right and an extraordinary generosity of spirit, and then as a wise adviser and kind friend. He has been pivotal in my thinking and revision of the manuscript. Thanks also to David Anthony, Joanne Barkan, Paul Buhle, Barbara Caress, Leo Casey, Darío Euraque, Barbara Fields, Moe Foner, Gary Gerstle, Jim Giblin, Michael Harris, Winston James, Mark Levinson, Peter Mandler, Tony Marx, Anne McClintock, Polly Moran, Rob Nixon, Warren Orange, Susan Pennybacker, Michael Pollak, Gyan Prakash, Haneen Sayed, Carl Schorske, Ellen Schrecker, Joe Schwartz, Nancy Sinkoff, Shelton Stromquist, Pamela Von Eschen, and Cornel West.

A Rockefeller Fellowship from Princeton University's African American Studies Program enabled me to complete this book and, and, most important, provided an endlessly stimulating and supportive intellectual community. I am especially grateful to Arnold Rampersad, Nell Irvin Painter, Judith Jackson Fossett, Jeffrey Tucker, Eddie Glaude, Jean Washington, and Hattie Black. Particular thanks to Judith Jackson Fossett for lending her sharp eye and intellect to the manuscript.

I am indebted to Peter Agree at Cornell University Press for his enthusiasm and his wise advice at critical moments and to Terence McKiernan for his expert editorial stewardship. I am extremely fortunate to have had Thomas Borstelmann and Carl Nightingale as initially anonymous readers for the Press. Borstelmann also generously shared his work at an early stage, and I have relied on his advice and scholarship to wade through the murkier waters of international politics. He has truly been a sympathetic and meticulous critic.

My first sense of egalitarianism and internationalism came from my parents, Avis and Clarence Von Eschen. I thank them for that, along with their unfailing generosity and enthusiastic love and support. Warm thanks also to friends and siblings Patrice Von Eschen, Lou Tilmont, Paula Von Eschen, Atta Orange, Diane Orange, John and Beth Von Eschen, Mary Ann Von Eschen, Kevin Fox, and Catherine Metzger.

Finally, it is absolutely impossible for me to imagine what the work on this manuscript might have been without the companionship and constant critical engagement of Kevin Gaines. His sensitive insights and spirited suggestions have enriched the book in many ways, and his love and support have made it a far more joyful adventure than I had ever dreamed possible. There are no words to express my gratitude or my love.

PENNY M. VON ESCHEN

Iowa City, Iowa

RACE AGAINST EMPIRE

INTRODUCTION

It is not culture which binds the peoples who are of partially African origin now
scattered throughout the world, but an identity of passions.
                                            —Ralph Ellison, *Shadow and Act*

ON NEW YEAR'S DAY IN 1940 Americans thrilled to Paul Robeson's
singing of "Ballad for Americans" over the CBS airwaves. The son of a former
slave and an internationally renowned singer and Shakespearean actor, Robeson
had the extraordinary artistic talent and the capacity for empathy to express the
hopes and dreams of a country just emerging from the Great Depression and
facing the prospect of war. Using the same imagination with which he embraced the world's music, languages, and peoples as his own, Robeson projected
in music a vision of a prosperous America not divided by race, ethnicity, or
creed. His deep, sonorous voice moved Americans from all walks of life with the
at once playful and somber lyrics. To the repeated question "Who are you?" the
song recounts an unfinished history of democratic struggle, naming and embracing all of America's peoples, until the answer is finally revealed: "America."[1]

Yet a decade later, Robeson was officially pronounced "un-American." In
1950 the United States government revoked his passport and rejected his appeal because as a spokesperson for civil rights he had been "extremely active in
behalf of the independence for the colonial peoples of Africa." Two years later
the U.S. attorney general subpoenaed the files of the Council on African Affairs, of which Robeson was chair, demanding "all [CAA] correspondence with
the African National Congress and the South African Indian Congress" and
with "all individuals and leaders" of those groups.[2]

As the Cold War emerged, the Truman administration was forced to contend
with Africans and African Americans articulating links between liberation

movements in Africa and the struggles of African Americans for civil and economic rights in the United States. For Robeson connected his own life and history not only to his fellow Americans and to his people in the South but to all
the people of Africa and its diaspora whose lives had been fundamentally
shaped by the same processes that had brought his foremothers and forefathers
to America. And in giving voice to what Ralph Ellison has called "an identity of
passions," Robeson was hardly alone. African American anticolonial activists of
the 1940s forcefully argued that their struggles against Jim Crow were inextricably bound to the struggles of African and Asian peoples for independence.
From Alphaeus Hunton's insistence that the liberation of Africa would make a
concrete difference the struggles of black Americans to Walter White's argument that "World War II has given the Negro a sense of kinship with other colored—and also oppressed peoples of the world," activists articulated a common
experience of racial oppression rooted in the expansion of Europe and the consequent dispersal of black laborers throughout Europe and the New World.[3]

This book traces the rise and fall of the politics of the African diaspora from
the late 1930s to the early Cold War years. At its heart is the story of a political
project among an international group of activists and intellectuals and how their
vision—for a time—animated African American politics. To make sense of their
project and its ultimate demise, one must keep an eye on several interrelated political processes. The rapid acceleration of Asian and African challenges to European domination and the crumbling of European hegemony during and in the
wake of World War II coincided with the creation of a U.S. wartime alliance with
the major European colonial powers and the Soviet Union, followed by the shift
of the Soviet Union from ally to adversary. Moreover, the United States emerged
as the dominant global power, a position from which the American government
fashioned new responses to Asian and African nation-building projects. In the
intersections of these broad processes one begins to understand the development
and collapse of the politics of the African diaspora.[4]

To illuminate facets of anticolonial politics and trace the relationship between anticolonial politics and the history of the United States emerging as a
world power, the book focuses on the most visible and defining anticolonial
projects, including African American participation in the 1945 Manchester
Pan-African Congress; support of Nigerian trade union struggles and the fight
against the British suppression of Nigerian newspapers; support for striking
South African miners; and the joint efforts of African Americans, South
Africans, and the government of India in the early days of the United Nations.

By the last years of World War II, internationalist anticolonial discourse was
critical in shaping black American politics and the meaning of racial identities
and solidarities. As the wartime challenges to colonialism reached fruition in
the unusually fluid situation following the war, and the formation of the

United Nations provided a forum for international debate and organization, diaspora identities had a powerful resonance and diaspora politics achieved a particular political efficacy. With the imminent independence of India and the promise of new Asian and African states in the foreseeable future, the possibilities for winning political and economic rights through international strategies looked much brighter than they would after the onset of the Cold War.

This politics in the making did not survive the beginnings of the Cold War. Differences proved stronger than the still fragile international institutions and ideologies. As African American liberals began to craft a dominant civil rights argument of the Cold War era, that discrimination at home must be fought because it undermined the legitimate U.S. leadership of the "free world," and the parallel argument for an anti-Communist anticolonialism, the Truman administration and the State Department embarked on far-reaching attempts to shape Asian and African perceptions of American "race relations." An integral part of these efforts was the systematic repression of those anticolonial activists who opposed American foreign policy and who fought for the visibility of the oppression of all black peoples against a bipolar reading of politics that rendered the opression of Africans and people of African descent a secondary issue. The embrace of Cold War American foreign policy by many African American liberals, as well as U.S. government prosecution of activists such as Robeson and the CAA, fundamentally altered the terms of anticolonialism and effectively severed the black American struggle for civil rights from the issues of anticolonialism and racism abroad. This book further explores the reshaping of black American political and rhetorical strategies in the early Cold War and the attendant rewriting of the meanings of "race" and "racism." The 1950s eclipse of 1940s anticolonialism had profound implications for the politics of the black American community as questions concerning political, economic, and social rights in an international context were neglected in favor of an exclusive emphasis on domestic political and civil rights.

The significance of the politics of the African diaspora lies both in its creative reinterpretation of a larger diaspora tradition and in its unique contribution to the world of the 1940s. The diaspora politics of this period stood in a complex relationship to African nation-building projects. Those black Americans who constructed diaspora identities did not posit themselves as members or potential members of a nation or advocate a return to Africa in the sense of a back-to-Africa movement. Yet the politics they fashioned did constitute a re-turning toward Africa and an identity defined in relation to Africa. With the demise of European hegemony and the emergence of strong anticolonial movements on the African continent, African Americans claimed a shared history and argued that independent African nations would help their struggles for political, economic, and social rights in the United States. The promise of new African and

Asian nations in the near future, coupled with hope that the United Nations would provide a forum in which issues of racial, colonial, and economic oppression could be addressed on an international scale, gave political immediacy to this vision.

Moreover, in articulating a democratic and internationalist politics, anticolonial activists spoke to issues at the center of the reshaping of America in the post–World War II era: the relationship of the United States to emerging Asian and African nations; definitions of democracy, freedom, and the very meaning of American citizenship and what it entailed; how political, economic, and civil rights were to be defined and who in America and across the globe was to have access to these rights. And in articulating common desires and ideals, black intellectuals and journalists increasingly elaborated a conception of democracy that put the struggles of black peoples at the center of world politics but encompassed *all* democratic struggle. The solidarities and identities they formed were necessarily racial, because they saw race at the heart of the processes shaping the modern world: the enslavement of Africans, the exploitation of colonial peoples, and the development of racial capitalism. At the same time, precisely because they recognized the importance of race, anticolonial activists could point beyond it to a vision of a genuinely democratic world.

As wartime political alliances and innovations in mass communications radically altered the boundaries of the possible, this shared democratic vision gave rise to new political strategies. The new international forums and plans for the United Nations Organization that emerged in the later years of the war enhanced the possibility of redefining political sovereignty and individual and group rights on an international scale. And African Americans—from the avant-garde international left of Paul Robeson and W. E. B. Du Bois to the National Association for the Advancement of Colored People (NAACP), churches, fraternities, and nurses' associations—came to see these forums as hopeful sites for their own struggles and brought to them a new vision of the rights and responsibilities of citizenship.

The power of the 1940s politics of the African diaspora came from its evocative linking of the 400 million black people scattered about the globe, as well as its descriptive and analytic value. Along with the political recasting of peoples denied political, economic, and civil rights from a national minority to a global majority, the notion of a diaspora invokes a profound history and materiality. The very concept of diaspora suggests a story about how a people got from one place to another—in this case, the story of the expansion of Europe and the consequent dispersal of black laborers throughout Europe and the New World.[5] It is not accidental, then, that the architects of the politics of the African diaspora were historians who, more systematically than most, understood racism and shared bonds in the context of the history of slavery, colonialism, and imperialism. Not only Du Bois, as the foremost historian and intellectual, but African American popular discourse in the 1940s linked African Americans with Africa and the Caribbean, not because there were biological blood ties but because their differing experiences of slavery and colonialism were all seen as part of the history of the expansion of Europe and the development of capitalism.

The international anticolonialism of the 1940s was a creative, political project among an international group of activist intellectuals. Activists who came from radically different regional political economies and lived within different national boundaries engaged in a lively debate about the nature of their bonds and the political strategies best suited to their common liberation. Far from assuming a homogeneity based on "race," they often saw themselves as engaged in an innovative project. For example, W. E. B. Du Bois argued in 1945 that "Africa is a vast and deeply separated continent and its unity must be a matter of future upbuilding rather than of past fact. Nevertheless, the people of Africa and more especially the darker peoples of Negro and mulatto origin, have in modern day, increasingly common oppression, desires and ideals."[6]

This book seeks to identify the political leaders, intellectuals, journalists, and activists who articulated the bonds between black Americans, Africans, and all oppressed peoples; to emphasize their creative interventions in a rapidly changing world of war; and to trace the processes by which their vision came to animate African American political discourse. Focusing on the Council on African Affairs, (led by Paul Robeson, Max Yergan, Alphaeus Hunton, and in later years W. E. B. Du Bois) and on the NAACP (led by Walter White) as the major organizations involved in anticolonial politics, it also emphasizes the critical role of the black press and trade unions in reshaping international political debates and crafting new political strategies.

The first four chapters trace the emergence and elaboration of anticolonial politics during World War II and the immediate postwar period. Chapters 1 and 2 show the forging of a new political language by activists and journalists whose vision of the fate of black Americans as inseparably linked to the fate of Africans and other colonized peoples animated African American political thought in a powerful and unprecedented fashion. The roots of this vision lay in the contested left of the 1930s, but it was the anticolonial challenges of World War II that gave it new power and substance. Chapter 3 explores the importance of trade union organizations to the politics of the African diaspora and looks at African American participation in the 1945 Manchester Pan-African Congress and support of African labor. Chapter 4 examines the diaspora-based strategies that coalesced in 1946 and 1947 as the black American Council on African Affairs, the South African Passive Resistance Campaign, and the African National Congress (ANC) came together at the United Nations to support India's challenges to the South African government. At the dawn of the modern civil rights movement, anticolonialism and civil rights marched hand in hand.

The later chapters trace the eclipse of the politics of the African diaspora and argue that this must be understood as the result of several related political processes. Chapter 5 probes the breakdown of broad anticolonial alliances following the widespread acceptance of the Truman Doctrine of 1947. For many liberals, the criticism of American foreign policy gave way to an acceptance of America's claim to be the legitimate leader of the free world. In a fundamental reshaping of black American political and rhetorical strategies, anticolonialism did not disappear but, for liberals, was increasingly justified by an anti-Communist agenda. The repression of the McCarthy era devastated the anticolonialism of the left as well, destroying the vestiges of the 1940s politics. Chapter 6 explores the American government's prosecution of anticolonial activists in the Council on African Affairs in the context of American political objectives in Africa, and the government's far-ranging responses to African and Asian nationalism.

Chapter 7 considers the impact of the destruction of 1940s anticolonialism on mainstream African American perceptions The eclipse of historical analysis led to a renewed trivialization, exoticization, and marginalization of Africa; the liberal definition of "freedom" in the 1950s reconstructed "race" and "racism" from something understood as rooted in the history of slavery and colonialism to something seen as a psychological problem and an aberration in American life, and from an international to a "domestic" problem. Discussions of international politics began to open up again in the mid-1950s but in radically altered terms from those of the 1940s. Chapter 8 probes the extent to which African American intellectuals, politicians, and journalists accepted the new position of America in the world as legitimate, exploring their participation in the Asian-African Conference in Bandung and the Congress of Colored Writers and Artists in Paris, and perspectives on Ghanaian independence.

In the opening epigraph, Ralph Ellison calls our attention to the power of human bonds across national and cultural boundaries. To speak of "an identity of passions" is to speak about an achievement, not something given but something that might be made. Architects of the politics of the African diaspora forged an identity of passions through a powerful cross-fertilization of socialist internationalism and the struggles of colonial peoples for independence. Yet if the anticolonial politics of the 1940s cannot be understood outside the context of 1930s internationalism, neither can it be subsumed under or fully explained by the leftist project. The intellectual and institutional links were tangled and complex as international solidarity movements among the colonized peoples of the globe creatively reshaped the language and ideologies of the 1930s and constructed the politics of the African diaspora.

CHAPTER ONE

THE MAKING OF THE POLITICS
OF THE AFRICAN DIASPORA

> In the deep, heavy darkness of the foul-smelling hold of the ship, where they could not see the sky, nor hear the night noises, nor feel the warm compassion of the tribe, they held their breath against the agony. . . . In a strange moment, when you suddenly caught your breath, did some intimation from the future give to your spirits a hint of promise? In the darkness did you hear the silent feet of your children beating a melody of freedom to words which you would never know, in a land in which your bones would be warmed again in the depths of the cold earth in which you will sleep unknown, unrealized and alone?
>
> —Howard Thurman, *On Viewing the Coast of Africa*

THE SENSE THAT AFRICAN AMERICANS shared a common history with Africans and all peoples of African descent had long been an important part of African American thought, but the global dynamics unleashed by World War II brought it to the forefront of black American politics and animated political discourse at an unprecedented level. Many African American political leaders and journalists analyzed the war through a prism of anticolonialism. A new political constellation emerged as anticolonial issues acquired a new prominence and stood side by side with domestic demands in the political agendas of leading African American protest organizations.[1]

From the 1935 Italian invasion of Ethiopia to the strikes that swept the Caribbean and West Africa in the late 1930s, from Nigerian responses to Roosevelt and Churchill's dispute over the meaning of the Atlantic Charter to India's dramatic challenge to the British during the war, African American political discourse was keenly informed by and deeply responsive to events in Africa, in the Caribbean, and throughout the colonized world. Even issues which on the surface appeared strictly domestic, such as the use of black American troops in the war, were approached from an anticolonial perspective and guided by the premise that the struggles of black Americans and those of Africans were inseparably bound. By the end of the war in 1945, even mainstream civil rights leaders such as Walter White, executive director of the NAACP, could declare that "World War II has given to the Negro a sense of kinship with other colored—and also oppressed—peoples of the world."

Black Americans, he continued, sense that "the struggle of the Negro in the United States is part and parcel of the struggle against imperialism and exploitation in India, China, Burma, Africa, the Philippines, Malaya, the West Indies, and South America."[2]

Although the articulation of inextricable ties between African Americans and others of African descent and the attention to anticolonialism were widespread among African American leaders and journalists by the mid-1940s, these issues did not arise uniformly. The crafting of a new international political language and new political strategies, as well as how these came to animate a broader political discourse, can be understood only by looking at the initiatives of the men and women who created this politics both through political organizing and through print capitalism and the black press. The years of World War II and its immediate aftermath were a golden age in black American journalism. Newspapers with national circulations such as the *Pittsburgh Courier* and the *Chicago Defender* more than doubled in size between 1940 and 1946. The *Courier* reached a circulation of more than a quarter-million, with an actual readership easily three times that size.[3] This was also the heyday of Claude Barnett's Associated Negro Press—a syndication service subscribed to by nearly two hundred papers, or 95 percent of black American newspapers—which made international reporting widely available to small black papers that otherwise would not have had the resources to carry reports on African, Caribbean, and international affairs.

The black press was the main vehicle through which public intellectuals spoke to one another and to their main audiences: the black middle classes and working classes, including teachers, ministers, other professionals, and blue-collar and domestic workers.

Moreover, creatively employing the new technologies and new possibilities in communication that came out of World War II, a cast of activists, journalists, and editors clustered in black American newspapers—the *Chicago Defender*, the *Pittsburgh Courier*, the *Crisis*, and the *New York Amsterdam News*—formed a dense nexus with journalists and publishers from London to Lagos and Johannesburg, marshalling the resources of important black middle-class and entrepreneurial institutions to create an international anticolonial discourse. From Pittsburgh to Lagos to Chicago to London to New York to Johannesburg—the nodal points of production—print journalism both provided the vehicle for the creation of this imagined diaspora and unified intellectuals and activists across the globe.[4]

THE ROOTS OF THE POLITICS OF THE AFRICAN DIASPORA

In linking the struggles of African Americans to African peoples worldwide, architects of the politics of the African diaspora drew on a body of thinking dating back to the eighteenth and nineteenth centuries. In the mid-nineteenth century black American nationalists such as Martin R. Delany and Henry Highland Garnet combined a vision of independent black organizing in the United States with calls for black emigration, sometimes to South America or Canada, sometimes to Africa. Delany, especially, pioneered the creation of a global analysis and a vision of black solidarity that embraced a truly Pan-African sensibility. Inspired by slave revolts that had revealed Pan-African aspirations—such as the South Carolina freedman and artisan Denmark Vesey's plans in 1820 to establish ties with Haiti—Delany created the character Henry Holland in his novel *Blake* (1859–61). Holland, a free black man, tries to organize a revolt involving all the slaves in the Western Hemisphere. Moreover, Delany's presentation of slavery as an international system of economic exploitation further links him to the politics of the 1940s.[5]

Although worlds apart from the projects and aspirations of the internationalists of the 1940s, the civilizing missions of black Christians such as the nineteenth-century black nationalist missionary Alexander Crummell, who spent twenty years in Liberia, and the Ethiopianist tradition in black thought also embodied a belief in universal black solidarity and salvation. Through their wide reach in black American middle-class institutions, these earlier projects were a critical part of the milieu in which later activists formed their own world views and aspirations.[6]

In the twentieth century, a vision of the African diaspora was given a voice in the NAACP's journal the *Crisis*—which, under the long editorship of W. E. B. Du Bois, consistently presented the struggles of the black world in international terms—and in Carter Woodson's *Journal of Negro History* as well.[7] In a life that spanned the rise and fall of colonialism, from the European partition of Africa in Berlin in 1884 and 1885 when he was still a child to his death in Ghana in 1963, six years after the new nation's independence, Du Bois possessed a keen awareness of history. He resisted the prevailing discourses that naturalized colonialism and race. From the earliest issues of the *Crisis*, readers were reminded that colonialism had a beginning. And in the gift of historical imagination, whatever has a beginning, constructed by human actions, may also have a middle and an end.

Du Bois was also a founder of the Pan-African Congress movement. From the turn of the century, Pan-Africanist intellectuals gathered in the 1900, 1919, 1921, and 1927 Pan-African Congresses to challenge the excesses of colonial rule, to establish intellectually the existence of a bond between Africans and persons of African descent in the diaspora, and to demonstrate the importance of Pan-African unity for building an emancipatory movement.[8] Delegates to the early congresses articulated an elite ideology and, more accommodationist than anticolonial, appealed as intellectuals to European powers to act more humanely (see Chapter 2). The carnage of World War I and the mistreatment of colonial subjects, however, demonstrated that colonial metropoles were unreceptive to humanitarian appeals. The war also deepened the integration of African societies into the world economy and unleashed a major migration of peoples of African descent within the Western Hemisphere, setting the stage for the emergence of new kinds of movements and new forms of Pan-Africanism.[9]

The early Pan-African Congresses, however, remained the province of intellectuals and a small African American elite. It was Marcus Garvey and his Universal Negro Improvement Association that brought the notion of the links between the black world and Africa to a mass audience, creating a new working-class diaspora consciousness. By linking the entire black world to Africa and its members to one another, Garvey made the American Negro conscious of his African origins and created for the first time a feeling of international solidarity between Africans and peoples of African descent. In a brutal era of Jim Crow, lynchings, and political disenfranchisement, Garvey transformed African Americans from a national minority into a global majority.[10]

Garvey remained ambiguous in his critique of the West. His thought and movement embodied unprecedented forms of organization and a modern diasporic sensibility, yet at the same time he embraced many of the ideals and forms of Western imperialism and colonialism. The same period, however, also saw a flowering of nationalists on the left such as Hubert Harrison, Cyril Briggs, and the African Blood Brotherhood, who unequivocally rejected beliefs in the superiority of Western civilization. Historians have documented the rich cross-fertilization of leftist and Pan-African movements, beginning most visibly after the Russian Revolution. Although these movements were partly inspired by Bolshevist ideals, the Soviet Comintern and the American Communist Party were also pushed to acknowledge—implicitly if not explicitly—the distinct histories of black laborers throughout the globe, leading to their advocacy of black self-determination and formations such as the Negro Trade Union Committee. As Robin D. G. Kelley has argued, the Communist Party often provided, if inadvertently, spaces in which black nationalists were able to carve out considerable autonomy. Thus, by the 1930s, not only had the left helped to reshape nationalist thought, but the internationalism of the left—responding to assertions of black nationalism—had already been transformed by its appropriation of Pan-African thought.[11]

In addition to traditions of Pan-Africanism and left internationalism, the broad anticolonial alliances of World War II built on the rich black oppositional politics of the 1930s. Through diverse protest efforts such as the "Don't Buy Where You Can't Work" campaign, the Scottsboro case, and the NAACP's anti-lynching crusade, the modern civil rights struggle was beginning to get under way with an increasing emphasis on economic issues. The development of alliances among liberals, leftists, and nationalists around a broad agenda for black working-class empowerment and social and economic justice crystallized in the formation of the National Negro Congress in 1936 with A. Philip Randolph as its president.[12] The loyalties forged in these movements, alongside continuing personal, ideological, and organizational divides, would all play a role in the new wartime alliances and shape the emerging anticolonial movement.

THE ETHIOPIAN CRISIS

The Italian invasion of Ethiopia in 1935 marked an especially critical moment in the articulation of diaspora thought and politics. Paul Robeson claimed it was a watershed for black American consciousness, since it exposed "the parallel between [black American] interests and those of oppressed peoples abroad."[13] As the historian William R. Scott has demonstrated, the black American press and churches played major roles in publicizing the Ethiopian crisis in the United States. The invasion also ushered in a new chapter in the organizational history of anticolonialism with the formation of numerous new nationalist groups such as the Ethiopian World Federation.[14]

Many black nationalists viewed the invasion of Ethiopia as a skirmish in a race war of European (and Japanese) colonial expansion, in which Ethiopia was the last holdout of real independence in Africa. Black nationalists also viewed as racist the indifference of Western nations to a clear fascist attack. Communists, in contrast, through the Provisional Committee for the Defense of Ethiopia (PCDE) in Harlem, attempted to redirect antiwhite sentiment toward a critique of fascism.[15] The tensions between these differing interpretations of the Ethiopian conflict, between the racial interpretations of the war held by many black nationalists and the strictly antifascist interpretation advanced by the Communist Party, would be overcome in part during World War II. Like black supporters of the Republican cause in Spain—who, as Kelley has demonstrated, combined Pan-African and internationalist sentiments in a way that "accepted the Communists' vision of internationalism and inter-racial unity" which "allowed them to retain their nationalism and to transcend it"—architects of the politics of the African diaspora would successfully bridge and transform these two world views by arguing that anticolonialism and antiracism were necessary pre-conditions for democracy everywhere.[16]

BLACK BRITAIN

In Britain, the invasion of Ethiopia led to the politicization of Harold Moody's League of Coloured Peoples, previously devoted to education, and to the formation of the International African Service Bureau.[17] The founding of the bureau in 1937 formalized the gathering in London of a remarkable group of black intellectuals. Led by Trinidadians George Padmore and C. L. R. James, along with Jomo Kenyatta, the future president of Kenya, the bureau attracted students, intellectuals, trade unionists, and political activists from Africa and the Caribbean, who had traveled to London (sometimes via the United States) for the educational, intellectual, and political opportunities it afforded.

To catapult back into the black Britain of the 1930s is to discover a tiny, close-knit community of intellectuals who had formed longstanding and dense relationships—social, intellectual, and political—that transcended personal and ideological differences. This group of transplants from colonial societies—who still maintained strong ties to their homelands and were aware of the burgeoning trade union and anticolonial activities there—grasped the vulnerability of colonialism and predicted its collapse over the next decade. In analyzing, interpreting, and helping to shape this process, they creatively reshaped the leftist politics of the 1930s.

George Padmore provides an ideal entry point into this world. Padmore's journey took him from a British colony in the African diaspora to black American colleges, to an interracial American and international left, and finally to international Pan-Africanism. Born in Trinidad in 1902, Padmore became a journalist while still in his teens. He wrote for student publications at Fisk and Howard universities while studying in the United States from 1925 to 1928. In 1928 he dropped out of Howard's law school to work full time in antiimperialist and national liberation movements.[18] He joined the U.S. Communist Party and became the secretary of its International Trade Union Committee of Negro Workers and editor of the *Negro Worker*. In 1930 he went on a speaking tour of West Africa and helped plan the First International Conference of Negro Workers, held in Hamburg, Germany, in July 1930.[19] Traveling between western Europe and Moscow, Padmore quickly rose to a position of prominence in the Communist International as its reigning expert on race and imperialism. Among the many pamphlets and essays he wrote for the Comintern was *The Life and Struggles of Negro Toilers*.[20]

By 1933 Padmore had broken with the Communist Party. By his own account, he resigned after the Comintern "liquidated" the Negro Trade Union Committee and suspended publication of the *Negro Worker*. According to Earl Browder, however, Padmore was expelled from the party because of his view that the "road to liberation of the Negroes lies through race war of these 'darker races' against the whites."[21] Padmore returned to England, where he published *How Britain Rules Africa* in 1936 and *Africa and World Peace* in 1937. In 1937 he cofounded the International African Service Bureau in London with C. L. R. James, an anticolonial activist and Trotskyist theorist, and I. T. A. Wallace-Johnson, a trade unionist and journalist from Sierra Leone. After James went to the United States and Wallace-Johnson returned to Sierra Leone, Padmore dominated the bureau until it merged into the Pan-African Federation in 1944. The federation in turn provided the core of organizers for the Manchester Pan-African Congress in 1945, a critical moment in the formation of diaspora politics and a key turning point in Pan-Africanism.[22]

These activists came together despite clearly articulated political differences. In fact, their broad ideological debates and substantive differences in interpretation, policy, and vision helped push Padmore's own intellectual development and gave rise to a new radical critique of colonialism. C. L. R. James exerted a critical influence on Padmore. Interestingly, Padmore's *The Life and Struggles of Negro Toilers* had been written for white workers; Padmore had believed that successful anticolonial revolt required revolutions in the metropoles in order to weaken the European powers. James, on the other hand, in his 1938 *A History of Negro Revolt*, placed black people at the center of world events and insisted that the western revolutionaries of the modern world needed Africans as much as the Africans needed them. Thus, in debates with James, Padmore developed a deeper sense of the centrality of the struggles of Africans and colonized peoples in global politics, an analysis that proved singularly appropriate and appealing as World War II unleashed an array of anticolonial challenges and accelerated the crumbling of European hegemony.[23] Organizations such as the International African Service Bureau and Caribbean and West African activists such as Padmore and Wallace-Johnson helped to impart a new urgency to anticolonial issues in America. They laid the foundation and created the context for a politics linking the struggles of African Americans with those of Africans and other colonized peoples.

Padmore especially, through his journalism, crafted a popular language for the international movement that animated black American discourse in the 1940s. Writing for the *Chicago Defender* and *Pittsburgh Courier* nearly every week from 1938 to the late 1940s, and providing in-depth essays for the *Crisis* several times every year, he had a profound impact on African American political thought. During World War II he served as African correspondent for the Associated Negro Press, making his reports widely available to black American newspapers. As a prolific journalist and essayist for African American, West Indian, West African, and British newspapers, he also facilitated communication among anticolonial activists in the United States, Britain, the Caribbean, and, in later years, West Africa.[24]

The African American anticolonial politics of the 1940s had a decided bias toward the Anglophone world. Political leaders and writers did monitor the entire range of colonial powers, emphasizing changes in French West Africa during and after the War, and devoting considerable attention to Dutch and Belgian colonialism. Yet the bulk of African American journalism, and almost all the political organizing and direct political support were related to British West Africa, the Caribbean, or southern Africa. This bias was clearly related to questions of language and culture, but was also the result of differences in types of colonialism, between the French model of assimilation and the British model of indirect rule.

PADMORE READING HIS FAVORITE NEWSPAPER

George Padmore occupies a unique position in the world of letters and has garnered international fame through his uncompromising fight for the rights of colonial peoples throughout the world. He is best known as London correspondent for The Courier. Mr. Padmore is shown in the library of his London apartment reading an issue of The Pittsburgh Courier.

George Padmore reading the *Courier* in the office of his London home, 1943. *Pittsburgh Courier,* July 31, 1943.

THE INTERNATIONAL BLACK PRESS

The early reshaping of internationalism through print capitalism can be observed in the sympathetic attention of the African American press to strikes across the Caribbean and West Africa in the late 1930s. A series of strikes began in Trinidad and swept the Caribbean region in 1937 and 1938.[25] African American journalists treated labor unrest and recurrent clashes with police in the West Indies not as isolated problems but as illustrations of the oppressiveness of the entire colonial system.[26] Journalists emphasized the worldwide impact of the strikes, noting similar revolts and discontent in Morocco, Tunis, and Algiers; Vancouver, British Columbia; and Batavia, Surabaja, and Bandung in the Dutch East Indies.[27] Moreover, discussion of the strikes enabled the analyses of labor and political economy that permeated black American journalism in the 1940s. Calling the riots in the West Indies "symptomatic of a general feeling of unrest throughout the whole colonial world," the *Defender* argued that the "prevalent poverty" of colonial workers was a consequence of "the imperialist policy of using both the people and their lands for the benefit of vested interests," thus forcing people into "semi-starved conditions."[28]

George Padmore was the most influential journalist writing on the strikes in the Caribbean. In a 1938 series of essays in the *Crisis* he discussed the repressive policies of the colonial governments and emphasized the intertwining of political and economic exploitation as workers were deprived of their "most elementary civil rights, such as freedom of the press, speech, and assembly."[29] Padmore typically offered careful analyses of political economy. In "Labor Trouble in Jamaica" he explained the economic differences between Trinidad, where petroleum and asphalt industries supplemented agriculture, and agrarian Jamaica. Because of high taxation, a rising cost of living, and a corresponding decline in the price of agricultural products, Jamaican peasants were losing their land or being forced to augment their incomes through work on plantations. Small banana growers fell completely at the mercy of foreign monopoly capitalists, the United Fruit Company of America and others, who controlled the export market and dictated the price of bananas.[30] Padmore played a dual role as journalist and activist. While he provided regular coverage from London and the West Indies of official British inquiry into labor conditions in Trinidad, African American newspapers highlighted the role of the International African Service Bureau in bringing issues affecting the peoples in the British colonies before the House of Commons.[31]

By the 1950s, as an adviser to Kwame Nkrumah in the newly independent nation of Ghana, Padmore had developed an extremely anti-Communist version of African socialism. But throughout the 1940s his antagonistic position toward the Communist International was aligned with neither anti-Soviet, anti-socialist, nor even anti-Stalinist Trotskyist socialist groups. Rather, in a powerful example of how the anticolonial project displaced classic political divisions, Padmore maintained close relationships with activists and trade unionists of several schools, from the Trotskyist James to the Communist Wallace-Johnson to a broad spectrum of American liberals and leftists. Sharp differences would arise among members of this anticolonial generation in the 1950s; the international movement fragmented when faced with the pressures of national liberation struggles unfolding on a Cold War terrain. But in the late 1930s and early 1940s, although political differences might foster debate or even personal antagonisms, they did not preclude cooperation.

If the black press was critical to the making of the politics of the African diaspora, freedom of the press—indeed, for African activists such as I. T. A. Wallace-Johnson, survival of the press—was always precarious.[32] Secretary of the Sierra Leone Trade Union Congress and Youth League, and one of the founding members of the International African Service Bureau, Wallace-Johnson was another important architect of 1940s anticolonialism. Beginning in the 1930s, he was one of the most important West African trade unionists and journalists over the next decade.[33] Though not as visible among African Americans as Padmore, he was an important anticolonial figure and provided access to African news for black Americans through his Sierra Leone–based *African Standard*. The *Courier*, for example, reprinted articles from the weekly and covered Wallace-Johnson's trade union activities.[34] Black American journalists monitored the suppression of Wallace-Johnson's *African Standard* in 1939 under colonial sedition, undesirable publication, and deportation ordinances and his subsequent imprisonment in 1940.[35] The *Courier* reported that Wallace-Johnson had been arrested and sent to a concentration camp without trial under the Colonial Defense Regulations, and the paper's editor and publisher were also imprisoned for publishing an attack on the Sierra Leone government for its treatment of Wallace-Johnson.[36]

African American newspapers followed boycotts and strikes in other West African colonies as well, always framing the disputes in the context of colonial oppression. As he had with coverage of the West Indies, Padmore provided a significant amount of the reporting on West African strikes, served as a liaison between the British, West African, and American press, and offered in-depth analyses in the *Crisis*.[37] A 1937 *Defender* article reported from London that "Gold Coast Africans have caused a panic among London and Liverpool export merchants" by declaring a boycott of British merchandise. Boycotters had sparked the publicity by adopting the tactics of Indian leader Mahatma Gandhi, paralyzing trade and disrupting the lucrative cocoa industry.[38] The *Defender* covered the cocoa strike as it continued into 1939 (involving "hundreds of thousands of native farmers"), reported the censorship of strike news in the British press, and publicized the International African Service Bureau's support. Stressing that the strike had given rise to an unprecedented cross-class political alliance and a new "African solidarity," the *Defender* announced that the farmers were backed by the Gold Coast youth movement, the Aborigines' Rights Protection Society, and the Nigerian youth movement.[39] Interest in the cocoa strike brought attention to many other conflicts engendered by colonialism. A single issue of the *Defender* addressed a wide range of issues: Arab opposition to the partitioning of Palestine, the reception in Germany of George Padmore's *How Britain Rules Africa*, the alarm of Belgian Congo officials at the influence of the labor movement in the French Congo, the setting up of a labor school in Mexico, the approval by the League of Nations of Italy's rule in Ethiopia, and the activities of Marcus Garvey in London.[40]

The world of the black left in Britain shaped the development of African American politics in yet another and perhaps equally profound fashion by attracting and influencing leading black American intellectuals such as Paul Robeson and Ralph Bunche. Robeson encountered this dynamic community in

London in the 1930s, where he got to know not only James and Padmore but such future African leaders as Nnamdi Azikiwe and Jomo Kenyatta, and, later, Kwame Nkrumah. Testifying to the impact of these meetings, Robeson recalled, "I discovered Africa in London." He studied African linguistics at the University of London, and his growing political involvement was deeply connected to his interest in African music and culture.[41] And just as that interest cannot be disentangled from his involvement in the diaspora circles of London, his commitment to anticolonialism cannot be severed from his growing commitment to the left.

As his biographer Martin Duberman has richly demonstrated, numerous forces shaped Robeson's personal and political development: travel to the Soviet Union in 1934 and 1937, a 1938 trip to Spain in support of the Republican cause in the Spanish Civil War, the friendship with Jawaharlal Nehru and his sister Vijaya Lakshmi Pandit that resulted from his support for Indian independence and the Indian National Congress in 1938.[42] The work of his wife, Eslanda Robeson, on Africa and her 1937 trip to South Africa also had a powerful impact. Still, without oversimplifying the array of his influences and experiences, it is clear that Robeson's sojourn in London was critical to his development. These activities and relationships fit very neatly into his world of popular-front socialism with its advocacy of broad democratic rights and—especially for black intellectuals and activists—of anticolonialism.

THE COUNCIL ON AFRICAN AFFAIRS

In 1937 Robeson helped to found the organization that became the Council on African Affairs.[43] Over the next fifteen years, black American anticolonial activists in the CAA helped keep the issue of colonial liberation on the U.S. agenda and provided links to international anticolonial networks and African liberation groups. With the onset of Cold War hostilities, splits in the CAA exposed tensions endemic to many of the late 1940s alliances of leftists and liberals. Finally, in the early 1950s, the CAA was at the center of anticolonial activists' dramatic confrontation with the government as the United States sought to stifle internal opposition and make itself the undisputed leader of the "free world."

Robeson, a major donor and fund raiser and chief policymaker, served as chair of the CAA for most of its life. Other leaders included W. Alphaeus Hunton, who joined the organization in 1943 as its educational director and later became executive director; and W. E. B. Du Bois, who served as vice-chair and, after 1948, chaired the CAA's Africa Aid Committee.

The CAA began as the International Committee on African Affairs (ICAA) under Max Yergan, an African American who had spent fifteen years working for the YMCA in South Africa, but its 1942 reorganization as the Council on African Affairs made it distinctly different from its predecessor. The ICAA, representing a cross section of interwar left and liberal politics, had included social gospel Christians and corporate philanthropists; the CAA's militant black international diaspora consciousness marked a shift to independent black leadership. A closer look at the character of the earlier organization and the problems it faced provides insights into the world of the left and the relationship between international and civil rights politics in the late 1930s and early 1940s.

The historian David Anthony has recounted the beginnings of the ICAA and the unique position of Max Yergan in the international interwar left.[44] Yergan was born in Raleigh, North Carolina, in 1892. Though educated at St. Ambrose Episcopal Academy and the Baptist-funded Shaw University, Yergan was also influenced, through his grandfather, by the African Redemption and Ethiopianism traditions of the late nineteenth century. At Shaw, he joined the segregated black YMCA. Following assignments in Bangalore, India, and in East Africa during World War I, Yergan arrived in South Africa in 1922.[45] During his fifteen years with the YMCA there he became disillusioned with liberalism and increasingly influenced by radicals in the African National Congress, the South African Communist Party, and a 1934 trip to the Soviet Union.[46] Paul Robeson, whom Yergan had first met in 1931, also motivated Yergan's turn to the left and was important as a financial backer, contributing $1,500 in 1937 to get the ICAA off the ground.[47]

Among the South Africans with whom the ICAA had especially close associations was A. B. Xuma, future president of the African National Congress; he and Yergan discussed plans for the creation of an American-based organization focused on Africa.[48] When Yergan returned to the United States he served as secretary for external relations for the All Africa Convention, of which Xuma was vice-president.[49] Xuma and D. D. T. Jabavu, a professor at South Africa Native College at Fort Hare and president of the All Africa Convention, were members of the ICAA, and the organization's first important public gathering—coinciding with a visit to the United States by Xuma and Jabavu in September of 1937—featured both as speakers.[50] Also in 1937, through Ralph Bunche, Yergan met African and Caribbean activists in London, including Jomo Kenyatta, Padmore, Wallace-Johnson, and Ras Makonnen. Yergan's discussions with Kenyatta and Xuma were important in crystallizing plans for the ICAA and shaped another goal: facilitating the education of Africans in the United States. Yergan and Bunche worked to raise money for this purpose and to bring Kenyatta to America for a lecture tour.[51]

The ICAA comprised leading black educators, lawyers, and artists such as Hubert T. Delany, Channing H. Tobias, Mordecai Johnson, Ralph Bunche, and the Paris-based but Martinique-born writer René Maran. Other members were Fred Field, an important funder; his wife, Edith Field, who later served as treasurer; Frieda Nuegebauer, the white South African secretary of the organization; Mary

Van Kleek, a social democrat who was director of the International Studies Department of the Russell Sage Foundation; and Raymond L. Buell.

Seeking to educate the American public about Africa, the ICAA remained an educational organization.[52] Its irregular meetings, however, led to internal frustration and criticism. Some of the conflict stemmed from Yergan's involvement with other groups; from an organizational standpoint his energies were spread too thin to provide adequate direction for the ICAA. From a broader political perspective, Yergan's association with the Communist Party, his adherence to its policies, and specifically his assumption of the presidency of the National Negro Congress (NNC) after A. Philip Randolph resigned in protest against that organization's political and financial associations with the Communist Party, infuriated or at least alienated many of Yergan's hitherto civil rights allies.[53] Directly after Yergan assumed presidency of the NNC, for example, Ralph Bunche resigned from the ICAA, complaining about its inactivity and lack of direction.[54] Other ICAA members, especially the professors at Howard University who were under pressure from the House Un-American Activities Committee under the chairmanship of the southern Democrat Martin Dies, also sought to distance themselves from Yergan.[55]

Despite this early disaffection of liberal educators and civil rights activists, and the considerable divisions among black intellectuals and activists, the CAA's influence and credibility with civil rights leaders and organizations revived enormously during World War II, reaching their height by the end of the war. Mary McLeod Bethune, for example, who had praised Randolph for his resignation from the NNC, became an active member of the CAA and is a prime example of the involvement of mainstream civil rights leaders in the anticolonial movement. More than any other event, the war underscored the unity of civil rights and antiimperialism.[56]

If the communist popular front of the 1930s had a second incarnation after Hitler's invasion of the Soviet Union and the formation of the U.S.-British-Soviet wartime alliance, black civil rights and anticolonial activists—invigorated by the crumbling of European hegemony and the domestic upheavals of war—created a black popular front. Crafted by the left but embracing the full range of black American liberals, church leaders, and professional and middle-class organizations, it arose at a crucial historical moment and endured until the dawn of the Cold War. A remarkable unity (and militancy) of outlook and purpose was displayed during the war by black leadership—ranging from Roosevelt's "Black Cabinet" to the NAACP, the left, and the churches—and black politics was deeply infused with a new internationalism.[57] Thus, to understand the credibility of the CAA, one has to examine both the changes in that organization and the sweeping changes in the broader political landscape that accompanied America's entry into World War II and the U.S.-Soviet wartime alliance.

When the ICAA was reorganized in 1942 as the Council on African Affairs, with Paul Robeson as chairman, it retained its emphasis on educating the American public about Africa but also adopted more expressly political goals: the political liberation of the colonized African nations, and improved economic and social conditions on the African continent. Its leadership sought to achieve these goals not only through education but by organizing broad political support for decolonization and lobbying the U.S. government on issues pertaining to Africa.

Most important, the new CAA embodied a militant and explicit diaspora consciousness, accompanied by a distinct shift to autonomous black leadership. Embracing an antiimperialist and anticapitalist politics, the CAA insisted that "our fight for Negro rights here is linked inseparably with the liberation movements of the people of the Caribbean and Africa and the colonial world in general."[58] Hunton's appointment to the staff in 1943 marked a major turning point in his life and in the life of the organization. The day-to-day work and policy was thereafter carried out by Hunton, with the much greater involvement than before of Paul and Eslanda Goode Robeson. Other newly active members included Bethune and the sociologist E. Franklin Frazier. They were joined by Charlotta Bass, a participant in the 1919 Pan-African Congress in Paris, a civil rights activist, a promoter of the West Coast "Don't Buy Where You Can't Work" campaigns, and editor and publisher of the *California Eagle*, the state's oldest black newspaper.[59]

Yergan remained an important figure in the CAA; with his wide connections and considerable political skills, he was a valuable bridge to the left and to the rich culture of the popular front. Moreover, his adherence to Communist Party positions was less problematic during World War II than in the period of the Dies Committee and the Nazi-Soviet pact. But Yergan's involvement in numerous organizations and his lack of focus on the CAA remained continual sources of criticism and tension. To Hunton and other CAA activists, impatient to get on with work for Africa and anticolonialism, Yergan seemed to be everywhere and nowhere and thus a problem for the organization.

It was Alphaeus Hunton (increasingly joined by Robeson and later Du Bois) who, animated by the concerns of Africa and anticolonialism, made the CAA a vital and important organization. That he, like Yergan, was close to the Communist Party should caution against a reading of CP alliances as either a definitive or a divisive issue in wartime left and liberal organizations. Until 1948 when, in a radically different political climate, the organization split over the question of its relationship to the left, most conflicts within the CAA concerned the question of how to work effectively on anticolonial issues—with those close to the CP often lining up on different sides.

The broad political and cultural connections of Yergan, the intellectual leadership of Hunton and Du Bois, and, perhaps most important, the cultural and political influence of Robeson made the CAA a strong and credible organization among black Americans, steeped in a rich world of black popular culture.[60] In its heyday, its rallies and fund-raisers featured not only Robeson but such major American artists as Marian Anderson, Lena Horne, the jazz composer and pianist Mary Lou Williams, the Golden Gate Jubilee Quartet, John Latouche, and Duke Ellington.[61] But it was World War II that brought about the increasing politicization and influence of the CAA.

CHAPTER TWO

DEMOCRACY OR EMPIRE?

In our church where Bee is the leader, we pray for the war to end too, so that the Yankees could go back home and the village could come back to its senses and the girls would come off the streets. Lots of people don't want the war to end. They wish the Yankees and their money stay forever. But to some of us, our life was draining away.

—Earl Lovelace, *The Wine of Astonishment*

THE OUTBREAK OF WORLD WAR II accelerated the already heightened sensitivity to colonialism among people of African descent in the diaspora. As scholars of Pan-Africanism have argued, the war raised in sharp relief such issues as the nature of liberty, the powers of the state, the rights of the individual, and racial prejudice.[1] Since World War I, nationalists and Pan-Africanists had trenchantly critiqued and debunked myths of white supremacy and the civilizing mission and had challenged the political and economic order on which they rested. In the 1930s especially, the scholarship of C. L. R. James and W. E. B. Du Bois had placed black peoples at the center of world events. But as the weakness of colonial powers during World War II opened up an unprecedented array of challenges to colonialism, these ideas took on new urgency and meaning. Mass anticolonial movements gathered momentum, and an international black press watched as European hegemony and colonialism began to disintegrate.[2]

In their specific interpretations of the war and anticolonial struggles, black intellectuals and journalists in the United States, Britain, West Africa, and the Caribbean elaborated a conception of democracy that focused on the struggles of black peoples and their potential democratic transformations, yet also embraced a universalism that linked all struggles for democracy and independence. Anticolonial solidarities and identities were necessarily racial because activists understood race to be a product of the global processes that had shaped the modern world: slavery, exploitation, racial capitalism. Nevertheless, at precisely the moment that anticolonial activists emphasized the centrality of the exploitation of

African peoples and the production of "race," they created a universalist vision of a genuinely democratic world. Understanding their analysis helps explain how these activists embraced all democratic struggles and enables an appreciation of their marvelously fluid sense of "we-ness" and the expansiveness of their democratic vision.

THE PACIFIC THEATER

Activists and journalists—supported by the vivid political cartoons of Jay Jackson, Holloway, and Ollie Harrington—seized on successful Japanese invasions of European-held territories in the Pacific in 1941 and 1942 to critique colonialism.[3] Reporting on a colonial conference in Britain at which speakers discussed the collapse of Malaya, Singapore, and Burma, Padmore wrote that native peoples either "remained passive, considering the war as a struggle between two sets of imperialists which did not concern them," or, as in Burma, "joined up with the invader in the hopes of getting back the land which had been appropriated from them."[4] In the *Chicago Defender*, John Robert Badger put succinctly what was to become the dominant argument: "Colonialism is incapable of defending a territory [or] population under its control."[5]

Walter White argued that British policy was making India as much a pushover for the Japanese as Burma, whose long-suffering people wondered, "If we are going to be exploited, what matters it if our exploiters be yellow or white?" With the caveat that this was "a dangerous assumption," White nonetheless asked, "Who can deny the basic logic of the Burmese whose men received a top wage of 35 cents a day and whose women earned 16 cents a day in the mines of Burma which paid in 1940 to absentee landlords in Britain dividends of 252 per cent?"[6]

Reflecting the new emphasis on colonialism and the Pacific theater of war, in 1942 the *Pittsburgh Courier* added two new columns that ran through the immediate postwar period: "As an Indian Sees It," by Kumar Goshal, a West Coast–based journalist who was also a member of the Council on African Affairs; and "China Speaks," by the journalist Liu Liang-Mo. Like White, raising a question that dominated the black American press over the next few years, Liu asked in 1942, "If Japan will attack India, will India be another Malaya, Singapore, Burma?" Insisting that colonial policy undermined the concerted effort necessary to win the war, Liu warned that the British imprisonment of Indian leaders and the shooting-down of Indian people "help the Axis fifth column tremendously."[7]

The course of the war would have been very different, an editorial stated, "if the darker peoples in the colonies had been given SELF-GOVERNMENT within the empire and made to feel that they had something to defend."[8] Drawing a parallel with the Pacific colonies, Ellis A. Williams warned, "The people of the West Indies

"Swearing Off Before It's Too Late"

Britain and the United States, too hung over from imbibing white supremacy to see that immediate independence for colonized peoples would be the best Allied wartime strategy. Jay Jackson, *Chicago Defender*, July 11, 1942. (Courtesy of the *Chicago Defender*.)

feel that they are not citizens," and unless this attitude changed immediately, the British and U.S. governments could have another Hong Kong, Malaya, Singapore, or Burma on their hands.[9] Even Egyptian "apathy" toward the war, a 1942 *Courier* editorial argued, was "added proof that chickens do come home to roost, for the conditions which England fostered and maintained in Egypt since 1882 may now lead to another disaster."[10]

'Dictators Vs. Democracies'

The litmus test for democracy applied globally to include freedom for colonized peoples and full citizenship rights for black Americans. Jay Jackson, *Chicago Defender*, April 20, 1940. (Courtesy of the *Chicago Defender*.)

THE ATLANTIC CHARTER

Anticolonial activists closely followed wartime debates among the Allies over the future of the colonies. Disagreeing with Winston Churchill's view that the principles set forth in the Atlantic Charter did not apply to colonial subjects, Franklin Roosevelt argued that they should apply to all peoples.[11] Debates over the interpretation of the Atlantic Charter became a central issue in African American political discourse and helped shape the subsequent politics of the African diaspora. Issued in August 1941, the charter did not interest the black press until the agitation of West and South Africans made it an important issue to black Americans.[12]

The Atlantic Charter was introduced in the black press in early 1942 by George Padmore's coverage of the organizational activities of West African groups in London. In early 1942, in the *Defender* and the *Courier*, Padmore reported demands that Prime Minister Winston Churchill clarify the meaning of the Atlantic Charter for Nigeria. Noting Churchill's statement in the Commons that the charter was not "applicable to Coloured Races in colonial empire, and that the 'restoration of sovereignty, self-government and national life' is applicable only to the States and the Nations of Europe," the Nigerians wondered if they were in fact "fighting for the security of Europe to enjoy the Four Freedoms whilst West Africa continues pre-war status."[13]

When the British informed Nnamdi Azikiwe, editor of the *West African Pilot* in Nigeria, that "the Prime Minister does not consider that any fresh statement of policy is called for in relation to Nigeria or West African colonies, generally," the *Defender* condemned the British response: "There can be no 'harmony' between England's 'high conception of freedom and justice' for white Englishmen, and Africa's hope for political redemption and economic salvation which can only come through removal of the oppressive, inhuman, British yoke."[14]

By the end of the year the Atlantic Charter had captured the attention of a wide array of African American activists such as Walter White and journalists Horace R. Cayton, P. L. Prattis, Kumar Goshal, and George S. Schuyler.[15] Seeking to ensure that Roosevelt would make good on his anticolonial reading of it, White and the NAACP lobbied the White House on the importance of the charter's application to all peoples. White warned that the document would be hypocritical if confined to those of the white race, but if applied to all, it could have an important effect upon peoples of color throughout the world and on American domestic racial politics.[16] With his inimitable sarcasm, Schuyler noted in his *Courier* column, "Soft-hearted people may feel that these African, Asiatic and Malaysian people should come under the provisions of the Atlantic Charter. They do not stop to think how many companies would go into bankruptcy, how many aristocratic Nordic families would be reduced to working for a living, how impoverished all the missionaries, explorers, archaeologists, artists and others who live off the bounties" of colonialism would be.[17]

The debate over the Atlantic Charter was essentially a debate over the future of colonialism. This became abundantly clear in November 1942 when Churchill, in response to criticism by Wendell Willkie, declared, "We mean to hold our own. I have not become the King's first minister in order to preside over the liquidation

Atlantic Charter For Whom?

As Winston Churchill argued that the Atlantic Charter applied only to Europeans, African Americans applauded Roosevelt's insistence that the Charter applied to all. Jay Jackson, *Chicago Defender*, April 17, 1943. (Courtesy of the *Chicago Defender*.)

of the British Empire." A *Defender* editorial replied, "Black America is truly shocked by the bold and brazen stand by Churchill. We have never known or believed him a friend but we hoped that he as well as the world is learning about democracy from the very 'blood sweat and tears' of war."[18] Tongue in cheek, the *Courier*'s "In Defense of Churchill" editorialized that "instead of censuring Mr. Churchill and his class, we should commend them for their self-interested defense of their income and capital, and wish that other leaders would be as frank in stating their war aims."[19] Two weeks later another *Courier* editorial demanded an African Charter, appealing to history to condemn as "nonsense" the arguments of white liberals who insisted on a period of "tutelage" for self-government: "Many of these African nations were self-governing for centuries before the Europeans subdued them with superior firearms (their only superiority)."[20]

Discussions of the Atlantic Charter increasingly articulated the links between black Americans and colonized peoples and scrutinized the role of the United States in the postwar world. Like the Churchill statement, President Roosevelt's opposing position that the charter's principles applied to all peoples received widespread publicity.[21] Black American anticolonialists took advantage of the disagreement to publicize the plight of the colonies and to gain leverage in their lobbying efforts.[22] Throughout the war journalists and activists continued to press for a strong American position on the Atlantic Charter. And in a clear demonstration of how international politics could bolster domestic struggles, many insisted that if the charter were extended to all peoples, it would logically extend to African Americans. *Defender* editorials called Secretary of State Cordell Hull "a bitter disappointment" because he "would not give his assurance that the Atlantic Charter applies to Negroes"; likewise, they praised Willkie's sharp criticisms of Churchill.[23] "Testing" the Atlantic Charter through an in-depth analysis of proposed peace plans for Africa, the African American historian L. D. Reddick argued in the *Crisis* that "what happens in Africa in the immediate future will reveal to the submerged masses everywhere, and to ourselves, whether our stirring declarations have meaning or whether this is just one more indecent war."[24]

THE INDIAN CHALLENGE TO COLONIALISM

The refusal of Indian leaders to support the British in the war without an immediate guarantee of independence had a powerful influence on black American political consciousness. As early as 1939 a caustic *Courier* editorial noted approvingly that Gandhi had "served notice on the British overlords that freedom for India must come BEFORE any co-operation to help England win the war against Germany"; the Indian leaders were "perfectly right in insisting upon freedom NOW when England is occupied elsewhere. Experience has amply shown that the word of English statesmen is not any better than that of Hitler."[25]

African American journalists and activists, then, carved out an advocacy of anticolonialism that refused to accommodate wartime national loyalties. Maintaining a course of principled independence, their support of India's demands for immediate independence was in no way mitigated by the entry of the United States into World War II. The *Courier* reported that in an October 1942 survey of 10,000 black Americans, 87.8 percent "responded with a loud 'yes'" to the question "'Do you believe that India should continue to contend for her rights and her liberty now?' . . . Southern Negroes joined with their Northern brothers in full approval of the Indian struggle for self-rule."[26]

The survey followed months of anticolonial agitation in the Council on African Affairs and detailed coverage of India in the African American press. In September 1942 more than four thousand people attended the CAA-sponsored Rally for the Cause of Free India at New York's Manhattan Center. Speakers demanded the release from prison of the Indian independence leader and future prime minister, Jawaharlal Nehru. Paul Robeson told the rally that his interest in

INDIA VITAL TO VICTORY OVER FASCISM!

A Free India will be a powerful Ally of the United Nations.

A Free India will strengthen democracy everywhere and speed the liberation of all colonial peoples.

HEAR

★ **PAUL ROBESON**   ★ **MAX YERGAN**

★ **MICHAEL QUILL**   ★ **C. H. TOBIAS**

★ **KUMAR GOSHAL**
AND OTHERS

MASS MEETING

MANHATTAN CENTER

34th Street, West of Eighth Avenue

WEDNESDAY, SEPT. 2, 1942   8:30 P.M. SHARP

On sale at: Tickets: 28c, 55c and 83c   (Tax Incl.)
COUNCIL ON AFRICAN AFFAIRS, 1123 Broadway, Room 802; AMSTERDAM STAR NEWS, 2340 Eighth Avenue; PEOPLES VOICE, 210 West 125th Street; NEW YORK AGE, 230 West 135th Street; 135th Street Y.M.C.A.; WORKERS' BOOKSHOP, 50 East 13th Street; INTERNATIONAL WORKERS ORDER, 80 Fifth Avenue; BOOKFAIR, 133 West 44th Street; ASHLAND PLACE Y.W.C.A., 221 Ashland Place, Brooklyn, N. Y.

Auspices: COUNCIL ON AFRICAN AFFAIRS, 1123 Broadway, Room 802

Council on African Affairs broadside publicizing the Rally for the Cause of Free India, Manhattan Center, New York, September 1942. (Courtesy of Lloyd Brown.)

India went back to the 1930s, when he had met Nehru and his sister Vijaya Lakshmi Pandit in London after touring Spain with Krishna Menon, the dominant force in the India League; he had found, Robeson said, that "we had much in common."[27] Other speakers included columnists Kumar Goshal and Liu Liang-Mo, New York City Councilman Adam Clayton Powell Jr., and Channing H. Tobias of the national YMCA.[28] Pointing to the hypocrisy of British democracy, the

African American journalists consistently praised the uncompromising refusal of Indian leaders to support the Allies unless immediate independence was granted. Holloway, *Pittsburgh Courier*, August 29, 1942.

CAA's early publication *News of Africa* proclaimed it "unthinkable that a great
anti-fascist like Nehru should today be languishing in prison because he represents the very principles for which the war is being fought."[29]

Complementing CAA efforts, A. Philip Randolph, head of the International
Brotherhood of Sleeping Car Porters, spoke on behalf of Indian independence at
the 1942 convention of the American Federation of Labor.[30] Walter White lobbied both Roosevelt and the State Department to urge that the American government intervene in the dispute between Indian nationalists and the British.[31]
White became a member of J. J. Singh's India League of America and joined fifty-
six prominent Americans in a full-page petition in the *New York Times* calling for
Roosevelt and Chiang Kai-shek to insist on a reopening of negotiations between
Indian nationalists and the British government.[32]

Indeed, for African Americans the litmus test for democracy acquired a global
reach, including freedom for colonized peoples along with full citizenship for
black Americans. Antifascism was crucial to democratic politics, but European
antifascism by itself did not challenge the global context of oppression. Their
support for India was predicated on a solidarity based not simply on race and
color but on a vision of democracy that condemned concentrating solely on European and Japanese fascism while ignoring the political and economic exploita-

tion of imperialism.[33] A *Defender* editorial declared, "Together we say with the millions of the Indian people 'We are entirely opposed to Nazism, (and Fascism) but we are also opposed to imperialism with which we have had (and are still having) bitter experience ourselves and which crushes our growth and exploits us."[34] Discussing Gandhi's 1942 threat of civil disobedience against British rule if independence were not immediately granted, Denton J. Brooks argued in the *Defender* the "paradoxical" nature of Britain's denial of India's demands, when India's concepts of equality and freedom were "the world's ideals."[35]

The African American theologian Howard Thurman had developed a deep interest in the Indian independence movement and a personal friendship with Gandhi and the Nehru family during a 1935 visit to India.[36] Describing Thurman "as a democrat who knows that political freedom is the condition precedent to human dignity," Peter Dana reported for the *Courier* that Thurman believed the Indian leaders had "reduced to moral absurdity" the British pretense "to fight a war for freedom on the so-called practical basis of denying India her political independence." Dana quoted Thurman: "There aren't enough jails in all India to imprison the spirit of present day India that articulates itself in Gandhi and Nehru."[37]

Journalists consistently praised the uncompromising positions taken by Nehru and Gandhi. Nehru, Padmore declared, believed his task was "to gain India's independence and defeat the Fascist Powers," and if circumstances placed him "simultaneously in opposition to Britain and to Britain's enemy Japan, he still could not do otherwise."[38] When three major radio chains in the United States refused to carry a Nehru speech giving the Indian side of negotiations, black journalists and the NAACP had a field day denouncing this blatant censorship.[39] A *Courier* editorial approvingly quoted Gandhi's statement "'There is no room left for negotiation—either they recognize India's independence or they don't.' . . . There is no question of 'one more chance,' the Mahatma asserted. 'This is open rebellion. I conceive of a mass movement on the widest possible scale.'" The editorial concluded that "if the United Nations were as eager to restore freedom to India as they are to restore freedom to the enslaved countries of Europe, their victory over the Axis would be assured."[40] Two weeks later the *Courier* quoted from Gandhi's weekly paper *Harijin*, that "Britain does not deserve to win the war if she is merely fighting to keep her Asiatic and African possessions."[41]

The attention to Gandhi as a militant antiimperialist—the coverage of his imprisonment by the British and publication of his scathing critiques of the United States—is especially worthy of note because (see Chapter 7) at the time of his assassination in 1948, Gandhi was reinvented in the American media as simply a great moral leader who fought "prejudice" and the caste system, with little mention of his struggle against British imperialism. The coverage of his death was a dramatic example of the shift from the 1940s critique of colonialism, imperialism, and racism to the dehistoricized version of racism, stripped of all analysis of political economy, that flourished in the Cold War era. But throughout World War II and immediately thereafter, Gandhi, Nehru, and the Indian movement for independence offered forceful critiques of imperialism from a perspective grounded in political economy. George Padmore reported in the *Defender* that "in the fight to throw the imperialist yoke from his people," Gandhi had adopted this slogan: "Complete abolition, root, and branch, of the process of exploitation of primary commodities, such as cotton, cocoa, palm-kernels, rubber, tea, tobacco, etc., as well as the agricultural masses of Asia, Africa, and the Pacific by the great industrial and imperialist powers of Europe and America."[42]

Growing criticism of American policy and the role of the United States in the international economy—a theme that would play an increasingly important part in postwar African American political discussion—was also part of the discussions on India. Arguing that "America's treatment of her 12,000,000 colored citizens is coming home to roost in India," a front-page *Defender* article quoted Gandhi: "We know what American aid means. It amounts in the end to American influence, if not American rule, added to the British [control]."[43] In October 1942, Gandhi told S. Chandrasekhar, who was soon to depart for study in America, that on his return to India he would have to "unlearn alot of things American." When Chandrasekhar asked for elaboration, Gandhi continued with a smile, "The American notions of democracy for instance," explaining that he was "thinking of the American Negro and the treatment he receives in American democracy." Asked if he wanted to visit the United States, Gandhi replied: "I don't think the American people are interested in me as a symbol of India's struggle for Freedom, not even as an exponent of non-violence. I think the average American is greatly interested in me as a social curiosity—my loin cloth and my goat's milk and things like that. That is why I don't think I will ever visit the United States."[44]

Denton J. Brooks Jr., writing for the *Defender* from New Delhi in 1944 about debates within National Congress Party circles, reported that "a wave of disillusionment" was sweeping the Congress about the American position on Indian independence; practically all Congress-controlled papers were carrying headlines asking "Will U.S. Go Imperialistic Too?" Indians feared, he claimed, that there had been an agreement whereby the United States would take control of Japanese territories, while Britain retained control of India and Burma.[45]

BLACK AMERICAN TROOPS

Although the U.S. armed forces were not effectively desegregated until well into the Korean War, the participation of black Americans in the military was a central concern within debates over desegregation during World War II.[46] Within the broader context of the sustained critique of colonialism, the black American press was initially skeptical about the participation of Africans or colonial peoples in what was seen as a European conflict. Discussing probable incursions by Mussolini into North Africa, a 1940 *Courier* editorial found it tragic that "black men will be fighting again on both sides over a matter which is an academic question to them."[47] Some journalists, however, predicted that arming colonized peoples would help to bring a speedy downfall to colonialism. One *Courier* editorial argued that Africans "were subdued and enslaved by Europeans with superior arms. With these superior arms now being placed in their hands they are in a position at last to effect their emancipation."[48] Another declared, "White people are scarce in Africa, and when multitudes of armed Negroes learn that European governments are too busy butchering each other to concentrate on Africa, their self-interest, patriotism and hatred of their oppressors will speedily be asserted."[49]

These editorials were written before the American entry into the war and before the *Courier* had declared its "Double V" campaign against both fascism abroad and racism at home. After the United States declared war, Padmore and others enthusiastically promoted the use of black American and African troops and argued for their importance to Allied war efforts.[50] With the fall of Dakar, Senegal, to the Germans in 1942, the *Defender* thought it doubtful that the Axis could hold Dakar if it were attacked by Anglo-American forces comprising black American and West African troops.[51] Even at the height of enthusiasm about the use of black troops, however, careful scrutiny of their role continued. There was fierce criticism of the Allies' coercive use of unarmed Africans for transport and labor battalions. This practice caused such high casualties, the *Defender* charged, that it was "a contradiction of the very principles of liberty and humanity for which we claim to be fighting."[52] Journalists further criticized Allied unwillingness to arm and use already trained African troops in Dakar because of racial prejudice and "fear of a widespread colonial revolt."[53] The same prejudice and fear motivated the refusal of the British to release I. T. A. Wallace-Johnson from prison; in the words of an official, the *Defender* reported, they thought it "unsafe to allow Johnson [*sic*] his liberty among the natives who are excitable and may get out of hand if feeling bec[omes] aroused."[54]

The enthusiasm of journalists and activists for the use of black troops derived from the potential for attacks on Jim Crow. But that enthusiasm, as well as the *Courier's* "Double V" campaign, must be understood in the context of criticism of Allied aims.[55] The fight against Jim Crow was seen as inseparably linked to the the fight against both imperialism and fascism, which could create tensions among the Allied powers. "Double V" perhaps should have been called "Triple V," for even after the American entry into the war and the development of a clear strategy of using wartime aims to attack Jim Crow, anticolonialism remained the

"The Man Who Came Back"

AMERICA 1619

The descendants of West Africans liberating West Africa from Nazi control, as black troops spelled the death knell of colonialism. Jay Jackson, *Chicago Defender*, November 28, 1942. (Courtesy of the *Chicago Defender*.)

central issue in the black press's editorial comment. Thus, in 1943 the *Courier* reminded readers: "The present war is being fought in order to destroy the military power of Germany, Italy and Japan so that they will be unable hereafter to threaten the status quo as established by the victorious Allied Powers, and that is all." Underlining the need for militancy at home and abroad, the *Courier* continued, "The only wars waged for the liberation of oppressed peoples are those which are fought by the oppressed peoples for that purpose. Freedom cannot be granted—it must be won."[56]

Journalists and writers analyzed the implications for the future of colonialism of using black troops and, in turn, linked the fate of Jim Crow to the fate of imperialism. The poet and writer Langston Hughes predicted that the effects of the participation of black soldiers in the war "will eventually shake the British Empire to the dust. That will shake Dixie's teeth loose too, and crack the joints of Jim Crow South Africa." The war, he asserted in early 1945, had weakened "the unmitigated gall of white imperialism around the world."[57] John Robert Badger argued that "mobilization of African peoples requires abandonment of the traditions and institutions of colonialism." Moreover, he exalted in seeing the descendants of Africans aid in the liberation of Africa: black American soldiers, many of whom were descendants of inhabitants of Senegal, Dahomey, and the Ivory Coast "who more than a century ago came to the United States in the shackles of slave ships, last week went back to African shores aboard an Allied invasion armada, to prevent the threatened re-enslavement of Africa by the goose-stepping slavers of 1942." For Badger, these black American troops were simultaneously defeating the Axis powers and destroying French colonialism: "The French empire arose on the accumulation of profits pilfered a hundred years ago from the theft and sale of living human beings. Today the descendants of those victims of barbarism have participated in destroying—in fact if not in law—the French Empire."[58]

THE CRITIQUE OF AMERICAN EMPIRE

Criticism not only of French and British imperialism but of the role of the American government and U.S. corporations in the rapidly changing global political economy—as well as questions about who would own and control the world's resources—increasingly animated black American political discourse. A *Defender* editorial linked the oppression of black Americans and Indians, charging that "Negro America" was as much "the victim of American imperialism, greed, terror and rapacity" as India was the victim of British imperialism.[59] In the same vein, L. D. Reddick argued that peace planning was taking place in the context of competition between British capitalism and American capitalism and that the penetration of American capital into Canada, India, Australia, and South Africa had been accelerated by the war.[60] Walter White applauded *Fortune* magazine's criticism of Britain's racial policy but added that "for an American magazine, it is a clear case of the pot and the kettle."[61] With the rise of the Cold War, such a denunciation of U.S. foreign policy would become out of bounds for such a prominent liberal as White and for the NAACP.

Journalists monitored those areas that had been transformed by American occupation during the war and had developed relatively new relationships with the United States, such as Trinidad, as well as those—Puerto Rico, Haiti, Liberia—whose direct economic and political ties with the United States were much older. Noting that "the war hit the Caribbean like a cyclone from the Gulf," John Robert Badger pointed out the impact on the West Indies of millions of American dollars, the introduction of American culture, and American military and naval construction and organization.[62]

None of the islands was more deeply transformed than Trinidad. The largest oil- and pitch-producing area of the British Empire, with air bases commanding

'No Joy Without Some Pain'

American occupation brought American dollars, but it also brought Jim Crow and economic and cultural dislocation. Jay Jackson, *Chicago Defender*, September 21, 1940. (Courtesy of the *Chicago Defender*.)

the Panama Canal and the oil fields of Venezuela, Trinidad was considered important to U.S. defense policy. American occupation brought immediate changes. "Trinidad's population of 450,000," the *Courier* reported, "has a universal topic of conversation—the American bases, the American soldiers, the American sailors. ... What will Uncle Sam gain by this? That is the big question."[63]

In the *Defender*, Ramona Lowe told the story of "Rum and Coca Cola," a calypso song written by Lord Invader (Rupert Grant), which became an American hit. Its "pert lines," wrote Lowe, "have a tragic portent to people aware of the complications Americans have invariably left after their occupation of the Caribbean islands." The song was about the impact of American money as Yankee occupation disrupted familial, gender, and sexual relationships.

> Since the Yankees came to Trinidad,
> They have the young girls going mad,
> The young girls say they treat them nice,
> And they give them a better price.
>
> Chorus: They buy rum and Coca-Cola,
>   Go down to Point Cumana,
>   Both mother and daughter
>   Working for the Yankee dollar.
>
> I had a little mopsey the other day,
> Her mother came and took her away;
> Then her mother and sisters
> Went in a car with some soldiers.
>
> A couple got married one afternoon,
> And was to go marayo on a honeymoon,
> The very night the wife went with a Yankee lad,
> And the stupid husband went staring mad.

Lowe laid bare the intertwined cultural and economic exploitation experienced by black artists. "Rum and Coca Cola" was popular in Trinidad, but unknown to Invader, the Andrews Sisters recorded the song, and it became a hit in the United States. Invader learned that "someone was getting rich on the fruits of his labor" only after *Time* sought him out as the original composer. He complained that "the song was copyrighted in Trinidad and I never sold it to anyone," and when he heard the Andrews Sisters' version he remarked caustically, "We don't speak like that."[64]

United States military presence and investment arrived also in Jamaica and Surinam during the war. Alfred E. Smith reported in the *Defender* that with the establishment of a U.S. air base in Jamaica, military interests were added to earlier economic interests such as those of the United Fruit Company.[65] Randy Dixon, a *Courier* war correspondent, described new U.S. bauxite mining in Jamaica as a "rush" on aluminum by American-controlled companies such as the Jamaican Bauxite Company, a subsidiary of the Aluminum Company of America

(ALCOA) and Reynolds Metals. Noting the increasing global reach of "New South" business interests, as well as astutely capturing the collapsing boundaries of time and space, Dixon argued that black Americans must take notice of American action abroad because "the consequences of any action in one section of the colored world are automatically manifested in the life of colored people everywhere."[66] Also attacking the dramatic new role of U.S. military intervention, John Robert Badger reported that American troops had arrived in the Dutch colony of Surinam in November 1941 to secure the booming production at Dutch and American mines: "The working conditions are worst, pay lowest and the treatment of the workers most severe at the American mine . . . controlled by the Aluminum Company of America, which means the Pittsburgh Mellon family's interests."[67]

Journalists' monitoring of new investment during the war stimulated inquiry into the political and economic history of the islands. In a series on Caribbean economics, Badger argued that the colonial political status of the islands had "its economic counterpart in the one money-crop plantation system." Cane sugar, he argued, "is the curse of the West Indies," and in Puerto Rico and Cuba "sugar is a double curse." Not only had American-controlled sugar interests built a one-crop economy, but U.S. tariff laws further contributed to exploitation by rewarding the cultivation of unsuitable land for that one crop and discouraging diversified farming.[68]

The political status of Puerto Rico as a U.S. holding engendered particularly detailed scrutiny of U.S. economic interests there. A 1943 *Courier* editorial argued that President Roosevelt and Secretary of the Interior Harold Ickes opposed Puerto Rican independence "because of its strategic value and the big investment of the sugar trust whose exactions have reduced the Puerto Rican to abject poverty and disease."[69] In a six-part series on Puerto Rico for the *Defender*, Denton J. Brooks argued that American interests were intent on strangling the reforms proposed by members of the Popular Party, elected in 1940.[70] Puerto Rico, argued Brooks, was a critical test case for the Atlantic Charter.[71] Following the Brooks series, the *Defender* charged the United States Congress with hypocrisy for discussing immediate independence for the Philippines, where the Japanese were still firmly in control: "If Congress wants to do something spectacular," it should grant independence to Puerto Rico, where, "far removed from the threat of Japanese or German invasion, the colonial system operates in all its ugly viciousness. And the United States must plead guilty as the powerful giant who operates it."[72]

U.S. economic and political ties to Haiti also received close scrutiny as diaspora politics took firm hold in the black American press. In 1941, when the Allies lost their major sources of rubber after Malaya fell to the Japanese, Haiti was among the places where the United States sought to introduce new rubber production to make up for the loss. The scheme turned out to be an utter failure: it produced no rubber but devastated the Haitian economy.[73] Although early press reports had expressed high expectations,[74] the disastrous consequences were exposed by Harold Preece in a 1944 *Defender* series. He reported that 250,000 black farmers had been driven from their lands, their houses and properties destroyed, and the fertile land made barren desert: the "crazy suicidal scheme produced no rubber . . . only starvation for Haiti's subsistence farmers." Through the U.S. government agency SHADA, Wall Street's "phony front," Preece argued, "Wall Street has sewed up Haiti" for American imperialism. Not only was Haiti responsible for paying back $17 million to the Export-Import Bank of Washington—also a U.S. government agency—but SHADA now had the "right to 'develop' any other Haitian 'resources' as it sees fit."[75]

Liberia, a nation settled by former American slaves and brought into being by an act of the U.S. Congress in 1847, found itself almost a century later in a strategically critical wartime location. Following the collapse of France and the German presence in Senegal, the United States and Liberia reached a formal defense agreement in March 1942 which permitted the construction of an American air base.[76] The African American press monitored the impact of the U.S. military presence on the political economy of Liberia, and analyzed the already thorny history between the two countries. In the *Crisis*, Ernest E. Johnson described the U.S. camp in the "legendary part of Central Africa which was once famous in the worldwide slave trade" as "the biggest American aerial operation anywhere outside the United States." And in keeping with the pattern in the Caribbean, economic penetration immediately followed the military presence: "It naturally followed that American troops would have to protect all this plumbing, wiring and concrete built by Pan American Airways with the aid of U.S. Army engineers, Firestone Tire and Rubber Company engineers, and local labor."[77] Similarly, Padmore saw the desire of the U.S. Army and Navy for bases in West Africa leading to a "further tightening of the grip of international finance on Liberia." In 1871 a group of "international financial tycoons, headed by J. P. Morgan and company" had advanced a refunding loan to the young nation; when Firestone took up the international loan, it became "the virtual ruler of Liberia."[78]

A 1943 visit by President Roosevelt to Liberia, followed by a visit of President Edwin Barclay and President-elect William Tubman of Liberia to the United States, further stimulated critiques of the United States–Liberia connection. So did the publication of Arthur I. Hayman and Harold Preece's *Lighting Up Liberia*, a scathing indictment of the Firestone Company and the ruling elite of "Americo-Liberian" leaders.[79] When Barclay and Tubman came to discuss the future of rubber production in Liberia, Badger called it "a mission to Firestone."[80] This cynicism, he explained, "was a result of awareness that Liberia had been established by act of Congress, that American capital has financed the new nation and had been the beneficiary of its economic development, and that one American trust—the Firestone rubber trust—dominates the economic life of the country."[81]

By the later part of the war the international perspective in African American popular writing was widespread. The sociologist and journalist Horace R. Cayton argued in 1943 that with an outlook gained "through an identification with the exploited peoples of the world . . . the Negro had placed his problems in a new and larger frame of reference and related them to world forces." Moreover, black Americans were "developing an international point of view more rapidly than the rest of the population."[82] Edgar T. Rouzeau, a columnist for the *Pittsburgh Courier*, argued that "colored people must think globally in terms of freedom and democracy for colored people everywhere," for even if the aspirations of black Americans were granted tomorrow, "those gains would be subject to constant threats as long as colored people were exploited in other parts of the world."[83]

Increasingly, black American journalists, intellectuals, and civil rights activists insisted that African Americans not only shared an oppression with colonized peoples but that their fate in the United States was intertwined with the struggles of those peoples. For example, Rouzeau argued that an independent India would help black Americans win rights and that "India's fate may well decide the future of the Black American."[84] According to Rouzeau, "the practice of prejudice against a sovereign nation is far too risky an undertaking even for powerful 'democratic' nations like Great Britain and the United States." The *Defender* also linked the plight of black Americans to that of Indians: "If India's cry for freedom is smothered, the position of the Negro people the world over will become increasingly precarious."[85] By the same token, the *Courier* reported, Paul Robeson "declared last week that an essential part of the solution of the Negro problem in this country will be the pressure of other countries on America from the outside."[86] Ironically, this theme would be reformulated during the Cold War.

African American leaders argued that the bonds black Americans shared with colonized peoples were rooted not in a common culture but in a shared history of the racism spawned by slavery, colonialism, and imperialism. The strongest version of this argument had its basis in left-wing theories of imperialism as developed in J. A. Hobson's *Imperialism* (1902) and Lenin's 1916 pamphlet, *Imperialism, the Highest Stage of Capitalism*. In this view, the drive for profit inherent in capitalism led to the constant search for new markets and new sources of raw materials and hence, necessarily, to colonial and imperialist expansion. To defeat colonialism, therefore, one must also defeat capitalism. Moreover, it followed that there was a systematic interdependence of oppressed peoples based on the international reach of modern capitalism.[87] In 1936, in *A World View of Race*, Ralph Bunche argued that "the imperialism of today is a product of modern capitalism, and the beginning of its application to Africa coincides with the deep penetration into the hinterland and the partition of the continent in the last quarter of the nineteenth century." These developments had given rise to theories of race that had "no scientific basis" but "lend themselves so conveniently to the exigencies of political and economic control."[88] Likewise, according to John Robert Badger, black Americans "recognize that our own status is connected with that of other submerged peoples, especially those of Africa and the West Indies, where the issue of race has been injected into politics and forms an ideological pillar of the repressive structure of world imperialism."[89]

The analysis of racism as something rooted in the history of specific economic, political, and social practices encouraged discussion in the popular press of the constructed nature of race. In 1942 the *Courier* carried the headline "'Race Is an Invention' Says George Schuyler." In a lecture at Hampton Institute, Schuyler had explained that there is "no such thing as white and Negro blood, though propaganda can make a great national issue out of its 'existence.' When you subjugate people, an excuse must be made and racial propaganda is a device used to say that an enslaved group is inferior."[90]

Indeed, as an understanding of race and racism as rooted in capitalism and imperialism increasingly came to permeate the popular press, the strong sense of the history of racism led to indignation and outrage at what were perceived as ahistorical and racist analyses of the war and the problem of fascism by the white press.[91] A *Defender* editorial criticized the *Chicago Tribune* for its "strange discovery": "It discovered, believe it or not, for the first time since the advent of the twentieth century, that 'the world seems to have entered into an era of senseless brutality in which people who have control over others are determined to make an end to humanity, justice and decency.' . . . The Tribune would have us believe that the age of hate began with the triumphal entry of Herr Fuehrer into Vienna. The age of hate [in fact] began with the slave trade and the intensification of prejudice which followed the liberation of the slaves."[92]

Turning this analysis to an argument for solidarity in broad antifascist alliances, Paul Robeson maintained that black Americans understood the "democratic significance of the present conflict" out of an "awareness born of their yearning for freedom from an oppression that predated fascism."[93] Other activists and journalists agreed that the war must be understood as a consequence of imperialism. As Max Yergan wrote in the *Courier*, "It must always be remembered that the Hitlerite scourge of today has its roots in the imperialism of which India and Africa have been the victims. Competition among the imperialist powers for more land and peoples to exploit brought on the fascist regime."[94] George Padmore asserted that for a real, lasting peace to be achieved, imperialism must be abolished. Behind the war lay "the standing conflict between bandit nations for colonies as markets, sources of raw materials and cheap labor, spheres for the investment of finance capital, and naval, military and air bases. . . . The fact that I spent three months in a Nazi prison does not blind me to the fact that in a capitalist world, as long as Britain and France reserve the right to rule over 500 million colored peoples and exploit their labor in the interests of plutocracy, they cannot expect Germany to be satisfied. Empire and Peace are incompatible."[95]

As World War II wore on, and black Americans had increasing knowledge of events in Africa and the colonial world, liberal spokespersons such as Walter White came not only to share the language of antiimperialism with leftists such as George Padmore and Alphaeus Hunton but also to share an analysis (or at least a description) of British and American exploitation of African nations. Historians have documented the militant anticolonialism and antiimperialism of the NAACP during the war.[96] The *Baltimore Afro-American* reported Walter White's warning to Roosevelt and Churchill that unless the problem of the color line was solved, "the colored peoples of India, China, Burma, Africa, the West Indies, the United States and other parts of the world will continue to view skeptically assertions that this is a war for freedom and equality." Moreover, "failure to solve this problem will inevitably mean other wars" caused by "the continuation of white imperialist exploitation of colored people."[97] A 1944 State Department report too noted the prevalence of critiques of imperialism by African Americans across political lines: "Leading Negro journals like *The Crisis*, official organ of the National Association for the Advancement of Colored People, the relatively conservative *New York Amsterdam News* and the militant left-wing organ, the *People's Voice* conduct a perpetual and bitter campaign against 'white imperialism.'"[98]

The language of antiimperialism could be so widely shared because the concept could mean different things to different people. A White and a Schuyler shared a description of exploitation with a Padmore or a Hunton but differed in their prescriptions for correcting this exploitation and their visions of a just and humane world. Yet it would be wrong to see the politics of the African diaspora as only a superficial convergence of liberals and leftists. At the heart of anticolonialists' core set of beliefs was a conception of democracy that embraced the struggles of colonial peoples and saw black peoples as part of the laboring classes of the world. Thus, although they believed that the abolition of colonial political and economic domination was the first condition for a democratic and humane world, they also believed that African Americans and colonized peoples had interests in common with other laboring classes.

As the war drew to a close, not only were critiques of imperialism widely shared, but the organization of new communication networks and a host of postwar planning forums created opportunities for African Americans to give sub-stance to their internationalist and democratic visions. In the years that followed, African American anticolonial and civil rights leaders would join with Africans and Indians in international trade union and Pan-African forums, in support of striking African workers, and in postwar planning bodies and the formation of the United Nations.

CHAPTER THREE

TO FORGE A

COLONIAL INTERNATIONAL

O kinsmen! We must meet the common foe!
Though far outnumbered, let us show brave,
And for their thousand blows deal one death blow!
What though before us lies the open grave.

Like men we'll face the murderous, cowardly pack,
Pressed to the wall, dying but fighting back!
—Claude McKay, "If We Must Die"

IN 1946, FOLLOWING A GENERAL STRIKE of Nigerian workers, the British banned a chain of militant pro-independence newspapers sympathetic to the strikers. Featuring the striking workers and the fight for the freedom of the press, the *Baltimore Afro-American* quoted Nnamdi Azikiwe, editor of the banned papers: "With our back to the wall, we have solemnly pledged our lives to the redemption of Africa, and are determined to face imprisonment or exile or a firing squad. . . . As we fight back with every constitutional energy at our disposal, if we must die, we shall repeat, to our last breath, Claude McKay's great poem, 'If We Must Die.'"[1]

Thus, in support of a workers' strike, an African American newspaper featured a Nigerian journalist and anticolonial leader who had been educated in black American universities, who was quoting a poem written by a Jamaican, which was inspired by the Chicago race riot of 1919. In such tributaries and connections one sees a glimpse of the depth and complexities of 1940s anticolonialism. Just as Azikiwe's appeal reflected his embeddedness in transnational and cross-class institutions—from Nigeria to Jamaica to Chicago, and from universities to newspapers to trade unions—his claims for the rights of workers to full constitutional protection resonated with black America's campaigns for jobs and housing during the war. And given that black advancement into housing or jobs often met violent white resistance—for example, thirty-four lives lost in Detroit in 1943—and that African American soldiers were suffering racist violence in army camps as well as from local police and civilians, Azikiwe's outspoken militancy for the right to self-defense had more than a metaphorical appeal.[2]

This marriage of Pan-African politics and union organizing was no accident. Trade union and labor organizations provided the most prominent ideological and institutional bases of Pan-Africanism in the 1940s. In the last months of World War II and the immediate postwar period, the importance of trade union organizations and the accompanying conviction that black peoples were foremost among the laboring classes were abundantly clear. They were demonstrated in African American participation in the 1945 Manchester Pan-African Congress and subsequent work with the Pan-African Federation; in support for Nigerian trade union struggles and the fight against the British government's suppression of Nigerian newspapers; in black American support for striking South African miners; and in relief efforts during the 1946 famine in the Ciskei region of South Africa.

LABOR AND THE 1945 PAN-AFRICAN CONGRESS

The emergence of a central place for trade union and labor organizations in Pan-Africanism can be observed by exploring two very different attempts to organize a Pan-African Congress in 1944 and 1945. In the first endeavor, Harold Moody (chair of the London Missionary Society and president of the London-based League of Coloured Peoples), Amy Jacques Garvey (Pan-African leader and the second wife of Marcus Garvey), and W. E. B. Du Bois began to plan a Pan-African Congress in early 1944.[3] Their efforts resembled the earlier phase of Pan-Africanism represented in the 1900, 1919, 1921, and 1927 congresses. More accommodationist than anticolonial, the early congresses were led by an elite who believed that educated Africans in the diaspora had a special role to play in the liberation of Africa by virtue of their education and their relatively greater access to political power.[4]

Their beliefs and assumptions were markedly different from those of activists in the Pan-African Federation such as George Padmore and I. T. A. Wallace-Johnson, who led the second initiative. This group, deeply influenced by Marxism, was tied institutionally to African labor movements and drew greater representation from the African continent, including trade unionists and future leaders of independence movements such as Kwame Nkrumah and Jomo Kenyatta. The paternalism that characterized earlier Pan-Africanism was mitigated by the decided shift to African initiatives and leadership. Moreover, the belief that colonialism was a child of capitalism, that black peoples were among the laboring classes, and that their struggles were therefore linked to those of other working people provided an alternative frame for understanding both the exploitation of the people and resources of Africa and strategies for African liberation. With leadership and inspiration drawn from African independence and trade union movements, these Pan-African activists argued that independent African and Asian states would aid concretely in the struggles of African Americans and others in the diaspora. While maintaining a sense of reciprocity, this argument inverted the old relationship wherein supposedly better educated and more powerful African Americans were to help the less powerful Africans.

Although only the second initiative actually reached fruition, exploration of the first attempt helps illuminate how decisively Pan-Africanism changed during World War II. Amy Jacques Garvey first approached Du Bois in January 1944 with Harold Moody's proposal to frame an African Charter and form an African Regional Council under the auspices of the United Nations.[5] In response, Du Bois proposed a Pan-African Congress to be held after the war.[6] Reiterating long-standing themes of ties of "descendants of Africa in America and the West Indies," Du Bois stressed the need for involvement from the diaspora. In fact, his proposal included only groups in the diaspora. Although Du Bois was in theory concerned about seeking African representation and "real popular support," in practice he lacked familiarity with African organizations and did not have the contacts to include them.[7]

The distance between many of the groups involved in the first initiative and the Pan-African Federation can be seen in their different arguments about what Africans and those of African descent shared. The objective of Amy Jacques Garvey's African Communities League was the "cultural and ethical development of people of African descent." Positing an intrinsic "cultural pattern" distorted by the "alien persecutors," and in the gender-laden language of nineteenth- and early twentieth-century Pan-Africanism, Garvey sought to "relink" Africans in the diaspora with Africa as the "motherland."[8]

The shift of initiative to the Pan-African Federation represented not just a change in institutional base and strategy but a profoundly different set of assumptions on which to build a politics and a definition of a people. Leaders with backgrounds in the Communist International, such as Padmore and Wallace-Johnson, combined both intellectual and ideological commitments to historical materialism and a Marxist tradition with institutional ties to the trade union formations that had mushroomed during World War II. They linked black peoples not just through culture but through positing a shared history. They saw vehicles of liberation not in cultural organizations and tools but in working peoples' organizations. Their emphasis on work and workers' organizations further linked the struggles of peoples of color to the struggles of other working people. And in the era of a burgeoning left and trade union movement, fueled by the central role of the left in antifascist resistance, this emphasis on the struggles of working people proved to be a powerful legitimizing factor in struggles for independence. The leaders of the Pan-African Federation assumed the legitimacy of independence and saw it as imminent, not something that needed to be argued or waited for.[9]

Norman Manley, founder of the People's Nationalist Party of Jamaica, told black Americans attending the 1945 convention of the Alpha Phi Alpha fraternity that the "fast spread of Socialist forces in Europe and the development of the World Trade Union Congress are two forces which promise true equality to all peoples. . . . It would be mad to ignore the promise of these forces and to cut ourselves off from them." Exemplifying the solidarity among peoples of African descent and the emphasis on labor characteristic of the politics of this period, Manley stated that "ultimate equality for you is inextricably bound with that of other peoples of African descent. You can strengthen your fight here in the United States by championing the cause of minority and colonial groups all over the world."[10]

Domestic and international dimensions of the new African American interest in labor worked as reciprocal influences. As Nelson Lichtenstein has pointed out, in the mid-1940s the fate of the trade unions and of the movement for black freedom were more closely linked than at any other time in American history.[11] The CIO's efforts to organize black workers, as well as a marked jump in the number of black workers in industrialized and unionized jobs during World War II, led to heightened expectations and a strong emphasis in African American communities on the issue of jobs.[12] Black civil rights activists focused on jobs, specifically on gaining entry into industrial and unionized jobs, as the key to community advancement. Black workers staged wildcat strikes, such as those at the Dodge Motor Company in Detroit in 1941, to enforce Fair Employment Practices Commission regulations, and in some cities entire African American communities mobilized to secure fair treatment in defense industries.[13] In the later years of the war there were numerous state and local FEPC initiatives. In 1945, for example, bills against discrimination in employment, fifty-five in all, were introduced in almost every large industrial state.[14]

All these domestic developments led the black press to take a new interest in international labor. At the same time, the views of international labor, especially in Africa, and colonial questions influenced black American views of U.S. labor. The interest of black American activists and journalists in 1944 and 1945 conferences of the International Labor Organization (ILO) and the World Federation of Trade Unions (WFTU) illustrates both the centrality of trade union struggles in the politics of this period and the impact of attention to Africa and the Caribbean trade union struggles on black American perceptions of U.S. labor.

African American journalists and activists often judged international trade union congresses, unions, and labor leaders according to the positions they took on black labor in Africa and its diaspora. In 1944, when Philadelphia hosted the twenty-sixth session of the International Labor Conference, Paul Robeson, speaking as chair of the Council on African Affairs, criticized the ILO for having no direct representation of colonial peoples.[15] Likewise, Thyra Edwards asked pointedly in the *Crisis* whether the leadership of the American Federation of Labor (AFL) was indifferent to questions involving colonies and racial minorities, adding that "racial minorities is hardly the term for a group which constitutes one and a half billion, 75 percent of the world's human population." She both criticized the AFL for not involving African American, Puerto Rican, Filipino, and Virgin Islander representatives in the conference deliberations and encouraged black American leaders to follow the example of Paul Robeson and the CAA, the African Methodist Episcopal Church, and Carter Wesley's chain of Texas papers in taking a greater interest in the conference.[16]

The Congress of Industrial Organizations (CIO) was affiliated with the World Federation of Trade Unions, formed through an alliance of CIO leaders and the British and Soviet labor movements.[17] The unprecedented African involvement in international trade union congresses of 1945 indicated the greater receptivity of the WFTU to African labor (in contrast with the ILO), and the growing strength of African labor. When the WFTU met in London in February, the *Defender* declared that it might be "the most significant conference in history for the colored peoples of the world," because colonial peoples would have a voice and a vote in international affairs for the first time. Moreover, "it is fitting and proper that this precedent-shattering event should come at a world labor meeting. Around the earth wherever men of color make their home, they are primarily working men who use their hands to earn their bread. Their past, present and future belongs with labor. In unions lies their salvation, because it is in the organization of men who toil that democracy reaches its full fruition."[18] The same issue covered "labor's sweeping victory" in Jamaica with the election of Alexander Bustamante, founder of the Bustamante Industrial Trades Union; a labor strike in Uganda; and a successful two-month transit strike in South Africa.[19] In the following weeks the *Pittsburgh Courier* and the *Chicago Defender* both featured front-page reports by George Padmore on African and Asian representation at the conference. Kenneth Hill of Jamaica demanded complete self-determination for all colonial peoples of Africa, the West Indies, and the Pacific area. Hill, representing Caribbean workers, and Wallace-Johnson, representing African workers, were among the delegates appointed to draw up a constitution and a program for the new federation.[20] Press accounts of the involvement of anticolonialists in the WFTU extended over the next several months.[21]

Padmore and other black American journalists sometimes intervened politically in the events they covered. Rayford Logan, then the *Courier*'s foreign affairs editor, cabled CIO president Sidney Hillman at the WFTU conference to urge "independence, self-government, autonomy, first-class citizenship in all dependent areas."[22] Henry Lee Moon, another African American journalist, worked for the CIO's Political Action Committee. First involved with the WFTU through the

CIO, he became instrumental in securing black American involvement in the Manchester Pan-African Congress and promoting interest in the event. Besides covering international labor conferences, he familiarized African American audiences with African trade union leaders. In a 1945 feature article, for example, he reported that after five years of exile and imprisonment the Sierre Leone trade unionist I. T. A. Wallace-Johnson had challenged WFTU conference delegates to "be prepared to fight against British and other colonial imperialism which, to us in the colonies, is even worse than fascism." Observing that Wallace-Johnson was "possessed of a rare charm, wit and humor" and "seems to derive a keen pleasure out of recounting tales of his imprisonment and exile," Moon sketched Wallace-Johnson's trade union activities, beginning in 1914 when he had led a strike of twenty-five customs service employees.[23]

Moon also assessed the stance of American labor organizations on colonial issues. In addition to noting that the AFL had been admonished for failing to send representatives to the WFTU conference, Moon praised Sidney Hillman for his outspoken support of colonial representation.[24] Later that year, however, at the October WFTU congress in Paris, the positive appraisal of Hillman was reversed: black American papers charged that he had betrayed the West African delegates by maneuvering in favor of the election of white South African delegates to the Constitution Committee.[25] The Hillman controversy continued for weeks. *Courier* writer Horace R. Cayton attacked Hillman's actions. George Schuyler, reporting that delegates at the Pan-African Congress "will be largely African students and labor leaders," argued that the "African labor leaders, doubled-crossed by Sidney Hillman, . . . will probably be in the mood for a pan-African gathering, realizing that the Negro must save himself if he is to be saved." Linking the betrayal of the Africans to the prospects of African Americans, a *Courier* editorial argued that Hillman's actions should warn black Americans to be wary of the CIO Political Action Committee.[26]

The October 1945 meeting of the WFTU was of particular interest to African American journalists and activists because of the participation of West African delegates, which in turn facilitated the organizing of the Pan-African Congress in Manchester.[27] At the February WFTU congress in London, the Pan-African Federation had taken advantage of the presence of African trade unionists to call for a Pan-African Congress in the fall. A meeting sponsored by the International African Service Bureau set up a provisional committee, which included Jomo Kenyatta of Kenya and Wallace-Johnson of Sierra Leone, to work on the Pan-African conference.[28]

It is significant that the first black American contact with the Padmore group about the conference was through the auspices of a labor organization. Henry Lee Moon attended the WFTU congress as staff for the CIO Political Action

Committee and over the next several years his work with the Pan-African Federation was instrumental in forming links between U.S. labor and anticolonial movements.

The conference planners hoped to include African Americans through the auspices of the NAACP. Walter White, visiting London in 1944, had met with members of the International African Service Bureau, the West African Students Union, and the League of Coloured Peoples. They discussed plans to form a "world-wide colored liberation front composed of Africans, West Indians, Afro-Americans, and other colored races."[29]

But it was from an article by Padmore in the *Defender* that Du Bois, already pursuing the idea of organizing a conference with Harold Moody and Amy Jacques Garvey, learned of the new initiative. Du Bois objected to the plans outlined in the *Defender*, questioning the location and the date, insisting that it was "of the greatest importance" that a Pan-African Congress be held in Africa.[30] This early correspondence between Du Bois and Padmore, from which grew a close political collaboration that would continue until Padmore's death in 1959, offers a unique glimpse into the intellectual and political history of Pan-Africanism. At the same time, the different perspectives hinted at in this letter illustrate Du Bois's political and intellectual distance from African organizations. For him, Pan-Africanism was a political project, but his sense of institutional possibilities was circumscribed by his lack of contact with the new trade union and anticolonial formations that had arisen in the previous decade. To White and the NAACP he wrote:

> There is no reason to think that the present congress is going to be more Pan-African than the others. In fact, Africa is a vast and deeply separated continent and its unity must be a matter of future planning and upbuilding rather than of past fact. Nevertheless, the people of Africa and more especially the darker peoples of Negro and mulatto origin, have in modern days, increasingly common oppression, desires, and ideals. It will be difficult to forge these into one united demand, but it will not be impossible.[31]

To Padmore, Du Bois argued that they should be very "catholic" and "avoid pushing people too far," given political differences among participants. He was concerned not to offend Moody, who objected to trade union and Communist participation. At times their correspondence offers almost a comedy of errors and misperceptions on the part of both Du Bois and Padmore about the political milieu of the other, starkly illustrating initial differences in a relationship that developed into close personal and political collaboration. Du Bois, for example, greatly encouraged by labor gains among black Americans but still ignorant of the centrality of trade unions in the new West African and British Pan-African formations, assumed that the British groups such as Moody's would be skeptical about working with labor. He explained to Padmore that "American Negroes . . . are much more radical and broadminded than they were a generation ago and wish to go far in cooperating with the labor movement."[32] Padmore responded with exaggerated claims of "complete unanimity of purpose and outlook among the colonial peoples of the British empire."[33] At the same time, he emphasized his interest in working with African Americans and reminded Du Bois that he had talked to Walter White during White's visit to England and had discussed the possibilities of a conference when White spoke to the West African Student Union.[34]

Despite Du Bois's initial reservations about the Padmore organization, communication from Henry Lee Moon persuaded him to support the effort. Moon asserted that there was a great deal of interest in a Pan-African Congress in Britain and described meetings in London, Manchester, Liverpool, and Cardiff, as well as with colonial delegates to the World Trade Union Conference. In Cardiff, for example, he had met with "a working class group composed of African and West Indian Seamen and factory workers." Impressed by activists such as James Taylor of the Gold Coast, Kenyatta, and Wallace-Johnson, Moon contended that Moody's reservations about the conference came from "doubting the wisdom of relating the conference in any way to the labor movement. The problem he maintains is humanitarian and not political or economic."[35]

Convinced, Du Bois next sought to address Moody's reservations. Holding a conference around the time of the Paris WFTU meeting, he wrote Moody, would make possible "direct representation from Africa and the Caribbean which would be impossible under other circumstances." More important, Du Bois now insisted:

the intellectual leaders of the Negro throughout the world must in the future make close alliance and work in close cooperation with the leaders of labor. . . . Africa cannot neglect this necessary extension of democracy. Our problems of race are not simply philanthropic; they are primarily economic and political: the problem of earning a living among the poorest people in the world, the problem of education, of health and of political autonomy, either within or without the empires.[36]

Du Bois's sense of the institutional base of Pan-Africanism had thoroughly changed. He quickly accepted trade union–based Pan-Africanism because it resonated with his own ideas about politics and economics. Moreover, his recent work with Alphaeus Hunton of the CAA had drawn his attention both to American labor and to the role of organized labor in anticolonial politics. Hunton had encouraged Du Bois to invite representatives of American labor to a Colonial Conference in New York City in the spring of 1945, on which they had collaborated, and had argued that changes in the CIO and AFL were an "index of the enhanced role labor will play in international policies."[37] Reflecting these discussions with Hunton, Du Bois told Moody that in the United States cooperation had been achieved between the intelligentsia and labor: "We see now that only in union can progress be made."[38]

The 1945 Pan-African Congress opened on October 15 in Manchester, England, with eighteen colonial trade unions and twenty-five political and cultural organizations represented.[39] As the organizers had hoped, the strong representation of organizations from the African continent and the leadership of what Imanuel Geiss has called the "the labour wing of the nationalist movement" distinguished the congress from earlier efforts led by middle class groups from the diaspora.[40] Yet the conference affirmed the strong ties of Africans to those in the diaspora. Employing the same international language that African Americans used to link their struggles to Africans and colonized peoples, the congress issued a declaration stating, "We believe the success of Afro-Americans is bound up with the emancipation of all African peoples and also other dependent peoples and laboring classes everywhere. . . . American Negroes continue their demand for full rights of American citizenship, economic, political and social."[41]

Although Du Bois and Moon were the only African Americans who actually attended, the Manchester conference received widespread and enthusiastic attention from African American leaders and journalists. African American trade unionists, including A. Philip Randolph of the Brotherhood of Sleeping Car Porters, sent fraternal greetings.[42] The *Afro-American* reported that "autonomy and independence for Africa were demanded by the 200 delegates representing 60 nations and groups of African descent" who attended this fifth Pan-African Congress.[43] In the *Defender*, Padmore charted the details of Congress declarations, including opposition to "the unequal distribution of wealth and also the rule of wealth and conduct of industry solely for private profit," and "a united effort with trade union labor."[44] Padmore's role as principal organizer and— through his reports for papers throughout the United States and West Africa— chief publicist of the conference highlights the thinness of the line separating journalism and organizing in this period, as well as Padmore's singular place in international anticolonialism.

The dearth of direct black American involvement was due mainly to a lack of travel resources but partly also to political tensions. Du Bois had trouble securing the involvement of the NAACP and further trouble in obtaining a visa, making his participation in the conference uncertain until shortly before it opened.[45] He later noted that he had not been able to ask the CAA to participate "officially because of the hesitation of the NAACP."[46] In an era of widespread left-liberal cooperation, Walter White was among those liberals most skeptical about cooperating with the left. And clear tensions existed between the CAA and the Pan-

African Federation, going back to the mutual suspicions between Padmore and Yergan evident in their 1937 meeting.[47] CAA reports on the Manchester congress did not mention Padmore, and it seems likely that Hunton and Yergan ignored him because of his expulsion from the Comintern. Moreover, Padmore had his own suspicions about the CAA. To Du Bois he launched into an attack on Yergan, who, he complained, "no doubt" had contacts with the Communists in South Africa.[48] Again, however, these differences among anticolonialists did not preclude cooperation. Padmore explicitly expressed a desire to cooperate with the CAA, and the CAA's *New Africa* reported favorably on the congress, praising its efforts "to forge a kind of Colonial International." The CAA later signed on to Pan-African Federation petitions and publicized its work.[49]

BLACK AMERICANS AND THE PAN-AFRICAN FEDERATION

Du Bois was elected president of the Pan-African Congress, Padmore explained in the *Gold Coast Observer*, as an expression of confidence and appreciation "for having guided the movement until it has at last found a mass basis among the darker peoples of Africa and other parts of the Colonial world."[50] After the conference, Du Bois served as a liaison between the Pan-African Federation and black American groups. As president of the federation, he organized a petition to the United Nations in 1946 requesting authorization to attend sessions of and send consultants to the General Assembly and any committees dealing with Africa, in order to "help voice the complaints and demands of African Negroes." Stating the federation's aim to establish freedom and political autonomy for African peoples, the petition also embodied the belief in political reciprocity, asserting that the Pan-African Federation "had far reaching and increasing influence among Negroes and has especially brought people of Negro descent in the Americas into sympathy with their African brethren."[51]

Black American organizations and individuals participating in the Pan-African Committee and approving the petition represented a very wide cross section of ministers, educators, philanthropic groups, trade unions, fraternal societies, and other groups. Organizations and individuals accepting membership on the committee included the Council on African Affairs, Southern Negro Youth Congress, National Council of Negro Women, Adam Clayton Powell Jr., Henry Lee Moon (for the CIO Political Action Committee, New York), W. H. Jernagin (director of the Washington bureau, National Fraternal Council of Churches, and president of the National Sunday School and BTU Congress), American Teachers Association, H. Councill Trenholm, National Bar Association, Alpha Phi Alpha fraternity; New York State Conference of NAACP Branches; and African Student Association.[52]

It is notable that black American support of the Pan-African Federation, as was typical of the politics of the African diaspora, had its major institutional base in black middle-class institutions, despite the political and ideological emphasis on labor and on black peoples as part of the laboring classes. Part of the explanation is that black Americans lacked a strong industrial or trade union base. Despite gains made by black workers during World War II, the majority of African Americans were still in nonunionized agricultural and service sector employment.[53] This points to an institutional weakness in the politics, but other factors too explain both the composition and the viability of the broad coalition. Of more immediate political importance than the continued dominance of unskilled labor for black workers were the striking changes of the World War II era, when, as the historian William H. Harris has demonstrated, "as many blacks left the farms for munitions and other industries as had gone north during the great migrations of World War I."[54] The marked growth in the number of black workers in unions and considerable job diversification led to raised expectations and a focus on jobs among civil rights activists. In addition, the overall political strength of unions in this era contributed to a greater influence for black workers in unions than the numbers would suggest.[55]

Moreover, as the historian Kevin Gaines has argued, the occupations within the black community that are widely perceived as middle class (teaching, the clergy, business, the professions) cannot be regarded as the equivalent of the business, managerial, and craft labor occupations among whites from which black peoples were largely excluded. The precariousness of the black elite and relative lack of access to capital meant that a material basis for a black middle class was always on shifting sands. If in periods such as the turn of the century, racial uplift ideology relied on strategies of class stratification, at other times, black middle-class ideology has emphasized demands for political inclusion articulated to broader movements for social justice. Indeed, the cross-class coalitions represented by black American support for the Pan-African Federation were typical of civil rights struggles in this era.[56]

THE NIGERIAN GENERAL STRIKE

Through the immediate postwar era, labor struggles in Africa continued to win the attention and support of black Americans. The 1945 general strike in Nigeria, and subsequent suppression of the Nigerian press by the British, not only stimulated widespread coverage in the African American press but led to ad hoc support organizations and efforts in the United States. Nnamdi Azikiwe, the leading West African anticolonial activist in the mid-1940s and editor of a chain of newspapers, was the key figure in the fight against British suppression of the Nigerian press. Azikiwe had studied in the United States at

Howard and Lincoln universities from the mid-1920s to 1934, working closely with Ralph Bunche and especially Alain Locke. It was at Howard that Azikiwe first encountered George Padmore, who spoke there on the 1928 American presidential elections. The two cooperated later in founding the International African Service Bureau in London in 1937 and in the Pan-African Federation and Manchester Pan-African Congress in 1945. Over the years Padmore was a frequent contributor to Azikiwe's newspapers in West Africa, and Azikiwe's broad contact with African Americans included writing for such African-American papers as the *Philadelphia Tribune* and the *Baltimore Afro-American*.[57] Back in West Africa, Azikiwe encouraged Kwame Nkrumah, Mbonu Ojike, K. O. Mbadiwe, and others to study in the United States. Azikiwe seems to have believed that Britain's muted racism encouraged a respect for the British system, whereas education in America, with its overt racism and large African American community, fostered dissatisfaction and at the same time provided the tools to fight colonialism and racism.

Azikiwe returned to American awareness in 1945 and remained a key figure over the next decade.[58] The general strike began on June 22, 1945, and lasted for ten weeks. Padmore reported that 500,000 members of the eighty unions in the Nigerian Trade Union Council were involved. Railroad workers started the strike after the acting governor refused to grant the demand of a united front trade union committee, deeply concerned with wartime inflation, for a 50 percent pay increase. Within one day, government employees—including postal and telegraph workers, electricians and helpers, lawyers and laborers—had walked out with the railroaders.[59] Harold Preece observed in the *Crisis* that "the organized workers of Nigeria" had "challenged that pseudo-civilization known as imperialism" with "the first general strike in Africa since the Hebrews under Moses staged a mass stoppage preparatory to a mass walkout from Egypt." Documenting the strike's effectiveness in "shutting down Nigeria," Preece reported that within three days it was impossible to ride a bus or train, to send a letter or a telegram. "House servants, employed by the British gentility, failed in many cases to show up to work, leaving the gentlemen and their wives to empty their own slops and brew their own tea."[60]

The CAA, which had been covering Nigerian trade union activity in its newsletter *New Africa* and monitoring labor conditions, warned of an impending general strike.[61] When it broke out, the CAA formed an emergency committee to support the strikers.[62] In London too, as Kwame Nkrumah reported for the *Gold Coast Observer and Weekly Advertiser*, a rally of thousands of Africans, Indians, West Indians, and other colonials pledged solidarity with the workers of Nigeria, and the Pan-African Federation issued appeals on their behalf to black leaders and labor and progressive organizations in America, the West Indies, India, China, Mexico, and elsewhere.[63]

In response to strike agitation and coverage, the British government first suppressed two daily papers published in Lagos, Nigeria—the *West African Pilot* and the *Daily Comet*—and then shut down others in the Azikiwe chain.[64] The strike and press ban stimulated a series of telegrams to Lord Halifax and the British Embassy in Washington and the Colonial office in London from African American and other progressive American organizations.[65] In the United States those included the NAACP, the United Auto Workers (UAW), the Garvey Club, the National Committee for India's Freedom, the Socialist Workers Party, the African Students Association, and the Universal Negro Improvement Association. On the basis of NAACP information that Azikiwe had been arrested, his life threatened, and his newspapers suppressed by order of Governor Richards for supporting strikers who were asking a sixty-cent daily wage, Walter White warned Colonel Oliver Stanley of the Colonial Office in London that these actions would "greatly discredit British and Allied claims" that the war was being fought for freedom of men everywhere. R. J. Thomas, UAW President, urged "full protection of editor Azikiwe in [the] right to advocate organization of Nigerian workers."[66]

In response, the British Colonial Office argued that the suspension of the newspapers had been ordered because of "a series of misrepresentations in the local press of the facts regarding the strike of the Government technical workers," and that the strike was illegal because the workers had repudiated the action of their trade union leaders, who had agreed to settle constitutionally.[67]

As the press ban wore on, it captured increasing attention in African American newspapers. The *Afro-American* reported in March 1946 that "the ban imposed by the British government on the chain of influential native newspapers edited and directed by Nnamdi Azikiwe, fearless publisher and his associates, still remains in effect."[68] Quoting Azikiwe's announcement to the government invoking Claude McKay's poem "If We Must Die," another front-page *Afro-American* article reported the formation of a "Zikist movement" by "Nigerian youths and progressive elements, resentful of this official effort to destroy the power and influence of the native press."[69] On the same day, the *Defender* described six different moves on the part of the British "to stifle the Zik chain."[70]

African American support of the Nigerian workers and press was part of the cross-fertilization of Pan-Africanism and world labor that peaked in 1946 and went in hand in hand with unprecedented worldwide trade union militancy. As 1946 began, two million industrial workers were on strike in the biggest U.S. industries and taking part in the first general strikes in twelve years.[71] A single issue of the *Afro-American* in February 1946 carried eight articles on different strikes in the United States, the Caribbean, and Africa, including those by workers in Liberia; steelworkers in Philadelphia; 35,000 steel, meat, construction, and electrical workers in New Jersey; General Electric employees in Philadelphia; the Oilfield Workers' Trade Union in Trinidad; railway workers in Jamaica; and packing-house workers in Kansas City, who were supported by Paul Robeson and Cab Calloway. Robeson told the workers: "I will be right on the picket line with you and if anything happens, let it happen to me too."[72]

Robeson's most sustained and visible strike support, however, involved South African mine workers in 1946, at the apex of a CAA-led pre-apartheid solidarity movement among African Americans. This movement involved not only strike support but extensive lobbying at the United Nations and a highly publicized famine relief campaign. The groundwork for these campaigns had been laid through Max Yergan's extensive South African contacts and by the 1943 recruitment of Alphaeus Hunton to the staff of the CAA.[73] In order to understand the emergence of this movement, one must examine the changes in the CAA.

HUNTON AND THE NEW CAA

William Alphaeus Hunton Jr., one of the most neglected African American intellectuals in studies of this period, joined the CAA in 1943 as educational director and editor of *New Africa* after seventeen years as an assistant professor of English at Howard University.[74] A person with exceptional talent, rare personal integrity, a deep commitment to humanistic values, and an enormous capacity for hard work, Hunton was described by one friend as a gentleman revolutionary and praised by Du Bois in 1957 for his thorough knowledge and understanding of the continent of Africa. Hunton's disarming modesty, self-possession, gentle sense of humor, and quiet tenacity rarely failed to impress those who knew him. If his failure to leave many personal records make him something of a phantom beside larger-than-life friends and colleagues such as Robeson and Du Bois, the history of his family reveals the rich traditions of democratic struggle that animated his vision and contributed to his unusual focus and energy.

Born in Atlanta, Georgia, in 1903, Hunton grew up in a remarkable family with a long history of social and political activism. His slave-born grandfather, Stanton Hunton, was surreptitiously educated by the Virginia woman who owned him. After three unsuccessful attempts to flee, he bought his freedom in 1840 and in 1843 moved to a small settlement of freedmen in Chatham, Ontario, Canada, where he made a living as a brickmason. In 1858 he became a close confidant of John Brown when the raid on Harper's Ferry was being planned.[71] Perhaps he met other associates of Brown's such as Martin R. Delany, or encountered the latter's Emigration Society. At any rate, his sixth son, William Alphaeus, would develop a deep interest in Africa.

Alphaeus Hunton's father, William Alphaeus Hunton, was born in Chatham in 1863 to Stanton and Ann Conyer Hunton, a free African American from Cincinnati. The elder Hunton graduated from the Wilberforce Institute of Ontario in 1884. In Ottawa he joined the local Young Men's Christian Association and in

1888 moved to Norfolk, Virginia, to become the first paid black YMCA secretary. In this post Hunton traveled widely in the United States, Europe, China, and Japan. He also read a great deal about Africa, was deeply concerned about its colonial oppression, and urged the extension of the YMCA movement there. As Addie Hunton recalled in her biography of her husband, "Again and again we had talked about Africa."[76]

If Alphaeus Jr.'s work was in many ways a secular continuation of his father's religious internationalism, it was perhaps even more squarely within the radical political traditions of his activist mother. Addie Waite was born in Norfolk in 1866; she was educated in the public schools of Boston and the City College of New York and taught sociology at Alabama A & M College. She married Hunton in 1893 and became his assistant and close colleague. After attending the founding convention of the National Association of Colored Women in 1895, she carried its work to the deep South. In 1899 the Huntons settled in Atlanta, where William Alphaeus Jr. was born in 1903. The 1906 Atlanta riots had a profound impact on the family: "In a moment," wrote Addie, "all our sense of security was gone, and we had to realize that we, as colored people, had really no rights as citizens whatsover. It left us very empty, for we knew in that hour that all for which we had labored and sacrificed belonged not to us but to a ruthless mob."[77]

Since William Alphaeus Sr. was about to embark on a tour of Asia for the YMCA, the Huntons left Atlanta and in early 1907 moved to their permanent residence in Brooklyn, New York, where Alphaeus Jr. grew up.[78] Perhaps the senior Hunton was moved by the juxtaposition of the violence of Atlanta and the democratic movements sweeping Asia at the turn of the century. At any rate, his resolve to extend the YMCA movement into Asia and Africa deepened, and before his death from tuberculosis in 1916 he had lived to see Max Yergan leave for India as the first black American assigned to an overseas YMCA station.

Returning from a two-year stint in Europe where she received a degree in linguistics from the Sorbonne, Addie Hunton continued her remarkable political activities. Active in the YWCA throughout her life, she became a leader in the fight for women's rights. She published articles on black women and the women's club movement in the *Atlanta Independent,* the *Voice of the Negro,* the *Colored American Magazine,* and the *Crisis.* Her "Negro Women Defended" castigated those who accused black women of immorality. She helped organize the first conference of black employed and volunteer workers in New York City, and in 1912 her survey of the conditions of three thousand industrial workers in Winston-Salem, North Carolina, was published by the national YWCA as "Beginnings among Colored Women."[79] After the death of her husband, Addie Hunton went to France with the YWCA to work among black American troops during

World War I. After the war she served as a field secretary for the NAACP and wrote about race relations in American-occupied Haiti. Continuing her efforts for women's rights, in 1921 she led a delegation of sixty black women from fourteen states to challenge Alice Paul and the National Woman's Party, addressing the disenfranchisement of black women and presenting their concerns.[80] Addie was also a principal organizer for the 1927 Pan-African Congress in New York City. She died in Brooklyn in 1943, the same year that her son Alphaeus Hunton Jr. joined the CAA.[81]

Alphaeus grew up in Brooklyn and attended the Boys High School. After the death of his father he worked for several years as a porter to finance his education. He graduated from Howard in 1924 and received his M.A. in English from Harvard University in 1925. Hunton accepted an appointment as assistant professor of English at Howard University, where he specialized in Victorian literature. He believed that social and economic studies were essential for understanding literature, and his study of the nineteenth-century imperialist development of Britain proved indispensable in his later African research.[82]

Hunton studied for his doctorate at New York University from 1934 through 1938. His approach to literature and his dissertation, "Tennyson and the Victorian Political Milieu," were influenced by his dissertation instructor, Edwin Berry Burgum, a Marxist and an editorial board member of *Science and Society*. Tennyson, argued Hunton, was above all "deeply concerned with the preservation of law and order in the state, and with the broadening and strengthening of the empire." The thesis examined British empire theory and the public reaction in England and America to the glorification of Britain's imperial role.[83]

Hunton also wrote on the socialist poet William Morris, whom he deeply admired. His reflections on Morris provide a rare glimpse into the more personal elements of his own humanistic values. Hunton admired what he saw as Morris's independence, arguing that whatever the influences on his work, he knew no master or guide and was "essentially himself," "too big to be bound up by petty influences." Hunton praised his simple and unostentatious way of life, noting that "he was always working." Above all, he stressed Morris's "appreciation of beauty" (interestingly, a trait Hunton's friends and associates ascribed to him as well, one that he shared with his father), which led him "to work against the sordid conditions under which most men lived, and it was that that gave him hope of creating true art."[84]

In studying with Burgum, Hunton began to delve into Marxism-Leninism and became increasingly engaged in politics. He was involved in organizing Local 440 of the American Federation of Teachers (AFL) and argued for CIO affiliation, since in the obsolete craft structure of the AFL there was no place for black unskilled workers. When the National Negro Congress formed in 1936, with John P.

Davis as national secretary and A. Philip Randolph as its first president, Hunton served as a member of the national executive board and chair of the Labor Committee. Through the NNC he was active in campaigns to break down barriers to jobs, housing, and education for African Americans.[85] In that work and at Howard, Hunton developed a close relationship with Doxey A. Wilkerson, also a professor at Howard and head of the Civic Affairs Committee of the NNC. At some point in this period Hunton joined the Communist Party, probably influenced by members such as Wilkerson and fellow travelers such as Yergan. Hunton was to remain a member for the rest of his life but did not participate directly in the party's organizational activities.

It was probably through the NNC that he first met Max Yergan and encountered the Council on African Affairs, which he joined in 1943. It was also in 1943 that Hunton married Dorothy, following a two-year courtship and the considerable hesitation arising from two failed marriages and his self-described restless commitment to his work. Yet Dorothy was to become a constant companion for the remainder of his life, a colleague and source of support throughout his work at the CAA and later exile in Guinea, Ghana, and Zambia.[86]

The addition of Hunton to its staff inaugurated the period of the CAA's greatest influence. Hunton developed widespread African contacts and gained access to information on colonial affairs through correspondence and subscriptions to African and European periodicals. As editor of *New Africa*, he enabled the CAA to publish extensive coverage of trade union and political organizing throughout Africa, with an emphasis on southern Africa, Nigeria, and the Gold Coast. Since it was collecting the most thorough information on Africa available in the United States, the CAA also functioned as a press service, providing information to black American organizations, newspapers, and journals and later to United Nations delegates from several countries including the United States.[87] Under Hunton's editorship, *New Africa* focused on various forms of organizing in Africa—trade unions, women's groups, church groups—and analyzed the political economy of colonialism, especially trade and industrial relations and foreign investment.[88]

As the reorganized CAA gave more attention to political rather than strictly educational work, it sought to increase its membership. Several prominent African American liberals joined its ranks in 1944, including the prominent educator Rayford W. Logan and Mary McLeod Bethune. Bethune brought to the CAA decades of activism, most recently as president of the National Council of Negro Women and as an appointee to the National Youth Adminstration agency in the Roosevelt administration—part of his so-called "Black Cabinet." She also brought a longstanding interest in Africa, pride in her family's African ancestry and her strong but unfufilled youthful desire to work in Africa as a missionary.[89] Another especially active new member was E. Franklin Frazier.[90] Besides adding prominent members, for the first time the CAA sought to broaden its base, which helped to set up its later campaigns. CAA representatives traveled around the country, including the South, *New Africa* reported, in an effort to establish "educational centers for the community" and "mobilize the sentiment of church people who are interested in seeing America interested in Africa."[91]

The most significant work of the CAA involved South Africa. In 1944–45 it lobbied the South African government, reported on conditions in South Africa, and publicized the work of the African National Congress.[92] *New Africa* typically carried ANC statements, policy reports, and news of such efforts as the 1944 campaign against the pass laws.[93] And just as the CAA provided information on conditions in South Africa—not only in the United States but in African newspapers and journals such as Wallace-Johnson's *African Standard*—CAA work on South Africa received its own coverage in the African American press.[94]

In addition to institutional ties, similarities in the color bars that emerged in the settler societies and the American South drew African American organizers and journalists to work on South Africa.[95] Before and during the war they analyzed the mutual plight of black Americans and South Africans. The *Crisis*, which had long covered South Africa under the editorship of Du Bois, argued that black Americans should immediately recognize in the pronouncements of South African whites the political philosophy that "holds sway in Dixie."[96] Likewise, in 1939 the *Courier* discussed protests against police brutality in South Africa, noting that "life among natives in Africa and Negroes in America" was "parallel in many respects."[97] George Padmore's regular reporting for the *Courier* and the *Defender* brought dramatic coverage of boycotts and strikes in South Africa to the pages of the black American press.[98] He wrote, for example, of the 1944 bus boycott, organized by the ANC and involving more than half a million people, and of the 1945 strike of "ten thousand African natives of Johannesburg" against the trolley lines.[99] Padmore also warned of the postwar plans of the Smuts government to extend European control in Africa, and of the organization of the "notorious anti-Negro, anti-Semitic, and anti-labor Ox Wagon movement headed by Dr. Malan," which would come to power in 1948 and implement apartheid.[100]

THE SOUTH AFRICAN MINERS' STRIKE

Although comparisons between South Africa and the southern United States preceded and would long outlast the 1940s, the emergence of South Africa as a visible issue in the 1940s and the birth of a mid-1940s pre-apartheid solidarity movement led by the Council on African Affairs were part of the growing emphasis among African American activists on labor and political economy. Journalists discussed differences between the political economies of South Africa and African colonies without white settler populations. In-depth *Crisis* essays examined the singular political and economic role of South Africa in the global economy, with an emphasis on southern Africa. L. D. Reddick cautioned against viewing Africa solely through the "traditional reference of European imperialism and colonial exploitation," for such a lens obscured the unique role of South Africa in the global political economy. Rather, he said, the exploitation of Africa should be understood in terms of a complex relationship between British capital and local government and industry.[101] Rayford W. Logan reviewed the career of Jan Smuts over the previous twenty-five years and argued that Smuts "ranks second only to Churchill in the influence that he wields both within and without the British Commonwealth and Empire."[102]

Thus, even before the miners' strike of 1946 that sparked a CAA-led American solidarity effort, journalists were monitoring conditions in South African gold mines. A June 1944 *Defender* editorial explained how Britain and South Africa's sparring for profits led to the greater exploitation of African labor: "It is expected that a compromise will be arrived at by allowing the mining companies to recruit cheap labor from those territories under the direct rule of the London colonial office. It is believed that by setting up regional councils on which powers with colonies participate, laws can be made to regulate this traffic and direct these Africans into mining and agricultural industries according to the needs of the European employers."[103]

The *Afro-American* reported in March 1946 that Britain was able to "operate her famous Witwatersrand gold mines, through economic pressure that forces African natives to work an eight-hour shift for 50 cents," while the mines "pay huge dividends yearly on billions of dollars worth of stock." Moreover, great discrepancies between the wages of white and black workers meant that white underground miners averaged 68 cents an hour plus time and a half for overtime, while black underground workers received an average wage of seven cents hourly regardless of overtime.[104] In April 1946 the African Mineworkers Union resolved to claim a minimum wage of ten shillings a day and a range of improvements in working conditions. In May, after a series of wildcat work stoppages, the mineworkers voted in favor of a general strike if demands were not met.[105]

CAA and American labor support for the workers was acknowledged in the local press. *Inkululeko*, a Communist Party newspaper based in Johannesburg, reported that Yergan had "sharply assailed the anti-labor policy of the ruling class in South Africa." Discussing CAA plans for a rally at Madison Square Garden, *Inkululeko* praised the involvement and sponsorship of prominent CIO and AFL leaders and emphasized the participation of the Communist Party's wing of the labor movement, quoting Michael J. Quill, the Transport Workers Union president, and Louis Weinstock, secretary-treasurer of District Council 9 of the Brotherhood of Painters, Decorators and Paperhangers. Quill argued that the conditions of "American workers are not secure as long as millions of workers suffer under the oppressive burden of miserable wages and conditions in South

At his camp in Pompton Lakes, N. J., Joe Louis yesterday told Paul Robeson, chairman of the Council on African Affairs, that he was 100 per cent behind the Council's June 6 Madison Square Garden meeting in the interest of food and freedom for Africa. Robeson will speak and sing *Ballad for Americans* at the rally.

Boxing champion Joe Louis, with Paul Robeson, endorsing the CAA famine relief campaign at his camp in Pompton Lakes, N.J. *PM*, June 4, 1946.

Africa and other colonial countries"; he hoped that trade union involvement in CAA support for South Africa would help the "efforts of the World Federation of Trade Unions to raise standards of workers throughout the world." Weinstock said it was "outrageous" that only white workers were allowed collective bargaining rights in the Union of South Africa and emphasized that the WFTU had "endorsed the appeal of the African delegation for free trade unions and removal of all restrictions placed on them by the Smuts government."[106]

In August 1946, sixty to seventy thousand South African mineworkers "refused to go on shift in at least twelve mines." The Council for Non-European Trade

Alphaeus Hunton addressing four thousand people at Abyssinian Baptist Church to open the famine relief campaign. Josh Lawrence, Paul Robeson, Rev. Shelton Bishop, and Adam C. Powell Sr. are seated behind the cans and bags of food. (Photographs and Prints Division, Schomburg Center for Research in Black Culture, The New York Public Library, Astor, Lenox and Tilden Foundations.)

Unions (CNETU) called for a general strike in sympathy. The strike lasted a week and the response of the state was ruthless: at least twelve Africans were killed and more than a thousand injured as the result of police action.[107] The CAA publicized the strike in the United States and supported the striking miners. The *New York Times* published a letter to the editor from Paul Robeson outlining the strikers' cause and arguing that the owners of the South African gold mines "represent a form of tyranny repugnant to decent practice in modern industrial employment." Robeson appealed to "my fellow Americans" to protest these conditions to the South African ministry in Washington and to express support for the workers.[108] The CAA organized a letter campaign directed to H. T. Andrews, a minister of the Union of South Africa, protesting the "brutal smashing of the gold miners strike," along with the continuation of the pass system and the denial of trade union rights and decent living to African workers.[109]

As in Robeson's appeal, the CAA combined appeals to black solidarity with explicit claims about the rights and responsibilities of U.S. citizens. Asking Americans for "direct action against fascist-like exploitation of black men" by the British and South African governments, the CAA stressed the "direct dependency" of the South Africa gold economy "upon U.S. favor." In view of that dependency, the CAA outlined a program of action for American citizens, including letters to President Truman, the State Department, and Hershel Johnson, American delegate to the United Nations.[110] But journalists and activists argued further that international organization and pressure were necessary to support the miners. Reporting that the World Federation of Trade Unions had received an appeal from the African miners union urging it "to exercise its influence in behalf of the African miners before the United Nations and the International Labor Conference," the *Defender* forcefully asserted the necessity and efficacy of diaspora politics: "The issue is unlikely to come before the bar of world opinion at all unless Negro Americans and colonials raise it in the United Nations Assembly."[111]

FIGHTING FAMINE, FIGHTING RACISM

Besides supporting the miners' strike, the CAA coordinated a highly visible campaign for famine relief in South Africa's Ciskei region, which culminated in a rally of nineteen thousand persons at Madison Square Garden. The rally was preceded by a week of radio programs on the famine, featuring Broadway stars—Betty Garret, Canada Lee, Judy Holliday, Kenneth Spencer—along with Paul Robeson and Alphaeus Hunton. Also drawing the support of such luminaries as Joe Louis, this campaign strikingly illustrates the extent to which attention to culture and political economy went hand in hand, as well as the importance and visibility of South Africa in 1946.[112]

The campaign was initiated by Betty Radford and Govan Mbeki of the Johannesburg-based *Guardian*.[113] Working with the *Guardian* and the ANC's R. T. Bokwe, who was also a member of the CAA and was in charge of food distribution in the Ciskei, Hunton and Yergan organized meetings in New York, Los Angeles, and other western and southern American cities. In addition to CAA members, sponsors included Marian Anderson, Lena Horne, Adam Clayton

Powell Jr., Mary McLeod Bethune, and Arthur Spingarn.[114] The campaign received publicity not only in the United States but in South Africa and West Africa, capturing the attention of the South African government.

The opening meeting on January 7, 1946, drew a crowd of 4,500 to the Abyssinian Baptist Church in New York City, with Judge Hubert T. Delany presiding. Robeson sang and delivered the keynote address. Other speakers included Marian Anderson and Rev. Ben Richardson, editor of the *Protestant* and a prominent Harlem activist. Five tons of canned food and nearly $2,000 in cash were collected.[115] By January 18 fifty-two cases of food had been shipped to South Africa, and $1,000 had been forwarded to the African Food Fund at Middledrift, Ciskei.[116]

The extent to which analyses of political economy permeated popular discourse is evident in this campaign: press reports and CAA literature located the causes of the famine in land policy, linked to a host of other discriminatory measures. The CAA emphasized that the "lack of land is the basic cause of the Africans' lack of food," and resolutions passed at the Abyssinian Church meeting and forwarded to Smuts argued that to avoid recurrent food shortages "it is imperative that the government remove the land restrictions and the various economic and civil barriers, such as the colour bar, pass laws, denial of trade union rights, and complete political disfranchisement, which are the fundamental cause of the Africans' present and recurring distress."[117] The *Afro-American* reported the CAA contention that "while food shortages in Europe are due to war . . . the main obstacle to food provision in Africa" was "a lack of arable land for the natives, since European settlers have cornered the best soil areas."[118] Similarly, in the *Defender*, John Robert Badger emphasized the political and economic causes of the famine, explaining that four million Africans were restricted to 13 percent of the total land area of South Africa.[119]

In arguing that Africans were "starving under South Africa's fascist racial discrimination," Robeson and others linked antiracism with exploitation in their critiques.[120] Hunton protested to the *New York Times* that the paper had given five inches of space to starving baboons in South Africa while ignoring human starvation there.[121] Badger deplored the lack of interest in the famine on the part of "the big money's press or the official government sources of London and Washington." Indeed, Badger complained, so far as Secretary of State James Byrnes of South Carolina was concerned, there didn't seem to be "any people in Africa." Badger urged black Americans to "demand that the Truman Administration give equal consideration in its food program to the peoples of Africa, Asia and other colonial areas."[122] In an effort to stimulate government action, the CAA wrote to American officials involved in providing food for foreign relief: "Negroes in particular, while supporting fully the efforts to help starving peoples in Europe and Asia, are at the same time disturbed by the apparent indifference to the needs of the people in Africa."[123] This "indifference," moreover, mirrored the racist hypocrisy of the Union of South Africa. Max Yergan pointed out that while officials were directing starving black Africans to "pray for relief" from the drought, Prime Minister Jan Christian Smuts had launched an $8 million campaign to send food to Great Britain, and his government was buying corn and oats from Argentina and the United States to save European-owned cattle.[124]

In March 1946 Robeson launched a nationwide appeal for famine relief and called upon community leaders, newspapers, and churches to set aside March 31 as "Help Africa Day."[125] Augmenting these efforts, Hunton collected canned food and money from schoolchildren and community organizations in Brooklyn, New York, and a wide range of church and community groups across the country contributed to the campaign.[126] By the end of March the CAA had sent $1,800 and seventy-seven cases of canned food to Cape Town for distribution in the famine-stricken areas.[127] Publicity in the African American press included the *Afro-American*'s front-page article "Murder of a Race Primed in South Africa: 8,000,000 Natives Slowly Starving to Death on a Pound of Meal a Day," in which Michael Carter featured the work of Hunton and Yergan.[128] John Robert Badger praised the campaign in the *Defender*, noting that "thanks to the Council on African Affairs," information on the famine was available to the people of the United States.[129]

Coverage of the CAA's famine relief campaign in West and South Africa emphasized the importance of international solidarity among Africans and people of African descent. The *Guardian* quoted a resolution, passed at the Abyssinian Baptist Church meeting, that underlined these bonds: "We want our brothers and sisters in South Africa to know that they have friends here in America who realize that the fight against discrimination in the United States can be won only as part of the war against human exploitation and oppression in South Africa and everywhere else."[130] The *Gold Coast Observer* noted that the ANC thanked Paul Robeson and Max Yergan "for the great stand your Council is taking on behalf of Africans who have implicit trust in your representation of their case in world councils which they themselves are barred from attending."[131] A June 1946 issue of the *Gold Coast Observer* reported that Robeson is "'the voice of Africa outside of Africa' to the native African.... Mr. Robeson represents all their hopes and aspirations." Froma Sand, a Hollywood screenwriter, added that South Africans, oppressed by the British and the Boers and forgotten by the outside world, "hold in high esteem Paul Robeson, and other persons and organizations like the Council on African Affairs," and regard the famine relief campaign "as fighting his battle and bringing his case before the world."[132]

Among contributors to the campaign was Caribbean-born Hugh Mulzac, captain of the S.S. *Booker T. Washington*, "the first Negro Captain put in charge of a U.S. Victory ship during the war." Another contribution came from the Bahamas "to assist in the effort to give some relief to our brothers and sisters across the seas—in the Mother Land." For Yergan, the latter was especially noteworthy, "indicating the common bond between the Caribbean people whose own condition is very low and the exploited peoples of Africa." Even poor women in the Bahamas who had been unable to contribute any money, he explained in the *Gold Coast Observer*, had sent an assortment of handmade straw articles to New York to be sold for South African relief.[133]

The South African consulate in New York, and legation in Washington regularly followed the activities of the Council on African Affairs, but the Ciskei famine relief campaign received particular attention.[134] The government of the Union of South Africa had reason to worry. Not only had the CAA's support for South African miners and the famine campaign mobilized an extraordinary array of Americans, but the belief on the part of African Americans that their struggles were linked to those of Africans and all colonized peoples found its greatest institutional expression in the forums surrounding the founding and the early years of the United Nations. And in 1946, as worldwide attention turned to the new organization, the CAA joined with the government of India, the South African ANC, the Joint Passive Resistance Council of the Transvaal, and Natal Indian Congresses of South Africa to challenge the policies of the South African government at the United Nations.

CHAPTER FOUR

THE DIASPORA MOMENT

We say even to the President of the United States, we say to King George VI. of England, to Winston Churchill. If all you White Imperialist Rulers of the world, . . . if you refuse to do justice to those of my race in America. In the West Indies. In South and Central America. . . . We say to YOU LET THE BLACK PEOPLE FREE! GIVE THEM BACK THEIR AFRICAN TERRITORY! . . . Give themselves their own SELF-DETERMINATION! Give themselves their own representatives and protectorate government in Africa! which belongs to 22 millions black people of America 400 million black people scattered all over the world. The New Negro everywhere wants African liberation. . . . The New Negro of Harlem wants Post War jobs. Decent living wages, . . . we want our houses be painted TODAY! according to sanitary conditions. We want work for our Negro painters, Plumbers, Carpenters and others.

— Community Progressive Negro Painters Union, Inc. and the New Harlem Tenants League, to the Mayor of New York City, May 15th, 1946.

IN A LETTER TO Mayor William O'Dwyer of New York City in 1946, the Community Progressive Negro Painters Union and the New Harlem Tenants League invoked their membership in a community of "400 million black people scattered all over the world" to legitimize their own local claims to jobs and decent housing. Just as striking is their sense of audience. In addressing demands to "all you White Imperialist Rulers of the world," including the President of the United States, King George VI of England and Winston Churchill, the organizations named their oppressors not as arbitrarily exploitive and cruel individuals or states but as powerful actors in a global system of empire and racial capitalism that exploited and appropriated the land, labor, and bodies of black peoples "scattered all over the world."[1]

Diaspora identities had a particularly powerful resonance in the unusually fluid politics of the immediate post–World War II period, a time when the wartime agitation and discussion about colonial independence reached fruition. From the formation of the United Nations to the first stirrings of the Cold War, African American activists brought an elaborate vision of the rights and responsibilities of citizenship to their anticolonial political strategies. The Council on African Affairs was the most visible African American group seeking to influence the direction of American foreign policy, and despite its left-wing radicalism, the

CAA stood at the center, not at the margins, of black American opinion on colonialism. A wide range of African American leaders, churches, and fraternal, business, and community organizations lobbied on anticolonial issues and sought representation in UN bodies. The black American press detailed anticolonial politics at the United Nations. In the aftermath of World War II an extraordinarily broad consensus on colonial issues existed among black Americans.

The formation of the United Nations Organization in 1945, providing a forum for international debate, offered new opportunities for a politics imbued with a sense of identity among African peoples everywhere. With the imminent independence of India and the promise of new Asian and African states in the near future, the possibility of winning political and economic rights through international strategies looked very hopeful in this period. Indeed, diaspora-based strategies coalesced in a unique way in 1946 and 1947. The black American CAA, the Joint Passive Resistance Council of the Natal, the Transvaal Indian Congresses in South Africa, the African National Congress, and the government of India came together at the United Nations to fight the attempts of the South African government to annex South-West Africa and to fight new legislation that would further restrict the rights of Indians within the Union of South Africa.

LOBBYING FOR GLOBAL DEMOCRACY

Through the first part of 1945 the policies of the American government toward colonialism were still indeterminate.[2] Given the continued wartime alliance of the United States and the Soviet Union, and President Roosevelt's real if ambiguous commitment to the independence of European colonies, William Roger Louis and Ronald Robinson have argued, "At least up to the summer of 1944 it seemed probable that the State Department's proposals for an international authority to preside over the liquidation of the European colonial empires had the backing of the president and might inspire American policy after the war."[3] Internal governmental squabbling on the question of the future of the colonies—described by then Secretary of State Edward Stettinius as "warfare between the 'Hottentots and Crusaders' in the State Department and 'hard-boiled realists' of the Navy and War Department"—created a situation in which anticolonial activists could lobby those sympathetic to their goals.

The strategies of the Council on African Affairs would change dramatically by the end of 1946, but in 1944, with wartime alliances still in place, it could lobby within a context of widespread support for new international bodies to promote world peace and security.[4] Conveying the sense of hope that the defeat of fascism and the end of European political dominance would open the door to a far more equitable world, Max Yergan declared in a February radio address that the framework of the Atlantic Charter and the Teheran Declaration offered "the realistic possibility, indeed, the necessity, of carrying forward a broadly conceived plan for meeting the health needs, providing the economic development, and insuring speedy advancement toward complete self-government for the African peoples."[5]

The CAA advocated postwar economic restructuring along the lines of a worldwide New Deal. Paul Robeson and Yergan argued that in order to avoid economic collapse in America and around the world like that of the 1930s, it was necessary to find new markets; this view was shared by a broad consensus of government, business, and labor leaders as well as journalists. The CAA further argued, however, that because the world economy was severely distorted by the political and economic exploitation of colonial peoples, "such markets can only be created by raising the purchasing power in those dependent areas where millions have hitherto known little but poverty and want. In somewhat the same way that the Southern region of this country is called the nation's number one economic problem, so the colonial territories all over the globe may be called the world's number one economic problem."[6] Summing up in a *Defender* article, John Robert Badger quoted Yergan: "Raising the living standards and well-being of the peoples of colonial countries to a new and higher level is an indispensable condition for gaining economic security in the postwar world. It is an indispensable condition for avoiding right here in the United States a repetition of the wholesale unemployment and privation that we experienced in the last decade."[7]

The CAA's contention that anticolonialism was a necessary feature of economic expansion was shared by a large liberal and left faction in the United States, including such politicians as Henry Wallace. Others, though agreeing on the need for economic expansion, emphasized instead the role of U.S. investment in the mode of Henry Luce's vision of the "American Century," which called for U.S. political and economic dominance in world affairs.[8] The resolution of this debate would not become clear until the Cold War years, but the lines were clearly drawn by 1944.[9] Capturing the heart of the differences over postwar policy—the question of who owns and controls the world's resources—Kumar Goshal warned in the *Courier* that "American dreamers of a super-imperialism wish to see a reactionary government in France through which they can gain a foothold in Europe and—through the French empire—in Africa and Asia as well. This policy will only lead to disaster." Goshal argued that "the only sane way out is the way visualized by such leaders as Henry Wallace and Philip Murray. It is to help industrialize the industrially backward—that is, the colonial—countries on the basis of freedom and equality, and free and equal access to all raw materials and natural sources." The necessary role of the leading industrial countries in this development, he continued, would be as collaborators rather than rivals: "They must forgo the luxury of imperialism, and accept as equal partners the peoples who are in bondage today."[10]

Thus activists promoted Africans' place in international commerce as free and equal trading partners with their own interests, distinct from those of the colonial powers. CAA lobbying regarding British government regulation of the West African cocoa trade illustrates their attempts to work for African economic independence. Wartime inflation had hit British West Africa especially hard. Commodities produced there and in the Belgian Congo became critical following Japanese victories in the Pacific, as the Allies lost access to raw materials in Malaya, Singapore, and the Dutch East Indies.[11] British policy on the wartime marketing of colonial exports was decisive in squeezing both producers and consumers: "The prices of colonial exports were controlled and kept at artificially low levels during the war by the British government at the same time that the cost of colonial imports rose dramatically."[12]

Calling the British handling of the cocoa crop "a classic example" of commercial exploitation of colonial peoples, the CAA's *New Africa* revealed that the British government's Cocoa Control Board was headed by John Cadbury, an owner of one of Britain's principal chocolate firms. Despite wartime difficulties, Cadbury Brothers had "recorded a profit of nearly fifteen million dollars—a profit not shared by the producers."[13] The Farmers Committee of British West Africa asked the CAA to help the growers gain an audience with the American Embassy in London about cocoa production and prices. When the U.S. State Department intervened on behalf of the U.S. cocoa trade and chocolate industry in response to British policy on cocoa prices, Yergan pressed for a meeting between State Department officials and the Farmers Committee, stressing that "African interests as well as American and British interests are involved in the issue of cocoa production."[14]

Yet work on such specific economic issues was limited by the CAA's lack of political leverage in influencing economic policies and its circumscribed contact with West African groups. The council sought to exploit ambiguities and differences within the U.S. government, pushing for clearer and stronger anticolonial policy. When the State Department's Division of African Affairs was formed in 1944 with Henry Villard as its chief, the CAA applauded Villard's promotion of the "open door" policy, as set forth in the Atlantic Charter, but described his policies as progressive but inadequate. The CAA endorsed Villard's positing of reciprocal dependence, whereby "Africa needs our skills and services . . . just as we need Africa's resources," but nonetheless cautioned that the open door policy would be worse than useless unless economic developments gave "primary consideration to the interests of the African peoples."

Moreover, the CAA found, Villard "falsely minimized the desire of the Africans for self-government."[15]

Continuing to push for stronger anticolonial policies, in April 1944 the CAA organized a conference for black American and American-based African organizations to develop strategies lobbying the United States and other governments.[16] The meeting's co-sponsors indicate the range of church, community and political groups that allied with the CAA on anticolonial issues. They included Mary McLeod Bethune, president of the National Council of Negro Women; Rayford Logan of Howard University; Cecelia Cabaniss Sounders, executive secretary of the Harlem YMCA; David H. Sims, president of the First Episcopal District, AME Church; and the African Students Association.[17] Kwame Nkrumah, future president of Ghana, was also a participating sponsor.[18] Insisting that promoting the welfare of Africans and other dependent peoples "must be an integral part of the projected international order," conference participants argued that abolishing "the inferior social, economic, and political status of Africans and all colonized peoples" was an essential prerequisite "for the achievement of international harmony and security." Resolutions asked that the United States take the lead in raising living standards and promoting the industrialization of the African economy, stressing that "Africans themselves" should be the "principal beneficiaries of this economic progress."[19] Calling for moves toward self-determination, other resolutions demanded accountability within proposed international bodies; existing or projected regional commissions within Africa, for example, "should be held accountable to the United Nations organization for the abolition of all forms of political discrimination based on race, creed, or color."[20]

The CAA invited Villard to the conference and representatives from other governments as well.[21] Representatives of the Soviet and Belgian governments and the French National Committee attended, as did the consul general for Ethiopia. Neither the U.S. State Department nor the British government participated, but the meeting did draw their attention. British Ambassador Viscount Halifax described increasing pressure in the United States "for an African Charter and guarantees of improved economic conditions and ultimate self-government for the African peoples." Noting that "the driving force behind this pressure" was the Council on African Affairs, Halifax complained that "widespread publicity was obtained through the Council's clever use of Paul Robeson's birthday on the 16th April. A birthday rally . . . to which 8,000 people turned up . . . provided a useful platform for the spreading of the Council's ideas. . . . The negro press, of course, has given full play to these developments, for Robeson's prestige among the colored people is very great."[22]

The wide array of African American institutions that participated in the conference underscores the CAA's leading role in shaping anticolonial discourse in the African American community.[23] Likewise, the nearly two hundred individuals and organizations that endorsed a CAA letter to President Roosevelt and Secretary of State Stettinius, setting forth the central recommendations of the conference,[24] illustrate the widespread support for the CAA's positions in this period.[25] They included editors and publishers of the *Chicago Defender*, *Baltimore Afro-American*, *Pittsburgh Courier*, *Norfolk Journal and Guide*, and *New York Age*, as well as Claude Barnett, director of the Associated Negro Press; leaders of professional organizations such as the National Bar Association, the NAACP, the West Indies National Council, and the National Council of Negro Women—and of church, fraternal, and educational groups; trade unionists such as Michael J. Quill, president of the Transport Workers Union; politicians such as Congressman Adam Clayton Powell; writers and artists, among them Countee Cullen, Langston Hughes, Alain Locke, and Theodore Dreiser.[26] In the fluid context of wartime liberal and left alliances, supporters and participants spanned the political spectrum from liberals such as Channing Tobias, senior secretary for Negro Work at the YMCA, to leading leftists such as Ben Gold of the Fur and Leather Workers Union and Earl Browder of the Communist Political Association (as the American Communist Party was briefly renamed in 1944).[27]

GLOBAL REACH: WARTIME CIVIL RIGHTS

The Council on African Affairs was not alone in its attempts to influence American policy. In September 1944 Walter White, as secretary of the NAACP, wrote to President Roosevelt, asking him to make it clear that "the U.S. government will not be a party to the perpetuation of colonial exploitation and to appoint qualified Negroes to serve at U.S. government conferences determining war or post war policies."[28] White had emerged during the war as a strong advocate of anticolonialism.[29] Despite strong disagreements with White on other issues, Du Bois had returned to the NAACP in July 1944 as director of special research, specifically to work on anticolonial issues. He hoped "to revive the Pan-African movement and to give general attention to the foreign aspects of the race problem."[30] The historian Robert L. Harris Jr. has demonstrated that the political agenda of many African American protest groups emphasized anticolonial issues. A. Philip Randolph and the March on Washington movement proposed a "Western Hemisphere Policy Conference for Free Negroes whereby people of color would meet to discuss the problems of Africa and the darker races and develop plans to submit to the world peace conference."[31] The National Council of Negro Women participated in regional meetings sponsored by the State Department across the country to discuss the Dumbarton Oaks proposals.[32]

The Dumbarton Oaks Conference of late summer and early fall 1944 marked the beginning of the negotiations about international postwar organization that led eventually to the founding of the United Nations. Representatives of Britain, the Soviet Union, China, and the United States drafted proposals for maintaining peace and security in the world. A resolution offered by China opposing racial discrimination was rejected by the other three nations in favor of the extraordinarily vague principle of the "sovereign equality of peace loving states." There was no mention of race or colonialism.[33]

According to Harris, "The most sustained critique of Dumbarton Oaks came from Du Bois, who observed that 750 million black people would have no voice in the proposed world forum."[34] In Du Bois's view, Dumbarton Oaks said to the peoples of Africa and Asia that "the only way to human equality is the philanthropy of masters who have historic and strong interest in preserving their power and income."[35] Representing the NAACP at a conference of Americans United for World Organization at the Department of State, he argued that the Dumbarton Oaks "emphasis on nations and states and the indifference to races, groups or organizations indicate that the welfare and protection of colonial peoples are beyond the jurisdiction of the conference's proposed governments."[36] Attempting to garner support for his position, in a speech before the Men's Club of the Arnet Chapel AME Church, Du Bois "blasted the Dumbarton Oaks conference for kicking out China's resolution on racial equality" reported the *Defender*, and warned that "the gate has been left open for another war."[37] Du Bois's criticism of the proposed representation through states in a new international organization marked the beginning of a challenge to the idea that human beings had rights and agency only as citizens of a nation-state. That idea would be contested at the United Nations in 1946 and 1947 by an alliance of black Americans, Indian and black South Africans, and the government of India.

Along with the efforts of organizations such as the CAA and the NAACP, leading articles in African American newspapers effectively promoted anticolonial issues, and black American journalists increasingly scrutinized the U.S. State Department. A *Courier* editorial criticized the Trusteeship Council established by Dumbarton Oaks to supervise the administration of the colonies, because it did not address self-government: "In short, the colonial colored folk are to be administered by white bureaucrats." To correct this, the editors argued, there "should be Negro representatives at the Peace Conference. . . . Somebody must be present to look after the interests of these colonial peoples except the representatives of the Allied powers."[38]

Despite widespread disillusionment with State Department performance at Dumbarton Oaks, attempts to influence the government continued. Rayford W. Logan, professor of history at Howard, was one of the important and visible African American intellectuals writing on colonial issues. A critic of the League of Nations mandates system, Logan had published his first analysis of it in the

Journal of Negro History in 1928. In 1942 he worked with Anson Phelps Stokes's Committee on Africa, the War, and Peace Aims; in 1943, directly lobbying President Roosevelt, he again criticized the proposed new mandates system and advocated a form of international administration that would guarantee the representation of Africans.[39] Writing in the *Defender* in December 1944, Logan captured the complexity of African American political strategy in the months before the founding of the United Nations. He first expressed "dismay" that Dumbarton Oaks proposals failed to make any reference to the colonial and other dependent areas, since their problems "were a fundamental cause of the first and second world wars and are likely to contribute to the outbreak of a third world war." Logan despaired that "what little hope there was has now been devastatingly weakened" by the actions of the Department of State. Nevertheless, he outlined a political strategy: since the State Department had recently created a division of public liaison to facilitate "the presentation to the Department of public opinion on international problems," he argued, "any failure on our part literally to bombard it with protests against the omission of the problem of dependent areas from the scheme just released" would be reprehensible and "perhaps fatal." Logan further suggested that Du Bois call yet another conference of African American organizations to draw up proposals on colonial and dependent areas that would complement Dumbarton Oaks.[40]

Du Bois began work in January 1945 on just such a meeting, and the Colonial Conference was held in New York City on April 6, 1945, at the 135th Street Branch of the New York Public Library. Participants included Logan, CAA representatives, Kwame Nkrumah, Kumar Goshal, Amy Ashwood Garvey, W. Adolph Roberts of the Jamaican Progressive League, George Harris of the Ethiopian World Federation, Charles Petioni of the West Indies National Council, Ethelred Brown of the Jamaica Progressive League, John Andu from Indonesia, and Maung Saw Tun from Burma.[41] Du Bois worked with Alphaeus Hunton on preparing the conference, and their growing collaboration was an important factor in Du Bois's later decision to join the CAA.[42]

Du Bois also invited Villard and Ralph Bunche from the State Department.[43] Neither attended, but Bunche deserves attention here, given his later prominent role in the United Nations. He had joined the State Department in January 1944, after working for the Office of Strategic Services (OSS) as an expert on Africa and for the intelligence division of the army's general staff. At the State Department he functioned as an expert on dependent areas and assisted in international organizational matters, including the Dumbarton Oaks Conference.[44] Although Bunche became very prominent among black Americans after 1949, his role as an insider in 1944–46 appears to have set him apart from black American political strategies and to have made him inaccessible to black American leaders; Essie Robeson and Walter White, for example, complained about his elusiveness.[45] Kenneth Robert Janken has argued that Bunche worked within the constraints of overall U.S. foreign policy objectives, and "his actions troubled other African American intellectuals who saw a severe disjunction between his words and deeds."[46]

The organizers of the Colonial Conference, seeking the widest possible consensus, demanded an international Colonial Commission to "oversee and facilitate the transition of peoples from colonial status to such autonomy as colonial peoples themselves may desire."[47] In fact, the agreement among African American leaders and intellectuals demonstrated at that conference masked political and philosophical differences. For example, Logan's opposition to immediate independence for African nations set him apart from Africans and Caribbeans in the Pan-African Federation and the leaders of the CAA.[48] Consequently, conference organizers intentionally avoided mentioning the demand for immediate independence. As the founding conference for the United Nations approached, debate on the future of colonialism centered on two questions: how to ensure the representation of colonized peoples in international bodies, and whether dependent areas would be administered under a system of international trusteeship or a League of Nations–style mandates system that would in practice give colonial powers unencumbered control. On these issues, African Americans were united.[49]

In the months immediately before the San Francisco conference that established the United Nations, anticolonialism was a central focus of African American political discourse. Leaders and journalists numbered both international and domestic concerns among their political priorities. A. Philip Randolph, in his 1945 New Year's speech from Durham, North Carolina, warned that Dumbarton Oaks was "under the control of the same nations that have exploited and oppressed, robbed and deceived, murdered and dominated the peoples of color for centuries." Linking the fight against Jim Crow with the fight against imperialism, he argued that the tasks lying before black Americans were to support bills for a permanent Fair Employment Practices Commission, to wage "an all-out struggle against discrimination and segregation in the armed forces," and to fight for "the freedom of Africa, a Negro at the Peace table, a National Commission on race, . . . and a Federal Education bill to provide educational opportunities for Negroes."[50] Thus, at the dawn of the modern civil rights movement, international issues went hand in hand with domestic concerns.

The evidence strongly suggests that this pioneering work in linking the oppression and political struggles of African Americans with those of Africans and other colonized peoples had a significant impact on the politics and world view of black Americans. African Americans analyzed and predicted the behavior of politicians on domestic issues on the basis of their actions in Africa and Asia. No one should be surprised, a *Courier* editorial remarked, that Secretary of State

Stettinius had transferred "most of the Negro clerks and messengers, who have long served the State Department" and placed "the remaining ones in obscure places," since "he is straight from Wall Street, which is exploiting and oppressing colored people all over the world."[51] Some African Americans even based their electoral decisions on international concerns. Assessing the 1944 presidential candidates, John Robert Badger rejected Thomas Dewey on the basis that Dewey's thinking was dominated by Herbert Hoover, who "made his fortune and his name as an exploiter of colonial labor." Hoover, Badger explained, had "wrangled from the Chinese the deed to the great Kaiping coal mines" through his "dictatorship" of Anglo-Continental Mines Ltd. Moreover, he had exploited black labor in South African, Nigerian, and Trinidadian gold and tin mines, and had been instrumental in Firestone's acquiring control over Liberia. "That," argued Badger, "is the specter which today haunts colonial peoples when they think of the November elections in the United States, and the possibility of Hoover's man Dewey becoming U.S. president."[52]

CITIZENS OF THE WORLD

When the founding conference of the United Nations opened on April 25, 1945, Metz T. P. Lochard, editor-in-chief of the *Defender*, declared that "the World Security Conference in San Francisco has but one meaning to the Negro people—that is, how far democratic principles shall be stretched to embrace the rights of our brothers in the colonies and to what extent the American Negro's own security at home shall be guaranteed."[53] African Americans and their allies brought to the United Nations deliberations an elaborate vision of the rights and responsibilities of citizenship. Delegates at San Francisco sought to correct the stark omissions of Dumbarton Oaks, where the final proposals had ignored colonialism and racial discrimination. Representatives of Egypt, India, Panama, Uruguay, Brazil, Mexico, the Dominican Republic, Cuba, and Venezuela, supported by numerous nongovernmental organizations, maintained that the purpose of the new organization should go beyond general ideas of peace and security: "Clear and explicit provisions supporting human rights" should be placed at the beginning of the Charter and throughout.[54] As Paul Gordon Lauren has shown, the negotiating power of states determined to insert provisions on human rights and racial nondiscrimination was considerable; in fact, numerous modifications of the Dumbarton Oaks proposals were made at San Francisco. Most significantly, Article 1 of the UN charter listed among the organization's major purposes the achievement of human rights and fundamental freedoms "for all without distinctions as to race, sex, language or religion."[55]

The inclusion of the demand for equality on the grounds of sex points to another critical dimension of 1940s anticolonial politics as well as an important shift in Pan-Africanism. In ideological terms, 1940s anticolonialism represented a radical departure from the earlier gendered language of, for example, Martin R. Delany's consistent masculinist positing of Africa as the fatherland and pervasive invocations of the motherland. In the politics of the African diaspora, Africa was neither a motherland nor a fatherland but the site of struggle for the extension of universal rights to all peoples regardless of race, nationality, or *sex*. The adoption of universalist notions of "rights," however, was by itself not sufficient to guarantee that gender inequalities would be challenged. Indeed, activists' concern about calling prevailing gender relations into question was limited; for the most part, they stopped short of critiquing the way gender hierarchies were reproduced within oppositional movements and institutions. Nonetheless, the language of rights helped make possible the critical leadership of women such as Vijaya Lakshmi Pandit, Charlotta Bass, and Mary McLeod Bethune and initiated the disruption of gendered political categories. Not only was women's leadership important, but the efforts of women in strikes against the pass system in South Africa and against the head tax in Nigeria were a critical and visible part of anticolonial politics.[56]

The broader representation of women was partly a product of the challenges to male authority and leadership in Pan-African politics over the previous two decades. The historian Barbara Bair has explored the critical role of women in the Garvey movement and their challenges to male authority, despite the movement's replication of Victorian gender norms.[57] But the leadership of women in the 1940s was also the result of both the greater space that opened for women during World War II and the broad conception of rights that dominated the liberal and left politics of the 1930s and 1940s.[58] And one of the consequences of the later collapse of the politics of the African diaspora was the reinscription of gender in discourses on Africa and anticolonialism and, arguably, within Pan-African politics.

Black Americans at San Francisco, contending that "the subjection of two-thirds of the world's people" was a threat to international security, supported efforts to include strong human rights clauses in the UN charter.[59] For Du Bois, "what was true of the United States in the past is true of world civilization today—we cannot exist half slave and half free."[60] He argued that the task of the NAACP was to "impress upon the American delegation and others [at San Francisco] that human rights among the great nations and especially among the colonies must be respected. Their flagrant disregard . . . toward colonial peoples has caused two wars in our day and will cause wars in the future."[61]

Although the number of black American observers was relatively large, including Max Yergan of the CAA, the NAACP was the only organization representing black Americans that was granted status as a consultant to the American delegation. Its appointment caused controversy among other African Americans;

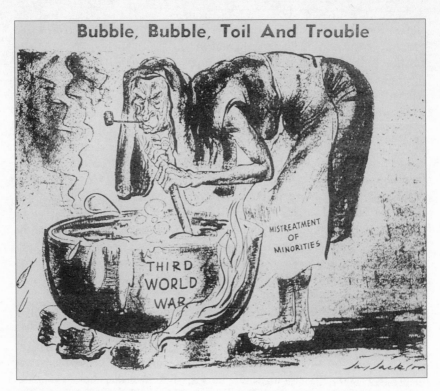

Bubble, Bubble, Toil And Trouble

THIRD WORLD WAR

MISTREATMENT OF MINORITIES

Anticolonial activists warned again and again that the consequence of continued economic and political oppression of colonized peoples would be unremitting war. Jay Jackson, *Chicago Defender*, April 14, 1945. (Courtesy of the *Chicago Defender*.)

the Fraternal Council of Negro Churches, for example, protested to the State Department that "no purely Afro-American group" was among the forty-two designated to advise the American delegation and several black organizations chose their own representatives.[62] Du Bois defended the selection of the NAACP, arguing that it "is not speaking simply for itself." In fact, the cooperation among African Americans and the broad interest in international politics is evident in Du Bois's list of groups that "have sent us special resolutions":

> We have been authorized to speak for the March on Washington Movement, the National Urban League, the Association of Colored Graduate Students, the Delta Sigma Theta Sorority, the National Association of Deans and Advisers of Men in Negro Educational Institutions, the Conference of Adult Education and the Negro, the National Medical Association, the National Bar Association, the National Association of Ministers' Wives, the National Dental Association, the Independent Order of St. Luke, the Independent Order of Good Samaritans,

the National Council of Negro Women, the National Negro Insurance Association, and a number of other organizations.[63]

Nonetheless, during months of front-page headlines on plans for the conference, African American journalists predicted that there would be controversy over colonial issues. George Padmore believed that the postwar status of dependent areas in Africa and Asia would "become one of the most important and controversial issues with which delegates to the forthcoming San Francisco Conference will be forced to grapple."[64] The *Defender* outlined key questions for "Negro Americans and other peoples victimized by forms of political oppression." Foremost among these were whether there was a substantial basis for hope for an enduring peace; what kind of world organization would be required to keep peace; and whether the representatives of the United Nations would deal with the interests of racial and national minorities.[65] Journalists analyzed the past support for racial equality of participating nations and based predictions on these records. Badger cited French plans for a "colonial New Deal in French overseas territories," Chinese challenges to racial discrimination, and recent declarations that "the abolition of racial discrimination was one of the USSR's basic peace aims" as positive indications that there would be support for racial equality augmented by the "voice of many smaller nations such as Latin American countries, Liberia, Ethiopia, Syria, Lebanon, Egypt and the Philippines."[66]

Kumar Goshal, less optimistic, warned that the British government would present the "'white man's burden' theory in its post–World War Second clothes." He predicted that the British would attempt to deny the colonial status of countries such as India and Burma, with evidence "furnished in the shape of three Indian stooges of the British government—Mudalier, Noon, and Krishnamacharl—attending as delegates."[67] Lively depictions of the conflict over Britain's handpicked Indian delegation included George Padmore's report of Gandhi's denunciation of "this camouflage of Indian representation through Indians nominated by British imperialism."[68] Du Bois recounted that he and Walter White "ducked" when photographers attempted to take a photograph of them with the Indian representatives "because these men were stooges of the British Empire appointed to represent India by Great Britain, and representing in no way the Indian people. It would have been a calamity for us to be photographed with them."[69]

Although the United Nations Charter did finally contain numerous clauses on human rights with provisions for equal rights and self-determination, these principles did not translate into a commitment to practical or effective means of implementation.[70] "The majority of states," Lauren explains, "remained unwilling to sacrifice elements of their sovereignty for the sake of human rights by authorizing the international community to intervene in their own domestic jurisdiction and internal affairs." John Foster Dulles, then a member of the American delegation, worried that human rights and nondiscrimination clauses would call attention to "the Negro problem in the South." Similarly, the British expressed apprehension about the implications of such clauses for restrictive immigration quotas in the dominions and their own policies in colonial areas. As Lauren has argued, "Human rights and racial nondiscrimination thus foundered, once again, on the rock of national sovereignty."[71]

As controversies over implementation were played out, the issue of trusteeship was especially important to the United States because it concerned the future of the Pacific islands then controlled by the U.S. military. Faced with questions that affected its own new global interests, the American government rhetorically continued its support of colonial freedom but narrowed the definition of that freedom. At Yalta the United States had chosen to make an alliance with the Soviet Union and China in support of colonial freedom against the British and the French. At San Francisco in May 1945 the American delegation, split between "crusaders" such as Charles W. Taussig and Isaiah Bowman and "realists" such as Navy Commander Harold Stassen, ultimately sided with the British against those advocating a broader definition of colonial independence.[72]

Black American journalists closely monitored the development of American policy. Badger saw the U.S. Army and Navy asking for "unilateral control over dependent territories" but believed the State Department "favorable to the establishment of a colonial body with considerably more authority than the old mandates commissions of the League of Nations" and hoped that the latter would prevail.[73] Rayford Logan, however, worried that the State Department was uncommitted to the principle of international trusteeship and, further, that the Navy Department actually had plans to annex the Pacific islands. To Logan, this distinct retreat from the anticolonialism of Roosevelt had ominous implications for UN colonial policy at the United Nations. Not only would the United States greatly increase the number of persons under its colonial administration, but America would forfeit its moral claim to oppose colonialism elsewhere in the world.[74] Obviously, he said,

> if the United States is not even considering placing any of her existing colonies under international trusteeship and if the policy of the Navy Department for the annexation of the Pacific islands should prevail, the delegates of the United States at San Francisco or anywhere else can hardly insist that the former colonies of Italy be denied to England if she contends that she needs them to protect her life line to India, Singapore and Hong Kong.[75]

Disillusioned criticism of the American government deepened as the conference continued. On May 26 the *Defender* reported, "Sweeping demands that the United States delegation end its opposition to freedom for colonial peoples poured into the United Nations here this week."[76] On the same day the *Courier* called the conference "a cruel buoying of the hopes of subjugated and oppressed peoples from one end of the earth to the other. . . . All the words about trusteeship add up simply to saying that each of the three powers is going to do as it pleases, whether the other people of the world like it or not."[77]

Another *Courier* editorial reassessed African American political strategies in light of the shifts in U.S. policy. Arguing that the United States had liberated the "Pacific peoples from Japanese rule, only to substitute American rule, rather than self-rule," the editorial called Du Bois, White, and Bethune of the NAACP delegation "naive" in pressing for an end to the colonial system by lobbying the U.S. government: "The hope of powerless peoples of the earth lies not in agreement between rival exploiters but rather in disagreement and the fear of conflict which forces concessions."[78]

Despite disappointed hopes for and criticism of the United Nations, it became a focal point for lobbying efforts on the part of black Americans and for joint projects by Africans and those of African descent. In the six months after the San Francisco meeting ended, African Americans organized two separate conferences "calling for the social, political and economic rights of African colonial peoples" and appealing for the "creation of machinery necessary to the participation of African colonial peoples" in the United Nations. The first conference, called by Du Bois, gathered twenty organizations to discuss proposals that had originated with the 1945 Pan-African Congress. The second was sponsored by the African Academy of Arts and Research.[79] The CAA continued its strategy of lobbying the American government on behalf of African interests. The CAA forwarded its "Text and Analysis of the Colonial Provisions of the United Nations Charter," a six-point program for Africa in the peace settlement, to new Secretary of State James F. Byrnes and Edward L. Stettinius Jr., then U.S. representative to the United Nations.[80] Robeson sent the document to the consul general of the Union of South Africa as well.[81]

African American international strategies reached their climax in 1946 and 1947. Through the UN, the Council on African Affairs joined with South African Indians and the African National Congress to challenge the South African government's attempt to annex South-West Africa and to restrict further the rights of Indians in the Union of South Africa. This moment stood on the cusp of two very different historical periods. The legitimacy and power of wartime alliances in which black American anticolonial politics had thrived were at their height. Yet this was also the moment when the seeds of destruction of these alliances began to take root. On the one hand, African American organizations continued to lobby the federal government on anticolonial issues; on the other hand, the same organizations took a sharply adversarial turn in their stance toward the government. Objecting to U.S. support for South Africa and the European colonial powers, and increasingly challenging the notion that America was the legitimate leader of the "free world" and therefore above censure, black Americans both criticized new directions in American foreign policy and attempted to use the United Nations as a forum in which to gain support for civil rights struggles in the United States.

South Africa was especially important to black American international politics in this period and significantly influenced its adversarial turn. As the historian Thomas Borstelmann has demonstrated, relations between the United States and South Africa grew "stronger and friendlier in the immediate postwar years as the Union's economic and strategic importance to Washington increased with the development of the Cold War."[82] In addition to its increasing importance to the United States, South Africa drew black American attention because of the links between the CAA, the ANC, and the South African Indian Congress. Moreover, African Americans, like non-European South Africans, faced color bars and turned to international forums as part of their political strategy.[83]

Through the CAA, black Americans were directly involved in two controversies at the United Nations that brought international attention and criticism to the government of South Africa: discrimination against Indians within the Union of South Africa, and South Africa's attempt to annex South-West Africa (now Namibia). In 1946 and 1947 the Indian government, South Africans in the ANC and the Joint Passive Resistance Council, and black Americans working through the CAA coordinated attempts to put pressure on the South African government through the United Nations. Leaders of these endeavors included the Indian delegate Vijaya Lakshmi Pandit; South Africans H. A. Naidoo and Sorabjee Rustomjee, representatives of the Joint Passive Resistance Council; A. B. Xuma of the ANC; South Africans Senator Hyman Basner, and E. S. Sachs; Rev. Michael Scott; and Alphaeus Hunton of the CAA. Owing to their combined efforts, issues of discrimination and colonial representation were at the heart of the first full session of the United Nations. Earl Conrad summed up the significance of this challenge for many black Americans when he reported for the *Defender* that despite the protests of Prime Minister Jan C. Smuts of the Union of South Africa, the fears of the U.S. delegates, and the opposition of the British, "the color and colonial issues hang like a specter over the entire proceedings of the United Nations General Assembly. . . . Matters concerning India, South

Africa, Negro Americans and other oppressed minorities have entered the United Nations to stay."[84]

The treatment of Indians within the Union of South Africa not only drew world attention but raised salient questions about representation of national minorities. In 1946 the South African government passed the "Asiatic Land Tenure and Indian Representation Act." Termed the "ghetto bill" by its opponents, the act prohibited Asians "from dealing in land with non-Asians" and from "living in certain 'controlled' areas."[85] In response, South African Indians formed the Joint Passive Resistance Council of the Transvaal and Natal Indian Congresses and launched a passive resistance campaign.[86] Just as black Americans linked their appeals in international forums to anticolonial struggles, South African Indians looked to India to challenge the government of South Africa at the UN on its treatment of Indians. In so doing, South African Indians reaffirmed their membership in a diaspora community. The *Passive Resister*, organ of the passive resistance movement, constantly affirmed the ties to India in articles such as "'You Are Bits of India'—Nehru's Message To Indians Abroad."[87] In "We Have Not Forgotten South African Indians," the *Passive Resister* reported a speech at the All India Congress Committee declaring that "with India becoming free 'our brethren in other lands are looking to us to bring about an amelioration of their conditions.'"[88]

The expectation on the part of South African Indians and black Americans that the independence of Asian and African states would make a real difference to their own struggles was not based on abstract notions of communion or solidarity. India's participation in discussions of anticolonialism and racial oppression at the founding of the United Nations fueled the belief that there was potential for organizing at the UN.[89] African Americans had argued since Dumbarton Oaks that representation by nation-states at international councils would exclude colonized peoples, noncitizens, and all persons discriminated against within states, since only states could file petitions and grievances. At the first session of the United Nations, India attempted to circumvent this problem by representing South African Indians and thus initiated a controversy about the nature of representation in the UN.

In 1946, with Vijaya Lakshmi Pandit—"the intense and articulate" sister of nationalist leader Jawaharlal Nehru—opening the debate, the interim Indian government filed charges with the General Assembly that Indians living in South Africa were discriminated against.[90] This claim was based partly on a new interpretation of individual rights in international law. Although India and its allies had failed to gain clear implementation measures in the human rights clauses of the UN charter, they argued that the charter, "as a legal document, recognized fundamental rights of the individual and thereby for the first time in history transformed individuals from mere objects of international compassion into subjects of international law."[91] Indian demands were also based on a historical claim to a relation of kinship with Indians in the diaspora. In a statement protesting their "anomalous status" and lack of representation within South Africa, delegates from the South African Indian Congress supported the complaint lodged by the government of India: "Our well-being since our advent to South Africa has been subject to the oversight and the concern of the people and government of India and, we now hope, the nations of your organization."[92] Arguing for the legitimacy of this position, the statement quoted the deputy prime minister of the Union of South Africa, J. H. Hofmeyr, who said: "We cannot blame the Local Indians, as we put it, running to Mother India unless we recognize them as South African citizens with rights of citizenship."[93]

The other side of the controversy sparked by the efforts of the Indian government on behalf of South African Indians was summed up by a *New York Times* editorial. The charges brought by India, said the *Times*, "raise serious questions for the United Nations itself, and may require a more precise definition of what its jurisdiction and its powers are." Pointing out that "the Indian Government complains about the treatment, not of its own citizens, but of racial kinsmen who have lived in South Africa for generations and are therefore South African citizens and outside the jurisdiction of the Indian Government," the editorial argued that "as long as the United Nations is not a world government representing all the people of the world directly, but rather an organization of states represented by their respective governments, it behooves every member state to respect the domestic jurisdiction of every other state."[94]

The CAA, however, embraced Indian efforts. The South African *Guardian* reported Yergan's declaration that "Prime Minster Smuts' characterization of the Indian issue as a strictly 'domestic' affair was exactly parallel to the argument of poll tax Congressmen in the United States who cry 'Hands Off!' whenever their 'white supremacy' rule is threatened by federal legislation."[95] The CAA also organized letters to President Harry Truman, the U.S. State Department, and Hershel Johnson, American UN delegate, urging "full support to the Indian government's petition to the United Nations protesting South African Government's discrimination."[96]

CAA appeals to the American government fell upon increasingly deaf ears. Thomas Borstelmann has demonstrated the growing economic and strategic links between the American and South African governments: "The need of the

United States at the end of the war to invest abroad to maintain American economic prosperity matched up well with what Truman's Commerce Department called 'the pivotal importance' to South Africa 'of uninterrupted capital flow from Abroad.'" Moreover, the war had ended American self-sufficiency in raw materials, and South Africa was not only mineral-rich but had the world's largest undeveloped reserves of uranium ore capable of early commercial development.[97] Given these ties, at the United Nations in 1946 the Truman administration sought to minimize criticism of South Africa by playing a mediating role in the dispute with India.[98]

In December 1946 the Indian strategy won a small victory when the UN General Assembly adopted a resolution asking the government of South Africa and India to discuss their problems, settle their dispute about the treatment of Indians in the Union, and report at the next assembly session.[99] Since the resolution did not contain binding provisions for enforcement, its backers claimed that the terms were so "mild that no one could possibly object." Nevertheless, opponents described it as "blatant interference into domestic affairs." The thirty-two nations supporting India included all states from Africa, Asia, and the Middle East. Among the fifteen siding with South Africa were the United States and Britain.[100]

Negative publicity at the United Nations, including the work of black American journalists, did not pass unnoticed by the South African government. Prime Minister Smuts declined an interview with A. M. Wendell Malliet, foreign editor of the *New York Amsterdam News*; in the words of South Africa's UN representative, he believed it would draw him into "a first class Press controversy."[101] British officials helped the South African government keep tabs on American opinion: for example, Ronald Sinclair, British consul in New York, sent newspaper clippings from the *New York Times* and black American papers such as the *Chicago Defender* and the *New York Amsterdam News* to the South African consulate general.[102]

THE CAA AND SOUTH-WEST AFRICA

CAA opposition to discrimination against Indians in South Africa went hand in hand with opposition to South Africa's plan to annex South-West Africa. When the war was nearing its end, activists and journalists had paid increasing attention to the regional ambitions of the Jan Smuts government. A June 1944 *Defender* editorial warned that if Churchill and the other Empire prime ministers, who had been meeting in secret conclave in London, should agree to Smuts's plan for regional control over the colonial areas, the South African "native policy based upon racial segregation will be extended to other parts of the African continent."[103]

The Union of South Africa's attempts during and after the San Francisco conference to annex South-West Africa were not its first; in fact, South Africa had tried and failed to do so after World War I. Officially made an international mandate under the League of Nations, South-West Africa had in practice been run, "with a minimum of interference," says William Minter, on "South Africa's terms."[104] At the end of World War II, South Africa's renewed efforts for official annexation were universally condemned in the African American press. The *Defender* emphasized the cooperation between the British, American, and South African governments: immediately after the announcement of an American and British proposal on trusteeship, which recommended that former mandated areas revert to the original nations in control, South Africa made its "proposal for extending its rule over Africa." The *Defender* also warned of the belligerence of South African delegates, who "contended that there is no prospect of the territory ever existing as a separate state."[105] *New Africa* pointed to the immediate danger that South Africa would annex not only the mandate territory of South-West Africa but the territories of Bechuanaland, Basutoland, and Swaziland, given Smuts's claim that "their eventual inclusion in the Union of South Africa is provided for in the South African constitution."[106]

Black South Africans actively sought the support of the international community for their opposition to annexation. In early 1946 A. B. Xuma, president of the ANC, cabled from Johannesburg appealing to the United Nations to "save their black brothers living in the mandated territory of Southwest Africa from annexation by the Jan Smuts' government of the Union of South Africa."[107] R. T. Bokwe, a South African member of the CAA, made a passionate argument for placing South-West Africa under the Trusteeship Council, pleading that if South-West Africa and the Protectorates of Swaziland, Basutoland, and Bechuanaland were handed over to the Union, "our doom is sealed for many generations to come."[108] But the ANC lacked resources for international work and became involved in UN lobbying only in a somewhat haphazard fashion, when Xuma traveled to the United States in the fall of 1946 for medical treatment.[109] Alphaeus Hunton expressed alarm to Xuma in 1946 that "the United Nations Secretariat has received very few expressions of protest against the annexation."[110]

CAA members, particularly Hunton, did extensive lobbying and publicity at the United Nations.[111] The CAA pamphlets "Facts about South-West Africa—Annexation or Trusteeship," and "South Africa Must Answer to the United Nations" (both written by Hunton), and "8 Million Demand Freedom! What about It, Gen. Smuts?" (on South Africa's treatment of its own African population) were widely circulated among UN delegations and within the United States and South Africa.[112] Members of UN delegations from India, the United States, Ceylon, and the Soviet Union relied on this material for their information on South Africa, and in a striking admission of the credibility and influence of the CAA, an American representative stated that it "has been considered by members of the Trusteeship Division of the Secretariat as an excellent pressure group."[113] Certainly, the erudite work of Hunton provided delegates with information otherwise hard to come by. "Annexation or Trusteeship," for example, explained South-West Africa's history as a "Class C" mandate under the League of Nations and its division into "reserves" and "police zones," with pass laws for all non-Europeans and a stringent vagrancy law that forced Africans to work for an employer. The pamphlet showed that the region's resources such as diamonds and vanadium were controlled by South African corporations, contended that South-West Africa functioned as "another reservoir of African labor for the gold mines in the Union of South Africa," and emphasized that members of ANC and other South African organizations who opposed annexation were prevented by the government from leaving the country because of this opposition.[114]

The CAA featured work on South Africa at its Big Three Unity rally at Madison Square Garden in New York City, which attracted approximately 19,000 people in June 1946. The *New York Times* reported that resolutions passed at the meeting not only rejected annexation of South-West Africa but demanded investigation of racial discrimination; abolition of pass laws, residential requirements, the color bar, and restricted land ownership; and the inclusion of South Africa in the starvation relief efforts of the American government.[115] This kind of attention again brought the anxious scrutiny of the South African government. H. T. Andrews, its secretary for external affairs, asked Robert Webster, consul general in New York, to attend the rally in order to prepare material "for use by the South African Delegation at the United Nations Assembly."[116] Webster responded that he feared the meeting might be the beginning of a movement to "queer the pitch for Field Marshal Smuts when he comes to the General Assembly in September to ask incorporation of South-West Africa into the Union."[117] He described the hall decorated with enormous posters, the most prominent showing "Africa in the grip of a huge octopus, the various tentacles being labeled with the names of the powers having control," including the Union of South Africa. Reporting the meeting "about 60% colored, 40% white," Webster worried that "the movement has reached dangerous proportions."[118] Alarmed and confused by a movement led by African Americans with "strong white organized support," South African intelligence concluded that the "aim appears to be Africa for Communist-organized Labour-controlled black Africans."[119]

In addition to high-profile meetings and lobbying, press conferences held by the Council on African Affairs facilitated publicity about South Africa. The CAA hosted nearly two hundred leaders of various American organizations at a press conference for the South African representatives Basner, A. B. Xuma, and H. A. Naidoo in late 1946. A number of UN member states were also represented.[120]

Shadow Of Coming Events

A sadly prescient warning of the decades of South African domination in Namibia and the rest of southern Africa that were to follow. Jay Jackson, *Chicago Defender*, December 7, 1946. (Courtesy of the *Chicago Defender*.)

Major Robinson reported in the *Defender* Basner's contention that "behind Smuts' request to the UN General Assembly to annex the mandated territory of South-West Africa is his desire to obtain more cheap labor to work the new gold fields discovered in his Union of South Africa," but a *Defender* editorial speculated that Smuts would make his case "behind a facade of pious phraseology and democratic pretensions." Reflecting the new sharp criticism of American foreign policy, the *Defender* predicted that the majority of U.S. newspapers would highlight Smuts's position because as a "defender of colonialism and imperialism, Smuts serves the interests of U.S. imperialism and the present makers of U.S. foreign policy."[121] Robinson further charged Smuts with causing the "threat of war for years to come, and the end of the UN as an agency for world cooperation."[122] And the *Defender*, though dismayed by the degree of American support for Smuts, urged that "to turn the tables on the senile old vulture is the best way of exposing him in his true character."[123]

In addition to its press conferences, the CAA organized a picket demonstration in front of the South African consulate on November 21, 1946. Some two hundred participants included representatives of thirty trade union, civic, and church organizations.[124] With print media still the major vehicle for trans-Atlantic communication, these pickets, meetings, and lobbying were visible in South Africa through frequent articles and photographs in papers such as the *Guardian* and the *Passive Resister*.[125]

As in the case of discrimination against Indians in South Africa, on the issue of South-West Africa the American delegation to the United Nations sought to reduce antagonism between South Africa and its critics. The U.S. government wanted to avoid provoking non-Western delegates but also feared that attention to South-West Africa had potential implications for American policy toward the mandated islands of the western Pacific, which the American military remained unwilling to place under UN trusteeship.[126] The United States therefore encouraged South Africa to accept a trusteeship arrangement for South-West Africa as a way of retaining its practical advantages there without provoking the anticolonial delegates.[127]

Regarding the weak form of trusteeship advocated by the American government as outrageously inadequate, in October 1946 the CAA petitioned the UN Human Rights Commission for an investigation of human rights in the Union of South Africa, the rejection of South Africa's request for annexation of South-West Africa, and the removal of South-West Africa "completely from under the jurisdiction of the South African government."[128] The *Afro-American* reported that the CAA had charged the South African government with "flagrant violation of the most elementary principles of human rights" and urged the Human Rights Commission to make "specific provisions outlawing all forms of social, economic, and political discrimination prevailing in the Union of South Africa."[129] The CAA argued that South Africa's racial policy and practices were not simply "a matter of local concern for that country, but rather a matter of international concern" because they "adversely affect the rest of Africa and also Asia, as well as causing concern to Negroes throughout the world."[130]

In November 1946 the Trusteeship Committee turned down the Union of South Africa's proposal to incorporate South-West Africa.[131] The United States opposed incorporation and, in fact, sponsored the resolution adopted by the committee rejecting South Africa's request; however, the United States also opposed and helped to defeat two separate resolutions—one introduced by India and Cuba and other by the Soviet Union—that not only would have rejected incorporation but would have placed South-West Africa under international trusteeship.[132] The U.S.-sponsored resolution that did pass merely requested but did not require that South Africa "follow the example of other mandatory powers by bringing South-West Africa under a trusteeship agreement."[133]

Reacting to this resolution, Paul Robeson outlined the CAA's position on South-West Africa and its objections to American policy in a letter to John Foster

Dulles, then an American delegate to the UN General Assembly. In response, Dulles admitted that the U.S. rejection of incorporation was "couched in more conciliatory language than in the case of some other proposals" and, nervously stepping around the issue of Jim Crow, added, "I did not feel that the United States, in view of its own record, was justified in adopting a holier-than-thou attitude toward the Union of South Africa."[134] The following year, when the government of South Africa had failed to submit the requested trusteeship agreement, the CAA complained in a memorandum to the General Assembly. Citing statements by both Smuts and Daniel Malan's Nationalist Party indicating that measures to incorporate South-West Africa were proceeding, the CAA quoted a Smuts government report that South-West Africa would be regarded as a fifth province of the Union. Given the "tremendous industrial development" of the Union and the "vast resources in raw materials" of South-West Africa, it was South Africa's intention to link the economies of the two. Pointing to the South African government's blatant disregard of the UN resolution, the CAA again insisted that the administration of South-West Africa should "be given over to an international body under the jurisdiction of the Trusteeship Council of the United Nations."[135]

When South Africa finally did submit a report to the Trusteeship Council, it acknowledged that no progress had been made in compliance with the General Assembly resolution based on the complaint of the government of India. Paul Robeson, the *Passive Resister* reported, warned that the South African government was arguing that the UN charter was neither explicit nor binding in its provisions concerning the guarantee of human rights and fundamental freedoms to all peoples without distinction as to race, sex, language, or religion, and that other nations also practiced discrimination in various forms. Consequently, said Robeson, the case against South Africa must be pressed "as a clear demonstration to the peoples of America, Africa and the world that the Charter's provisions are NOT mere empty idealist expressions which can be ignored and violated with impunity by members of the organization."[136]

Seeking support for its opposition to the South African report, the CAA distributed to UN representatives its "Analysis of the Report of the Union of South Africa on the Administration of South West Africa for the Year 1946," covering education, health, land, and labor.[137] In April 1947 at the 71st Regiment Armory the CAA held a rally for "Africa and Colonial Freedom through a Strong UN." The rally featured the CAA work on South Africa and a special show written by John Latouche, lyricist of "Ballad for Americans" and "Beggar's Holiday," which dramatized the struggles of African and colonial peoples. Latouche had been deeply affected by spending a year in the Belgian Congo working on the Warner Brothers documentary *Congo*. Arguing that "our fate is bound up with that of colonial peoples," and despite growing Cold War tensions and the warnings of "well-meaning people" not to do the show, Latouche declared that "I regard this show as a statement of myself as an American writer." He added on a more personal note that he wanted to present the play to Robeson as a birthday gift.[138] In September 1947, Ashwin Choudree and A. I. Meer joined Robeson, Lena Horne, and Henry Wallace at a rally of 15,000 people at Madison Square Garden in New York.[139] On the South African side, the *Passive Resister* publicized messages to Paul Robeson and the CAA from Nehru, vice-president of India's interim government, and from the South African Passive Resistance Council; CAA reports were read at meetings and rallies in Johannesburg as well.[140]

On October 15, 1947, a resolution introduced by India placing South-West Africa under international trusteeship passed the Trusteeship Committee of the UN by a vote of twenty-seven to twenty. The United States not only voted against it, as did the United Kingdom and all colonial powers, but lobbied afterward to ensure that the resolution would not get the two-thirds majority it needed to pass the General Assembly. Robeson, Yergan, and Hunton voiced their objections to the American vote in a meeting with Francis B. Sayre, American representative on the Trusteeship Committee of the UN General Assembly, who maintained that the resolution as it stood "could not secure the necessary two-thirds majority in the Assembly."[141] Indeed, two weeks later the General Assembly reversed five Trusteeship Committee decisions on Africa and colonial areas. In the words of the CAA, "More than three weeks of work in Trusteeship Committee was largely undone." On South-West Africa the General Assembly adopted a resolution merely expressing "hope that the Union Government may find it possible" to submit a trusteeship agreement by the next meeting.[142] The CAA charged that the American bloc, led by Dulles, won not through legitimate democratic channels but through the procedural maneuver of securing a two-thirds majority requirement. Three decades passed, with a protracted war between the government of South Africa and the South-West African People's Organization (SWAPO), before the United Nations Security Council explicitly stated its intent to secure independence as Namibia (the name adopted in 1968).[143] And it was yet another decade before Namibia celebrated independence.

The year 1946 had begun with promise and hope for anticolonial activists in America, in Africa, and throughout the diaspora. Fascism had been defeated, and European colonialism seemed on its last legs. But the unprecedented challenges to global political and economic inequality and the work of the CAA, the Joint Passive Resistance Council, and the ANC at the United Nations were sharply disrupted by the Cold War. CAA strategy had depended on lobbying a government that was open, at least in principle, to supporting political and economic democracy for colonized peoples. But as the United States consistently chose to support South Africa and its colonial wartime allies, the CAA increasingly viewed the

CAA broadside publicizing the Rally for African and Colonial Freedom, Regiment Armory, New York, April 1947. CAA rallies typically featured music and dramatizations. (Courtesy of Lloyd Brown.)

American government as an adversary rather than a potential ally. The broad anticolonial alliances among African Americans and the fledgling politics they represented did not survive the early Cold War. To understand what was at stake and how the 1940s anticolonial alliances disintegrated, one must look more closely at the foreign policy of the Truman administration in 1946 and 1947.

CHAPTER FIVE

DOMESTICATING ANTICOLONIALISM

Not only do human beings and nations exist in narrow economic margins, but also human dignity, human freedom, and democratic institutions. It is one of the principal aims of our foreign policy today to use our economic and financial resources to widen these margins. It is necessary if we are to preserve our own freedoms and our own democratic institutions. It is necessary for our national security. And it is our duty and privilege as human beings.
—Undersecretary of State Dean G. Acheson, address to the Delta Council, Cleveland, Mississippi, May 8, 1947

THE IRONY OF GIVING A SPEECH on freedom and human dignity in Mississippi in 1947 may have been lost on Dean Acheson, but it was impossible for black American leaders at the end of World War II not to read proclamations about freedom and democratic institutions abroad in the context of domestic politics. This was especially so in Mississippi, the state with the highest recorded number of lynchings, five hundred and thirty-nine, of black Americans.[1] By 1946 a sharp rise in violence against returning black soldiers echoed the disillusion of the post–World War I period: heightened expectations followed by brutality, and collapsed opportunities accompanied by severe repression.[2] Further, with anxiety widespread among Americans about the postwar economy, economic reconversion was already reversing gains made by black labor during the war. The labor market was effectively resegregated as black workers, lacking seniority, were replaced by returning white soldiers.[3] In 1946 the prospects for black Americans appeared precarious indeed, and those denied political and economic democracy at home anxiously watched postwar international developments and questioned the implications for black Americans and colonized peoples.

As the Cold War first emerged, a broad spectrum of black American leaders continued to view international politics through the prism of anticolonialism. Escalating tensions between the United States and the Soviet Union were read by black American leaders and the black American press as intransigence on the part of American and British imperialism. Moreover, journalists and activists consistently linked the foreign policies of Secretary of State James Byrnes of South Carolina with the Jim Crow of his home state, and the violence of imperialism with the lynchings and brutality in the American South.

But despite scathing criticism of the initial developments of the Cold War, with the issuing of the Truman Doctrine in 1947 and the acceleration of domestic political repression, the terms of anticolonial politics began to change rapidly. Critiques of American foreign policy gave way to an acceptance of the Truman Doctrine and its claims that America was the legitimate leader of the "free world."[4] The embrace of the Truman Doctrine by many African American leaders reshaped black American political and rhetorical strategies and fundamentally altered the terms of anticolonialism. Many leaders abandoned criticism of foreign policy in favor of the dominant argument that racial inequality at home should be opposed because it undermined the legitimate global goals of the United States. Popular anticolonialism was increasingly limited to a focus on America's colonialist allies and warnings that the United States would inadvertently bolster colonialism by supporting Britain and France. Moreover, as the Cold War escalated, the affirmation by many black American leaders that "Negroes are Americans" left no room for the claim of commonality with Africans and other oppressed peoples.

BOLSTERING EMPIRE

When Winston Churchill called for an anti-Soviet Anglo-American military alliance in his "Iron Curtain" speech of March 1946, there was still broad agreement and cooperation among African American activists and journalists on anticolonial issues. African Americans, like most Americans, disapproved of Churchill's proposal, which—along with the loan to Britain being debated in Congress—was widely seen as a betrayal of the United Nations.[5] But condemnation by African Americans was distinguished by its emphasis on the implications for imperialism and colonialism. The Council on African Affairs sent a letter to President Truman accusing Churchill of aiming to "preserve the British imperialistic system with the help of American troops and military power."[6] Paul Robeson further denounced Churchill's scheme for "Anglo-Saxon domination" at a CAA meeting at the Second Baptist Church in Los Angeles, where he was joined by Lena Horne in calling for "united action of all democratic forces to achieve freedom for all colonial and subject peoples."[7]

Strong reactions to Churchill's speech and broader critiques of imperialism among African Americans were not confined to the left. Given Walter White and the NAACP's swing to embracing American foreign policy by early 1947, it is critical to appreciate how adamantly that organization too had rejected the

Post-war uncertainty for African Americans as resegregation of the labor market and growing violence against returning black soldiers threatened to erode wartime gains. Jay Jackson, *Chicago Defender*, June 19, 1946 and February 23, 1946. (Courtesy of the *Chicago Defender*.)

actions of the United States and Britain as late as mid-1946. The NAACP charged that Churchill's plan "would virtually insure the continuation of imperialism," and declared his address "beyond question one of the most dangerous and cynical made in contemporary history by a presumably responsible man." Warning that the proposed Anglo-Saxon bloc might destroy the United Nations, the NAACP further charged that it "would have direct and immediate effect upon all Americans in its underwriting of empire."[8]

Successful wartime alliances and support for the United Nations had created a context in which a wide range of African American intellectuals and activists elaborated a democratic politics that viewed the abolition of colonialism as a necessary condition for a democratic and just world. Worried about the potential destruction of the United Nations and the impossibility of resolving colonial issues if a U.S.-Soviet alliance were not maintained, Mordecai Johnson, president of Howard University, charged that since the formation of the

Oh Boy! Peace And Quiet

United Nations, the United States had forfeited "the moral leadership of the world" in order to "pacify the imperial bloc."[9]

The mainstream black press shared the fear that superpower political realignments would be devastating to anticolonial movements.[10] According to the *Afro-American*, "Mr. Churchill's message was 'historic' because of the danger and cynicism implied." Churchill's proposed Anglo-American alliance would assure a "continuation of imperialism and eventually plunge us into a war with Russia on the other side." Arguing that British interests were in jeopardy in Greece, Egypt, India, Indonesia, and the Near East, the editorial concluded, "We shudder to contemplate the fate of colonials already oppressed under the British heel should such an imperialist partnership become a reality."[11] For the *Defender,* imperialism and democracy were simply incompatible. If the United States would "apply the principles of democracy it need have no fear of the Soviet Union or the communist way of life," but it "cannot do this and support British imperialism."[12] It was British imperialism that threatened the United Nations, and "the Soviets are no threat to American security if we do not intend to be tied to British policy."[13] As an alternative, the *Defender* supported Henry Wallace's plea for U.S.-Soviet amity, arguing that

Let ME Bear The Burden

African Americans watched in dismay as the United States took over the tasks of empire from the British. Jay Jackson, *Chicago Defender*, April 6, 1946. (Courtesy of the *Chicago Defender*.)

"such friendship and cooperation is a fundamental condition for a progressive settlement of colonial questions."[14]

Like Robeson and the CAA, journalists tied the American military to colonialism and warned that American-made arms were being used by the armies of colonial powers "in oppressing colonial peoples in far flung trouble centers throughout the world."[15] Charging that Churchill had "proposed that the English speaking peoples assume the task of policing and ordering the entire world to their way of life," John Robert Badger offered a political strategy to block the British-U.S. military alliance. Black Americans, he wrote, must attempt to "drive Secretary of State Byrnes from office, to curb the imperialist drive of U.S. big business, and to prepare now to elect national and state legislators who will provide the opportunity of voting out a Truman or a Republican counterpart of Truman in 1948."[16]

Critics of Churchill and imperialism drew on the legacy of President Roosevelt's opposition to British colonialism. The *Afro-American* reminded readers that Roosevelt had been gravely concerned about the post-war status of colonials and had warned Churchill that "retention of the imperialist status quo would jeopardize the peace." Moreover, he had "infuriated" Churchill by proposing to send a delegation to Africa to investigate conditions there. Promoting Elliott Roosevelt's forthcoming book, *As He Saw It,* the *Afro-American* praised the younger Roosevelt's emphasis on his father's commitment to ending colonialism and his forthright disagreements with British and French attempts to "maintain their hold on their colonies."[17]

Much of the alarm expressed in the African American press over the new American role in the global political economy focused on oil. American corporations, with the help of the U.S. government, had been consolidating their control over Saudi Arabian oil since the late 1930s. World War II had underscored the strategic and economic importance of oil, leading the State Department to declare Saudi Arabian oil "a stupendous source of strategic power, and one of the greatest material prizes in world history."[18] In the immediate postwar period, corporate and government cooperation continued to safeguard the private interests of the oil companies while furthering U.S. efforts to control world oil reserves, combat economic nationalism, and contain the Soviet Union.[19] The black American press followed these developments closely. Kumar Goshal charged Britain and the United States with "carrying on some of the crudest imperialistic deals in many parts of the world." Goshal described the increasing control of Middle Eastern oil by the Arabian-American Standard Oil Co. (composed of Texaco and Standard Oil of California) and Standard Oil of New Jersey and Socony-Vacuum, American partners of the Iraq Petroleum Company.[20] Similarly, the *Afro-American* criticized the granting of exclusive oil rights in Ethiopia to an American oil company, citing the troubled histories of American oil interests in Mexico, British interests in Iraq, the Dutch in Sumatra and Burma, and Firestone in Liberia.[21]

One central goal of American foreign policy was to maintain Iran as a buffer zone between the Soviet Union and the oil fields of the Persian Gulf. When a dispute developed in early 1946 over the date of the withdrawal of Soviet troops from Iran, the United States encouraged Iran to present the case at the United Nations.[22] In 1946 Walter White blasted the United States and Great Britain for hypocrisy in pressing the Iranian issue before the UN Security Council. Small wonder, argued White, that Russia should have "difficulty in understanding why the two 'Anglo-Saxon' nations should manifest any interest in the presence of Russian troops in Iran as long as Britain retains troops in Greece, Egypt, Indonesia, the Levant, Iraq and Palestine." Charging that the United States was also underwriting British military, administrative, and economic domination in India, Nigeria, Ethiopia, Shanghai, South Africa, Kenya, and the West Indies, White expressed further bewilderment that the United

Some One Should Remind Him

The alliance with the Soviets had been decisive in the defeat of fascism, but faltering superpower cooperation threatened the hopes of colonized peoples for postwar democracy. Jay Jackson, *Chicago Defender*, January 27, 1946. (Courtesy of the *Chicago Defender*.)

States and Britain, which both held oil concessions in Iran should object to the Soviets having the same. He concluded that "the USSR is absolutely right in bluntly telling Britain and the U.S. to clean up their own houses before they presume to criticize the housekeeping of other nations."[23]

White's defense of the Soviet Union was hardly unique. The *Chicago Defender* was an especially strong advocate of continued cooperation between America and the Soviet Union and consistently espoused the view that it was corporate America that endangered cooperation—against the interest of the American people. In "Iran and American Business," the *Defender* argued that the "Affair Iran" should be interpreted as a "battle between a force that is desperately seeking to make the United Nations an instrument for peace and a combination of forces driving fiercely toward the Century of American imperialism, World War III and the virtual enslavement of the great masses of American people." Pointedly bringing the analysis back home, the *Defender* further declared that the enemy of America was not the Soviet Union but

Ambassador For Democracy

The appointment of a Jim Crow secretary of state, South Carolinian James Byrnes, signaled more trouble for black Americans at home and for colonized peoples abroad. Jay Jackson, *Chicago Defender*, September 21, 1946. (Courtesy of the *Chicago Defender*.)

"American Big Business" and its attempts "to carry abroad the system that prevails in South Carolina."[24]

FIGHTING POSTWAR JIM CROW IMPERIALISM

One of the most significant expressions of popular antiimperialism, was the CAA-organized Big Three Unity rally held on June 6, 1946, at Madison Square Garden in New York City. The CAA called the rally to organize "anti-imperialist and democratic forces" to influence American foreign policy, hoping, as Robeson put it, for "a mighty blow on the side of real democracy for our people here as well as our brothers on the continent of Africa."[25] Given Robeson's still high credibility among Americans across a broad spectrum, the day before the rally the *New York Herald Tribune* printed his lengthy letter to the editor, which sketched the problems of land and labor in West Africa, Kenya, and South

Africa and spelled out the inadequacies of American policy on Africa and the attempts by the South African government to annex South-West Africa.[26]

Nineteen thousand people attended the rally. Representing the apex of the popular front, Paul Robeson and Max Yergan were joined by black American and labor leaders such as W. E. B. Du Bois and Mary McLeod Bethune; William Hayes, president of the New England Baptist Convention; and Michael Quill, head of the Transport Workers Union. Participating artists included the jazz composer and pianist Mary Lou Williams, the Golden Gate Jubilee Quartet, and Pete Seeger. Joined by the CIO chorus, Paul Robeson sang "Ballad for Americans." Alan Lomax arranged and directed a "brief history in song of the intergrowth of African and American folk music, featuring Josh White, the Golden Gate Quartet, Pete Seeger and Sonny Terry."[27]

Speakers focused on American policies as well as South Africa. The CAA argued that American economic penetration into Africa had been accelerating since the end of the war. Pointing out that the American government was getting uranium from the Belgian Congo for atomic bombs and that American companies were prospecting for oil in Ethiopia and for minerals in Liberia, Hunton and Robeson asserted that U.S. corporations were increasingly "linked with international cartels which dominate Africa's mineral production."[28] Robeson saw these new developments as "stifling the democratic development of colonial Africa." A small but extremely powerful group of Americans, he warned, were "interested in Africa for the wealth they can extract from it and from the labor of the people there. You can be sure that their ideas for the future of Africa do not include freedom."[29] Adam Clayton Powell Jr. promoted the fund for South African famine relief, and, exemplifying the vision of extending democracy in its substance and scope, declared, "We did not fight to make the world safe for Churchill. We did not fight to make the world safe for whites only, nor for an upper class, nor a little group of American-British tories—we fought to make it safe for democracy and that means everybody."[30]

With the CAA still at the height of its credibility, the rally, including Robeson's speech, was widely covered by the mainstream press, including the *New York Herald Tribune* and the *New York Times*.[31] The *Times* reported that the Truman administration was accused of "helping to bolster up crumbling European empires in Asia and the Middle East, of defeating the cause of freedom for African colonial peoples, and of striking a blow against the American peoples themselves."[32] Throughout the remaining months of 1946 the CAA and anticolonial activists could still enjoy public visibility and a central place in black American politics. The CAA closed out the year with a benefit, the Christmas night opening of the musical theater collaboration between Duke Ellington and John Latouche, *Beggar's Holiday*.[33]

American actions at the United Nations continued to come under heavy scrutiny in the black American press. When an American resolution in the General Assembly called for a delay in setting up the Trusteeship Council, George Padmore charged that "American Big Business, Army and Navy men advising the delegates are certainly out to make the world safe for 'American imperialism' and to establish the 'American century' in the five continents and seven seas."[34] From Southeast Asia and the Pacific—where, the *Crisis* reported under U.S. Navy "democracy" in Guam "natives are deprived of basic civil rights"—to Latin America, Africa, and the Caribbean, journalists investigated and criticized U.S. State Department, military, and corporate activities.[35]

Postwar reporting on two areas that had been heavily covered by African American journalists during the war, Liberia and Haiti, exemplifies the widespread criticism of American political and economic interests in the African American press.[36] During World War II black journalists had reported on deepening American military and corporate involvement in Liberia. After the war Padmore, for example, described a "Wall St. Invasion of Liberia," arguing that American industries were attempting to secure markets and raw materials there in efforts to avert a postwar slump. He cited the plans of the Raymond Concrete Pile corporation of New York to construct a harbor in Monrovia as an example of the "pattern of American post-war economic imperialist penetration in Africa and backward colonial and semi-colonial territories."[37]

The Raymond Concrete Pile company had received a contract from the U.S. Navy to construct dock facilities for a port in Monrovia. In January 1946 Liberian workers went on strike against the company, which was backed by American troops. Workers struck over pay and working conditions, with demands including the reduction of an eighty-four-hour work week and access to canteen privileges (then limited to white employees), but also to protest the company's demands for concessions on iron deposits in Liberia as well as a railroad concession to a mining area of nearly a half-million acres.[38] The strike received front-page coverage in the African American press throughout the first half of 1946. James L. Hicks reported in the *Defender* that "colored American troops were alerted to protect American property, while United States Navy officials had drawn pistols on Liberians to force them to return to work on the project."[39] The following week, an *Afro-American* article headlined "Huge Concession Granted in Liberia as Ships Stand By" reported that while "a flotilla of American warships stood threateningly off shore," the Liberian government, against popular opposition, turned over to American interests for eighty years a huge three-million-acre mining and railroad concession, dispossessing a half-million people.[40] In following weeks, identifying with the African point of view and criticizing U.S. actions, journalists highlighted the conditions of the workers, the disciplining of

Liberian judges who had opposed the concession, and denials by the U.S. State Department that coercion had been employed in getting the mine concession.[41]

In Haiti, too, journalists had monitored the consequences of American wartime involvement, as well as the history of U.S. occupation and financial control.[42] When the government of Elie Lescot was ousted in January 1946 in a military coup that followed a popular uprising, the role of the U.S. government and American corporations figured prominently in the post-coup analyses of African American papers.[43] Enoc P. Waters Jr. argued in the *Defender* that "the interference of the United States government in the political affairs of Haiti" and the economic dislocation caused by the failure of the U.S. government rubber program had contributed to the revolt. Many believed, Waters reported, that Sumner Wells, undersecretary of state under the late President Roosevelt, had been "more instrumental in the 'election' of Lescot to the Presidency than were the masses of Haitian people."[44]

After the May 1946 election of President Dumarsais Estime, journalists analyzed the dilemmas of the new government and its attempts to "free itself from the tentacles of a giant octopus."[45] The *Afro-American* and the *Defender* documented the Haitian debt to the United States government through the Export-Import Bank and to private U.S. bondholders. President Estime, the *Defender* reported, faced "the difficult operation of soliciting continued U.S. aid and still refusing to deliver his nation's economy to Wall Street in a neatly wrapped parcel." And according to the *Afro-American,* Haitian Ambassador Joseph D. Charles charged that the Haitian government had to submit to political and financial control by the American government.[46]

The African American press looked at the failure of Haiti to obtain the aid it sought in the light of Truman administration plans to lend money to Europe. The *Afro-American* reported that "although willing on one hand to lend fantastic sums of money to foreign governments which are not even expected to repay them, the American Government has refused to help Haiti obtain a new loan to assist in restoring Haiti's agriculture, which was severely damaged during America's experiment to raise rubber there."[47] Journalists contrasted American willingness to appropriate millions of dollars for Greece and Turkey with the flat refusal of the State Department to aid Haiti.[48] In the *Courier,* Rayford Logan sharply criticized the Truman administration for refusing loans to Haiti in its efforts to "free itself from American financial imperialism," while giving "millions for the defense of a decadent, fascist-minded Greek monarchy."[49] Likewise a *Defender* editorial charged that the refusal to refinance the loans to Haiti "came at a time when Uncle Sam was offering four hundred million dollars to Greece to bolster a tottering throne, to say nothing of the untold millions that have poured into China toward the support of the Chiang Kai-

Chek government, 50 million recently granted to Italy, and the three billion given Great Britain."[50]

The pervasive monitoring and censure of U.S. government and corporate activities by the black press ceased abruptly after the first months of 1947, marking the beginning of a precipitous decline in the anticolonial politics that had emerged during the war and presaging far-reaching changes in African American politics. The reasons for these changes are complex, located in the very different responses of African American leaders to changes in Truman's foreign policy and civil rights in the early Cold War. But most important, after the Truman Doctrine and the Marshall Plan, the criticism of American foreign policy that had been an integral part of the politics of the African diaspora fell beyond the bounds of legitimate dissent, and the broad anticolonial alliances of the 1940s were among the earliest casualties of the Cold War.

To follow the developments of the split in the black American anticolonial coalition, and to understand the abruptness of the shift in opinion of many African American leaders, one must start with the Truman Doctrine. In early 1947, to President Truman and those around him, the most important obstacle to his foreign policy, and specifically to aid for Greece and Turkey, was the continuing public optimism about American-Soviet cooperation. Prevailing attitudes toward international affairs were guided by opinions formed during the war, including the belief that U.S.-Soviet cooperation could be preserved and confidence that the United Nations would be the dominant force in shaping international postwar developments. With policymakers dwelling on the constraints posed by public and congressional attitudes, the Truman Doctrine was intended, in the words of Senator Arthur Vandenberg, to "scare hell" out of the American people.[51] Unveiled by the president before a joint session of Congress on March 12, 1947, it asked Americans to accept the "great responsibilities" entailed in the struggle against Communism and the national mission to protect "free institutions, representative government, free elections, guarantees of individual liberty, freedom of speech and religion, and freedom from political oppression" throughout the world.[52] Explicitly outlining global security and military interests, the doctrine proclaimed that American security was involved wherever "aggression" threatened peace and "freedom." It was necessary for the United States to "support free people who are resisting attempted subjugation by armed minorities or outside pressure."[53]

Initial responses varied tremendously. To many Americans, including some liberal critics, the Truman Doctrine seemed a frightening abandonment of the United Nations. Henry Wallace and the Progressive Citizens of America organized in opposition to Truman and the increasing U.S.-Soviet polarization. The PCA condemned Truman for "dividing the world into two armed camps and for inaugurating a program of American imperialism which will take over the policies, methods and failures of the British Empire."[54] But many other liberals, including the newly formed Americans for Democratic Action, supported Truman's foreign policy. The Marshall Plan for European Recovery was proposed in June 1947. In promising to raise European living standards (and, thereby, U.S. exports), it embodied at least part of the strategy many liberals and leftists had promoted, which helped it win adherents such as the ADA.[55] And as the historian Nelson Lichtenstein has demonstrated, through tripartite business, government, and labor structures such as the Harriman Committee, labor leaders were offered power-sharing in the new economic order.[56]

Henry Wallace and the PCA opposed the Marshall Plan on the grounds that without Soviet support, it would increase the chance of war. Left-wing African American anticolonialists such as Robeson and Du Bois joined with the liberal Wallace and the Progressive Citizens in opposing not only the belligerence implied in the Truman Doctrine but the fact that the Marshall Plan would bolster the economies of colonial powers without consideration of economic and political democracy for colonized peoples. Robeson argued that Western European bankers could repay Wall Street only in raw materials from Africa, Asia, and South America, thus intensifying the exploitation of colonial peoples.[57] Thus, for Robeson and his allies, the Marshall Plan embodied the victory of the American Century, and its advocacy of U.S. political and economic dominance in world affairs, over a genuinely democratic worldwide New Deal.

Initially, their position was shared by some liberals and found a voice in the press.[58] Yet after initial skepticism, like most liberals and critical segments of the labor movement, important sectors of African American leadership and crucial institutions such as the leading newspapers backed the Marshall Plan and embraced the Truman Doctrine.[59] Walter White of the NAACP, for example, joined the Citizens' Committee for Support of the Marshall Plan and became a strong advocate of Truman's foreign policy.[60] John H. Sengstacke, editor and publisher of the *Defender*, became a founding member of ADA and a staunch supporter of Truman, leading to dramatic editorial changes in the paper.[61] Thenceforth these liberals would shun association with the left.

To some extent, it is not surprising that differences in the anticolonial coalition would emerge over political and economic policy. Although leftists and liberals shared the indictment of the exploitation of colonized peoples, leftists saw the problem as inherent in capitalist organization, whereas liberals sought a solution in antidiscrimination measures. Moreover, some African American leaders who supported Truman shared with many others a genuine fear of Communism and the Soviet Union. But these factors alone cannot explain the sudden embrace of American foreign policy by previously harsh critics, the severity of the polarization that occurred, or the sharp swing to anti-Communism by some black American leaders. Members of the ADA and other liberals had long been anti-Communist, but for many black liberals the shift to a Cold War brand of anti-Communism was incongruous. Walter White did not have a Manichaean world view that could comfortably accommodate the binary oppositions of the Cold War. Although a strong anti-Communist, he initially resisted red-baiting tactics within the NAACP.[62] Most important, his anti-Communism during the 1930s and his continued wariness of Communists throughout the war had not stopped him from reacting to the early stirrings of the Cold War with a passionate defense of wartime United Nations alliances, attack on U.S. hypocrisy, and defense of the concerns of the Soviet Union.[63] White had been a militant critic not only of the colonial powers but of American policy as well. In other words, for him and many other African American liberals, genuine—often scathing—critiques of the Communist Party had *not* then entailed an embrace of U.S. foreign policy.

Given White's extensive experience in international politics, and his long-standing critical view of the Soviet Union, it seems implausible that he became so quickly convinced of a new Soviet threat that he was willing to abandon years of work and commitment to a very different kind of internationalism. Moreover, though White and other NAACP leaders would later be confronted with the stark, and ultimately tragic, choice of supporting U.S. foreign policy or facing the destruction of their organization, it is unlikely that he or anyone could have foreseen in late 1946 the coming level of repression or understood these stakes. White, however did grasp the fact that criticism of United States foreign policy was becoming fundamentally unacceptable to the Truman administration at the same time that new opportunities were emerging to influence the government on *domestic* civil rights. White's support of Truman's foreign policy, then, was strategic. As anti-Communism came to dominate politics, he moved toward an anticolonialism that was justified by anti-Communism, arguing that the abuses of colonialism opened the doors to Communists and that it was imperative that Asia and Africa remain in the Western orbit.[64]

ANTI-COMMUNISM AND CIVIL RIGHTS

The acceptance by White and other key African American leaders of the proposition that the United States, as the legitimate leader of the free world, was engaged in a fundamental struggle with the Soviet Union had a profound impact on civil rights politics. As early as 1946, with the formation of Truman's Committee on Civil Rights, White and others began to craft the dominant argument of the anti-Communist civil rights liberals. The new argument seized on international criticism of American racism to argue that antidiscrimination measures were necessary for the United States in its struggle against Communism. The dominant liberal argument against racism, using anti-Communism to justify the fight against domestic discrimination and for civil rights, conceded the high ground to anti-Communism.[65] The liberals continued to link foreign and domestic policies but adopted a strategy that embraced American foreign policy while pushing for domestic rights. For example, White told the Senate Committee on Foreign Relations in early 1948 that discrimination against minorities in the United States must be eliminated if the Marshall Plan was to succeed.[66]

A glimpse of the varying responses of African American leaders to Truman's policies can be seen in late 1946 during Robeson's American Crusade to End Lynching and the separate NAACP antilynching initiative that followed a series of horrible murders in the South. Indeed, it is critical to consider the domestic context of rising violence against African Americans, especially against returning veterans.[67] The specter of a repeat of the post-World War I violence and repression animated the attempts of many African Americans to carve out a space in the Truman administration where they could create and seize opportunities to influence domestic civil rights. To this end, an NAACP group led by Walter White and Channing Tobias met with Truman on September 19 and quickly reached an accord. Although the administration avoided any commitment to intervene to stop the violence, White and Tobias joined Truman in setting up the President's Committee on Civil Rights, established by executive order in December 1946. The fifteen-person committee was chaired by Charles E. Wilson, president of General Electric. Sadie T. Alexander, a prominent black American lawyer, and Channing Tobias, a director of the philanthropic Phelps-Stokes Fund, were the two black American members.[68]

Whereas the Committee on Civil Rights, with its pronounced business leadership, represented the new opportunities for power sharing in a tripartite, corporate-led structure, Robeson's American Crusade—with participants from the African American press, black churches, the National Council of Negro Women, and the Southern Conference for Human Welfare—represented the broad wartime black coalitions. Robeson's group met with Truman only a few days after the White meeting and immediately came to loggerheads with the president. One disagreement was over how quickly the administration should act.[69] Robeson, outraged by Truman's claim that it was not expedient for the federal government to take action on lynching, complained that antilynching measures remained "in White's committee while Negroes are still being lynched."[70] But his most pronounced disagreement with Truman, and the issue separating his approach from that of the NAACP group, had to do with "America's moral position in world affairs."[71] The Robeson delegates ar-

'Pointing Out The Resemblance'

For Robeson and his allies, the government's refusal to intervene to stop barbaric lynchings demonstrated the blatant hypocrisy of democracy. Jay Jackson, *Chicago Defender*, October 12, 1946. (Courtesy of the *Chicago Defender*.)

gued that the federal government's refusal to fight lynching was inconsistent with the principles it had put forward at Nuremberg. In response to Truman's "reminder" that the United States and Britain represented "the last refuge of freedom in the world," Robeson replied that the British Empire was "one of the greatest enslavers of human beings." For Robeson, the new wave of brutality and terror directed especially against returning black soldiers underscored the relationship between antiblack violence in Jim Crow America and the violence of colonialism. Foreign intervention, Robeson warned Truman, would be in order if mob violence was not stopped.[72]

Fearing that his position would be undermined, Walter White accused Robeson's campaign of creating "confusion in the public mind" and introducing "extraneous issues" into the antilynching campaign.[73] Dropping his indictments of American foreign policy, White endorsed the right of the United States to moral leadership in the world and argued that discrimination at home must be abolished so that America would not be discredited in the eyes of the world. Shortly after the announcement of the Truman Doctrine, White told the president that "acts of discrimination against minorities abroad were being used to discredit the United States and convince the people of the world that Americans were incurably addicted to bigotry." White urged Truman to "let the people of the world know that while Americans frequently failed to live up to their declarations of democracy, we were constantly at work to narrow the margin between our protestations of freedom and our practice of them."[74] The combination of embracing the Truman Doctrine and U.S. world moral leadership, and insisting that American racism be reformed framed the Committee on Civil Rights statement *To Secure These Rights.* Issued in October 1947, this document charged that America treated black Americans as second-class citizens. Quoting Acting Secretary of State Dean G. Acheson's contention that "the existence of discrimination against minority groups in this country has an adverse effect on our relations with other countries," it argued that the United States could not neglect the "international implications" of civil rights violations.[75]

This argument, defining the parameters of the new liberal agenda on civil rights, would profoundly affect anticolonial politics. Ultimately, using the Cold War as a rationale for fighting discrimination left no room for the internationalism that had characterized black American politics through the mid-1940s. Walter White again serves as the paradigmatic case. He had been one of the most forceful voices articulating the links between the struggles of black Americans with those of Africans and other colonized peoples, yet after two years of the Cold War, White asserted that "Negroes are American" and that "in the event of any conflict that our nation has with any other nation, we will regard ourselves as Americans and meet the responsibilities imposed on Americans."[76] Ironically, this statement followed a *defense* of Paul Robeson and a warning that the government could not afford to ignore the issues Robeson was raising.

On the one hand, then, White's longstanding anti-Communism fit well with his new anti-Communist civil rights argument. And making good on his promise to "meet the responsibilities imposed on Americans," he plunged into international work, defending U.S. policy, for example, in the 1949 Town Hall of America Round the World Tour, during which he participated in radio broadcasts and seminars with leaders throughout the Near East.[77] On the other hand, despite his virulent anti-Communism, White was a reluctant Cold Warrior, pulled by the increasing hysteria and dynamics he could not predict or control into a politics that ran counter to his political and intellectual proclivities as well as his social and personal loyalties; eventually, he participated in the discrediting of Robeson and the left.

While African American liberals were supporting Truman, those on the left, including Robeson and Du Bois, backed the 1948 campaign of Henry A. Wallace.[78] Wallace's opposition to Truman's foreign policy, and his insistence that the Truman administration be more flexible in its approach to the Soviet Union, led to his forced resignation as secretary of commerce in September 1946 and eventually to his third-party challenge in the presidential election of 1948.[79] When Wallace formally declared his candidacy in December 1947, Robeson immediately announced his support and, according to his biographer, appeared on behalf of the Progressive Party ticket "at rallies ranging from the anonymity of high school gyms to the hoopla of Madison Square Garden—and in every section of the country."[80] The CAA, although its focus as an organization was still on South Africa and the growing U.S. corporate involvement throughout Africa, believed that a U.S.-Soviet split would be disastrous for colonial peoples fighting for their independence and therefore participated in meetings and rallies of the Progressive Party.[81]

The Wallace campaign ultimately foundered (he received only slightly more than one million votes), partly because of the administration's attempts to link his campaign with the Communists, but also because Truman shifted to the left on domestic issues during the campaign, successfully wooing much of Wallace's black and liberal support.[82] Courting the black vote in the 1948 election, and pressured by the ADA-led revolt in the northern sector of the Democratic Party—which insisted on strong civil rights platforms—Truman issued two civil rights executive orders in July 1948, establishing a fair employment board within the Civil Service Commission and the President's Committee on Equality of Treatment and Opportunity in the Armed Services.[83] Although the scope of these initiatives was limited, Truman's new aggressive stance on civil rights led to a revolt of the southern Democrats and the candidacy of segregationist Strom Thurmond.[84] It also helped Truman to secure 69 percent of the black American vote in the election, and that support—concentrated in the cities of heavily populated northern and western states—helped deliver crucial electoral votes in his victory over Dewey.[85]

The shifts in Truman's civil rights politics not only had a dramatic impact on the 1948 election, but encouraged the trend toward new political and rhetorical strategies that focused on domestic discrimination as a liability to American objectives abroad. Yet it must be emphasized that Truman's initiatives came *after* major shifts in black American politics had already occurred. The new lines had been clearly drawn in 1947, well over a year earlier, and deeply shaped perspectives and debate on desegregation. Moreover, scholars who have argued that Truman administration policies legitimized civil rights and raised expectations among civil rights leaders have exaggerated the importance of Truman's 1948 initiatives in fueling the civil rights movement.[86] As the historian Robert L. Zangrando has shown, the campaign promises of 1948 failed to translate into legislation, and "the Eighty-first Congress became a graveyard for the items in the civil rights package and the resting place for the NAACP's thirty-two-year-drive toward a federal anti-lynching law."[87] Further, new scholarship exploring previously unexamined dimensions of the 1940s civil rights movement demonstrates that, rather than raising expectations, civil rights politics narrowed during the Truman administration, as a result of the contraction of public discourse and the collapse of the left in the early Cold War years.[88]

Nelson Lichtenstein and George Lipsitz have argued that between 1946 and 1948 a powerful remobilization of business, which afforded anti-Communist labor leaders power within the circles of the corporate elite, blocked the broad social agenda of labor evident during World War II. And like Barbara Griffith and Michael Honey, who have traced the pulling back of labor's efforts to organize in the South and labor's abandonment of a civil rights agenda, these scholars have tied the curtailment of civil rights to the growing conservatism of the labor movement.[89] And the narrowing of labor's agenda had yet another critical effect on the fate of anticolonialism. In what the historian Patrick Renshaw has described as the fusion of domestic and foreign policies, as Communists were expelled from unions in America, American labor supported anti-Communist unions abroad even when that meant collaborating with former Nazis and other fascists. In 1949 CIO unions left the World Federation of Trade Unions, and both the AFL and the CIO took the lead in setting up the new anti-Communist International Confederation of Free Trade Unions.[90] CIO membership in the WFTU and WFTU support for African labor had helped to spark interest in and legitimize black American and Pan-African Congress support for African labor, as well as providing institutional linkages. The CIO's departure from the WFTU not only marked the end of the legitimizing stamp of world labor that had been crucial for the politics of the African diaspora, but destroyed critical embryonic institutional connections. Thereafter, the role of U.S. labor in Africa, and in well-documented European cases as well, would be filtered through the close liaison of the AFL and the State Department—with the financial support of the CIA.[91]

SHATTERING ALLIANCES: THE CAA AND THE NAACP

Historians have argued that the primary casualty of Truman's campaign to win support for his foreign policy was open public debate about foreign policy.[92] This resulted not only from the demise of the Wallace campaign and the left but from the defeat of the isolationist camp in the Republican Party and the rise of bipartisanship. During the 1948 election campaign, Republicans led by Robert A. Taft in the Senate and Joseph Martin in the House—those who objected to Truman's global commitments as well as to cooperating with

Democrats in an election year—lost out to Senator Arthur H. Vandenberg and other advocates of cooperation with Democrats on an internationalist foreign policy. Ultimately, Dewey committed himself to Vandenberg's bipartisan strategy.[93] At the same time that traditional isolationist voices were marginalized, the demise of the Wallace campaign and growing repression curtailed the criticism of Truman's policies from the left. President Truman's loyalty order of March 1947, the creation of Attorney General Thomas C. Clark's list of subversive organizations, and the deportation arrests and indictment of Communist leaders under the Smith Act all helped to isolate American left-wing critics of Truman's foreign policy.[94] Organizations that continued to challenge the Truman Doctrine—including the Council on African Affairs, the Council for a Democratic Far Eastern Policy, the Council for Pan-American Democracy, and the Council of Greek Americans—all faced harassment and prosecution by the Justice Department.[95]

As early as 1942 the FBI had branded the CAA "active in creating considerable unrest among the negroes [sic] by stressing racial discrimination" and had tracked the activities of the organization and especially of Paul Robeson, its chair, through 1946. In addition to following the CAA's anticolonial activities, the FBI investigated the ties of several leaders to the Communist Party. For example, as chair of the American-Soviet Friendship Committee and part owner and publisher of the militant Harlem weekly the *People's Voice,* Yergan had been widely identified with the left and, though not formally a member of the party, was very close to its leadership.[96] Before the onset of the Cold War, however the organization had operated unobstructed, and its views were still widely shared by many Americans.[97] But with the beginnings of the Cold War, the CAA's opposition to Truman's foreign policy, its emphasis on the growing American involvement in Africa and American uranium interests in the Belgian Congo and South Africa, and its support for African liberation groups placed the CAA outside mainstream opinion and increasingly at odds with the Truman administration.[98] In 1947 the Attorney general included it on his official list of subversive organizations. By that time the CAA was exhibiting the tensions endemic to left and liberal politics in this period, and many members began to drift away.

In 1948 the organization underwent a major split when its founder Max Yergan took a sharp turn to the right in perhaps the most pronounced political about-face among African American activists and intellectuals of the Cold War era.[99] David H. Anthony, his biographer, has astutely argued that Yergan's shift was a consequence of the Manichaeism through which—first as a Christian, then as a leftist, and finally as an anti-Communist—he consistently viewed the political and moral universe in simple binary oppositions of good and evil.[100] In February 1948, now fearful of association with the Wallace campaign or the

Communist Party, Yergan argued that the CAA should publicly declare its "non-partisan character." Robeson and Hunton objected, insisting that doing so would play into the hands of "reactionary red-baiters and would not help the Council."[101] When the matter was referred to the policy committee, Yergan so obstructed its work that Du Bois resigned the committee's chairmanship in protest. Yergan attempted to take over the organization by firing Hunton and publicly announcing that a "Communist faction" was attempting to use the CAA "to swing the Negro vote to the support of Henry A. Wallace."[102]

Paul Robeson, Eslanda Robeson, and Hunton organized their supporters, including E. Franklin Frazier, to save the CAA from a Yergan takeover. Yergan was suspended by the board and expelled from the organization in September 1948. Much of the significant work of the CAA was yet to come. Du Bois had joined the CAA in 1947 and had moved his office to its headquarters when he left the NAACP in 1948. As the Robeson-Du Bois-Hunton alliance solidified, the organization's contact with African groups continued to deepen.[103] But with Yergan's departure, such prominent civil rights leaders as Hubert T. Delany, Adam Clayton Powell Jr., Rayford W. Logan, and Channing Tobias resigned from the organization, and others—among them Mary McLeod Bethune—stopped attending its functions. Over the following four years several former members, most notably Max Yergan and Channing Tobias, cooperated fully with the FBI and the attorney general's office in prosecuting the CAA.[104] The CAA increasingly found its support from the left, rather than from the broad cross section of black American institutions and leadership that had sustained it through its first decade.

A rift between W. E. B. Du Bois and Walter White over foreign policy contributed to Du Bois's dismissal from the NAACP in 1948. Their differences were evident in their conflict over the organization's 1947 petition to the United Nations, which exemplified the NAACP's new exclusive focus on domestic discrimination and its silence on foreign policy issues. On October 23, 1947, the NAACP formally presented to the UN Commission on Human Rights "An Appeal to the World: A Statement on the Denial of Human Rights to Minorities in the Case of Citizens of Negro Descent in the United States of America."[105] In the words of the *Afro-American* the document charged the United States with "failing to practice what it preached."[106] It read in part:

> Because of caste custom and legislation along the color line, the United States is today in danger of encroaching upon the rights and privileges of its fellow nations. Most people of this world are more or less colored in skin; their presence at the meetings of the United Nations as participants and as visitors renders them always liable to insult and to discrimination; because they may be mistaken for Americans of Negro descent . . . This question, then, which is without

a doubt primarily an internal and national question, becomes inevitably an international question."[107]

Hugh Smythe of the NAACP drew a parallel between this petition by African Americans and "the Pan-Nigerian movement"; he argued that the petition had significance for South Africans and Kenyans, noting South African efforts to petition the United Nations and a 1946 conference of the Kenya Africa Union.[108] Yet despite Smythe's effort to link the petition to African struggles, the argument it contained marked a departure from the internationalism of the World War II period. Du Bois had wanted the petition to embrace the problems and concerns of Africans; the actual document took a more limited position. It focused on the hypocrisy of the United States and argued that the "color line" in America undermined its status as the leader of the free world. Widely hailed in leading American newspapers and periodicals such as the *New York Times,* the *New York Herald-Tribune,* the *New York Post, PM,* the *Nation,* and nearly all the leading African American publications, the petition embodied the argument that dominated African American political discourse during the Cold War era.[109] And in accepting the legitimacy of the United States as leader of the free world, it departed from the argument that linked the struggle of black Americans against Jim Crow with that of Africans against colonialism.

For Du Bois, to suggest that race was an international question because discrimination within the United States would inevitably violate the rights of foreigners distorted the deeper meaning of the international dimensions of race. In a memo to Walter White, he objected that the NAACP petition had "nothing to do with Africa or African problems." Whereas in the early 1940s African American activists had posited a reciprocal and interdependent relationship between the struggles of Africans and those of African descent, Du Bois lamented that—despite his personal efforts and urgings since his return from the Pan-African Congress—the NAACP had "taken no stand nor laid down any program with regard to Africa." He noted his authorization "to prepare a petition on the rights of the Negro Minority in the United States," but he complained that "I asked two years ago to have authority to collect and publish the various demands of Africans for freedom and autonomy. Permission was never given me."[110]

Du Bois's differences with White over foreign policy escalated with White's support of the Truman Doctrine. Since the United States "has become international in its action," argued Du Bois, "so the NAACP is called upon to take a stand concerning Africa, Asia, Indonesia, and Israel." In the absence of a clear NAACP position on foreign policy, he said, White's acceptance of a consultancy to the American delegation to the United Nations for the Truman administration "ties us in with the reactionary, war-mongering colonial imperialism of the present administration."[111] Following his statement of opposition to White in a memo that was obtained by the press, Du Bois was dismissed from the NAACP in September 1948.[112] Thereafter, the NAACP was no longer connected to the Pan-African Federation.[113] Thus the relationship between the black American freedom struggle and the Pan-African Federation, developed at the 1945 Manchester Pan-African Congress, was severed.[114] In 1956, on the eve of Ghanaian independence, Kwame Nkrumah complained to Carl Murphy, publisher of the *Afro-American,* that the "time has come for the NAACP to change policies and not be exclusively concerned with domestic race policies."[115]

THE COLLAPSE OF A TRANSNATIONAL BLACK PRESS

If a major casualty of Truman's campaign to win support for his foreign policy was open public debate on foreign policy, many black American journalists were among the particular victims. Despite the rich extant literature on internal repression during the Cold War, the story of its impact on the African American press remains to be told.[116] The tradition of criticism of American foreign policy was devastated; writers such as John Robert Badger, Kumar Goshal, and George Padmore quickly disappeared from the bylines and were often blacklisted. In the white press too, from the right-wing Hearst chain to the liberal *New York Times,* views that questioned Cold War policies were widely censored, and reporters who did not oblige were often fired in the period following the announcement of the Truman Doctrine.[117] Given the greater susceptibility of black Americans generally to this wave of repression, however, and the fact that civil rights activities also came to be suspect, the black American press was even more vulnerable.[118] The deleterious effects of the Cold War are strongly suggested by the sharp drop in circulation of national black American newspapers—including the *Courier,* the *Defender,* the *Journal and Guide* and the *New York Amsterdam News*—after 1947. What is clear is that they made rapid and dramatic changes. As late as April 1947, the *Defender* and the *Courier* still questioned aid to Europe, as they did in discussing the Haitian debt. But thereafter, both rallied behind the Marshall Plan and declared their wholehearted support for Truman's foreign policy. Calling Republican opposition indistinguishable from that of Communists, the *Defender* declared that "our approach to problems in which the security of the country is involved cannot be a purely partisan or racial approach." The most crucial questions should be whether a policy "safeguards the vital interests of the nation" and stabilizes national unity: "Does it checkmate the foe within? If it falls within this category, then it is beneficial to Negroes."[119] Arguing for the desegregation of the armed services in early 1948, the *Courier* compared the efforts of A. Philip Randolph and Walter White and blasted Randolph for his "extremist" advocation of civil disobedience against conscription unless the military abandoned segregation. Black Americans were the only group of Americans that had "never produced a traitor," insisted the *Courier:* "It would be extremely dangerous, and perhaps catastrophic, if the idea became widespread that there was any intention on the part of even a small segment of the colored population to hamper national defense in any way."[120]

The criticism that had blossomed during the war and had peaked only a year before the Truman Doctrine had raised sharp questions about ownership and control of the world's resources. With the onset of the Cold War, direct criticism of American foreign policy or the terms of government or corporate involvement was beyond the bounds of legitimate debate. Supporters of Truman's foreign policy could retain their anticolonialism—still the official position of the U.S. government—but their acceptance of the idea of political exigencies in a bipolar world fundamentally altered its terms.

The difficulty of maintaining a broadly anticolonial position while avoiding criticism of American policies is starkly illustrated in discussions of the Marshall Plan. The fact that Marshall aid was extended primarily to colonial powers posed a dilemma for its new enthusiasts, but they resolved it by advocating—in an unspecific way—"assurance of social and economic democracy in the colonies." Accepting the terms of the Cold War, the *Courier* stated that "the U.S. *must* put up the money."[121] The *Defender,* arguing that black American leadership should endorse the Marshall Plan, added that "some effort" should be made by the United States to extend aid to "non-white nations."[122] A 1949 *Courier* editorial first worried that black Americans, "opposed as they are to colonialism . . . are committed nevertheless through the Marshall Plan to the support of these nefarious enterprises." Then, drawing back from the implications of the argument, it noted that the imperialist powers might be reforming as a result of "pressure of American purse strings" and, seemingly resigned, added that the Russians were also imperialist and that there was "nothing Negroes can do about the use of their taxes to bolster governments exploiting darker peoples over the globe."[123]

Militant African American criticism of the Dutch in Indonesia stands out as the exception that proves the rule. Although on the whole the United States supported its colonial allies in the postwar period, in the case of this particularly intransigent colonial power, the U.S. suspended $5 million in Marshall aid designated for the Netherlands East Indies, believing that Dutch actions "encouraged the spread of Communism in Southern Asia."[124] Thus African American arguments for Indonesian independence did not conflict with the acceptance of the United States as the legitimate leader of the free world and they could be couched in terms of anti-Communism.[125] Praising the United States for withholding funds from the Dutch, the *Defender* asserted that America "must lead the way in the fight for freedom of colonial peoples" and support Nehru's demands that the Dutch get out of Indonesia.[126] Truman supporter Walter White praised the United States for its "forthright stand" at the United Nations "against the cold-blooded attempt of the Dutch to use armed force." If the Dutch were not stopped, he said, "revolt will play directly into the hands of Russia, will sweep throughout Asia, Africa, and other places where men are robbed for the sake of absentee landlords in Europe and other places."[127] Similarly, the *Defender* argued that "the Netherlands government is playing directly into the hands of Joe Stalin and his Communist bandits who are anxious for an excuse to penetrate the Pacific islands." It was the responsibility of the United States as "the greatest power on earth" to use that power to oppose the Dutch.[128]

In summary, then, the transnational press—the Pittsburgh-Lagos-London-Chicago-Johannesburg-New York nexus that had helped create and disseminate the politics of the African diaspora—was no longer an institution through which American government foreign policies and corporate prerogatives could be challenged. This loss, along with the massive changes in the labor and civil rights organizations that had supported black American anticolonial politics, left anticolonial activists of the late 1940s without an institution and ultimately without a voice in American society. In 1955, Du Bois lamented that "one of the curious results of the current fear and hysteria is the breaking of ties between Africa and American Negroes"; it was "tragic" that "American Negroes are not only doing little to help Africa in its hour of supreme need, but have no way of really knowing what is happening in Africa."[129]

In short, the politics of the African diaspora, as represented in the broad African American anticolonial alliances of World War II and the immediate postwar period, did not survive the Truman Doctrine and Marshall Plan. The new liberal argument on civil rights was intimately linked to changes in foreign policy, arguing that discrimination within the United States was undermining America's legitimate global strategies. As India and then Indonesia won independence, and nationalist movements accelerated throughout Africa and Asia, this argument played an increasingly important role in the shaping of U.S. policy. Moreover, as civil rights politics itself came to be suspect in the deepening Cold War hysteria, White and other liberals—facing as the alternative the destruction of the NAACP—moved more and more to protect civil rights by grounding its justification firmly in anti-Communism and support of U.S. foreign policy.

But if doing so made possible some form of dissent in an otherwise repressive era, the cost was very high. The greatest irony of this liberal civil rights strategy was that neither the Truman nor the Eisenhower administration acted decisively on civil rights. Instead, the preoccupation of the Truman administration with America's "Achilles heel" led to frenetic efforts to shape the world's *perceptions* of race in America. To understand the thoroughness of the severing of relationships between black American activists and Africans, one must examine the new State Department programs in Africa and Asia and the government prosecution of anticolonial activists that devastated the left and destroyed the vestiges of the 1940s movement.

CHAPTER SIX

HEARTS AND MINES

They tell us we are in a free country. . . . Yes, we are free. Free to starve, free to live in shacks, free to be idle and unemployed, free to die for want of medical attention. Free to work for low wages, free not to have anything to save. . . . It is possible that democracy and freedom have different meanings for different people.

—West African Youth League of Sierra Leone

DESPITE THE FRAGMENTATION OF anticolonial alliances and the split of the Council on African Affairs in 1948, remaining CAA leaders such as Hunton, Robeson, and Du Bois continued to support African liberation movements and to monitor American corporate initiatives in Africa.[1] The CAA's African Aid Committee, chaired by Du Bois, raised money in 1950 for striking coal miners at Enugu, Nigeria, and the Nigerian National Federation of Labor.[2] Hunton followed the activities of Edward R. Stettinius Jr., the former secretary of state who, Hunton contended, controlled virtually the entire economy of Liberia through his Liberia Company.[3] Alarmed by these activities, colonial powers sought to undermine the CAA's visibility in Africa. In fact, by 1950 the CAA's *New Africa* was banned from the mails of the Union of South Africa, Kenya, and the Belgian Congo.[4]

The historian Sterling Stuckey has argued that Robeson's efforts on the behalf of the liberation of African and Asian peoples intensified in the period after 1949.[5] The Marshall Plan and the new American corporate inroads into Africa and Latin America deepened his critique of the relationship between imperialism and Jim Crow and his sense of connection with black peoples in the Caribbean, South America, and Africa. For Robeson, the Marshall Plan meant "enslavement of our people all over the earth, including here in the United States on the cotton and sugar plantations and in the mines of the North and South."[6] Moreover, again linking the violence of imperialism with the violence in the American South, Robeson argued that the new U.S. foreign policy was—and could only be—backed by militarism. The Atlantic Pact gave "legal sanction for sending guns and troops to the colonies to insure the en-slavement and terrorization of our people. They will shoot our people down in Africa just as they lynch us in Mississippi."[7]

Thomas Borstelmann has aptly observed that for most of the peoples of Africa and Asia, "the Cold War and the supposed dangers of communism were merely distractions from the historic opportunity provided by World War II for ending the European colonialism that had long dominated the lives of most of the world's people."[8] As the Truman administration chose to interpret interna-tional, national, and even local politics in terms of a fundamental struggle with the Soviet Union, Robeson and other anticolonial activists struggled to shift the focus of the debate to colonial peoples' and working people's control of their labor, their land, and their resources. For Robeson and his allies the conflict was ultimately over the meaning and terms of freedom. In response to Truman's ar-gument that sources of the most vital raw materials including uranium would be lost if the free countries of Asia and Africa should fall to the Soviet Union, the *African Standard,* published by the West African Youth League of Sierra Leone, asserted the vacuity of Truman's brand of freedom and its irrelevance for colonized peoples.[9]

Yet this was a struggle that anticolonial activists would ultimately lose. The work of the CAA was increasingly encumbered by government efforts to silence the organization and its leadership. Robeson's biographer, Martin Duberman, has asserted that Robeson was *misquoted* by the Associated Press from the Paris Peace Conference in 1949 as saying, "It is unthinkable that American Negroes would go to war on behalf of those who have oppressed us for generations against a country [the Soviet Union] which in one generation has raised our peo-ple to the full dignity of mankind." Nevertheless, following the dispatch, Robeson faced fierce denunciations from both the white press and black leadership, as well as the wrath of government agencies.[10] As Duberman has explained, Robeson had been for many the showcase black American—proof that a "deserving" black person could make it in America—and even better, someone who talked with pa-triotism and optimism about the country's democratic promise. But the AP ac-count from Paris, following four years of increasingly disenchanted public pronouncements, suggested that he had turned out to be an unsuitable represen-tative, and it became imperative to isolate and discredit him.[11]

In fact, Robeson did believe that the Soviet Union offered hope for colonized peoples, but he critiqued the U.S. role in fostering the Cold War not because he supported the Soviet Union but because of what he believed would be devas-tating consequences for anticolonial and democratic projects. For the rest of his life he would struggle to make oppression of black peoples visible against a bipolar reading of global politics that rendered the oppression of Africans and peoples of African descent a secondary issue. Seeking to protect free speech and civil liberties, the right to speak his mind as an American citizen, and the integrity and independence of black politics, Robeson saw his silencing by the U.S. government as an "un-American" violation of civil liberties. The government's inability to accept the independence of anticolonial struggles and its persistence in viewing antiracist projects in terms of the Cold War seemed to him forms of racism rather than roadblocks to Soviet expansion in the United States. Responding to attacks after the Paris Peace Conference, he declared: "They can't imagine that our people, the Negro people, forty millions in the Caribbean and Latin America, one hundred and fifty millions in Africa, and fourteen million here, today up and down this America of ours,—are also determined to stop being industrial and agricultural serfs."[12]

Unable to silence Robeson through fear and intimidation as it had silenced other critics, in 1950 the federal government revoked his passport. The rejection of Robeson's subsequent appeal plainly revealed that the government regarded anticolonialism and civil rights activism as interlocking issues that threatened national security. The State Department contended that even if the passport had been canceled "solely because of the appellant's recognized status as spokesman for large sections of Negro Americans, we submit that this would not amount to an abuse of discretion in view of the appellant's frank admission that he has been for years extremely active in behalf of the independence for the colonial peoples of Africa."[13] The government's brief in the Court of Appeals stated that while working for the liberation of African peoples "may be a highly laudable aim, the diplomatic embarrassment that could arise from the presence abroad of such a political meddler, traveling under the protection of an American passport, is easily imaginable. After all, 'the President is the sole organ of the federal government in the field of international relations.'"[14] Clearly the U.S. government would not tolerate criticism of its foreign policy by civil rights leaders.

In the three years following the revocation of Robeson's passport, the Council on African Affairs itself faced two sets of charges by the U.S. attorney general: first as a Communist-front organization according to the Subversive Activities Control Board; second, as a foreign agent under the Foreign Registration Act. Evidence for the second case rested on the CAA's relationship with the African National Congress, the South African Indian Congress, the Kenya Africa Union, and the Nigerian mine workers.[15]

U.S. RESPONSES TO AFRICAN AND ASIAN NATIONALISM

Before considering the details of those cases, and in order to appreciate what was at stake one must look at American objectives in Africa and Asia. Government prosecution of the CAA for links to African liberation groups did not directly cause the eclipse of the politics of the African diaspora; as noted previously, the precipitous decline of anticolonial politics began earlier in 1947. But the full dimensions and the implications of the decline can be understood only in the context of America's confrontation with Asian and African nationalism. Between 1945 and 1960, as the United States emerged as the dominant global power, forty countries with a total of eight hundred million people—more than a quarter of the world's population at that time—revolted against colonialism and won their independence. Policymakers in the Truman and Eisenhower administrations wanted to ensure that these new nations remained friendly to the United States, so by 1950 the Truman administration was increasing its attention to Africa.[16] A 1951 State Department directive, for example, emphasized that because "Africa provides a sizable proportion of the critical commodities now required by the Free World," it was imperative to "insure that Africa will remain firmly fixed in the political orbit of the Free World."[17]

Several factors made parts of Africa strategically crucial in the early Cold War. During World War II, when Japan occupied much of the Pacific, the Allied Powers had turned to Africa for natural resources. By the late 1940s, following the independence of India and Indonesia and the establishment of a Communist regime in China, the United States and its European allies viewed Asia as "lost" to the West and relied even more on Africa.[18] Until the discovery of uranium deposits in Colorado in 1952, for example, the Congo's Shinkolobwe mine was the primary source of uranium used in U.S. atomic bombs; thus the large supplies of uranium in the Belgian Congo and South Africa gave the region a unique significance in the eyes of the Truman administration.[19] The Korean War made Africa's strategic raw materials even more critical.[20]

The outbreak of the Korean War, moreover, greatly heightened American policymakers' fears that resentment of American racism might cause Asian and African peoples to seek closer relations with the Soviet Union, exacerbating what the historian Melvyn P. Leffler has characterized as the obsession of U.S. officials with the Communist threat in Third World areas and their exaggerated fear of the Soviet Union's ability to capitalize on the rising tide of nationalism.[21] As the State Department told the American consul in Lagos in 1951, no one should assume "for a moment that the Soviet directorate is unaware of the importance of Africa to the Free World . . . We must never forget that the anticolonial feeling in certain African territories constitutes a formidable problem for the Free World because all of the Colonial Governments are aligned on the side of the Free World."[22] Given the increasing strategic and political importance of Africa to the United States, policymakers in the Truman administration walked a tightrope between allegiance to colonial powers and their desire to win the loyalty of new Asian and African states. But the projects of Robeson and the CAA clashed with the explicit aims of the American government to foster pro-Western independence movements in Africa and Asia.

The scope and contours of the conflict can be understood only in terms of the federal government's all-encompassing ideological vision of national security. George F. Kennan observed in 1952 that "national security" is not simply a "negative quality: the absence of something we call military attack . . . or the successful repelling of it." Rather, he said, "customs and public policies in race relations" profoundly affect "the feelings of other peoples toward us and the dispositions they make of their physical and military resources, and accordingly on the demands we make of other peoples."[23] Accordingly, the Truman administration saw racial discrimination in America as its Achilles heel in a propaganda battle with the Soviet Union for the allegiance of Africa and Asia.[24] Yet as Thomas Borstelmann has demonstrated, once the Truman administration was preoccupied with Korea, it paid little further attention to domestic civil rights programs and was unwilling to challenge the southern wing of the Democratic Party. Thereafter, black protest, not segregation itself, came to be seen as the threat to U.S. security.[25]

Acting on these fears, the administration, instead of genuinely addressing problems of discrimination, violence, and the denial of rights to black citizens, became increasingly energetic in efforts to shape perceptions of America in Africa. Voice of America broadcasts and the State Department's "Cultural Affairs, Psychological Warfare, and Propaganda" programs, attempted to defend American foreign policy, to manipulate African perceptions of black American life, and sometimes to discredit Robeson and Du Bois. The fact that many such programs were in place by 1950 and that they coincided with the prosecution of Robeson and the CAA locates the genesis of this relationship between U.S. domestic and international racial politics earlier than is often assumed. Commonly, examples of the connection are taken from the Kennedy years or seen as an outgrowth of civil rights struggles in the 1950s and 1960s.[26] But the reconstruction of race, from the rejection of formulations of international solidarity by black American liberals such as Walter White as early as 1947 to the government's attempts to win the hearts and minds of Africa and Asia, began with the Cold War itself.

State Department officials in West Africa were deeply concerned about the impact of prominent anticolonial activists such as Robeson and Du Bois. The arrest in 1951 of Du Bois and other Peace Information Center officers led to "urgent" requests from diplomatic personnel in Lagos, Nigeria, for information to quell publicity on the case, and a U.S. 1953 intelligence report on the Mau Mau uprising in Kenya linked Jomo Kenyatta to Paul Robeson.[27] But the most dramatic example of State Department apprehension about relationships between African Americans and Africans is revealed in the deliberate attempt to discredit Paul Robeson. The revocation of his passport drew widespread international attention and provoked scathing criticisms throughout Asia as well as Africa.[28] U.S. officials in West Africa were particularly alarmed about the ramifications of the case, and were also dismayed by the repercussions of Robeson's criticism of American intervention in Korea. In August 1950 the American Consul in Lagos complained that Robeson's criticism of U.S. intervention had been widely publicized in the Nigerian press: "It is tragic that the most poisonous anti-American propaganda comes from the United States itself."[29] In 1951 Roger Ross, a U.S. public affairs officer in Accra, Gold Coast, sent a memo to the State Department suggesting that a disparaging article be written about Robeson and distributed in Africa.

[USIS, i.e., the United States Information Service] in the Gold Coast, and I suspect everywhere else in Africa, badly needs a thorough-going, sympathetic and regretful but straight-talking treatment for the whole Robeson episode. . . . The universality of its usefulness to us in Africa ought to warrant whatever it costs in time and money. Because there's no way the Communists score on us more easily and more effectively, out here, than on the U.S. Negro problem in general, and on the Robeson case in particular. And, answering the latter, we go a long way toward answering the former.[30]

Ross wanted the story of Robeson "told sympathetically, preferably by an American Negro devoted to his race," and presented as a tragedy. To be convincing, it should "pay homage to the man's remarkable talents as an artist" and, with regret rather than rancor, treat his political views as a "spiritual alienation from his country and the bulk of his own people" and as an "illness of the mind and heart, . . . not easily recognized, yet contagious, and thus a deadly danger."[31] Predicting that he could get such an article "serialized in practically every newspaper" in the Gold Coast, Ross requested a printing in booklet form, with pictures. He stressed that to make the article credible, it should be "written by someone independent of the Department, published in an American periodical," and then reprinted.[32]

An article of this precise description appeared in the November 1951 *Crisis*, the official NAACP organ, as "Paul Robeson—The Lost Shepherd," by Robert Alan. Alan was identified only as "the pen-name of a well known journalist." Through the willingness of the *Crisis* to publish such an article, along with Walter White's very similar "The Strange Case of Paul Robeson," published in *Ebony*, the NAACP cooperated in discrediting Robeson.[33]

"CULTURAL AFFAIRS, PSYCHOLOGICAL WARFARE, AND PROPAGANDA"

A struggle over the meaning and significance of race was a critical ideological component in the U.S. pursuit of global hegemony. In addition to direct attempts to discredit Robeson, the State Department intervened culturally and politically to influence the terms of solidarities among black Americans and Africans and to shape world perceptions of the status of African Americans. The State Department's "Cultural Affairs, Psychological Warfare and Propaganda" originated in World War II's Psychological Warfare Board of the Office of War Information.[34] Many books about the United States Information Agency (USIA) mention Africa only in the 1960s.[35] Yet some critical programs were in place as much as twenty years earlier. The United States Information Service (USIS) in the Gold Coast, Nigeria, Kenya, and South Africa used radio broadcasts, films and publications to win recognition for the U.S. as the champion of African and black American aspirations.[36] The State Department personnel throughout Africa also reported bi-weekly on local press coverage of United States foreign policy and American "race relations" and worked to counter the poor image of America abroad stemming from domestic racial discrimination.[37]

Much USIS effort went into crafting representations of black American life. Citing feelings of solidarity between Africans in the Gold Coast and African Americans, Hyman Bloom of the American consulate in Accra observed in April 1951 that "among Gold Coast Africans, who consider themselves more or less the parent stock of U.S. Negroes, there is a deep, wary, almost psychotic concern with the whole issue of race-relations in America," which gave the Communists "a perfect theme."[38] To counter this perceived "psychosis," the USIS attempted to project positive images of black American life. Drawing on the economist Gunnar Myrdal's *American Dilemma*, the State Department developed a clear strategy that acknowledged that discrimination existed but hastened to add that racism was a fast disappearing aberration, capable of being overcome by a talented and motivated individual. Indeed, this Myrdalian twist characterized the dominant liberal discourse on racism in the late 1940s and early 1950s. A stress on the achievements of individual black Americans as examples of American democracy at work was often deemed more desirable than the image of group advancement. Toward this end, the USIS released articles such as "Working for World Peace: Dr. Bunche in History," "The United States Negro in Business and Economic Progress," and "Negro Hurdler Is Determined to Win Olympic Event," which were successfully reprinted in Lagos, Nigeria, in June 1952.[39]

As one effort of USIS, the Nairobi-based Regional Public Affairs Officer John A. Noon and his staff created a series of radio broadcasts in Swahili called *The Jones Family of Centerville USA.* Noon explained that this "family serial" was designed to "broaden understanding of life in the United States; increase the African's understanding of and appreciation for democratic institutions and processes by presenting democracy in action; present the role of Negro-Americans in American life." The program was aired in a twenty-minute spot immediately preceding the 6:00 P.M. newscast. Noon boasted that the "geographical coverage for these broadcasts includes Kenya, Uganda, Tanganyika and Zanzibar with an estimated listening audience of 3,000,000."[40]

In a not very subtle case of pointing to anxieties through a denial of their importance, Noon discussed the "many problems" in scripting the show: the Joneses were "Negro-Americans. Should this fact be revealed at the outset or would it be more effective to give ethnic identity at a later time?" After "extensive debate" in a classic case of Myrdalian bad faith, the staff decided "to avoid ethnic labels for a time in order to impress the audience that this was not a factor defining status in American life." Only after the audience had realized that the Joneses were able to participate in the full round of community activities, would the "Negro-American identification" be introduced "most indirectly."[41]

But while attempting to defend American racial practices and foreign policy, the USIS itself sometimes became the object of biting criticism and wit. Its arguments, the *Eastern Nigerian Guardian* charged, were "calculated to veil the truth and bamboozle Nigerian opinion."[42] The *Labour Guardian* launched a similar attack: "To laud to the sky the isolated case of a successful Negro may be tolerated. But to present it to the people as the lot of the Negro community across the Atlantic is a claim tantamount to fraud. We know the lot of our brothers there. . . . The Nigerian people cannot afford to have their minds poisoned by a people who though they are free would not allow others to be free."[43]

USIS officers were frustrated not only by these criticisms but by what they considered alterations or deliberate misuse of their material in the West African press. In an account of the presentation of an award to the singer and actor Harry Belafonte, the toastmaster's praise of Belafonte's "crusade for Americanism" was translated in the Gold Coast's *Daily Mail* as "crusade for Africanism."[44] In Lagos, Willard Quincy Stanton complained that Azikiwe's press was intentionally using USIS material out of context. Harold Null, the public affairs officer of the American consulate general had given a series of radio broadcasts extolling the virtues of voluntarism in American civil society against statist control in the Soviet Union. Null explained that "when Americans combine toward a common end, the combinations are brief and easily dissolved by other unions." Instead, in the satirical hands of the *West African Pilot,* Null's defense of civil society was modified into the contention that "the American government has always been an unstable equilibrium of contradictions." Indeed, such instability was offered as an explanation for lynching. Since "American society moved into the wilderness well in advance of legal institutions, the frontier justice of vigilantes and lynch law have lingered on to become instruments of oppression in the orderly society that replaced the frontier."[45] No wonder USIS officials were furious. In placing racism and violence at the heart of American life and institutions, the *West African Pilot* thoroughly undermined the attempts of the U.S. government to define racism as an aberration, as well as their claim that civil society is necessarily morally superior to the state. Here, civil society was unmasked as a source of terror, suggesting the state's ineffectiveness as a protector of black rights.

In South Africa the State Department faced the dilemma of wanting to court the black majority by fabricating an image of American racial harmony and simultaneously not wanting to embarrass its white supremacist allies by pretending to believe in this very fabrication. Thus, State Department programs had a much slower start in South Africa than in Nigeria, Ghana, or Kenya, and programming was significantly different. U.S. officials in Johannesburg and Cape Town argued that materials on "the race problem" risked alienating and embarrassing the white minority government and white citizens. Nonetheless concerned that "the majority, which is black, is frankly skeptical of America's stand on the issue of color," they recommended programs on "Negro culture, or with opera, drama and music by Negro performers," and again suggested emphasizing the progress and accomplishments of individuals.[46] By 1955 and 1956, Voice of America and State Department projects highlighting individual achievements and culture, were having considerable success in capturing publicity in black South African papers. For example, the *Bantu World*, the largest Soweto-based paper, carried a series called *Cartoon History of the United States*, along with extensive reports on musicians and athletes.[47] These and more general information about American politics were found useful elsewhere as well. A. W. Childs, the American consul general in Nigeria, after reviewing the pamphlet program outlined by the Department of State, ordered two thousand copies of the *Cartoon History*, and accorded the political pamphlets *Freedom Is Winning* and *What Shall Men Believe* "considerable effectiveness at this post."[48]

Given the economic and strategic importance of South Africa to the United States, the relationship between their governments sometimes dictated parameters for programs in other parts of the continent. A 1955 report to Secretary of State John Foster Dulles from the consulate in Leopoldville, Belgian Congo, fretting over negative publicity in the local media about racial discrimination in America, blithely recommended that U.S. consulates throughout Africa host Fourth of July celebrations for black Africans, which "would have a happy effect on millions of Africans." The Leopoldville consulate planned such an event for months before reality set in and it was canceled. In the words of the U.S. representative at the Trusteeship Council, it would have made the American ambassador to the Union of South Africa "persona non grata," and "this indeed would be a serious loss without comparable benefits and without consideration of the issues of defense and strategic materials."[49]

In Africa as elsewhere, education quickly became a major tool of "psychological warfare." The Fulbright student and professor exchange program began in 1946.[50] In 1948, the American consul in Accra declared "a miniature cold war for the students." Expressing regret that Britain's worst antagonists (Azikiwe and Nkrumah) had been educated in America, George M. Atkinson, American vice consul, insisted that the education of Africans visiting the States be controlled to prevent such antagonism: "With the full realization that an international exchange of students can be an immense source of good will and propaganda, the consulate and the Gold Coast Government are now closely cooperating on all matters relating to students going to the United States."[51]

To augment these broad cultural and political efforts to capture the sympathies of African peoples, State Department personnel designed programs to justify and defend American foreign policy. In 1950, with the imperative of keeping colonized peoples on the side of the "free world," the USIS in Africa was concerned to reconcile American intervention in Korea with the claim that America was on the side of freedom for colonized peoples. A typical USIS release in Nairobi stated, "President Truman says the free peoples of the world will help the people of Communist ravaged Korea because it is in the nature of brotherhoods to assist the unfortunate."[52] Twentieth Century Fox distributed Department of State newsreel films, *President Truman Reports on Korea* and *United Nations in Korea*, in theaters throughout Kenya, Uganda, Tanganyika, and Zanzibar. Angus Ward, the American consul in Nairobi, monitored the showings and relayed to Washington his "town and theater breakdowns."[53] USIS articles such as "General Ridgeway Pleads for Peace in Korea" and "Truman Stresses Aid to Korean People" were reprinted in West and East African newspapers such as the *Daily Success* in Lagos.[54] Besides addressing U.S. involvement in Korea, USIS officials attempted to portray the Soviet Union as a nuclear aggressor and the United States as a savior by distributing booklets and pamphlets such as *Survival under Atomic Bombing Attack* in East Africa. The consulate in Mombasa, Kenya, furnished this pamphlet, for instance, to the editor of the *Mombasa Times,* which published it in January 1951.[55]

The production of USIS material involved the active cooperation of consulate staff and headquarters in Washington, and staff in Africa often struggled to apply Cold War hysteria there. Perceiving that it was a hard sell to make Cold War geopolitics relevant to colonized African peoples, Willard Quincy Stanton wrote to the State Department from Lagos that material on Communism tended to "fall flat"; therefore, the USIS needed to emphasize "Russian imperialism" instead and promote the idea that assistance to "Communist agents" would lead to the establishment of "Russian slavery": "A line such as this preached in simple terms might be understood by hundreds of thousands, perhaps millions of West Africans who do not like Whites but could perhaps be led to fear Russia."[56] Stanton's proposal materialized later that year with the publication in the local press of the USIS release "Attempt to Stamp Out Islam in Central Asia" and the distribution in Muslim areas of the USIS leaflet *Red Star over Islam.*[57] Still, State Department personnel also continued to attack Communism overtly in areas such as Nigeria, that had important trade union movements, using releases such as "U.S. Labor *versus* Communist Aggression."[58]

The USIS also addressed the challenge posed to American foreign policy by India's position of nonalignment with either side in the Cold War. Despite India's opposition to U.S. policy at early United Nations sessions, the United States had continued to court Prime Minister Jawaharlal Nehru and had hoped for a strong alliance with India.[59] But Nehru's visit to the United States in October 1949 quickly dashed such wishful thinking; his discussions with Truman and Acheson, writes the historian Robert J. McMahon, "revealed a deep chasm between New Delhi and Washington on key international issues, including the nature of the Soviet threat and the character of the new Chinese government."[60] Despite the U.S. failure to win the support of India, the State Department tried to capitalize on any contact with Nehru and to avoid the impression of an adversarial relationship between the two nations. Robert W. Stookey, American vice consul in Nairobi, distributed to schools and organizations throughout British East Africa an early USIS film on Pandit Nehru's visit to the United States.[61] Likewise, the USIS release "Communism and Gandhism Not Alike: A Visit to Red China" was distributed in Nigeria and reprinted in the *Daily Success* (Lagos) and *New Africa* (Onitsha) in June 1952.[62]

Unable to win the support of India, the United States turned to Pakistan as a South Asian ally. In contrast to the Indian government, as McMahon has pointed out, "Pakistani officials unequivocally pledged their nation's willingness to cooperate with the United States in long-range defense planning."[63] The Pakistan-U.S. alliance was shored up by Prime Minister Liaquat Ali Khan's visit to Washington in May 1950. In the Cold War battle for hearts and minds, the U.S. sought to make the most of this alliance with a new Asian state. In January 1951 Secretary of State Dean Acheson informed the American consul in Nairobi that the department had ordered 35mm Urdu prints of *Prime Minister Pakistan,* a film about the visit of the prime minister and his wife to the United States. After showings in Dar es Salaam, Tanganyika, were deemed "highly successful" by USIS personnel, U.S. officials secured the agreement of the Indian Film Combine to distribute the film in areas with significant South Asian populations, in Kenya, Uganda, Tanganyika, and Zanzibar, including Nairobi, Mombasa, Dar es Salaam, Tangam Kampala, and Jinja.[64]

(MIS)READING NATIONALISMS

An examination of U.S. officials' readings of African nationalism further illuminates what was at stake in the creation of African policy. Postwar security and State Department documents on African nationalism in many ways echo the story familiar from the more extensively studied nations of Southeast Asia and the Middle East. The State Department saw itself "caught in . . . the jaws of a vice of our own design and fabrication."[65] Although it did not want to antagonize other NATO members, it was convinced that "indigenous disturbances" created conditions favorable to Communism and worried that the excesses of its colonialist allies engendered this dangerous instability. Moreover, the political and economic interests of the United States would best be served by decolonization. Thus, policymakers saw their task as one of encouraging independent states that would be securely in the Western orbit.[66] A 1951 State Department memo warned against getting trapped into "strong or weak" support of either "African nationalist aspirations" or "colonial policies" and provided "guidance" on measures to "insure the unwavering loyalty of the African to the cause of freedom as we perceive it."[67]

Of course, the State Department was not monolithic, and proximity to nationalist movements had much to do with differences in interpretation: whereas officials in Washington understood such movements through the ideological prism of the Cold War, consulate staff in Africa were to some extent cognizant of the independence of nationalist challenges and did not make the mistake of attributing them in any simple way to Communism. In the early 1950s, for example, the USIE in Kenya targeted the Asian population, planning a radio station in Zanzibar with programs aimed at South Asian audiences.[68] But with the rise of the Kenya Africa Union and the Kenya Land and Freedom Movement, popularly known as the Mau Mau, USIE strategy shifted toward targeting the African population, indicating responsiveness to indigenous nationalism.[69] State Department and intelligence reports on Kenya clearly stated that the United States and Britain had found no evidence of Communist influence in the Mau Mau uprisings or in the Kenya Africa Union. Nonetheless, they believed that the unrest had created conditions that Communists could take advantage of, and they were concerned that the indigenous leadership in Kenya be sympathetic to the West.[70] John A. Noon, Public Affairs Officer in Nairobi argued that "interest in the Kenya disturbances centers in their reaction to world communism," but he fully acknowledged that Kenyans were not receiving "type one" direct Communist assistance and that "Kenya authorities are entirely convinced that the subversive movement is entirely propelled from within."[71] Similarly, State Department political reports from Nigeria, focused on the intricacies of nationalist movements, especially the rivalry between Azikiwe and Obafemi Awolowo.[72] American Consul General, Erwin P. Keeler reported in 1953, "there is no evidence to indicate any significant Communist participation in the Nigerian agitation and action toward gaining what the Nigerians call 'self-government,' nor any critical danger that they might move in to take over the nationalist movement at this time."[73]

Still, these insights about the independence of nationalist movements remained anomalous and did not alter or challenge the bipolar Cold War paradigm. Ultimately, taking a racist and simplistic vision of world affairs, the United States could not see African nation-building projects as anything other than potentially dangerous tools of the Soviet Union. Indeed, recognition of the integrity of African and Asian nationalist and nonaligned movements, would have required acceptance of the legitimacy of African and Asian demands for genuine political and economic equality on a global scale, whereas, in fact, U.S. officials remained unwilling to challenge either the prerogatives of corporate capital or American domestic racial policies. Domestically, the same blindness and evasions about the nature and allegiances of African nationalist movements was reflected in the suits filed against the Council on African Affairs.

THE CASE AGAINST THE CAA

Reexamining the prosecution of the CAA in light of American objectives and activities in Africa illuminates what was at stake, not simply for the domestic Cold War but for African nationalist movements and U.S. foreign policy. In 1952 the U.S. Attorney General's Subversive Activities Control Board (SACB) stated that "the Council on African Affairs (CAA) is substantially directed, dominated or controlled by the Communist Party, USA," and charged the organization with failing "to register with the Attorney General as provided in Sec. 7(b), (c) and (d) of the Internal Security Act of 1950."[74] Although it would be another year before the CAA was charged directly for its support of African groups, evidence for the first case rested on its work on Africa and, crucially, on its position against American intervention in Korea.

The CAA denied the charges of Communist affiliation and stated that it was "non-partisan, independent and not directed, controlled or dominated by the CP or any other organization." Asserting the integrity and independence of anticolonial politics against bipolar readings, its chief line of defense was to demonstrate the breadth of work in support of African liberation movements. The CAA noted especially its function as an "information service," citing subscriptions to CAA publications by U.S. libraries and colleges and African library and research services; its sustained work at the United Nations, which included relationships with American and other government officials; and its efforts in "responding to African emergencies." Moreover, the defense argued, its criticism of American policy on Africa "reflects the views of Africans themselves." The CAA substantiated its case with citations from Africans and from "parallel criticisms by Americans who are not communists," asking, "Is all such opposition to U.S. policies to be officially regarded as pro-communist and subject to McCarran Act prosecution?"[75]

Evidence and testimony used against the CAA seldom related specifically to links with the Communist Party but, rather, simply assumed that support of African liberation groups was Communist and therefore treasonous. In arguing that the CAA had failed to register with the Attorney General as required by provisions of the Internal Security Act of 1950, the Subversive Activities Control Board and Attorney General Herbert Brownell Jr., cited among supporting "facts" that "the Council seeks to create and further hostility among the negroes in this country to the United States for the purpose of rendering this segment of the population susceptible to Communist indoctrination."[76] One witness for the FBI (whose name is blacked out in the records) testified that "the purpose of the CAA was to stimulate the Negroes here to a sense of hostility to the U.S. by stimulating the consciousness of Africa, to show that Negroes were part of the African nationality, and divorce American Negroes from the American life, and stimulate such consciousness. I heard discussions of this at political meetings."[77]

Proponents of the 1940s politics of the African diaspora had seen no conflict between the status of black Americans as Americans and the view that their struggles were linked to those of Africans and other colonized peoples. They believed that independent African and Asian states would help black Americans to win their rights as Americans. But in the 1950s the prosecution and its witnesses viewed these formulations of solidarity as incompatible with American citizenship. The CAA defense repudiated charges that "the council seeks to create and further hostility among the Negroes in this country to the U.S." and asserted that "the real purpose of the attack on the Council" was "to intimidate and stop Negro people from speaking out for African freedom and identifying their struggle with that of Africans." Not only had the State Department withheld Robeson's and Du Bois's passports for alleged political meddling, but "now the organization headed by these two leaders is to be outlawed because it does not endorse U.S. policies on Africa." Finally, the CAA reiterated "the moral right" of black Americans to support the struggles of Africans.[78]

Bittersweet reunion: Alphaeus Hunton on his release from prison, with his wife, Dorothy Hunton, Paul Robeson, and W. E. B. Du Bois. (Photographs and Prints Division, Schomburg Center for Research in Black Culture, The New York Public Library, Astor, Lenox and Tilden Foundations.)

The attorney general dismissed these arguments and cited the CAA's position against U.S. intervention in Korea as evidence that the organization "never knowingly deviated from the views and policies of the Communist Party." The prosecution's brief claimed that the CAA had advocated the party's view of the United Nations by calling the UN "an instrument for war and imperialism, rather than as an instrument for peace."[79]

Defending its opposition to American intervention in Korea, the CAA contended that self-determination for the Korean people was a prerequisite for a genuine achievement of peace in that area. Responding to charges about its criticism of the United Nations, it recalled the history of its efforts at the UN and its repeated calls for public support of the objectives set forth in the UN Charter. Reiterating what had been the dominant position among African American leaders only six years earlier, the CAA charged that "as long as the demands and rights of subject peoples are neglected by the United Nations, and as long as the organization remains primarily an instrument of power politics, no one, regardless of his political philosophy, can truthfully say it is fulfilling its functions as an instrument for peace."[80]

Not only the CAA as an organization, but its individual leaders faced government charges. Du Bois was indicted in 1951 as an unregistered foreign agent for his work with the Peace Information Center, a New York-based anti-Cold War lobby.[81] Alphaeus Hunton was imprisoned in 1951 for contempt of court, as were Dashiell Hammett, Frederick Field, and Abner Green, when these four trustees of the Civil Rights Congress Bail Fund refused to divulge the names of fund contributors to a federal court.[82] Hunton spent six months at the segregated federal prison in Petersburg, Virginia.[83]

BEYOND LEGAL ENTANGLEMENTS

As the case against it wore on, the CAA struggled to continue and intensify its support of African liberation groups. But its own position grew more and more precarious. The domestic isolation of the CAA in its efforts to aid the ANC's Campaign for the Defiance of Unjust Laws in South Africa in 1952 and 1953 stands in dramatic contrast to its widespread legitimacy in 1946. Then— in the midst of its famine relief campaign for South Africa, lobbying on South Africa at the United Nations, and support of striking South African miners— 19,000 people had attended its Madison Square Garden mass meeting. This time around, Hunton labored in vain to organize a similar coalition of civic, labor, and religious leaders.[84] Despite its weakness, however, the CAA managed to send over $2,500 to the Defiance Campaign, held a series of outdoor rallies in Harlem and an Emergency Conference on the Crisis in South Africa, and picketed the South African consulate.[85] But these efforts took place on the sidelines, for domestic anti-Communism had cast a pall on the burgeoning postwar urban civil rights movement.[86]

In a bittersweet chapter closing this era of diaspora politics, the weakening of the CAA in the United States came at precisely the moment when its ties to the ANC had deepened. Throughout the Defiance Campaign, Hunton, Du Bois, and Robeson corresponded with R. T. Bokwe, Walter Sisulu, Z. K.

Persistence in the face of adversity: Alphaeus Hunton picketing the South African consulate during the Campaign for the Defiance of Unjust Laws, 1952. (Photographs and Prints Division, Schomburg Center for Research in Black Culture, The New York Public Library, Astor, Lenox and Tilden Foundations.)

Matthews, and Oliver Tambo. Robeson's international stature as an artist facilitated their relationship. Writing to Hunton in 1953 to thank the CAA for funds, Bokwe elaborated on the difficulties faced by the ANC "with practically all the leaders banned and court case after court case being instituted against them in an all out effort to break the Congress." He asked that Hunton "remember us kindly to Paul and his family. His voice at least we are still privileged to hear over the gramophone and radio and thus we feel we have him with us always."[87]

Among ANC activists in this period, Sisulu was in especially close contact with black Americans and other African activists. His efforts in 1953 and 1954 to organize a Pan-African Congress provide rich insight into the institutional and ideological relationships between international anticolonial networks and the left. Sisulu had been deeply influenced by Du Bois and the Pan-African tradition, as well as by Azikiwe of Nigeria. In turn as a leader of the ANC Youth League in the 1940s, Sisulu had profoundly influenced the slightly younger generation of leaders that included Nelson Mandela and Oliver Tambo. Gathering in study groups in the 1940s, Youth League members discussed books by Du Bois along with Azikiwe's newspapers.[88] The Communist Party and other socialist formations were at various times enabling for anticolonial projects but certainly not defining or even necessarily supportive. When Sisulu, with the aid of the Communist Party, traveled to London, Eastern Europe, and Moscow in 1953, he used the opportunity to hold meetings of any Africans present and to make plans for a Pan-African Congress in Africa. When leftist antiimperialists such as Fenner Brockway suggested that these plans were unrealistic and a London location was more feasible, Sisulu insisted that "even if I fail," it was important to make an "effort of bringing about consciousness in the people of Africa and . . . of focusing the attention of the people of Africa to something which is Africanist and held in Africa."[89]

Sisulu wrote to Du Bois in 1953 about his project, arguing that "the eradication of imperialism and oppression in Africa will be as a result of the struggle by the peoples of Africa themselves."[90] Noting Du Bois's CAA connection and his efforts for "the assistance of the African people for the last fifty years," Sisulu asked for advice on sponsoring a conference in Africa.[91] In reply, Du Bois lamented the difficulty in realizing such a conference and his own inability to obtain a passport to leave the United States or to get a visa to enter Africa. Agreeing, however that a Pan-African Congress in Africa would have great "value and significance," Du Bois recommended that Sisulu "write to all African organizations in Africa and to the various governments which would be interested" and offered his assistance in making such contacts. He also sent Sisulu George Padmore's London address and passed Sisulu's letter along to Padmore with the notation, "I think it would be splendid to push this movement even if at present it seems almost impossible."[92]

Sisulu took Du Bois's advice; he wrote to Padmore and sent a conference call to African national organizations and governments.[93] His appeal not only received a wide response from countries throughout Africa—including Ethiopia, Egypt, and the Sudan—but, like CAA activities, drew the attention of U.S. intelligence agencies. CIA staff wrote to FBI Director J. Edgar Hoover requesting information on Du Bois and the CAA concerning instigation or participation "in any recent project for holding a pan-African conference." Hoover responded with information on CAA references to the 1945 Manchester Pan-African Congress, and 1953 reports from the CAA's newsletter *Spotlight on Africa* (obtained from the U.S. Army Headquarters in Heidelberg, Germany) on independent plans for Pan-African conferences in (the Gold Coast) and South Africa.[94] The American consul in Accra regularly reported plans for a 1953 meeting in the Gold Coast involving Nkrumah and the Convention Peoples Party, and for a conference of the Congress of Peoples against Imperialist Oppression involving Fenner Brockway.[95]

Sisulu's dream of a Pan-African conference to mobilize African independence movements during the height of the Cold War never materialized. Not until 1958 was the All African People's Conference called by the newly independent nation of Ghana. The failure of Sisulu's initiative—and of other attempts at Pan-African conferences in the early 1950s—exemplifies the difficulties in sustaining international projects in this period. The institutional basis of these efforts had always been precarious, and they became impossible in these years. South African and black American activists faced prosecution within their own countries, and there was no independent commitment to such projects on the part of the Communist Party.[96]

Moreover, the unity of 1940s anticolonialism broke down as specific leaders and nations became enmeshed in the political exigencies of moving closer to independence. Tensions can be seen in the CAA's altered relationships with anticolonial activists in Nigeria and the Gold Coast. By 1954 the CAA had become sharply critical of developments in those countries. Its June 1954 newsletter attacked Azikiwe's visit to the United States, quoting him as saying, "We want to meet rich people and prove to them that we can best spend their money in Eastern Nigeria."[97] The CAA believed that Azikiwe had made concessions not only to British and American capital but to McCarthyism as well. Reporting that the Gold Coast government had issued an order prohibiting the importation of allegedly Communist-sponsored publications and that the Nigerian government had followed suit, the CAA endorsed protests against these actions by the All-Nigerian Trade Union Federation, the National Council of Civil Liberties, the United Working People's Party of Nigeria, and the Gold Coast *Ashanti Sentinel*.[98]

Tensions between anticolonial activists did not necessarily lead to a severing of relationships along classic Cold War lines, however. Hunton and Du Bois continued to maintain close ties with Azikiwe and other West African allies, even as they vigorously debated their differences.[99] In addition to assisting the Defiance Campaign in South Africa, the CAA coordinated efforts with the Kenya Committee in London to support the Kenya Africa Union and its imprisoned leader, Jomo Kenyatta. In 1954 the CAA held "A Working Conference in Support of African Liberation" in New York and established the Kenya Aid Committee with a goal of raising $5,000.[100] The committee organized delivery of dried milk, vitamin pills, and first aid supplies and sought to establish local aid committees nationwide and monthly educational forums in New York City.[101] At a series of summer street-corner meetings in Harlem in support of "the Kenya Africans' struggle," speakers stressed the "the common objectives for which the Kenya Africans and Negroes in Mississippi and Harlem struggle."[102] The CAA also contributed funds to the legal defense of imprisoned Kenyan nationalists.[103]

The CAA's work on Kenya reveals that solidarity did not simply mean one organization supporting another; rather, it was embedded in international networks. The ANC's Walter Sisulu had met Kenyan trade unionists, including J. A. Z. Murumbi of the Kenya Africa Union and Peter Koinage, at a conference in Poland in 1953.[104] Writing to Hunton in June 1954, Sisulu related "the mass murder and atrocities carried out by the British troops against innocent and defenseless Africans in Kenya," and argued that the campaign for a cessation of the war and a release of the leaders of the Kenya Africa Union must be intensified. Sisulu asked that the CAA contact the London Kenya Committee, stating his confidence that a call by Paul Robeson and Du Bois would have "tremendous support in various parts of the world."[105]

THE DEMISE OF THE CAA

The attorney general's office closely followed the CAA's support of these African liberation groups and renewed its aggressive prosecution. In defending itself against Communist-front charges in 1952, the CAA had used support of African liberation groups as its primary line of defense. But it was precisely this support that the government had interpreted as Communist-influenced, and in the midst of the first case another line of investigation emerged. In a 1953 memo to J. Edgar Hoover, Assistant Attorney General Warren Olney III argued that information previously submitted by the FBI for the case before the Subversive Activities Control Board "reveals that the subject may have incurred an obligation to register with this Department under the terms of the Foreign Agents Registration Act of 1938."[106] Olney implied that the attempts to link the

CAA to the Communist Party U.S.A. had been "a mere fishing expedition" and outlined a new case: the council's work on South Africa could be taken as evidence that "the subject is acting as 'a publicity agent' for a foreign principal," and money raised to support striking Nigerian mineworkers and the Defiance Campaign as evidence that "the subject is soliciting contributions for a foreign principal."[107] Olney further cited "general information to the effect that the subject maintains contact with individuals and organizations in Africa," emphasizing the Kenya Africa Union and the ANC. He noted, however, that the Justice Department did not have direct evidence that the CAA was acting "at the order, direction or request of a foreign principal." Therefore, Olney recommended a subpoena of CAA documents: "It may be that an examination of the subject's books, records and correspondence will reveal the necessary evidence to establish an agent relationship."[108] The final page of this memo obtained through the Freedom of Information Act is blacked out. Whatever its contents, Olney did subpoena CAA correspondence with the African National Congress, the South African Indian Congress, and their leaders.[109] Moreover, the FBI stepped up its surveillance.[110]

African activists understood charges against the CAA as intimately connected to support of African liberation groups. Writing to Robeson in 1953, Sisulu described South African government attempts to "discredit the liberatory movement by branding it subversive and anti-white," and linked the repressive tactics used against the ANC to those against the CAA: "It is not accidental that your organization has become the victim of the reactionary Eisenhower-McCarthy ruling clique who are conniving with other imperialists for the oppression and exploitation of millions of colonial and semi-colonial peoples."[111]

The CAA was finding it increasingly difficult to operate as an active organization. In the 1940s Du Bois had seen African Americans as the American base of opposition to imperialism. After five years of the Cold War, he felt estranged from black American politics and abandoned by its leadership. In late 1952 he wrote to Hunton protesting the move of the CAA's offices from 23 West 26th Street to Harlem: "No international agency belongs today in Harlem. It has neither the contacts nor the inspiration there. . . . Our programs go far beyond the provincial American Negro program into the programs of Africa and Asia, and we have a great center here, in the accessible part of New York."[112] Hunton's response contested Du Bois: "I fully share your view that the Council's program should *not* be limited by Harlem's horizons. At the same time however, I do feel that the main base of our work ought to be among Negro Americans, who as a group, have the most direct interest in Africa. I think it should be possible to have our headquarters in Harlem and yet maintain close ties with white progressive groups."[113]

If Hunton's assessment failed to grasp the impossibility of restoring the old coalitions, ultimately Du Bois's strategies proved no more effective. In the Mc-Carthy era both men were already marginal to black American and progressive American politics.

The government's case against the CAA never reached a resolution because in 1955, financially crippled by defense costs and further weakened by the restrictions placed on its individual leaders, the organization disbanded.[114] Having made an enormous contribution to the definition of black American politics and its relation to Africa, in the amnesia of the 1950s the CAA was quickly forgotten. The exile of its leaders from black American politics was swift and dramatic. Thereafter, work in the United States on Africa was dominated by new organizations thoroughly shaped by their birth in the Cold War era.[115]

The American Committee on Africa, established in 1953, became the major American political group concerned with Africa.[116] Lacking the relationship to the black American community and the radical domestic civil rights movement that had characterized the CAA, the ACOA typified the new anti-Communist anticolonialism. Led by George Houser, a Methodist minister who had worked with the pacifist Fellowship of Reconciliation, and Donald Harrington, another prominent minister, it was a bastion of anti-Communist liberalism, avowedly committed to stopping the spread of Communism in Africa. The ACOA advocated independent nations with close relations to the West and supported such pro-independence and pro-West leaders as Tom Mboya, a Kenyan legislator who was also the head of the CIA-backed Kenya Federation of Labor.[117]

The ideological gap between the CAA and the ACOA was clear even before the latter group's formation, during the South African Defiance Campaign in 1952. When Houser and Harrington held meetings to support the campaign, Alphaeus Hunton suggested consolidating their efforts. Houser replied that they would not work with the CAA because it had "many people who are not by any means unsympathetic to the communist party." He added, "The Communists will tend to make the most of the South African conflict, not because of basic concern for the South African people, but because they may be able to use the situation to bolster their own partisan position in the international power struggle."[118] Houser's *No One Can Stop the Rain: Glimpses of Africa's Liberation Struggle* does not even mention the CAA or its leaders in recounting American support for the Defiance Campaign.

The thoroughness of the severing of the links between the African American politics of the 1940s and the liberal African solidarity movements that emerged in the 1950s cannot be over-emphasized. Du Bois wrote in 1956, "The American Committee on Africa is a right-wing organization with Christianity and some big money behind it. Naturally, it is doing some good work and publishing some facts about the present situation, but fundamentally it is reactionary. . . . You cannot depend on it to tell the whole African story. . . . We have nothing in America that is at all worth while."[119] To understand the depth of Du Bois's disillusionment and the implications of the purging of radical anticolonialism, one must further examine the new politics and discourse on Africa that emerged during the Cold War.

CHAPTER SEVEN

REMAPPING AFRICA,

REWRITING RACE

The lack of interest of the black bourgeoisie and its mouthpiece, the Negro press, in the broader issues facing the modern world is due to the fact that the Negro has developed no economic or social philosophy except the opportunistic philosophy that the black intelligentsia has evolved to justify its anomalous and insecure position.

—E. Franklin Frazier, *Black Bourgeoisie*

IN 1954 W. E. B. DU BOIS COMPLAINED that the post–New Deal American Negro leadership had no interest in Africa.[1] On the face of it, this comment may seem incompatible with the rapt attention of black American journalists to the negative publicity and reaction that segregation in America was provoking in Asia and Africa. Civil rights leaders were deeply aware of the response around the world to American Jim Crow policies and sought to exploit it to their own advantage. As Mary Dudziak has argued, foreign policy concerns played a critical role in *Brown v. Board of Education*.[2] But a closer analysis of international coverage and the precise links made between domestic and international politics brings Du Bois's comment into sharper focus. African American anticolonialism had been profoundly changed by liberal leaders' acceptance of the proposition that the United States was the legitimate leader of the "free world." As former critics of American foreign policy—Walter White, Rayford Logan, A. Philip Randolph—came to oppose domestic discrimination by embracing anti-Communism, they emphasized their distinctiveness as Americans, not as persons of African descent. The politics of the African diaspora was eclipsed by the emphasis of African American leaders, intellectuals, and journalists on differences between African Americans and Africans, rather than on the bonds that had been so forcefully articulated during and after World War II.

With the demise of the transnational press that had been the critical means of creating and disseminating the politics of the African diaspora, its journalists were blacklisted or dropped from leading African American papers. Instead, anti-Communist liberals who put their hopes in securing for black Americans a share in American postwar prosperity dominated African American journalism and shaped the discussions of anticolonialism and Africa.

By 1950 there was a fundamental transformation of anticolonial discourse and a dramatic narrowing of coverage of Africa and the Caribbean in the black American press. Headlines concerning anticolonial movements, labor strikes, and the changing role of American corporations had disappeared. The greatly reduced volume of discussion of colonialism and Africa mirrored U.S. security concerns that British or French colonial excesses might open the door in Africa to the more dangerous Communists. Racism at home was presented as fundamentally at odds with the "American Creed," as an aberration that could mislead those in Asia and Africa about the true nature of the superior American democracy and drive them into the hands of the Communists. Black journalists focused on the image of the United States, not on the realities of American policy that had occupied them until 1947. At its worst, the new journalism trivialized and exoticized a homogenized and remapped Africa. Concrete discussions of the political economies of particular countries gave way to renderings of what was called "the great dark continent."

TOWARD A POLITICS OF SYMBOLISM AND FEDERAL PATRONAGE

The striking changes in the views of African American leaders and journalists on U.S. foreign policy can be seen in responses to the Korean War. In contrast to the interest in Asia and Africa during World War II, the absence of attention to the Korean War in the African American press is conspicuous.[3] Such sparse coverage as there was stressed the involvement of black American troops and the issue of segregation in the military.[4] In retrospect, one can identify the Korean War as the time when the U.S. armed services were integrated, but as the historian Richard Dalfiume has shown, integration during the war itself proceeded very unevenly against resistance, and by early 1951 there was still no definite assignment policy for black soldiers. Some units were integrating, others were not; thus, to black American observers and certainly to the press, continued segregation and discrimination were as conspicuous as the integration that did take place. The *Courier* charged that the black Twenty-fourth Infantry was being "framed" and called for an end to segregation; the NAACP charged discrimination against black soldiers in courts-martial.[5] But even though the moment appeared to be one of continuing struggle rather than victory, and the administration had once again failed to act decisively on civil rights, many activists and journalists felt that struggles for integration were legitimized by the Cold War and followed the path of least resistance through an endorsement of American foreign policy.

The meagerness of criticism of United States intervention in Korea or of American policy regarding China was part of the rise of bipartisanship throughout U.S. society. Being American meant agreeing with the government on foreign policy. In the atmosphere of the Cold War, any international identification became a liability, and African Americans insisted that they were first and foremost American. In late 1950 a *Courier* editorial announced that the American way of life "is in the greatest peril" and strenuously argued that this fact "must have as much meaning to Negro citizens as it does to other segments of the population. As long as there is a United States of America, the American Negro has a chance to fight for and win, everything that every other American enjoys. . . . If our nation should be struck down by some ruthless totalitarian power, we would lose even the chance to fight for our own advancement."[6]

Whereas in the 1940s journalists had consistently linked Jim Crow and imperialism, they drew sharp distinctions in discussions of Korea. Taking a position that inhibited criticism of domestic discrimination as well as of U.S. foreign policy, Joseph D. Bibb distinguished between colonial oppression and the American support of freedom in Korea, and declared, "Colored Americans admit that despite jim crow, discrimination and exploitation, . . . capitalism is better than communism."[7] In a striking reversal of its widespread condemnation of U.S. empire over the previous two decades, the *Courier* defended American intervention in Korea, arguing that the U.S. record on imperialism was "a good one": the United States had freed the Philippines while "Russia grabbed Outer Mongolia, Sinkiang, parts of Finland and Poland, all of Latvia, Estonia, and Lithuania, and set up puppet governments in Romania, Czechoslovakia, Bulgaria and Hungary."[8]

While championing American leadership of the "free world," civil rights leaders sought to exploit negative publicity on American racial discrimination to their own advantage. In 1950 Mordecai Johnson, president of Howard University, argued that independence for colonial peoples and an end to discrimination in the United States were, together, the best defense against Communism. According to *Afro-American* reporter James Hicks, Johnson "attributed communism's edge in the struggle to the discrimination against colored people by the capitalistic and imperialistic forms of government." China "has already gone over to the Communists," said Johnson, and the British Empire's "stupid blunder of treating the people of India as the United States has treated colored citizens in Alabama and Mississippi has created in India the best possible setup for communism in the world."[9] Warning that "in addition to a campaign to crush Soviet lies, there must be a campaign to crush Soviet truth," the *Courier* suggested as remedies, an end to discrimination in all federal departments, desegregation of the armed forces, and integration and liberalization of the foreign service.[10]

With criticism of American foreign policy off limits, analyses of the nuances of foreign relations were replaced by demands for putting black American staff in foreign policy positions. Journalists and civil rights leaders argued that black Americans in foreign service posts would be good for American diplomacy. Insisting that "the expansion of opportunities for Negroes would strengthen the moral position of the United States," the *Courier* launched a campaign for improvement in State Department hiring policies.[11] *Courier* reporter Dunbar S. McLaurin contended that appointing a black American ambassador to India "could do more to bolster sagging American prestige than millions of dollars in aid or relief—and knock the props from beneath most Communist argument."[12] Similarly, for *Afro-American* reporter Chatwood Hall, the United States was missing "the propaganda bus in the colored world": "A few dozen colored diplomats spread about these countries or some colored engineers, geologists or technicians would be more effective in gaining the good will of these people than hundreds of Voice of America broadcasts and Information Service bulletins."[13]

Thus, the mass politics of the earlier anticolonial alliances had been superseded by a middle-class politics of symbolism and federal patronage, which continued to be advocated by black American leaders throughout the 1950s. A. Philip Randolph, now international president of the Brotherhood of Sleeping Car Porters Union, recommended that the State Department should hire black Americans for service in Asian countries and that white personnel sent to Asia "should be screened for freedom from racism."[14] Adam Clayton Powell Jr. told President Eisenhower in 1955 that "one dark face from the U.S. is of as much value as millions of dollars in economic aid."[15] In response, the State Department did in fact begin to recruit more black American personnel and sponsored tours of Asia by prominent black Americans, among them the writer J. Saunders Redding, who toured India in 1953, and the journalist Carl T. Rowan, who traveled throughout India and Southeast Asia in 1954 and 1955.[16]

In the mid-1940s Rayford W. Logan had written extensively on the United Nations, becoming an expert on trusteeship. He had also been a leading African American critic of American foreign policy, highly visible through his journalism and involvement in anticolonial conferences. But according to Logan's biographer Kenneth Robert Janken, as a member of the United States National Commission for the United Nations Educational, Scientific, and Cultural Organization (UNESCO) from 1947 to 1950, Logan "defined his role as increasing the representation of African Americans in State Department policy."[17] And as the *Courier* adviser on foreign affairs, Logan was a leading proponent of placing African Americans in the U.S. foreign service. He argued that Secretary of State Acheson's "total diplomacy requires total democracy in the United States." Above all, "there should be no discrimination in those divisions of state that are concerned with the implementation of United States foreign policy."[18]

Logan's shift from criticizing to ratifying American foreign policy, with the proviso that black Americans be represented, exemplifies the dominant ideology of African American liberals in the early 1950s. In addition to his UNESCO position, Logan had become an NAACP adviser on international affairs following Du Bois's dismissal from that organization in 1948. Representing the NAACP at State Department conferences and meetings of nongovernmental organizations, and working with UNESCO, Logan had pushed for stronger clauses on international human rights—a position that sometimes brought him into conflict with the State Department, but even these disagreements remained within the bounds of an overall embrace of American foreign policy.[19] He was increasingly at odds with his former allies, suggesting in 1956, for example, that Africans were moving too quickly toward independence and worrying that emerging nations might abandon the United States and turn toward the Soviet Union.[20]

Walter White's attempts to link the fight against segregated housing to the American "national interest" sharply illustrates the limits of the strategy of using international anti-Communism to justify the fight against racial discrimination. Speaking for the NAACP at the 1950 Conference on Democracy in Housing, White warned that Africans and Asians "are being sold on the proposition that the United States talks democracy glibly, eloquently and frequently, and that it is one of the most backward places on the earth as far as democracy is concerned." Citing Nehru's lack of faith in the United States because of "lynching, of segregation, of ghettos, of the Ku Klux Klan," White declared that civil rights activists should sell the idea of unsegregated housing to all national interest groups in the country—including Metropolitan Life and the National Association of Real Estate Dealers—on the grounds that "to save themselves, they must take a stake in this whole issue and that their [present] practices are helping to create an unfavorable impression of America in other parts of the world."[21] Given the resegregation in housing brought on by urban renewal and suburbanization—all underwritten by federal housing policy—White's counsel starkly underscores the impotence of moral appeals in the face of widespread changes in the political economy. And by acquiescing in a narrowed civil rights agenda, many civil rights leaders forfeited the means to address these structural changes.[22]

It was precisely this retreat from challenges on fundamental social and economic issues that so troubled E. Franklin Frazier and animated his attacks on the black middle-classes in the 1955 *Black Bourgeoisie.* The book must be read

not solely as an indictment of the black middle classes but also as an indictment of Cold War liberalism. To be sure, Frazier harshly criticized black
middle-class leadership for breaking with the "traditional background of the
Negro" for rejecting its social heritage, and for its dependence on white philanthropy.[23] But Frazier also lamented the lack of interest in world affairs,
specifically colonialism, on the part of the black press. Black journalists, he
said, were careful "never to offend the black bourgeoisie or to challenge white
opinion on fundamental economic and social issues.[24]

Frazier's concerns are intelligible only in light of the dissolution of the broad
left and liberal coalitions of the 1940s that had fought for economic, political,
and civil rights in an international context. Frazier himself had been an active
member of the Council on African Affairs, remained a loyal supporter of Paul
Robeson and W. E. B. Du Bois throughout his life, and bequeathed his library
to Ghana.[25] He recognized that "the few Negro intellectuals who have dared to
express disapproval of the existing system of control over race relations have
been labeled Communists,"[26] and in a 1962 essay, he would complain that
"even today (the middle classes) run from Du Bois and Paul Robeson."[27] *Black
Bourgeoisie* also described as capitulation to Cold War red-baiting the
NAACP's refusal to "associate itself with unions or groups in which Communists might possibly be members."[28]

Frazier reserved some of his most vehement criticism for the black press,
which he described in "The Negro Press and Wish-Fulfillment" as "the chief
medium of communication by which the Negro creates and perpetuates the
world of make believe for the black bourgeoisie."[29] To appreciate the vehe-
mence of his attacks on the black middle classes and especially the press, as well
as the irony of the submergence of his critique of the Cold War despite the
considerable influence of *Black Bourgeoisie,* one must more fully examine
African American liberal discourse in the early Cold War.

PATERNALISM REVISITED

Sources of Frazier's dissatisfaction can be seen in the writings of those
intellectuals and journalists in the 1950s who overtly attacked the dominant
arguments of the 1940s. *Courier* columnist Marjorie McKenzie warned against
identifying with Africans. Recalling the argument that freedom for black
Americans rested upon a free Africa, she declared it "a frightening idea," one
that discounted American citizenship and "consigns us to thinking in racial
terms, a practice we have asked our white friends to abandon." What intellectuals in the 1940s had seen as commonality—that black Americans, Africans,
and all colonized peoples shared a common history of oppression—McKenzie
read as difference: "Does it make no difference that black men were trans-

planted from Africa to America 300 years ago and that a war was fought ninety years ago between brothers over the status of those emigrés and their descendants? Would it make no difference to us if our ancestors had never seen America?"[30] McKenzie actually found "some pride" in the fact that black Americans shared in the general American ignorance about Africa, because it demonstrated that "we identify culturally rather than racially." Instead of viewing the relationship between black Americans and Africans as reciprocal, McKenzie saw in Africa a tumultuous "march from the dark into the light" and thought that it was "America's duty to offer Africa a leadership that is true to our own best lights." Why, she asked, would black America want to "tie its star to the faltering gleam over the dark continent?"[31]

With the end of a belief in reciprocity, came a renewed paternalism. Africa became a "burden." A. N. Fields argued in the *Defender* that "the redemption of Africa rests upon the enlightened Negro of various civilized countries if hope is to ever be properly entertained for the complete realization of an intellectual and civilized Africa."[32] Although this sort of paternalism toward Africa had deep roots in African American and Western thought, it had been displaced during the 1940s by claims about commonalities and political reciprocity. Thus, its reemergence must be analyzed in the context of the 1950s and not simply taken as the persistence of an enduring strain of thought. "Let's Get Acquainted," an editorial spot in the *Courier,* typified both the newly paternalistic attitude and the assumption that a longstanding ignorance among black Americans about Africa was now gradually being dispelled. Portraying Africans as "people in various stages of civilization who are moving inexorably toward freedom and self-government but are mainly illiterate and industrially retarded," the *Courier* apprised readers that Africans "need sympathetic understanding and economic assistance." Black Americans, on the other hand, were "almost completely LITERATE, industrially advanced and have a brotherly INTEREST in the problems, struggles and advancement of their kinfolk across the Atlantic."[33]

In sharp contrast to the earlier assertions of bonds among black peoples worldwide, the press began to stress not only differences but hostilities. William Gardner Smith complained in the *Courier* that black people from European colonies felt superior to black Americans, and a letter to the editor called those from the Caribbean "clannish and cantankerous."[34] Although ethnic tensions among black people in the United States were certainly not unique to the 1950s, one rarely if ever found such views expressed in the mid-1940s; they reflected the collapse of a widespread identification with colonized peoples. Of course, the pervasive argument that black Americans were American first involved a positive emphasis on American citizenship that was crucial to the civil rights movement. But activists in the 1940s had also made positive claims to American citizenship yet had seen no contradiction between their struggles as Americans for political, civil and economic rights and their support for the struggles of Africans and other colonized peoples. It was in the atmosphere of McCarthyism and the Cold War that claims about citizenship often took an exclusivist form.

Further with the coming of the Cold War, journalists increasingly portrayed Africa as a U.S.-Soviet battleground and were preoccupied with Africa's importance to the "free" capitalist world. A 1953 *Courier* editorial declared that "Africa is not only a vast reservoir of raw materials necessary for the Allied war machine, but its 200 million people are virile, ambitious and resourceful folk who only need a little aid and encouragement to become a most valuable adjunct to the forces of the free world."[35] In 1952 the *Courier* carried a series on Africa and international politics by its United Nations correspondent, the sociologist Horace Cayton. He argued that the United States must take the lead in espousing self-determination in order to keep "these countries in their desperation and despair" from turning to the Soviet Union.[36] Cayton portrayed "a War of Words now going on for the minds of Black men," and warned that the East was "trying to identify the African's struggle for national autonomy with that of the Communist philosophy."[37] A front-page headline accompanying the opening article asked, "Will Reds Use African Troops to Conquer World?" A map of Africa bore the legend "Rumbling with unrest, majestic Africa is a mass of 'hot spots' as the entire continent from north to south is beset with riots and violent disturbances." Next to the map, a picture of a "typical Tuareg of Southern Libya" was captioned "Does Russia Plan to Use Men like These to Conquer World?"[38]

The Cold War vision of Africa permeated the press and other black institutions. At a speech at Lincoln University, Harlem minister James Robinson, who had earlier suffered Red-baiting for his alliances with the left in local civil rights politics, predicted "an Africa torn by revolt and Communist aggression." Although much of Asia was "already lost" to Communism, Africa, "need not be lost at all." For Robinson, treating racism as an aberration, it was urgent to show colonial peoples that the failures of democracy were not due to the political mechanism of democracy; rather, "trouble develops when a monkey wrench such as racial segregation is thrown in by those who want to wreck the machine itself."[39] In 1954 the *Defender* put in its "two cents worth on the problem of how to stop the Communists": we must tell the Asians "about our own revolution in 1776 and prove to them that they can get rid of their masters without embracing Godless Communism." Prescribing what the United States would in fact eventually do in Vietnam, the *Defender* argued that the United States should have given guns to "anti-communist native Indo-Chinese," not to the French. "Asians would prefer to be on our side but won't trust us if we give guns to their overlords."[40]

The most extreme portrayals of Africa as a Cold War battleground assumed that nationalist movements there were caused by Communism. The *Defender* reported that "part of the strategy of international Communism is a drive for Africa, the raw material base of Europe." Kent A. Hunter, a former newspaper reporter, had testified before the Internal Security Subcommittee of the Senate Judiciary Committee that Africa was in the "infiltration state" where Asia had been from 1920 to 1945 and "is to be steered to local nationalism and freedom and then incorporated in world Communism."[41]

Altered political and rhetorical strategies in the fight against discrimination during the Cold War era had far-reaching consequences for the definitions and meanings of racism. Some civil rights activists equated racism with Nazism in order to legitimize their struggle. Throughout World War II, black Americans had portrayed Nazism as one consequence of imperialism and one manifestation of racism, seeing antifascism as a critical component of democratic politics but not to the exclusion of anticolonialism. Now, Nazism became the standard of evil, and antiracist struggles appealed to similarities between racism and Nazism for their legitimacy. According to the new syllogism, Hitlerism was evil and un-American; Hitlerism equals racism; therefore racism is evil and un-American. The actions of Alabama police against black Americans were called "Gestapo tactics."[42] It was a powerful argument, but it took the case against racism out of its American context and out of the context of colonialism as well. And in positing Nazism and racism as unique, ahistorical evils, it took racism out of the context of history.

Along with the American South, South Africa was explained as the other site of this ahistorical evil. According to the *Defender,* "The Hitlerite, anti-Negro, anti-Jewish government of the Union of South Africa, under the leadership of the notorious racist, Dr. Daniel F. Malan, is apparently determined to create a Nazi state."[43] In the early Cold War the issue of South Africa was not eclipsed, as were many other international issues. Indeed, the election of Malan's government in 1948 and the beginning of apartheid brought renewed international censure to South Africa. Yet the collapse of a vibrant African American movement concerned with South Africa at the very inception of apartheid and the birth of the antiapartheid movement on a Cold War terrain had profound implications: South Africa was reframed as a paradigmatic liberal issue and became one of the most important sites of the rewriting of race. In lamenting the Malan victory, African American journalists and activists held up Nazism and Communism as the exemplars of racism and oppression; not the racial practices engendered by Dutch and British settlement and the development of the richest mining industry in the world.

New trends in journalism echoed and were perhaps influenced by Alan Paton's *Cry, the Beloved Country*.[44] As the critic Rob Nixon has argued, this 1948 novel played a singular role in shaping an international understanding of apartheid. Although it helped to bring international censure to South Africa for its racial injustices, Paton romanticized rural life and portrayed the city as corrupt, thus misrepresenting the many South Africans who viewed cities as a place of relative economic opportunity and cultural freedom. It also obscured the history of forced relocations and removals from the land and the grossly exploitive rural labor practices.[45] In a similar vein—and in sharp contrast to the sustained discussions by black American journalists in the 1940s of South African land, labor, and mining policies—Chatwood Hall, reporting for the *Afro-American* in 1950, also targeted restrictive racial policies in urban areas, going so far as to claim that the mining areas were free of exploitation. Hall quoted Charlotte Gilbert, a New Yorker who had visited South Africa: "In . . . the mining districts near Johannesburg and native settlements elsewhere, I found the natives to be fine and charming people. But when they come into Johannesburg, for example, they are treated like dogs."[46]

Moreover, Hall linked the argument against racism in South Africa with anti-Communism: it was "a glaring and nonsensical contradiction" that the South African government intended to fight Communism at the same time that it was bringing "more grist to the Communist mill" by "turning the racial oppression screw tighter on the native population."[47] Similarly, the *Defender* argued against a U.S. loan to South Africa because it "would play directly into the hands of Joe Stalin and his gangsters who are busy trying to discredit us in the eyes of the world."[48] In appealing to Cold War logic to argue for pressure against the South African government, activists and journalists conceded the high ground to anti-Communism: fighting racism was secondary to fighting Communism.

The same logic influenced African American views of the Defiance Campaign. In 1951 and 1952, when the ANC in South Africa organized nationwide passive resistance against the "unjust race laws" of Prime Minister Daniel F. Malan, acts of nonviolent civil disobedience such as the breaking of pass laws, residential restrictions, and curfews were widely reported in the African American press.[49] Yet just as political organization among African Americans with regard to South Africa was being disrupted by the marginalization of the CAA, the same fragmentation and disorganization pervaded popular discussion as liberal journalists and activists groped toward a new vocabulary to fit an anti-Communist terrain.[50] The African American press reported possible Communist involvement in the campaign and, in the years following, continued to worry that Malan's laws were opening the door to Communists.[51] Activists from the Congress of Racial Equality (CORE) and the American Committee on Africa (ACOA) explicitly—and misleadingly—insisted that the militant campaign in Port Elizabeth, where there was a strong trade union and Communist element, was "not in any way connected" with the broader passive resistance movement.[52]

The eclipse of a radical anticolonial politics should also be examined in the context of American intellectual life in the 1940s and 1950s and particularly, in light of the changes in historical analysis that accompanied the rise of Cold War liberalism. The marginalization of Du Bois and Robeson as critics of America's place in the postwar world must be set in the broadest possible context of the "end of ideology." The collapse of the politics of the African diaspora was accompanied by a powerful rewriting of "race" in popular African American discourse, evident in discussions of civil rights and domestic politics as well as international politics. The rewriting of race and racism involved a shift away from a sophisticated analysis rooted in history and toward psychological and social psychological research on race relations. The historian Walter A. Jackson has argued that this shift resulted from a variety of factors, including the influence of the economist Gunnar Myrdal, the priorities of funding agencies, and the national political climate.[53] In the social sciences these trends were in full swing during World War II. But despite the involvement of Ralph Bunche and other African Americans in the production of Myrdal's *American Dilemma* (1944), new liberal definitions of race had a negligible effect on African American discourse at that time. It was only with the ideological crisis engendered by the Cold War and the Truman Doctrine—which in effect created a political and ideological vacuum—that these vocabularies gained currency among African Americans.[54]

In the 1940s, racism had been widely portrayed not only by African American intellectuals but also in popular discourse as located in the history of slavery, colonialism, and imperialism. In the 1950s, the equation was reversed: rather than the result of slavery and colonialism, "race" and "color" were now offered as explanations for them. Marjorie McKenzie argued, for example, that "color" was the "sufficiently blinding" barrier that prevented the West from knowing what to do about colonialism.[55] In the retreat from explanations grounded in political economy, some of the dominant metaphors are easily identifiable. Racism was portrayed as a "disease," and as a psychological or spiritual problem, or as a characteristic of backward peoples which could be eradicated by "modernization" or, in more psychological language, "maturity."[56]

In the mainstream African American press discussions of racism were increasingly dominated by metaphors of disease. A 1949 *Defender* editorial headed "Curing the Disease" observed, tongue in cheek,

Students of race relations and social scientists often refer to racial prejudice as a disease of the mind. Whether racism is a disease or not, it has all the attributes of one. The children catch it from their parents and everyone who comes in contact with the virus becomes infected and suffers hallucinations of one sort or another. A great many of our Southern friends are obviously ill in the head, particularly those in Congress, and we would rejoice if some scientist could come up with a miracle drug to cure the brothers.[57]

Similarly, Albert Barnett wrote that efforts were being organized by "world leaders" to "fight the virus of prejudice," and a *Defender* editorial wondered where "race sickness" was leading the Western world.[58]

The *Defender* went so far as to make a psychologically grounded argument that racial discrimination caused nationalism, maintaining that the color bar "is the root cause of African inferiority, which in turn leads to resentment and revolt; it warps the minds of white and black man both." Nationalism and discrimination were linked, the *Defender* continued, "because it is the color bar more than anything else that makes Africans turn nationalist." Pursuing the psychological argument, it called Africa an "emotional volcano that may erupt at any time."[59]

Portraying racism as a primordial trait of "backward" peoples and countries, not a modern development located in specific social and economic practices, a *Courier* editorial on communal violence in India commented that prejudice "goes back to dim antiquity." Noting antagonisms among nationalities in Asia and the continuing role of anti-Semitism in Europe, the editorial argued: "By contrast the United States seems to be a model of tolerance and unity, and the prospect of eliminating prejudice seems very bright indeed. This is not to condone our vicious prejudices, but to remind our people that those changes take time, patience, and the general practice of tolerance."[60] In "Outmoded, So Outlawed," the *Courier* explained that "racial segregation in the nation's schools had become outmoded, and recognizing this fact, the Supreme Court outlawed it."[61] Like the functionalist modernization paradigm that emerged in the social sciences, the popular notion of racism as an outmoded, dysfunctional practice that would gradually disappear as nations progressed obscured human agency and responsibility in the creation and maintenance of political, economic and social institutions.[62]

African American journalists in the mid-1940s, demonstrating that racist practices led to enormous corporate profit, had implicated American and British imperial interests in the oppression of black South Africans. In the 1950s, liberal economists, historians, and journalists argued that racism was bad business, and bad business was bad for America. The *Defender* reported, for example, that South Africa's "rigid racial laws are creating a serious labor shortage which is beginning to affect the supply of uranium for the United States."[63] Horace Cayton saw the Malan government in South Africa, and Belgians in the Belgian Congo as "backward" and "out of step with the rest of the world"—in contrast to the American Metal Company Ltd. which, he said, acted as a progressive force in central and southern Africa.[64] In the 1940s, African Americans had debated the terms on which investment in Africa should take place, advocating a worldwide New Deal rather than the American Century. But in the 1950s, journalists tended not to be concerned with whether investment took place on democratic or exploitive terms; rather, they assumed that capitalism, and specifically American business, was a progressive force. In 1954 the *Courier,* evoking the spirit of Booker T. Washington, argued that even in South Africa progressive leadership was coming from industrialists who realized the need to tap "the vast reservoir of Negro energy, skill and talent." Moreover, "some of the big business firms that are sparking the drive for liberal racial policies are American controlled. This would seem to dispute the oft repeated assertion that it is the white Americans who spread racism around the world."[65]

The portrayal of racism as "prejudice," divorced from an analysis of institutions of domination, is strikingly illustrated in African American press coverage of the case of Seretse Khama. In 1950, after two years of silence in the black press on politics in various parts of Africa and the Caribbean, this case received consistent and even front-page coverage. Seretse Khama, chief designate of the 150,000 Bamangwatos in British Bechuanaland (Botswana), was exiled by the British from his homeland for marrying a white British woman.[66] In fact, there was more behind the exile than Seretse's marriage. Bechuanaland was said to contain some of the richest coal mines in the world and rich iron ore deposits. Seretse was a powerful leader who presented a challenge both to Britain and to the regional ambitions of the Union of South Africa. But the black press, for the most part, failed to address these issues, framing the case instead as a personal affront and a problem of "prejudice." [67]

Such an interpretation illustrates the rewriting of racism as an anachronistic prejudice and a personal and psychological problem, rather than as a systemic problem rooted in specific social practices and pervading relations of political economy and culture. From the early 1940s through 1946 the *Defender* had rarely published an issue without at least one editorial that addressed issues related to Africa and anticolonialism. In the first five months of 1950 there were only four editorials related to Africa, and two concerned Seretse's marriage, reducing the struggle for African and black American liberation to a fight against prejudice: "We are pleased to report that the African tribesmen are making their loyalty to Seretse Khama painfully evident to the uniformed thugs of Great Britain who are determined to punish the African prince for marrying a London typist . . . No nation that adopts an official anti-

Negro policy of government should be permitted to stand."[68] Likewise, as the *Afro-American* reported plans among Seretse's backers to stage a boycott against the British in protest, the *Courier* blasted the British charge that Seretse was a menace to his people, arguing that the real reason for the government's action "is the fact that the black ruler took unto himself a white wife."[69] The controversy continued until the end of March, when the British government, under mounting domestic and international pressure, allowed Seretse to return to Bechuanaland.[70]

The pervasive psychologizing of racism marginalized intellectuals, such as Du Bois and Hunton, who located racism in the history of slavery and colonialism. Moreover, the ascendancy of empiricism in the social sciences, encouraging narrower, "scientifically verifiable" objects of inquiry, went hand in hand with the eclipse of historical analysis, further marginalizing the work of scholars who inquired about something so broad as the place of the United States in the shifting global economy or the history of colonialism. These trends also had popular manifestations. In a triumph of empiricism, in 1953 the *Courier* began running a weekly column, "Facts about Africa," by Harold L. Keith. One such spot presented a list of 1952 crime statistics from South Africa; others offered short statements (often beginning and ending with ellipses, underscoring their lack of contextualization or development) such as "Ivory weapons were brought to Europe from Africa before 1600," and "In 668 A.D. Hadrian, an African, was named Archbishop of Canterbury but declined the honor because of his age."[71]

Likewise in the mid-1950s African American newspapers began adding foreign news sections, typically a quarter-page or half-page comprising short reports that were a far cry from the typical news stories of the mid-1940s.[72] Even their restriction to a small space—contrasted with earlier front-page coverage and extended analysis—indicates the reshaping of the relationship between domestic and international politics. Race, once seen as the product of global processes at the heart of the shaping of the modern world, had become domesticated in more ways than one. Contained, the concept no longer linked the struggles of black Americans and colonized peoples; tamed, its critical content was blunted.

New approaches also favored a vision of objectivity that made African Americans the least qualified persons to comment on racism in America. *Courier* columnist Marjorie McKenzie commented on the work of the Swedish social scientist Gunnar Myrdal and a *Collier's* article, "The Negro in America Today," by the white South African Alan Paton. According to McKenzie, the similarity between Paton and Myrdal lay in their objectivity: "Both are able to look at us with fresher eyes than we have for seeing ourselves."[73] A 1953 *Defender* editorial alerted the reader to "the first feature on Africa we have carried by a white writer. We make this point because practically all that we have published on Africa has been reports as seen through the eyes of Negroes who have more than a professional concern about what is happening in this land so vital to all the world at this time."[74]

Despite the claims of objectivity, and in keeping with the new emphasis on disembodied facts, the journalistic style of the feature article—highlighting "troubled spots"—came increasingly to replace coverage of politics and economics that analyzed the agency and accountability of individuals and organizations. In the early and middle 1940s, concrete reporting of strikes and political organizing told stories of specific agents who creatively interpreted and shaped the world they lived in. Thereafter news coverage of Africa and the Caribbean declined precipitously. Indeed, in 1947–48, it was almost as if the shift in discourse had become so awkward that reporting simply stopped for a time. The *Defender,* declaring itself "matured" in its 1947 New Year's editorial, abruptly discontinued its coverage of West African trade union and political organizing. Instead, Claude A. Barnett traveled to West Africa and reported in the *Defender* that "Sierra Leone might as well have stepped out of the pages of a story book. . . . Many of their bodies are beautiful as a sculptor's model and since both women and men carry bundles on baskets on their heads almost constantly, their posture is excellent."[75]

"EXOTIC" AFRICA: REINSCRIBING PRIMITIVISM

Barnett's powerful position as head of the Associated Negro Press, his new-found interest as a travelogue writer, and his capitulation to the demands of the Cold War go a long way toward explaining the abrupt drop in the coverage of African and Caribbean politics in black American newspapers. Another factor was the absence of George Padmore's work. As ANP correspondent for Africa in the 1940s, his writings had been accessible to a wide audience. When he was relieved of that post in 1947, his departure had a devastating impact on news coverage of Africa. The transformation of Barnett and the loss of Padmore were accompanied by far-reaching changes in editorial policy. In place of discussions of politics and the economy, ANP articles in the early 1950s reported such matters as the imprisonment of Nana Kobina, chief of the British Protectorate of Sekondi, Gold Coast, for "beating war drums and making a general nuisance of himself";[76] inflation in "bride prices in the eastern provinces" of Nigeria; and the meeting of South African explorers with "a rare tribe of Makwengi bushmen" in Southern Rhodesia. United Nations coverage included the complaint to the UN of an "ex-African chief" in the Belgian Congo who threatened to commit suicide unless his land was restored.[77]

In the 1950s journalists portrayed Africa as an undifferentiated monolith "of vital interest to Americans and free peoples everywhere" who were "concerned with the dangers of Communism." Writers depicted Africa contradictorily as a "troubled continent" in "ominous turmoil" and, at the same time, a place where nothing happened except the Cold War being fought by the United States and the Soviet Union.[78] Concrete discussions of the political economy of Uganda, Liberia or South Africa gave way to abstract renderings of "the great dark continent." At its worst, newspaper coverage exoticized and trivialized a now homogenized Africa. A former *Chicago Defender* reporter wrote from Addis Ababa in 1953 of the "strange though interesting" people of Ethiopia who "as a rule walk very gracefully—such as professional dancers do," and then of a police drive to "rid the streets of beggars, thieves and other undesirables due to an upcoming visit of Rita Hayworth and Aly Kahn who are on Safari and expected soon."[79]

The view of Africa as primitive and exotic was certainly not new in the United States, even among African Americans.[80] But representations of "the primitive" had been radically disrupted in the late 1930s and 1940s, dwarfed by the focus on political economy, by the pervasive argument that the struggles of African Americans were bound to those of Africans, and by the claims of political reciprocity between Africans and African Americans.[81] Moreover, the 1950s tendency to portray Africa as a place outside of history was an especially pernicious reinscription of ideas of the primitive. These ideas, though long served by science and disciplines such as anthropology, were now cloaked—and legitimized—by emerging modernization and development theory.[82] With discussions of history, political economy, and political dissent out of bounds in the Cold War, "Africa's problems" were explained as timeless, not something created by and potentially capable of eradication by the actions of human beings. William Townsend wrote in the *Defender* in 1948 that "the white man has not carried his burden well," since "the typical African peasant" was "still as hungry, diseased, unskilled, illiterate and enervated by a climate unsuitable for sustained work some 250 years after the coming of the white man as at the time of his coming." Even though Townsend was in no way endorsing colonialism, he attributed poverty in Africa to timeless natural and climatic factors, not to the policies of colonial governments and corporations.[83]

Employing metaphors from developmental psychology, many journalists interpreted political conflicts as normal growing pains. The goal of a free Africa, the *Courier* argued, "will not be reached smoothly. There will be controversy, cruelty and bloodshed sometimes, as there have been in the past and as there are today."[84] Thus, the notion of growing pains as inevitable in normal development replaced analyses that looked at change in terms of political conflict and global, regional, or class relations.

Journalists hailed cooperation and slow progress as the best route to change. A celebratory series in the *Defender* argued that the Belgian Congo was "progressing slowly without bias." This "huge overland frontier in the heart of restless Africa, rich with uranium and other raw materials vitally needed by the free world," had not been affected with the "native unrest, terrorism and anticolonialism" that had beset other parts of Africa and Asia.[85] According to the *Courier*, cooperation in the Belgian Congo between the Union Miniere (the controlling force behind the Katanga region's copper, cobalt, and uranium mining interests) and the colonial government was "increasing the purchasing power of the natives" each year, and "such people do not desire African nationalism, unrest, Communism, industrial disturbances or the organized crime seen elsewhere in Africa."[86] The Belgians, Allen R. Dodd Jr. argued in the *Defender*, could point with "justifiable pride to the work they are doing to raise the standards of a primitive people." Dodd quoted a Belgian official who explained, "You must understand that some of the people with whom we deal are primitive, very primitive." After relating "gruesome stories from the bush," the official argued that the British had made the mistake of sending Africans to European universities, thus imposing "advanced political ideas" on "very primitive emotions." Fully accepting the concept of modernization as the solution to "the problems raised by a primitive generation in the bush and a black generation in transition in the cities," Dodd compared the attraction of the Belgian Congo for Belgians "to that of the western frontier in America during the 1800s."[87]

With the political and ideological vacuum opened by the collapse of the left, but long before the visible shift to religious leadership in the civil rights movement marked by Martin Luther King Jr. and the 1956 Montgomery bus boycott, journalists turned to religious and moral discourse for an alternative vocabulary. Anti-communist religious movements in particular gained a new legitimacy. Moral Rearmament (MRA), a nondenominational Christian revivalist movement founded in the 1920s by Frank N. D. Buchman, had its greatest influence after World War II when it sent "task forces" throughout the "free world" to fight Communism and win converts. Buchman argued that the world could avoid war if individuals experienced a moral and spiritual awakening. Moral Rearmament was supported by President Truman, and a bipartisan committee of the House of Representatives attended the movement's 1949 world assembly. A 1949 Department of Justice memo described the MRA objective as "adequate ideological preparation of free nations for the ideological conflicts in which the world is now engaged" and called it "worthy and helpful in the strengthening of democratic forces throughout the world."[88]

Moral Rearmament launched campaigns in many parts of Africa, including South Africa, Northern Rhodesia, Kenya, and Nigeria.[89] African American papers reported that MRA assemblies "aimed at meeting the global Red threat, particularly in the dark continent."[90] John R. Barrow, the American consul in Nairobi, Kenya, described a camp where a Moral Rearmament-trained "Rehabilitation Officer" worked with the detainees, half Mau Mau "cooperators" and half "hard core resistors." The camp was administered on the premise that "economic and social" solutions to the "terrorist movement" were an "incomplete and inadequate answer to the whole psychological problem of Mau Mau. The basic problem in Mau Mau is ideological and can only be attacked through spiritual and ideological means."[91] According to Barrow, MRA representatives "stressed that MRA is the dynamic answer to Communism" and related stories of "changes of heart" that the movement had "caused among Communist-inclined leaders in Nigeria."[92]

The shift from a vocabulary of political economy to the language of moralism is illustrated further in the press treatment of Gandhi and India. Gandhi's militant stand against British imperialism and his sharp criticisms of the U.S. had been regularly covered in the African American press throughout World War II.[93] Yet by the time of his assassination in 1948, Gandhi had become, in the hands of the American press, a "moderate." The *Courier* announced that India had "lost its apostle of peace and her most powerful moderating influence." Noting his fight for India's independence, reporter Frank E. Bolden assured readers that "Gandhi was a social reformer but essentially a conservative."[94] Similarly, a *Courier* editorial, giving a sanitized version of "the winning of freedom from the British crown," argued that "Gandhi's greatest boon to mankind was the impress of love, brotherhood and peace." Portraying the Mahatma as more Christian than the Christians, the editorial noted, "It is difficult for Christians to appreciate the scope of Gandhi's contribution in this respect. Love and brotherhood are at the core of the concepts and teaching of Christianity. . . . But Gandhi was born into an environment where such concepts are largely alien."[95]

Gandhi was thus portrayed as a heroic individual who rose out of a barbaric Hindu civilization. The focus on his non-violence was understandable, given the wave of communal violence in India of which his death was in fact a part. Yet it also represents a shift from the wartime idea of solidarity between Indians and African Americans on the basis of their struggles to an identification with Gandhi because of his perceived similarities with Western civilization—a reinvention that does tremendous violence to his ideas and legacy. It is especially ironic, given one of Gandhi's more famous quips. When asked by a journalist what he thought of Western civilization, Gandhi is reported to have replied, "I think that would be an excellent idea."[96]

The abandonment of analyses of political economy was already apparent at the time of Gandhi's death; by the early 1950s he had been fully resurrected as a moderate. The *Chicago Defender* in 1954 could assure readers, in comparing him with Nkrumah, that "Gandhi did not believe in 'giving' his people anything 'too fast.'"[97]

By the early 1950s, African American critiques of the role of the American government and U.S. corporations in Haiti and Liberia had also disappeared. Along with exoticizing and trivializing of Africa and the Caribbean, the African American press was discovering "the new Haiti." Presumably referring to the declaration of Haitian independence in 1804 and rewriting history to suggest that the American refusal to recognize the black republic had instead been a Haitian rejection of North Americans, I. J. K. Wells reported for the *Courier:* "Contrary to the policy established nearly two hundred years ago, Haiti today is changing its attitude towards North Americans and welcoming them with open arms." Explaining the "drive to modernize Haiti," Wells predicted that "when Negro America discovers the new Haiti, thousands will flock there, not only as tourists but to build homes and to relax in both winter and summer. Haiti is really mellow."[98]

Stressing the achievements of the Haitian revolution rather than lassitude and leisure, Mary McLeod Bethune argued in the *Defender* that "Haiti has been, for generations, a symbol of attainable freedom for untold thousands." Yet forsaking the broad anticolonial coalitions she had helped to build, Bethune fell back on a gendered and sexualized language of empire. Haiti, she explained, is still "virgin territory, politically, economically, fraternally." The country's "marvelous possibilities . . . are still largely untapped. Her fertile soil is capable of making great contributions to the food needs of the world and to her own commercial development. She has impressive mineral resources. Her agriculture, her industry, her commerce lie fallow, ready for the plow of the pioneer."[99]

In the 1940s, journalists had critically documented the exploitation of Haiti's land, resources, and people by the American government and Wall Street. By 1950, journalists were suggesting that black Americans could share in the fruits of exploitation. Featuring "the paradise of the greater Antilles," where "happy vacationers" can "live like . . . millionaire[s]," the *Defender*'s magazine section reported that "Negroes who have long held regal dreams of living like a native prince can have these dreams come true in Port-au-Prince, Haiti."[100] Claude A. Barnett, in his new-found role as travel writer, previewed Haiti for a *Defender* popularity contest in which the three winners would "have an opportunity to view the tropical beauty of Haiti and the 1950 Bi-Centennial Haitian exposition." Describing the waterfront fair site, formerly "a slum district and an eyesore . . . transformed as if by magic wand into a place of charm and beauty," Barnett praised the "progressive steps" of President Dumarsais Estimé who realized that "for Haiti to really swing into the orbit of world affairs and progress more people had to become acquainted with her resources and possibilities."[101]

Barnett's adoption of the vocabulary of modernization, with no critique of power relations, stands in sharp contrast to previous journalistic analyses of Haitian debt. Barnett explained that Estimé's plans to "attract industry [and] secure outside capital" would result in "the eventual launching of enterprises large and small." Reviewing hotels, beaches, and food, Barnett reported that Estimé "was especially anxious to have American Negro business people come to Haiti to establish business."[102] Also exemplifying the depoliticized modernization paradigm, Roy Garvin described Haiti in the *Afro-American* as a poor country, something "to be expected" given its "primarily agricultural" economy. Yet with its "very large untilled acreage," its "wealth of cheap labor," and an American loan, Garvin argued, Haiti could have "unlimited opportunity for increasing its gross national income."[103] The ousting of Estimé by Paul E. Magloire in a military coup later in 1950 had little impact on these perceptions.[104] In what began to sound like a broken record, Magloire, like Estimé, was hailed for bringing in new stability and development.

In the 1940s journalists had analyzed the history of U.S. military invasions of Haiti and the role of the American government in propping up an antidemocratic but pro-American political and financial elite. In 1953 the *Defender*, in an egregious distortion of history, saw Haiti's instability as a product of independence and American ties as the best cure: "In her brief history Haiti has seldom known peace long enough to accomplish anything. Starting with the destruction of the French civilization in the revolution of 1804, periodic revolt and invasion have been constant threats." The *Defender* portrayed American money as the source of hope for future stability and the U.S. military as having brought stability in the past: "The nation felt no security until it was occupied by the United States Marines in 1915. The occupation was a bitter thing for Haitians, but it provided them with stability until 1934, when the Marines withdrew." Under Marine occupation, the country had "made the beginnings of a new economy with agricultural, social and political reform."[105]

Journalists' continued celebration of the "stability" to be found in Haiti's close relationship with the United States and their promotion of tourism as a favored means of economic "development" left no basis for grasping the upheaval of 1956–57, with its succession of five provisional governments within six months.[106] When Magloire was forced to resign in 1956, Haiti became the "troubled island." The *Courier* found his departure "saddening" but offered as causes only "bad advice from his henchmen and adverse economic circumstances."[107] In 1957, in "Haiti, Lovely Land of Woe," the *Courier* reported that with the election of the new provisional president, Frank Sylvain,

"Haiti is happy again." The article mentioned a general strike but offered no explanation except that "rival political leaders scrambling for power" had instigated a strike that "tied the normal life of the country into knots" until "stable elements" pieced together a provisional government.[108] When the dizzying rotation finally ended in the dictatorship of François Duvalier ("Papa Doc"), journalists lacked even a vocabulary with which to analyze the implications.

Liberia, like Haiti, had been the subject of penetrating and pervasive criticism by African American journalists who in the 1940s analyzed American corporate and government interference in the country's economic and political life. The contrast between that criticism and the celebratory reporting of the 1950s is starkly illustrated in the coverage of the 1952 inauguration of President V. S. Tubman for his second term. Claude Barnett, writing in the *New York Amsterdam News,* lauded "international harmony between Liberia and other nations of the world" and Liberia's "march of progress." He described "pageantry symbolizing its progress during its 104 years as an independent nation" and emphasized "the spiritual side of Life," business achievement, and progress in education.[109] Likewise, with progress the watchword of the day, the *Defender* reported that the inauguration would "climax the progress of an African nation illustrating Africa's ability to run a democracy with peaceful elections."[110]

Mary McLeod Bethune attended the inauguration and declared that Liberia had "walked hand in hand with the best of American foreign policy and the best of world policy." She had come, she explained, "to get the feel of the great continent from whence my forefathers were drafted to help build the economic and cultural structure of the New World"—thus depicting slavery as part of the march of Western progress and celebrating the role of Africans and African Americans in that march. According to Bethune, "Economic opportunities in Liberia are plentiful and American businessmen are rapidly discovering that profitable and mutually beneficial enterprises of all kinds can be carried on there without resort to exploitative methods or attitudes objectionable to the native population."[111] As a young person, Bethune had dreamed of going to Africa as a missionary. As president of the National Council of Negro Women and a member of the Council on African Affairs, she had been an important anticolonial activist. As an elderly person in 1952, she fulfilled her dream of visiting Africa, but with the collapse of the broad movement for political, economic, and social rights for black Americans and Africans that she had done so much to promote, Africa had become something not to analyze or understand in terms of global power relations but to "feel": President Tubman had fallen on his knees "in the midst of thousands, petitioning God for wisdom and guidance. It was profoundly moving. 'This,' I thought, 'is Africa.'"[112]

Coverage of the Kenyan Land and Freedom (Mau Mau) Movement stands out during these Cold War years for the sustained attention it received in the black press. To be sure attention to Kenya was an example of extreme exoticization; like other American and European portrayals, African American coverage adopted a voyeuristic stance.[113] The Mau Mau "cult" engaged in "waves of terror," and "Mau Mau depredations continued to rock this blood-drenched and terrified colony."[114] There was speculation that "membership in secret societies" was a consequence of the denial of "certain sexual outlets," along with suggestions that Mau Mau was a religious problem.[115] At the same time, however, there was considerable discussion of land policy and the political and economic background of the Land and Freedom Movement.

Two reasons stand out for this exception to the era's journalistic norm. First, the war in Kenya was associated with British, not American, policy. The British were seen as responsible for the conflict because of their ruthless and exploitive expropriation of Kenyan land and their brutal treatment of Kenyans. Combining sensationalism with an analysis of the causes of conflict, Horace Cayton described the "secret Mau Mau society" as "ruthless, desperate and frantic"—but, he continued, "there is no attempt on the part of the British to get to the root of the trouble. It has not occurred to them to examine their economic system."[116] The *Defender* reported that since the turn of the century the best agricultural land in Kenya had been taken by Europeans, while Africans were "segregated into grossly overcrowded areas called native reserves."[117] In 1954 the *Defender* reported "little doubt" that "the whole rebellion started over the land question."[118]

Second, although the American government prosecuted the CAA for ties to Kenyans whom U.S. officials believed to be sympathetic to Communists, the United States was also overtly and covertly aiding anti-British, pro-U.S. Kenyans such as Tom Mboya. Mboya and the Kenya Federation of Labor were affiliated with the Western-oriented International Confederation of Free Trade Unions.[119] Thus, neither sympathy toward freedom fighters nor criticism of the systems of domination in Kenya involved criticizing the United States, as would have been the case for Liberia, Haiti, or South Africa.

A final factor explaining the discussion of political economy in Kenya is that by 1953 and 1954 the most constricting effects of the Cold War had begun to loosen. New challenges and alternatives to Cold War paradigms were emerging—though in a drastically different context from that in which the politics of the African diaspora had thrived. The contours of the new international politics had further implications for the demise of the politics of the African diaspora.

CHAPTER EIGHT

NO EXIT:

FROM BANDUNG TO GHANA

I remember . . . the invasion of Ethiopia and Haile Selassie's vain appeal to the League of Nations, but they remember the Bandung conference and the establishment of the Republic of Ghana.

—James Baldwin, *The Price of the Ticket*

AFTER THE MOST REPRESSIVE YEARS of the Cold War, discussions of international politics began to open up, but on radically different terms from those of the 1940s. International gatherings such as the 1955 Asian-African Conference in Bandung, Indonesia, and the 1956 Congress of Colored Writers and Artists in Paris were surrounded by controversy. Who could travel, and who could not? Who could speak for America and its foreign policy? In Robeson's passport case the latter question was made explicit and by the mid-1950s continued to receive direct if unexpected answers. With Du Bois and Robeson barred from international travel, the State Department sought to enlist its own black American representatives, not only in its hiring practices but by sponsoring the Goodwill Ambassador tours of jazz artists such as Louis Armstrong and Dizzy Gillespie and sports heroes such as the high-jump world record holder Gil Cruter and the Harlem Globetrotters. But if internationalism had come to stay, the terms remained contested, and the new terrain was defined by a wide array of actors, from the State Department and Vice-President Richard Nixon to Congressman Adam Clayton Powell Jr., the rapidly growing Nation of Islam, and Kwame Nkrumah, the first president of Ghana.

African American participation in the Bandung and Paris conferences revealed both the extent to which African American intellectuals, journalists, and politicians accepted the new American position in the world as legitimate and the tensions in this legitimation. New State Department programs such as the Armstrong and Gillespie tours continued to underscore the critical role of race in the forging of U.S. political and cultural hegemony. At the same time, the programs exposed the limits of recasting the meanings and perceptions of race in America as long as the federal government refused to protect the rights of American citizens. Finally, although the new nation of Ghana stood as a beacon to a new generation of African Americans who defined and shaped new diaspora identities, their perspectives on the independence of Ghana in 1957 remained deeply shaped by the Cold War and the absence of an internationalist perspective.

NONALIGNMENT: THE BANDUNG CONFERENCE

The 1955 Asian-African Conference at Bandung helped to widen the terms of debate about international politics after the most constricted years of the Cold War. In the early 1950s, nations around the globe announced with growing frequency that they would not be subjugated by either the West or the East and declared their intentions to be neutral, "nonaligned" states, forming their own "Third World." For example, in 1954 when the United States, in order to combat Communism, established the Southeast Asian Treaty Organization (SEATO) and wanted to include all the states in that region, India, Burma, Ceylon, and Indonesia resisted pressure to join and asserted their resolve to remain "neutral" in the Cold War.[1] The Asian-African Conference was the most important and influential of several attempts to gain and then maintain independence from Cold War politics.[2] The conference was called for April 18–25, 1955, by five sponsoring nations: India, Pakistan, Ceylon (later Sri Lanka), Burma (later Myanmar), and Indonesia. Neither the United States nor the Soviet Union was invited. According to Prime Minister Nehru of India, the purpose was to "remove tensions and help Asian nations to develop."[3] Premier John Kotelawala of Ceylon explained that "Moscow and Washington must realize that there are others, too, in the world and that the main concern of these others is peace."[4]

Among black Americans, broad support for the position of nonalignment and the tremendous prestige of the conference represented a challenge to the acceptance of the United States as the legitimate leader of the free world, which had come to frame dominant African American political and rhetorical strategies. The existence of a powerful alternative vision of global politics as presented by Nehru and President Sukarno of Indonesia had the effect of opening up political discussion. The African American press widely hailed the conference as "a turning point in world history" and potentially the most important event of the twentieth century.[5] Noting the "clear challenge to white supremacy that this gathering of the world's yellow, brown, and black races represents," the *Afro-American* saw in it an "undisguised implication" that "the majority of the world's people think there is an alternative to following blindly the lead of either Russia or the United States."[6] Western nations, it argued, must accept "the new found solidarity of the colored peoples of the world" and independence for Asian and African nations, or "lasting peace in the world will never be possible."[7] For the *Courier,* the conference call issued in January 1955 bridged conflicting ideologies and politics and was based upon "a common interest of all the participating powers in the elimination of colonialism and the 'color line.'" Noting that African and Asian nations, "representing more than two-thirds of the earth's human beings" were to "meet in a 'peace parley' in April, thus demonstrating the growing importance of black, brown and yellow peoples in the world," it described the conference as "a slap in the face to both the West and Russia."[8] Similarly, the *Defender* predicted that the Asian-African Conference would "undoubtedly pose a problem for the United States, Great Britain, and anti-capitalist Russia": would the colored peoples of the world "who are now considered 'outsiders' enter the closed fraternal circle of modern mankind by the front door, if opened, or the back door, if need be?"[9]

Richard Wright observed in *The Color Curtain* that "Bandung was no simple exercise in Left and Right politics; it was no minor episode in the Cold War; it was no Communist Front meeting."[10] Despite Wright's own deep cynicism about Communism, he was impressed by Chou En-lai's "refusal to let himself be baited" into answering charges against Communism. Chou En-Lai, he said, "surrendered his opportunity to use the conference as a forum for the ideas and policies of Red China" in the interest of unity and thus gained the moral high ground over pro-West delegates such as those from Iraq, who were constantly attempting to inject Cold War issues into the agenda.[11]

But if Wright realized that the significance of the conference lay in its refusal to be defined by terms dictated by the United States or the Soviet Union, the participation of Chou En-lai from the People's Republic of China, along with SEATO bloc nations such as the Philippines, represented by President Carlos Romulo, immediately raised speculation about Communist–anti-Communist tensions. Despite the challenge nonalignment posed to Cold War ideologies, in the United States discussions of the Bandung meeting and perceptions of nonalignment remained framed by Cold War concerns. Ethel L. Payne's assignment to cover the conference for the *Defender* was part of a five-week tour of Asia and Europe "to report on the attempts of world communism to win the darker peoples away from the West, and what Europe is doing to meet this challenge."[12] From Bandung, Payne reported that "one of the questions uppermost in the minds of the Western Powers is will Red China and its compatriots like the communist Viet Minh faction seize the initiative and turn it into a Communist show?" Payne thought this unlikely because of the pro-West sentiments of delegates from the Philippines, Pakistan, Turkey, and Iraq.[13]

The West, as Paul Gordon Lauren has observed, "reacted to the Bandung Conference with silence, vacillation, or opposition. Secretary of State John Foster Dulles, in fact, even went so far as to condemn Third World neutrality as 'an obsolete . . . immoral and shortsighted conception.'"[14] In a March 1955 radio and television address from Washington, Dulles made his contempt clear, noting that America's Asian allies were meeting with "other Asian countries at a *so-called* Afro-Asian conference."[15] But Dulles and the State Department, especially personnel in the Gold Coast who monitored relations with India, were not unconcerned with the meeting's ramifications in Africa and Asia.[16]

New York Congressman Adam Clayton Powell Jr. had been one of the most prominent participants in the liberal and left coalitions of the 1940s that had become impossible during the Cold War. A former member of the CAA, he had worked closely with both the CAA and NAACP on international issues. After the Truman Doctrine, however, he became a staunch advocate of American foreign policy and left the CAA when Yergan departed in 1948. Powell wanted the United States to send a team of observers to Bandung, but as part of their strategy of playing down the significance of the meeting, the State Department refused the request and actively discouraged him from attending.[17] Powell insisted that the United States needed a "person of goodwill" at the conference and blasted the State Department for not recognizing the importance of representation at a gathering where Communism *would* have representatives. He defiantly declared, "I am going to go to this conference with or without the approval of the State Department unless they refuse me a passport and that will be quite a thing to do to a Congressman."[18] Resisting vigorous efforts by the State Department to stop the trip—including an invitation to tour Africa and Asia *after* the conference—a recalcitrant Powell left for Indonesia.[19]

In Bandung, despite attacking the Eisenhower administration for declining to send a message to the conference and for its blindness in failing to recognize the significance of the meeting, Powell opportunistically stepped in as an unabashed defender of the West. No sooner had he arrived at Bandung than he began to attack Chou En-Lai, calling him a "liar" for suggesting that "the U.S. and the western powers are trying to sabotage the conference."[20] Powell also went out of his way to rebuke Robeson and staunchly defended America, though invoking the dominant Cold War pro–civil rights argument that "America must 'clean up' her own race problem as swiftly as possible in order to reassure the people of Asia."[21] Ensuring that his efforts would not go unappreciated, Powell told the press that if he had not been at Bandung, the Communists would have "exploded the color question," but he had "stopped all that with a press conference that I held."[22]

Back in the United States, Powell's actions won him praise from Republicans and Democrats alike, as well as from the elite press.[23] In the African American press, however, his performance received mixed reviews. The *Defender* contrasted him with the "ill-advised Paul Robeson" and praised Powell for "upset[ting] the Communist strategy with a brilliant exhibition of loyalty to and love for his country and a realistic attitude toward his country's failures. At Bandung, when Communists were preparing to make capital use of the race issues to further their insidious aims, Adam Clayton Powell stoutly defended the progress made in America toward better race relations and more perfect social justice."[24] The *Afro-American* concurred that Powell had quickly dispelled any State Department reservations about his trip: the "glib New Yorker painted such a glowing picture of the racial situation in the United States, those officials who opposed Mr. Powell's going must now be overcome with mortification."[25] Yet the *Courier,* though "glad to see this new Congressman Powell in the role of defender of God's country," wondered about the "complete somersault" of the "fire-eater of the extreme left of the Democratic party who could find little to praise in America."[26]

Some responses exemplified the contradictions in the Cold War strategies of many journalists and civil rights leaders. A skeptical P. L. Prattis pleaded that he was too "dumb" to get the point of Powell's statement that it was "a distinction to be a Negro in the United States" and reminded the congressman that "while the white press has been publishing 'raves' about you, the writers in the Negro papers have been somewhat non-committal, or downright critical."[27] Even more strongly, James L. Hicks thought that "Mr. Powell sold colored people down the river at a time when they had nothing up for sale."[28] For these journalists, Powell's celebration of American institutions rang hollow, undermining his attempt to curb censure of American foreign policy.

Notwithstanding Powell's claims to have rescued the image of the United States at Bandung, for many in the Third World the absence of Du Bois and Robeson, both still banned from traveling, was as conspicuous as Powell's presence. The *Afro-American* carried texts of the messages from Robeson and Du Bois that were read at the conference. Du Bois declared that "because of my 50 years of service in the cause of 25 million colored peoples of America I venture of my own initiative to address you in their name, since the United States will not allow me to attend this meeting."[29] Robeson's statement that "the time has come when the colored peoples of the world will no longer be exploited and expropriated by the Western world" was cited by the Justice Department in an August 1955 hearing as evidence against Robeson in his continuing passport case.[30]

Although crippled by government accusations and charges, the Council on African Affairs persevered in its coverage of African events through its newsletter, renamed *Spotlight on Africa* in 1952.[31] The CAA during its last months focused on the Bandung conference and embraced the position of nonalignment. Writing against the grain of the 1950s, when "race" had been abstracted from its historical and material origins, Du Bois elaborated on the history that bound the participants of Bandung together: "Before the Renaissance such a meeting would have had no meaning," but since the Renaissance "skin color has been made a reason for oppression, discrimination and war, and therefore it is of great significance that the peoples of Asia and Africa have recently arranged to have a joint meeting in Indonesia to discuss their common problems."[32]

Most important for CAA leaders facing the destruction of their organization, Bandung vindicated their support of the struggles of colonized peoples over bipolar Cold War politics. The CAA applauded Sukarno's argument that conference participants were "united by a common detestation of colonialism in whatever form it appears, by a common detestation of racialism and a common determination to preserve and stabilize peace in the world."[33] To Alphaeus Hunton, the "signal contribution of the Asian and African conference to the Cold-War weary world" was its demonstration that "it is possible and practicable for Communists, non-Communists and anti-Communists to live together, meet together, speak together, and contribute toward the common good of all mankind."[34]

At the same time, CAA leaders criticized the Bandung gathering for its relatively meager African attendance. Of the twenty-nine nations represented, only six were from Africa: Egypt, Ethiopia, Liberia, Libya, the Gold Coast, and the Anglo-Egyptian Sudan. The CAA did applaud the participation of Moses Kotane of the African National Congress and the South African Communist Party, and Maulvi Cachalia of the South African Indian Congress, as well as the attention given to South Africa. But Nigeria, which like the Gold Coast was in transition to self-government, had not been invited; the CAA hoped "that this would not be the case in future meetings" and also argued that the "grave situation" in Kenya merited attention that it did not receive.[35]

Max Yergan surfaced at the conference as a reporter for the *Courier*. Following his departure from the CAA in 1948, he had reemerged in the early 1950s as an "expert" on Africa. His trips as a State Department representative included stops in South Africa, Nigeria, Liberia, and Senegal.[36] His 1953 *U.S. News and World Report* article, "Africa: Next Goal of Communists," argued that a "sympathetic and constructive" attitude must be cultivated toward the white South African government.[37] His presence in South Africa during the Defiance Campaign infuriated his former allies. A second visit, in 1957, caused a mild flurry in the South African government circles, since his so-called expertise had not been enough to alert him that bringing with him his new wife, who was white, would pose a problem. The government quietly arranged to have Mrs. Yergan spend some time in Uganda while her husband visited South Africa.[38]

Yergan echoed State Department policy by downplaying the significance of the Bandung conference and by stressing East-West ideological differences rather than unity of purpose. From the beginning he predicted that "sharp divisions of interests between Communists and anti-communists" and attempts to "develop overwhelming anti-West sentiment" would overshadow the intended "demonstration against white imperialism and colonialism."[39] He overtly disagreed with Powell's contention that the meeting "put the U.S. on the spot" by challenging it to clean up its own racial policies; Yergan asserted that the United States was not on the defensive but had "gained as a result of the conference," while "Nehru lost influence" and "Chou En-Lai was exposed."[40] Dismissing as "sentimental" the argument that conference participants had suffered racial discrimination and colonial and imperialist oppression, he argued that color occupied a secondary place in basic world affairs. The conference, Yergan concluded, "was not world shaking," because the nations who met at Bandung were economically dependent on the West, and "cold war ideologies are a most important factor in national self-interest."[41]

Despite Yergan's hopes for its irrelevance, the conference not only had worldwide ramifications but was tremendously important in opening up African American discourse after the most repressive years of the Cold War. Bandung and nonalignment created an alternative to viewing global politics through the prism of the Cold War and helped to create a new vocabulary for critiquing American policies. The salience of Bandung was reflected in discussions of the United Nations. In October, James L. Hicks reported that the General Assembly had voted (twenty-eight to twenty-seven) to include the question of the freedom of Algeria on the agenda: "The darker races" had "turned the United States and the colonial powers around in the first major test of strength in the UN since the dark races held their own conference at Bandung."[42] "The white people of the Western world," he said, "laughed last spring when the dark nations sat down together for a conference at Bandung, but the darker nations . . . are now having the last laugh."[43]

THE NATION OF ISLAM

The Nation of Islam provided another alternative space in the 1950s for an expression of diaspora sensibilities amid dominant bipolar and pro-American perspectives on international politics. The work of Ferruccio Gambino has located the sources of Malcolm X's internationalism and his conversion to the Nation of Islam in his experiences in prison and as a worker. From that base, Gambino argues, he attempted "in the wilderness of America" (an expression often repeated by Malcolm in these years) to build a bridge to the rising "darker races."[44] In the late 1940s and early 1950s Malcolm X was one of a group of prisoners, who, influenced by the Nation of Islam, were debating the Cold War and taking very antiimperialist positions. For Malcolm and other black nationalists, the United States was on the wrong side. Out of prison, between November 1953 and May 1954, for example, he talked about the Viet Minh siege of Dien Bien Phu and the Mau Mau in Kenya.[45]

Black nationalists such as Malcolm X were attracted to the Nation of Islam not because of a consciousness of Africa per se but because the Nation, arguing that one cannot serve two masters, disavowed allegiance to the United States.[46] Thus, following the collapse of a broader and more mainstream critique of U.S. foreign policy, the Nation of Islam permitted a space—for the most part unthinkable in the Cold War era—for an anti-American critique of the Cold War. In the 1950s nationalists such as Malcolm X had to juggle beliefs in anticolonialism and the rising "darker races" with Elijah Muhammad's apocalyptic religious prophecies. Tensions between Malcolm's growing demands for political justice in the courts and Elijah Muhammad's apolitical teachings would shape their relationship and eventually led to a break. But these tensions between an internationalist politics and the religious teaching of Elijah Muhammad, were not unique to Malcolm X and would continue to characterize the Nation of Islam. The weekly newspaper *Muhammad Speaks*, launched in 1960 and edited by Richard Durham, a non-Muslim leftist, became in the 1960s and 1970s one of the most sophisticated sources of information on Africa available to Americans.[47]

TOWARD A NEW SCHOLARSHIP

Even though Bandung offered an alternative to the Cold War and a new language for grappling with global politics and American policy, and the Nation of Islam offered yet a different alternative, the middle to late 1950s remained very much dominated by the Cold War. This was illustrated at another and very different conference, the first international Congress of Colored Writers and Artists, held in Paris in 1956. American participation (though as at Bandung there were conspicuous African American absences) dramatized the political and intellectual dimensions of the narrowing of black American anticolonialist discourse and the silencing of leading critics of the United States in the postwar world.

The meeting was attended by about sixty delegates from twenty-four countries. The American delegation included John A. Davis, professor of political science at the City College of New York; Horace Mann Bond, president of Lincoln University; and James Ivy, editor of the *Crisis*. Their trip was sponsored by the American Information Committee on Race and Caste.[48] Du Bois did not attend because the State Department still refused him a passport, and according to Ollie Stewart in the *Afro-American,* when a letter from him explaining his absence was read to the assembly, it "did not go over big with the American delegation."[49]

The most prominent Americans in attendance were James Baldwin, Richard Wright, and Chester Himes. Baldwin's consideration of what he termed "our relationship to the mysterious continent of Africa" in many ways echoed the exoticization of Africa seen in the mainstream black press in the early 1950s.[50] To Baldwin, the most disturbing event of the conference was the reading of Du Bois's message: "I am not present at your meeting because the U.S. government will not give me a passport." For him, Du Bois's "ill-considered communication . . . made the more seductive his closing argument" that Africa should not be "betrayed backward by the U.S. into colonialism." Du Bois, Baldwin insisted, obscured what

> at bottom, distinguished the Americans from the Negroes who surrounded us, . . . the banal and abruptly quite overwhelming fact that we have been born in a society, which in a way quite inconceivable for Africans, and no longer real for Europeans, was open, and in a sense which has nothing to do with injustice or justice, was free. . . . This results in a psychology very different—at its best and at its worst—from the psychology which is produced by a sense of having been invaded and overrun, the sense of having no recourse whatever against oppression other than overthrowing the machinery of oppression.[51]

Where Du Bois and Robeson had concretely examined the increasing similarities in the plight of Africans and of black Americans and had located the parallels in the internationalization of capital, Baldwin emphasized distinctions in political systems. That one of the most searching critics of America in the twentieth century could in this context defend the United States as a society that was "open" and "free," somehow beyond "justice or injustice," profoundly underscores the hegemony of this particular framing of Cold War anticolonialism.[52]

The American representation at the Paris meeting symbolized the rise of a new generation of African American scholars. The American Society of African Culture (AMSAC), formed following the conference, was a group of "scholars, writers, and activists" whose purpose was "to examine, record and cultivate the culture of the emerging African continent" and to study the contributions of African culture to American life.[53] Like the Congress for Cultural Freedom, founded in Berlin in 1950 as an attempt to mobilize a response to left-wing intellectuals, AMSAC was explicitly anti-Communist, albeit avowedly apolitical. It defined its goal as defending "the great cultural contributions of man against the perversions of political, economic and national movements." In fact, AMSAC received clandestine funding from the CIA.[54]

But the society's most important legacy lay in the area of scholarship. Its collection *Africa Seen by American Negro Scholars* was published as a special edition of *Présence Africaine* in 1958 and republished in the United States in 1963.[55] Although the volume offered some overlap with work done in the 1940s, it represented a new scholarship framed by the Cold War. St. Clair Drake, Martin L. Kilson, and Horace Mann Bond, all contributors, were among the most important scholars shaping the new academic study of relations between black Americans and Africans. St. Clair Drake in particular was deeply influential in framing a typology for the study of the African diaspora.[56]

These scholars were not Cold Warriors, but the questions they asked, and the histories they constructed were very much structured by the Cold War—as were the questions they did not ask.[57] The sources of the lacunae were evident in Drake's 1951 article "The International Implications of Race and Race Relations" in the *Journal of Negro Education*.[58] Drake accepted that the United States was "impelled, whether it desired the role or not, to assume leadership in international affairs." In part, this meant responding to Communism, which "not only attempts to manipulate racial sentiments" but also "exposes, attacks, and ridicules any evidences of racism among the free nations."[59] The article's short section "Pan-Movements and Contemporary Race Relations" noted that "significant interaction between Africans, West Indians, and American Negroes seems to have increased since the Second World War," but the examples conspicuously omitted any mention of political interaction or support.[60] And just five years after many African American organizations had viewed the United Nations as a forum in which to fight discrimination in the United States and to challenge American support of South Africa and the policies of the South African government, Drake predicted that the most important influences of the United Nations on race relations would be "indirect and informal," as "non-white participants in the United Nations are success symbols."[61]

Over the next three decades Drake developed sophisticated and synthetic work on the African diaspora, but the silences remained. Despite his acknowledgment of political Pan-Africanism—which he saw as less influential than "small p" or cultural pan-Africanism—and his argument that political Pan-Africanism was organically related to but not subsumed by movements of oppressed working people, his otherwise very comprehensive view of black Americans and the diaspora overlooked black American anticolonialism in the 1940s. The work of Paul Robeson, Alphaeus Hunton, and the CAA was invisible. Padmore's *Pan-Africanism or Communism* and Nkrumah's politics were discussed with scant mention of their roots in the left and without reference to their early alliances with African Americans or the repercussions of the Cold War for that generation of anticolonial activists.[62]

In addition to attempts to shape the terms of solidarity among African Americans and Africans through anti-Communist organizations and scholarship, the American government also ventured into the area of popular culture. Beginning in the early 1950s the State Department sponsored tours by African American athletes. Gilbert Cruter, who once held the world high-jump record, toured West Africa to help train athletes for regional Olympic trials.[63] Between 1951 and 1955 the Harlem Globetrotters made appearances in Berlin ("to combat the popular East German youth rallies being staged by the Communists"), and Indonesia, Burma, and Italy.[64] The South African *Bantu World* reported that the Globetrotters "blended basketball and buffoonery with their own special brand of diplomacy to become one of the United States' most effective weapons in the Cold War against communism." Owner-coach Abe Saperstein explained that by appearing "at the request of the U.S. Department of State in areas where communism is a threat," they played an "unusual role in helping combat the spread of communism."[65]

Goodwill Ambassador tours by African American jazz musicians were among the State Department's most highly publicized cultural efforts. One does not have to see the "jambassadors" as endorsing American policy—and for the most part they did not—to see the marked change in the representation of relations between African Americans and Africans that these tours represented. Initially proposed by Congressman Adam Clayton Powell, the jazz tours were part of a State Department strategy of not denying that discrimination existed in the United States but showing "progress" and emphasizing what a talented and motivated individual could achieve.[66] Widely celebrated in the African American press, the Goodwill Ambassadors symbolized the legitimacy of U.S. claims as leader of the "free world." "American jazz—hot, blues, Dixieland, bebop or rock 'n' roll—has at last been publicly acknowledged as the principal asset of American foreign policy," declared the *Afro-American*. "State Department squares at first scoffed" at Powell's idea, but when "they finally gave up out of sheer exhaustion and shipped the number one be-bopster," Dizzy Gillespie, to the Near East and Europe, "the result was electric" and the "only problem was finding auditoriums large enough to house the new converts to the American viewpoint attracted by Dizzy's bent trumpet, rhythmic beat, and unorthodox style."[67]

Gillespie's United States Information Service tour in 1956 included Abadan, Iran; Dacca and Karachi, Pakistan; Beirut, Lebanon; Damascus and Aleppo, Syria; and Ankara and Istanbul, Turkey. The *Courier* celebrated an editorial in a Pakistani newspaper proclaiming that "the language of diplomacy ought to be translated into the score for a bop trumpet," and reported a "miracle" in

Abadan, where Arabs who were "completely ignorant of what jazz was" eventually "started to catch the beat" and made the theater "as hot as any American jazz spot where Diz performed for long-standing fans."[68] Following that tour, Gillespie went to South America for three weeks, sponsored by the State Department and ANTA (American National Theatre and Academy).[69] Defending the tours against critics such as Louisiana's segregationist Senator Allen Ellender, Gillespie telegraphed to Eisenhower, "Our trip through the Middle-East proved conclusively that our interracial group was powerfully effective against Red propaganda. Jazz is our own American folk music that communicates with all peoples regardless of language or social barriers."[70]

Ironies abound in the choice of Gillespie as an ambassador. An unlikely ambassador as a former draft dodger, Gillespie had once been a card-carrying member of the Communist Party because it enabled him to get gigs in CP-run halls. Likewise, for him the tours meant a chance to work. "I sort've liked the idea of representing America," he said, "but I wasn't going to apologize for the racist policies of America." He managed to avoid his official State Department briefing, remarking, "I've got three hundred years of briefing. I know what they've done to us and I'm not going to make any excuses."[71] Though deeply aware of the politics involved, Gillespie didn't hesitate to defy State Department and local convention on the tours or to promote his version of America, which was considerably more egalitarian than the State Department's. He later recalled that the tour skipped India because it was nonaligned; his band played instead in Karachi, Pakistan, where the United States was supplying arms. But Gillespie refused to play until the gates were opened to the "ragamuffin" children, because "they priced the tickets so high the people we were trying to gain friendship with couldn't make it."[72]

Still, the State Department got tremendous mileage from these tours, and even jazz artists not sponsored by the State Department, such as Lionel Hampton in his 1956 seven-month tour of Europe, were proclaimed "U.S. jambassadors at large."[73] The enthusiasm reverberated well beyond the immediate areas visited by artists. For example, Africa-wide *Drum* magazine and the *World*, based in Johannesburg, carried feature articles on Louis Armstrong's 1956 tours.[74] Following on that enthusiasm, the Voice of America broadcast jazz programs in Africa in the 1950s and 1960s. In South Africa in 1956, the Voice of America carried two hours of jazz every night as well as special programs such as the Newport Jazz Festival.[75]

Louis Armstrong's celebrated yet "unofficial" 1956 visit to the Gold Coast drew crowds of up to 100,000 and attracted worldwide publicity.[76] The American consulate in Accra reported that Armstrong and his band received an "outpouring of press and public enthusiasm." The government and many private firms even gave employees a half-holiday to attend an outdoor performance, for which an audience of 30,000 showed up. The consulate considered the visit an outstanding success, citing the Ghanaian *Daily Mail*, which applauded the State Department and praised the "unbiased support for the African's course. . . . And they don't just talk thousands of miles away. They come to our land to see for themselves."[77] The tour was deemed such a triumph that a State Department–sponsored trip through the Soviet Union and South America was planned for the following year. Calling it "Satchmo's romp through the land of the Reds,"[78] the *Courier* named Armstrong one of the "brightest lights" of 1956 for "the easy manner in which he won friends for Uncle Sam overseas."[79]

Nevertheless, although the State Department no doubt benefited from tours by black American artists, many jazz musicians who performed under its auspices—Gillespie, Armstrong, and later Duke Ellington—not only challenged U.S. policy but disrupted claims to an exclusively American identity by promoting solidarities among black peoples. Music and, in this era, particularly jazz became a critical arena in which diaspora identities were elaborated and contested.[80] In fact, Gillespie's ties to Brazilian and South American artists were built partly by means of his government-sponsored tours. What he discovered in Brazil was "a lotta brothers, Africans—and their music is African."[81] And the significance of the crowds who came to hear him in Accra was clear to Armstrong: "After all, my ancestors came from here and I still have African blood in me."[82] Horace Cayton argued in the *Courier* that "there is a deep symbolic meaning underlying the visit of Louis Armstrong to the African Gold Coast"; it was a "dramatic illustration of the deep bonds of mutual sympathy between American and African Negroes, deeper and wider than the oceans and centuries between us."[83] A veteran journalist who in the 1940s had promoted solidarity between black Americans and Africans, Cayton recouped his argument in the 1950s, not through politics but through music. Armstrong, Cayton argued, represented not simply America but black Americans: "The hundreds of thousands of Africans were not only cheering Louis Armstrong as an artist and musician, or as an American. They were cheering Louis Armstrong as the representative of 15 million American Negroes."[84]

But the deepest ironies and limits of the U.S. strategy of promoting black American jazz artists as pro-American propaganda came to light the following year with Armstrong's widely publicized denunciations of Eisenhower and Governor Orval Faubus of Arkansas, after Faubus ordered units of the National Guard to surround Central High School in Little Rock and block the entry of black students. Armstrong abandoned his plans for a government-sponsored trip to the Soviet Union, declaring that "the way they are treating my people in the South, the Government can go to hell." Calling Faubus "an uneducated plow-boy," Armstrong said the president was "two-faced" and had allowed Faubus to run the federal government: "It's getting so bad a colored man hasn't got any country." The impact of Armstrong's not only criticizing and refusing to tour for the government but announcing that black people in America had no country sent a very alarmed State Department scrambling to get "perhaps the most effective un-official goodwill ambassador this country ever had," to reconsider (in the end Benny Goodman made the Soviet tour).[85] Armstrong did praise Eisenhower when he finally sent in federal troops to uphold integration, but against a flurry of attacks and canceled concerts and television appearances, he continued to express outrage over Little Rock, remarking in October 1957 that he'd rather play in the Soviet Union than Arkansas because Faubus "might hear a couple of notes—and he don't deserve that."[86]

There is great poignancy in Armstrong's making such a statement. Only seven years earlier the State Department had revoked Paul Robeson's right to travel and had expended considerable energy to discredit him in the Gold Coast, insisting in part that his contention that the Soviet Union was less racist than America made him un-American. Indeed, no one was more pleased by Armstrong's castigation of the administration than Robeson, who praised Armstrong for his "heartfelt outburst," and for criticizing the government "in stronger terms than I ever have." Particularly sensitive to the "virtual necessity for the Negro artist" to travel, given the dearth of opportunities for black artists in the United States, Robeson appreciated Armstrong's risk. Indeed, while denouncing black spokepersons who "have set out to calm the clamor of world humanity against racism," Robeson defended performing artists who "went on these government sponsored tours because they needed work and who were out to show the world, as they did, that the American Negro has talent and dignity deserving of respect everywhere." In an interesting coincidence, just as the Armstrong controversy exploded in late September, the October 1957 issue of *Ebony* hit the stands carrying an interview with Robeson by Carl T. Rowan, "Has Paul Robeson Betrayed the Negro?"[87] Noting that the name of one of "the most fabulous characters of our time" had become anathema, Rowan asked, "Why? What caused this almost unbelievable turnabout that sent an international hero plunging into seven years of obscurity?" And "why was the State Department out to get him?"

> "Nobody will ever convince me that the foreign and domestic policies of this country do not come straight from the South," explains Robeson. "This country is run by Jim Eastland and Lyndon Johnson and Richard Russell and that crowd." And Robeson figures that these men feared him, that they saw in him a symbol around which the Negro masses might rally to join hands with "the black power that is now flexing its muscles in Asia and Africa."[88]

For Robeson, the issue came back to the American South. The real reason he was silenced was that he challenged colonialism and racism in the South, not for what he considered the false charges that he was pro-Soviet. But if there is irony in this story, the imploding of State Department efforts to manipulate perceptions of race was perhaps inevitable. As Robeson told Rowan, "They can keep me from going overseas but they can't keep news of Emmett Till and Autherine Lucy from going over there."[89] The State Department could silence Robeson and promote other black artists in Ghana, but ultimately it could not contain American racism or the violence and lawlessness of the American South.[90]

GHANA

On March 6, 1957, Kwame Nkrumah was inaugurated as the first president of the new nation of Ghana. The independence of the former Gold Coast has often been taken as a starting point for a greater interest and more sophisticated understanding of Africa on the part of African Americans. Indeed, the approach of independence there prompted an outpouring of interest not only in Ghana, but in Africa as a whole on the part of black Americans.[91] Politicians and journalists celebrated the leadership of Kwame Nkrumah and analyzed the impact of Ghanian independence on Africa, on world politics, and on black American–African relations.[92] African American leaders such as Martin Luther King Jr., Ralph Bunche, Adam Clayton Powell Jr., Mordecai Johnson, A. Philip Randolph, Claude Barnett, and Horace Mann Bond attended independence ceremonies.[93]

Yet African American perspectives on the independence of Ghana also illustrate the ways the Cold War limited relationships between black Americans and Africans. The avoidance of politically sensitive issues in the preceding years had a dampening effect on the analysis of independence. In a milieu where change was far more likely to be explained under the rubric of modernization or development than of political conflict, there was little attention to the political history of independence. The *Defender,* for example, explained that "after following the usual pattern of political evolution under the crown colony system [the Gold Coast] was granted a constitution in 1950."[94] Even the wide interest among African Americans about Ghana in 1957 was deeply shaped by the Cold War.

The narrowing of political debate pertaining to Ghana was influenced by politics in West Africa as well as by the American context. Manning Marable has argued that although George Padmore claimed to represent a nonaligned position in the Cold War, "his polemics against Communism were not aimed at the African proletariat as much as at US government and corporate interests, which might underwrite many of Ghana's state expenses after independence."[95] Indeed, as the single most important architect of the vision embracing the commonality of the struggles of Africans and those of African descent in the diaspora, in the 1940s Padmore had walked a sophisticated line that allowed him to reject the Comintern without becoming anti-Communist or even anti-Soviet. In the 1950s, however, facing the exigencies of independence politics on the Cold War terrain, he became virulently anti-Communist, and in practical terms his "African socialism" steered a course toward the West.[96] But despite Padmore's influence, and especially after his death in 1959, Nkrumah and the nation of Ghana did elaborate a neutral, nonaligned Pan-Africanism, exemplified by Nkrumah's advocacy of the neutralist All Africa Trade Union Federation (AATUF) as a nonaligned alternative to the anti-Communist International Confederation of Free Trade Unions (ICFTU) and the World Federation of Trade Unions. This new politics was represented at the All African People's Conference held in Accra, December 8, 1958.[97]

Since the African socialism advocated by Nkrumah and his adviser Padmore was too complex to fit into a neat bipolar model, African American journalists and observers tended simply to pass over the politics of Ghana and ask what its independence meant to the United States or to the Soviet Union. The *Defender* argued that Russia saw it as "a golden opportunity to secure a political foothold through a Marxist introduction of an economic, materialistic way of life for Africans."[98] Politicians and journalists asked whether Ghana might accept Soviet aid.[99] According to Ethyl L. Payne, "a reliable source" predicted that once in the United Nations, Ghana would "not vote with the Asian-African group but . . . steer an independent course," "stick close to America," and ask for U.S. aid.[100] Demands for the appointment of "more qualified U.S. Negroes to the diplomatic and consular corps" replaced scrutiny of the policies these people would represent.[101]

The critical perspective of the 1940s about American government and corporate involvement in West Africa gave way to discussions of opportunities for American investment.[102] Warning that the West had lost Asia to "Sovietism and neutralism," the *Courier* urged U.S. aid to Ghana and other independent African nations. A *Defender* editorial argued that the United States should not repeat mistakes in Africa that had been made in Asia, where "the prevalence of Neutralism, anti-Western sentiment and the Communization of China have troubled the conscience of America and her political allies on the Western Hemisphere." America must meet "the swift rise of nationalism in Africa" with technical and financial assistance to protect U.S. investment there and ensure the "permanent goodwill of Africa and the commercial and political benefits that would flow thereby."[103] Albert Barnett praised Ghanaians for "ignoring politics" and demonstrating the "admirable qualities of perseverance and patience" by concentrating on "raising their economic levels."[104] Reporting "bauxite waiting to be prospected" in northern Ghana, the *Defender* noted that "American Negroes have been particularly welcomed." As another example of opportunities, the *Defender* noted an African American insurance company established in Accra.[105]

In the next decade a new generation of African American scholars, activists, diplomats, and entrepreneurs would define and articulate new diaspora identities and politics, and Ghana would be very significant to that generation.[106] But in 1957, after years in which African Americans emphasized their exclusive American citizenship and disclaimed international ties, and in which the American government discouraged international politics, the connections were weak. The disruption of the ties between African Americans and Ghanaians—bonds that had been built through the 1945 Pan-African Congress and the Pan-African Federation—was dramatized by the fact that Du Bois was prevented from attending the independence ceremonies by the United States government.[107] The new relations were of a different kind. One newspaper noted that Martin Luther King "finally caught up with the Vice President, Richard Nixon" in Ghana, but the subject of their conversation was Montgomery, not Ghana-and-Montgomery.[108]

Indeed, it was Nixon who stole the show and set the tone for the discussion of Africa, not King, Randolph, Powell, or any African American activist. Nixon attended independence ceremonies as part of a three-week African tour. Ethel L. Payne reported in the *Defender* that "Ghanians admiringly bestowed [on him] a new title, American Show Boy," a term used to show approval of a performance.[109] Nixon, wrote William Theis in the *Defender,* will tell Eisenhower that the "right amount of aid in the right places will tip the ideological scales definitely to the side of the free world"; for the new nation of Ghana, funding for a Volta River hydroelectric power project to operate a new aluminum industry was especially important.[110] Nixon also argued that what happened in U.S. race relations would determine whether Africa "will go Communist or not."[111]

Along with the new generation of African Americans drawn to Ghana, Du Bois and Hunton both moved there to work on the *African Encyclopedia.* Du Bois and Robeson both regained their right to travel in 1958, when the Supreme Court ruled that the secretary of state had no right to deny a citizen a passport because of political beliefs.[112] Noting that "I felt like a released prisoner," Du Bois traveled outside the country for nearly a year.[113] In 1960 he relocated to Ghana, and when the United States refused to renew his passport because he had joined the Communist Party, he became a citizen of Ghana on February 17, 1963. Hunton remarked that Du Bois had "simply formalized the fact that he was also a son of Africa," but just as striking, his move demonstrated that there was no longer a home in America for his generation of anticolonial activists. Du Bois died in Ghana on August 27, 1963, one day before the historic civil rights "March on Washington."[114]

Paul Robeson remained throughout the 1950s a political pariah in his own country. By the time of the Montgomery movement in 1955 and 1956 his influence had been neutralized, and his attempts to support the civil rights struggle were ignored or even seen as a hindrance. In 1957 he told Carl Rowan in the *Ebony* interview that "I think a good deal in terms of the power of black people in the world. . . . If I could just get a passport I'd just like to go to Ghana or Jamaica just to sit there for a few days and observe this black power."[115] But when "black power" was articulated in the 1960s, Robeson's enormous contributions to an internationalist black politics were largely unappreciated.[116] Following prolonged isolation, harassment, and exclusion from work and travel, he suffered a series of emotional and physical breakdowns and spent his last years virtually forgotten. A doctor who treated him in 1965 recalled that Robeson was anguished at not having received recognition from the current generation of civil rights activists. He died in 1976.[117]

Alphaeus Hunton, Howard– and Harvard– and New York University–educated Ph.D., was unable to find work in the United States. Following the closing of the CAA he explored in *Decision in Africa: Sources of Current Conflict* the history of the exploitation of land and labor in Africa, and the contemporary conflicts between African aims and American interests. After the book's publication in 1957, Hunton worked for some years as a seasonal employee in the unskilled division of the Hudson Bay Fur Company. In 1960 he and his wife, Dorothy, went first to Guinea, where he taught English, and then to Ghana to work with Du Bois. Following Du Bois's death in 1963, Hunton continued the *Africana Encyclopedia* project. Deported after the coup that ousted Nkrumah in 1966, he spent his last years in Zambia, where he wrote for the ANC publication *Mayibuye* and worked on a history of the Zambian labor movement.[118] He died in Lusaka, Zambia, in 1970.[119]

CONCLUSION

Let us be dissatisfied until the empty stomachs of Mississippi are filled and the idle industries of Appalachia are revitalized. Let us be dissatisfied until brotherhood is no longer a meaningless word at the end of a prayer but the first order of business on every legislative agenda. Let us be dissatisfied until our brother of the Third World—Asia, Africa, and Latin America—will no longer be the victim of imperialist exploitation, but will be lifted from the long night of poverty, illiteracy, and disease. Let us be dissatisfied until this pending cosmic energy will be transformed into a creative psalm of peace and "justice will roll down like waters from a mighty stream."
— Martin Luther King Jr., February 23, 1968

AFTER THE MCCARTHY ERA, the towering figures of anticolonialism in the 1940s—Du Bois, Robeson, and Hunton—were never again to have a voice in American politics. But although these individuals were marginalized in U.S. and African American politics, the issues for which they had fought—most fundamentally a conception of democracy that embraced political, economic, and civil rights on a global scale, and a radical democratic critique of American foreign policy—were once again debated in the 1960s. Critical discussion of American policies in Africa involving attention to political economy began to revive at the end of the 1950s with the anticolonial struggles in Algeria and the Belgian Congo, and the nonalignment strategies of such leaders as Patrice Lumumba and President Sekou Touré of Guinea.[1] As more radical elements emerged in the civil rights movement, antiimperialism was an important part of the new politics. African Americans would once again contest American policy at the United Nations, protesting for example, American CIA involvement and UN complicity in the 1961 murder of Lumumba.[2] The global vision of democracy developed by Malcolm X just before he was slain embraced antiimperialism. He also joined forces with the Student Nonviolent Coordinating Committee (SNCC), explicitly linking his internationalism with the fight for civil rights in the United States.[3]

The events of the late 1950s and 1960s vindicated the 1940s anticolonialists' analysis of the forces that were reshaping the world in the twentieth century. African American intellectuals, journalists, activists, and political leaders had argued that the liberation of Africa and Asia would have a significant impact on the struggles of African Americans, and the birth of new African and Asian states did indeed have far-ranging repercussions in American domestic politics and civil rights. The concern with America's image in the world, which had loomed so large for the Truman administration, continued to appear in civil rights rhetoric. As Martin Luther King Jr. told a rally at St. John's Church in Birmingham in 1963, "The United States is concerned about its image. . . . Mr. Kennedy is battling for the minds and the hearts of men in Africa and Asia . . . and they aren't gonna respect the U.S. of America if she deprives men and women of their basic rights of life because of the color of their skin. Mr. Kennedy knows that."[4] But the fact that King was making this argument in 1963 points to the enormous failure of the liberal civil rights strategy of the Truman era: embracing American foreign policy in the hope of furthering a domestic civil rights agenda. The preoccupation of the Truman administration with America's "Achilles heel" had led instead to frenetic efforts to shape the world's perceptions of race in America and ultimately to the effective disruption of leftist anticolonial politics. It did not lead the administration to act decisively on civil rights. It was only after the mass mobilization of African Americans and their allies in the southern civil rights movement from 1955 on that the Kennedy administration, in the summer of 1963, set in motion the events that would lead at last to the passage of the Civil Rights Act of 1964.

Moreover, the severing of international and domestic politics in the early Cold War and the silencing of antiimperialist and anticapitalist politics had profound implications for the politics of the black American community and for American society. It may be true, given the political terrain of the 1950s, that the moderated civil rights agenda contributed to the movement's dramatic successes, but it also meant that a host of questions concerning political, economic, and social rights in an international context were neglected in favor of an exclusive focus on domestic political and civil rights. Anticolonial activists of the 1940s had advocated freedom for Africans and those of African descent within an antiimperialist, anticapitalist framework. They also elaborated a profound vision of the rights and global responsibilities of American citizenship. But civil rights activists of the 1950s and 1960s negotiated in an international and national terrain dominated by the Cold War. Although civil rights leaders such as Martin Luther King Jr. and Bayard Rustin were personally interested in anticolonialism, it was not a programmatic part of the civil rights movement. And though placing hope in America's postwar prosperity did indeed carve out spaces for some middle-class African Americans, in retrospect, as a strategy for civil rights, it appears to have been a tragically narrow choice. For most black Americans, as the sphere of struggle narrowed from an embrace of economic, political, and social justice to a more circumscribed notion of civil rights, the post–World War II resegregation of the labor market and housing created new structural and institutional inequalities and barriers to advancement.

At the end of his life W. E. B. Du Bois commented that black Americans "are becoming Americans. But then what are Americans to become?"[5] Du Bois never lost sight of the global context of American politics, and he recognized the deep ramifications for domestic politics of expanding U.S. empire. If in the immediate postwar period the U.S. role in the international economy brought unprecedented prosperity to many, the militarization of the U.S. economy that fueled U.S. invasions and financed wars in Asia, Africa, and Latin America skewed investment toward high-tech "national security" needs and not only away from the social services of the New Deal and the Great Society but also away from basic industry and infrastructure. And in a cruel irony, as the inequitable social relations of empire came back home, these processes eventually eroded the industrial and public sectors where African American workers had made significant gains.

Cold War repression and historical amnesia made for striking discontinuities between previous and newer forms of democratic internationalist politics. Anticolonial opinion remained far more fragmented than had been the case in the 1940s—resurfacing at the margins, not in the mainstream, of black American politics—and there was a deep fissure between the new forms of activism and the 1940s political culture. With the silencing of intellectuals and political leaders such as Du Bois, Robeson, and Hunton, the antiimperialist and anticapitalist critique of the global political economy no longer had powerful and credible advocates within the African American community. Consequently, in the 1960s, young activists such as members of the Black Panthers and SNCC were cut off from an older generation and compelled to reinvent the wheel as they developed their own critiques of American capitalism and imperialism.

But despite these fissures in the history of anticolonialism and the American government's aggressive attempts to suppress antiimperialist politics, one sees profound implications of the politics of the African diaspora in the continuing challenges to empire and the continuing relevance of the analysis of the 1940s activists. The fate of the 1940s politics of the African diaspora tells us much about the stakes involved in challenging economic inequality and insisting on a global understanding of economic exploitation and the fight for human rights. The collision of anticolonial politics with Cold War liberalism illuminates the political and economic conditions faced by later democratic projects—from those of Malcolm X, Patrice Lumumba, and the ANC to Maurice Bishop, Michael Manley, and Haiti's Jean-Bertrand Aristide—as well as the vulnerability of these projects to internationally organized state repression.[6]

The challenges of Du Bois, Robeson, Hunton, and many lesser-known journalists and activists went to the heart of U.S. relations with new Asian and African nations and the emerging global political economy. They had advocated a democratic politics and an equitable distribution of the world's resources, warning that the consequence of continued political domination and economic exploitation would be unremitting war. And indeed the supposed "Cold War" was very hot for many of the world's peoples, costing the lives of millions in military conflicts in Africa, Asia, and Latin America. Throughout, the struggle to articulate a policy of nonalignment was undermined by the U.S. and Soviet arming of brutal dictatorships and by mercenaries and dictators willing to do the bidding of the superpowers. The death of Patrice Lumumba in a 1961 CIA-backed assassination recalls Robeson's tragic prescience in his graphic discussion of the emerging political economy: workers in the Congo, he warned, were mining tin for the manufacture of guns that would eventually be turned against them. In our hemisphere an American-backed elite has continued to rule Haiti, presiding over decades of the brutal Duvalier dictatorship and a coup ousting Aristide and the first democratically elected government. And South Africa not only extended apartheid internally but carried out years of war in Angola, Mozambique, and Namibia—with American money and arms—before the country's first democratic elections were finally held in 1994.[7] If the 1940s activists had still been living, surely they would have had deep satisfaction in seeing their allies from the late 1940s and early 1950s— Walter Sisulu, A. M. Kathrada, and Nelson Mandela—officiating in an ANC-led government, after having spent nearly three decades in prison for their challenges to the apartheid state.

The implications of the silencing and exile of these American critics and their democratic and internationalist vision for American politics can be further seen in the fate—only a decade later—of another African American leader. In the last years of his life Martin Luther King Jr. developed a critique of the American capitalist economy and embraced antiimperialist politics, challenging the United States to address its gross disparities in wealth and condemning its intervention in Vietnam as immoral. But as King attempted to reconnect the international and domestic politics that had been so thoroughly severed during the Cold War, he was increasingly isolated and chastised, abandoned by both white liberal and black establishment allies. The intellectual and political culture and the forms of institutions and alliances necessary to sustain his vision—a vibrant black press, a vigorous labor movement, and cross-class coalitions uniting liberals and the left—had been lost in the early Cold War.

On February 23, 1968, in a speech honoring the hundredth birthday of W. E. B. Du Bois (the last formal speech of his life), King told his audience that Du Bois had recognized the bonds between black Americans and the land of their ancestors, thus "alarming imperialists in all countries and disconcerting Negro moderates in America who were afraid of his black genius." Reminding white America of its debt to this African American thinker for his gift of truth about the history it had distorted, King insisted above all that people remember his radicalism and antiimperialism. Du Bois, King argued, "would readily see the parallel between American support of the corrupt and despised Thieu-Ky regime and northern support to the southern slave-masters in 1876."[8]

Moreover, King was aware that these insights must be brought to the legislative table. Like the anticolonial activists of the 1940s, he knew that gross inequalities and war were the result of policies and the people who made them. And also like those activists, he connected the possibility of change—a genuine transformation of American society and global power relations—to an ongoing struggle of memory against forgetting. The moral imagination to create a genuinely democratic world depended on remembering and bearing witness to the enslavement of Africans, the exploitation of colonial peoples, and the development of racial capitalism.

As new activists and dreamers of democracy struggle to realize their visions, perhaps like King they will look to the anticolonial activists of the 1940s—not to take comfort in the past but to find inspiration in their profound knowledge of history, their imagination, their capacity for hope in the face of adversity, and their remarkable faith in the possibility of human solidarity.

NOTES

Introduction

1. See Martin Bauml Duberman, *Paul Robeson* (New York: Knopf, 1988), pp. 236–37.

2. W. A. Hunton Papers, box 1, folder 19 (CAA Organizational, 1945–55), MG 237, Schomburg Library, New York.

3. See James L. Roark, "American Black Leaders: The Response to Colonialism and the Cold War, 1943–1953," *African Historical Studies* 4, no. 2 (1971): 253–70; Hollis R. Lynch, *Black American Radicals and the Liberation of Africa: The Council on African Affairs, 1937–1955* (Ithaca: Africana Studies and Research Center, Cornell University, 1978); Mark Solomon, "Black Critics of Colonialism and the Cold War," in *Cold War Critics: Alternatives to American Foreign Policy in the Truman Years*, ed. Thomas G. Paterson (Chicago: Quadrangle Books, 1971), pp. 205–39; Duberman, *Paul Robeson*; Manning Marable, *W. E. B. Du Bois: Black Radical Democrat* (Boston: Twayne, 1986); Paul Gordon Lauren, *Power and Prejudice: The Politics and Diplomacy of Racial Discrimination* (Boulder, Colo.: Westview Press, 1988); Sterling Stuckey, *Slave Culture: Nationalist Theory and the Foundations of Black America* (New York: Oxford University Press, 1987). See Imanuel Geiss, *The Pan-African Movement: A History of Pan-Africanism in America, Europe, and Africa* (New York: Africana, 1974); and P. Olisanwuche Esedebe, *Pan-Africanism: The Idea and Movement, 1776–1963* (Washington, D.C.: Howard University Press, 1982), for discussions of international Pan-African networks. See also J. Ayodele Langley, *Pan-Africanism and Nationalism in West Africa, 1900–1945: A Study in Ideology and Social Classes* (Oxford: Clarendon Press, 1973).

4. The many works that have made feasible a study of African Americans and international politics include William Minter, *King Solomon's Mines Revisited: Western Interests and the Burdened History of Southern Africa* (New York: Basic Books, 1986); Thomas Borstelmann, *Apartheid's Reluctant Uncle: The United States and Southern Africa in the Early Cold War* (New York: Oxford University Press, 1993); Robert J. McMahon, *Colonialism and the Cold War: The United States and the Struggle for Indonesian Independence, 1945–49* (Ithaca: Cornell University

Press, 1981); Christopher Thorne, *The Issue of War: States, Societies, and the Far Eastern Conflict of 1941–1945* (London: Hamish Hamilton, 1985).

5. Paul Gilroy, '*There Ain't No Black in the Union Jack': The Cultural Politics of Race and Nation* (Chicago: University of Chicago Press, 1987), pp. 157–58. See also Sidney Lemelle and Robin D. G. Kelley, eds., *Imagining Home: Class, Culture, and Nationalism in the African Diaspora* (New York: Verso, 1994).

6. Du Bois to Walter White, NAACP memorandum, 1945, W. E. B. Du Bois Papers, microfilm collection, Columbia University, reel 57, frame 1043.

CHAPTER ONE   The Making of the Politics of the African Diaspora

1. See Mark Solomon, "Black Critics of Colonialism and the Cold War," in *Cold War Critics: Alternatives to American Foreign Policy in the Truman Years*, ed. Thomas G. Paterson (Chicago: Quadrangle Books, 1971), pp. 205, 209; James L. Roark, "American Black Leaders: The Response to Colonialism and the Cold War, 1943–1953," *African Historical Studies* 4, no. 2 (1971): 255; Gerald Horne, *Black and Red: W. E. B. Du Bois and the Afro-American Response to the Cold War, 1944–1963* (Albany: State University of New York Press, 1986), pp. 20–21; Manning Marable, *W. E. B. Du Bois: Black Radical Democrat* (Boston: Twayne, 1986), pp. 159–61.

2. Walter White, "Kinship of Colored Peoples: People, Politics, and Places," *Chicago Defender*, March 3, 1945; Walter White, *A Rising Wind* (Westport, Conn.: Negro Universities Press, 1971), p. 144.

3. The circulation of the *Pittsburgh Courier* was 126,962 in 1940; by 1946 it had reached 257,519. The *Chicago Defender* grew from 82,059 in 1940 to 129,156 nationally and 74,475 locally in 1946. All figures are from N. W. Ayer & Sons, *Directory of Newspapers and Periodicals*, 1940 and 1946. See also Beth Bailey and David Farber, "The 'Double-V' Campaign and W.W. II Hawaii: African Americans, Racial Ideology, and Federal Power," *Journal of Social History* 26 (Summer 1993): 834, on the circulation and importance of the black press and the response of the U.S. government.

4. See Benedict Anderson, *Imagined Communities* (London: Verso, 1991), esp. pp. 113–40.

5. Martin R. Delany, *Blake; or the Huts of America*, ed. Floyd Miller (Boston: Beacon, 1970); original serialized version in *Anglo-African Magazine* and *The Weekly Anglo-African* from 1859 to 1862. See Wilson Jeremiah Moses, *The Golden Age of Black Nationalism, 1850–1925* (New York: Oxford University Press, 1978), pp. 151–54; Vincent Harding, *There Is a River: The Black Struggle for Freedom in America* (New York: Harcourt Brace Jovanovich, 1981), pp. 127, 129–33, 184–87, 207–8; Paul Gilroy, *The Black Atlantic: Modernity and Double Consciousness* (Cambridge, Mass.: Harvard University Press, 1993), pp. 27–28. On Delany, see also Sterling Stuckey, *Slave Culture: Nationalist Theory and the Foundations of Black America* (New York: Oxford University Press, 1987), pp. 226–31.

6. See Wilson Jeremiah Moses, *Alexander Crummell: A Study of Civilization and Discontent* (New York: Oxford University Press, 1989); Wilson Jeremiah Moses, *The Wings of Ethiopia* (London: Oxford University Press, 1990); William R. Scott, *The Sons of Sheba's Race: African Americans and the Italo-Ethiopian War, 1935–41* (Bloomington: Indiana University Press, 1993), pp. 8–11.

7. James W. Ivy, "Traditional NAACP Interest in Africa as Reflected in the Pages of *The Crisis*," in *Africa Seen by American Negro Scholars* (New York: American Society of African Culture, 1963), pp. 229–46; Moses, *Golden Age of Black Nationalism*, pp. 225–26.

8. Sidney Lemelle and Robin D. G. Kelley, eds., *Imagining Home: Class, Culture, and Nationalism in the African Diaspora* (New York: Verso, 1994), p. 3. On the earlier Pan-African Con-

gresses, see W. E. B. Du Bois, *The World and Africa: An Inquiry into the Part Which Africa Has Played in World History* (New York: International, 1987), pp. 7–12, 240–44; George Padmore, *Pan-Africanism or Communism* (Garden City, N.Y.: Anchor Books, 1972), pp. 107–13, 117–22; P. Olisanwuche Esedebe, *Pan-Africanism: The Idea and Movement, 1776–1963* (Washington, D.C.: Howard University Press, 1983); Imanuel Geiss, *The Pan-African Movement: A History of Pan-Africanism in America, Europe, and Africa* (New York: Africana, 1974); J. Ayodele Langley, *Pan-Africanism and Nationalism in West Africa, 1900–1945: A Study in Ideology and Social Classes* (Oxford: Clarendon Press, 1973).

9. Marable, *W. E. B. Du Bois*, pp. 100–107; Paul Gordon Lauren, *Power and Prejudice: The Politics and Diplomacy of Racial Discrimination* (Boulder: Westview Press, 1988), pp. 64, 77–79, 83–84, 106–7; Horace Campbell, "Pan-Africanism and African Liberation," in Lemelle and Kelley, *Imagining Home*, p. 289.

10. The quote is from Robin D. G. Kelley's introduction to C. L. R. James, *A History of Pan-African Revolt* (published 1938 as *A History of Negro Revolt*; Chicago: Charles H. Kerr, 1995), pp. 16–17; Robert A. Hill and Barbara Bair, eds., *Marcus Garvey, Life and Lessons: A Centennial Companion to the Marcus Garvey and Universal Negro Improvement Association Papers* (Berkeley: University of California Press, 1987); Barbara Bair, "True Women, Real Men: Gender, Ideology, and Social Roles in the Garvey Movement," in *Gendered Domains: Rethinking Public and Private in Women's History*, ed. Dorothy O. Helly and Susan M. Reverby (Ithaca: Cornell University Press, 1992), pp. 154–66; Tony Martin, *Race First: The Ideological and Organizational Struggles of Marcus Garvey and the Universal Negro Improvement Association* (Dover, Mass: Majority Press, 1986).

11. Robin D. G. Kelley, "Africa's Sons with Banner Red," chap. 5 in *Race Rebels: Culture, Politics, and the Black Working Class* (New York: Free Press, 1994), pp. 108–9, 116–20; Cedric J. Robinson, *Black Marxism: The Making of the Black Radical Tradition* (London: Zed Books, 1983); Paul Buhle, *Marxism in the USA: Remapping the History of the American Left* (London: Verso, 1987); Robin D. G. Kelley, *Hammer and Hoe: Alabama Communists during the Great Depression* (Chapel Hill: University of North Carolina Press, 1990); Lemelle and Kelley, *Imagining Home* (this entire collection is relevant, but see esp. the editors' introduction, "Imagining Home: Pan-Africanism Revisited").

12. Mark Naison, *Communists in Harlem during the Depression* (New York: Grove Press, 1983); Kelley, *Hammer and Hoe*; Robert L. Zangrando, *The NAACP Crusade against Lynching, 1909–1950* (Philadelphia: Temple University Press, 1980), pp. 98–165.

13. Paul Robeson, "American Negroes in the War," Speech at the Twelfth Annual Herald Tribune Forum, November 16, 1943, in *Paul Robeson Speaks: Writings, Speeches, and Interviews, 1918–1974*, ed. Philip S. Foner (New York: Citadel Press, 1978), p. 147.

14. Scott, *Sons of Sheba's Race*; William R. Scott, "Black Nationalism and the Italo-Ethiopian Conflict, 1934–1936," *Journal of Negro History* 63 (April 1978); Hollis Lynch, "Afro-Americans and the Italo-Ethiopian Conflict, 1935–1941" (unpublished), p. 29; Cedric J. Robinson, "Fascism and the Intersection of Capitalism, Racialism, and Historical Consciousness," *Humanities in Society* 6 (Fall 1983): 344; Elliott P. Skinner, "The Dialectic between Diasporas and Homelands," in *Global Dimensions of the African Diaspora*, ed. Joseph E. Harris (Washington, D.C.: Howard University Press, 1982), p. 32; Joseph E. Harris, *African-American Reactions to War in Ethiopia, 1936–1941* (Baton Rouge: Louisiana State University Press, 1994). For a contemporary in-depth history of Italian-Ethiopian relations, see Makonnen Haile, "Last Gobble of Africa," *Crisis* 42, no. 2 (1935): 70.

15. Kelley, *Race Rebels*, pp. 130–32; Naison, *Communists in Harlem*, pp. 138–40, 173–77. For examples of the popular argument that the invasion was a natural outcome of inevitable conflict

between imperialist and fascist European powers, see George Padmore, "Ethiopia and World Politics," *Crisis* 42, no. 5 (1935): 138; Harold Preece, "War and the Negro," *Crisis* 42, no. 11 (1935): 329; "An English Trick," *Chicago Defender*, April 23, 1938, and "The Double-Crosser," May 21, 1938; "Helping Ethiopia Now," *Pittsburgh Courier*, February 8, 1941.

16. Kelley, *Race Rebels*, pp. 157–58. On black Americans in the Spanish Civil War, see Danny Duncan Collum, ed., and Victor A. Berch, chief researcher, *African Americans in the Spanish Civil War: "This Ain't Ethiopia but It'll Do"* (New York: G. K. Hall, 1992), comprising documents from black American participants and an introduction by Kelley.

17. Geiss, *Pan-African Movement*, pp. 341–56.

18. W. Randy Dixon, "Calling George Padmore: Aggressive Fighter for the Rights of Colored Peoples throughout the World," *Pittsburgh Courier*, July 31, 1943, p. 5.

19. James R. Hooker, *Black Revolutionary: George Padmore's Path from Communism to Pan-Africanism* (New York: Praeger, 1967), p. 17.

20. Ibid., p. 22.

21. George Padmore, "An Open Letter to Earl Browder," *Crisis* 42, no. 10 (1935): 302; "Earl Browder Replies," *Crisis* 42, no. 12 (1935): 372. See Naison, *Communists in Harlem*, pp. 131–32, for the repercussions in Harlem of Padmore's ouster and the *Amsterdam News* support of Padmore's case.

22. Hooker, *Black Revolutionary*, pp. 49–50. On the International African Service Bureau, see Padmore, *Pan-Africanism or Communism*, pp. 124–27.

23. Kelley, introduction to James, *History of Pan-African Revolt*, pp. 1–33. See also, Robert A. Hill's remarkable essay on James, "In England, 1932–1938," in *C. L. R. James: His Life and Work*, ed. Paul Buhle (London: Allison & Busby, 1986), pp. 61–80.

24. Hooker, Padmore's only biographer to date, portrays Padmore as an exception to what he terms black American "parochialism" and thus not only misreads the 1940s, which were anything but parochial, but ironically trivializes Padmore by failing to do justice to his pivotal role in bringing anticolonial issues into the heart of African American discourse. See James R. Hooker, "Africa for Afro-Americans: Padmore and the Black Press," *Radical America* 2, no. 4 (1968): 14–19; and Hooker, *Black Revolutionary*.

25. "Trinidad Swept by Wave of Terrorism and Intimidation," *Chicago Defender*, January 8, 1938, p. 24; "60 Injured as British Troops Fight Rioters," *Chicago Defender*, June 4, 1938, p. 24; "Strikes Spread as Natives Are Terrorized," *Chicago Defender*, June 18, 1938, p. 24. For background, see Thomas C. Holt, *The Problem of Freedom: Race, Labor, and Politics in Jamaica and Britain, 1832–1938* (Baltimore: Johns Hopkins University Press, 1992), pp. 345–402; Khafra Kambon, *For Bread, Justice, and Freedom: A Political Biography of George Weekes* (London: New Beacon Books, 1988).

26. Metz T. P. Lochard, "Panorama of World News," *Chicago Defender*, June 4, 1938, p. 24; "West Indian Leader Exposes Shocking Poverty in Jamaica," *Chicago Defender*, May 14, 1938, p. 24.

27. "Trouble in the W. Indies Stirs Subject Races: Unrest Spreads to Dutch East Indies, Morocco, and British Columbia," *Chicago Defender*, July 9, 1938, p. 24.

28. Ibid. On the same day, under the headline "Riots Loom in British, French Colonies," a series of articles covered the Royal Commission survey of conditions in the West Indies, a labor conference in British Guiana, and the prediction of a general revolution in Jamaica.

29. George Padmore, "Fascism in the West Indies," *Crisis* 45, no. 3 (1938): 78–79.

30. George Padmore, "Labor Trouble in Jamaica," *Crisis* 45, no. 9 (1938): 287, 288, 308.

31. "Isles Plight Aired in the House of Commons: African Bureau Exposes Labor Conditions in West Indies," *Chicago Defender*, January 15, 1938, p. 24. See also "Begins Inquiry of Wages in West Indies: Quizzes Colonial Minister about Unrest in Trinidad," *Chicago Defender*, January

22, 1938, p. 24. The International African Service Bureau also received attention in the African American press for its efforts to protect Abyssinian refugees seeking asylum in Kenya. The *Defender* reported on a petition which was signed by George Padmore, chairman of the bureau; F. H. Wallace-Johnson, organizing secretary, West African Youth league; Jomo Kenyatta, general secretary, Kikuyu Central Association; and T. R. Makonnen, secretary, Pan-African Federation, seeking to "draw the attention of the British friends of colonial peoples and all subject races to the terrible conditions of the Abyssinian refugees in Kenya and the danger of their repatriation." See "British Plot Is Exposed by Colonials," *Chicago Defender*, October 18, 1937, p. 24.

32. See Alphaeus Hunton, "Upsurge in Africa," *Masses and Mainstream* 3, no. 2 (1951): 15–16; Patrick S. Washburn, *A Question of Sedition: The Federal Government's Investigation of the Black Press during World War II* (New York: Oxford University Press, 1986).

33. Leo Spitzer and LaRay Denzer, "I. T. Wallace-Johnson and the West African Youth League," *International Journal of African Historical Studies* 6, no. 3 (1973); Spitzer and Denzer, "I. T. Wallace-Johnson and the West African Youth League, Part II: The Sierra Leone Period, 1938–1945," *International Journal of African Historical Studies* 6, no. 4 (1973).

34. "Laborers in Africa Strike," *Pittsburgh Courier*, September 30, 1936, p. 5; "Expose Conditions in British African Colonies: Natives Earn $25 Year, Live in Huts, Menaced by Snakes," *Pittsburgh Courier*, September 9, 1939, p. 5.

35. "English Pass Strict Laws on African Publications," *Pittsburgh Courier*, July 29, 1939, p. 2.

36. "British Send Native Editors to Prison: Sierra Leone Leaders Jailed," *Pittsburgh Courier*, November 30, 1940, p. 13.

37. E.g., George Padmore, "Cocoa War on the Gold Coast," *Crisis* 45, no. 2 (1938): 52.

38. "West Africa Uses Tactics of Gandhi: Natives Boycott British Goods to Register Dissatisfaction," *Chicago Defender*, October, 18, 1937, p. 24.

39. "African Youth in Support of Cocoa Strike: 100,000 Farmers of West Africa Are Involved in Struggle," *Chicago Defender*, April 2, 1938, p. 24. See also in the *Defender*, "Farmers of the Gold Coast May Strike," December 11, 1937, p. 24; "Natives Work Together in Cocoa Fight," April 30, 1938, p. 24; "Natives Fight for Economic Emancipation: Entire Population Has Refused to Work for Exploiters," January 29, 1939, p. 4; and "British Press Censors News on W. Africa: London Dailies Suppress Information about Farmers' Plight," January 29, 1938, p. 24.

40. *Chicago Defender*, January 29, 1939.

41. Stuckey, *Slave Culture*, pp. 320–23; Martin Duberman, *Paul Robeson* (New York: Knopf, 1988), pp. 170–71.

42. Duberman, *Paul Robeson*, pp. 185–90, 210, 215, 222, 224–27.

43. Hollis R. Lynch, *Black American Radicals and the Liberation of Africa: The Council on African Affairs, 1937–1955* (Ithaca: Africana Studies and Research Center, Cornell University, 1978), p. 17.

44. David H. Anthony, "Max Yergan and South Africa: A Transatlantic Interaction," in Lemelle and Kelley, *Imagining Home*, p. 191; David H. Anthony III, "Max Yergan in South Africa: From Evangelical Pan-Africanist to Revolutionary Socialist," *African Studies Review* 34, no. 2 (1991). On the founding and early evolution of the CAA, see also Lynch, *Black American Radicals*, pp. 17–21.

45. Anthony, "Max Yergan in South Africa," pp. 27–31.

46. Ibid., pp. 40–42.

47. Duberman, *Paul Robeson*, p. 210; Anthony, "Max Yergan in South Africa," pp. 40–42.

48. See Max Yergan, General Secretary, Student Christian Association of South Africa, to A. B. Xuma, June 18, 1935, ABX 350618; Xuma to Yergan, February 19, 1937, ABX 370219a; and Yergan to Xuma, March 10, 1937, ABX 370310c, all in A. B. Xuma Papers, Historical Papers Library, University of the Witwatersrand, Johannesburg.

49. Yergan to Xuma, February 4, 1937, Xuma Papers, ABX 370204, contains a lengthy discussion of their plans, and Yergan's view of the impact of the new organization on his duties with the All Africa Convention.

50. W. A. Hunton Papers, box 1, folder 16 (CAA Correspondence), MG 237, Schomburg Library, New York. See Yergan to Xuma, September 3, 1937, Xuma Papers, ABX 370903, for details of the speeches to be given by Xuma and Jabavu, who were members of the CAA from 1937. R. T. Bokwe, with whom the CAA would work closely during its 1946 famine relief campaign, joined in 1942. See *News of Africa* 1, no. 2 (1942): 2.

51. Jomo Kenyatta to Bunche, November 22, 1938; also Bunche to Paul and Essie Robeson, December 27, 1938, both in Ralph Bunche Papers, box 1, University of California, Los Angeles. Kenyatta mentioned sending Bunche his book and that he was attempting to arrange through Max Yergan a visit to the United States.

52. Yergan, Bunche, and the anthropologist Melville J. Herskovits, all of whom had just completed work on Africa, collaborated closely on academic presentations of African issues. See Bunche to Herskovits, October 5, 1938, and Herskovits to Bunche, October 10, 1938, Bunche Papers, box 1.

53. Jervis Anderson, *A. Philip Randolph: A Biographical Portrait* (New York: Harcourt Brace Jovanovich, 1973), pp. 232–40; Anthony, "Max Yergan and South Africa," p. 192.

54. On the split in the NNC, see Bunche Papers, box 179, folder "Allegations," 1, 2, 6. On Bunche's resignation from the ICAA, see box 179, folder "Allegations," 3; and box 180, folders "Max Yergan: Notes for Intervention" and "Max Yergan: Additional Data."

55. Bunche to C. L. R. James, November 29, 1938, Bunche Papers, box 1.

56. Anderson, *A. Philip Randolph*, pp. 239–40.

57. See esp. Roi Ottley, *New World A-Coming: Inside Black America* (Boston: Houghton Mifflin, 1943). On the popular front, see Buhle, *Marxism in the USA*; Kelley, "'Africa's Sons with Banner Red': African-American Communists and the Politics of Culture, 1919–1934," in his *Race Rebels*, pp. 103–21; Kelley, *Hammer and Hoe*; Naison, *Communists in Harlem*.

58. Paul Robeson, "A Message from the Chairman to Members and Friends of the Council on African Affairs," in Foner, ed., *Paul Robeson Speaks*, p. 224.

59. On Charlotta Bass, see Gerald R. Gill, "'Win or Lose—We Win': The 1952 Vice Presidential Campaign of Charlotta A. Bass," in *The Afro-American Woman: Struggles and Images*, ed. Sharon Harley and Rosalyn Terborg-Penn (Port Washington, N.Y.: National University Press Publications, Kennikat Press, 1978), pp. 109–88.

60. See, e.g., the editorial applauding the CAA's work on famine relief for the Ciskei, *Pittsburgh Courier*, January 19, 1946; an interview with Paul Robeson, "American Foreign Policy Supports World Fascism," *Pittsburgh Courier*, January 19, 1945; report of the CAA publication *New Africa* and its summary of events in 1944, *Chicago Defender*, February 17, 1945.

61. On the role of black gospel quartets in expanding and legitimating unionism, see Kelley, *Race Rebels*, pp. 40–42.

CHAPTER TWO   Democracy or Empire?

1. P. Olisanwuche Esedebe, *Pan-Africanism: The Idea and Movement, 1776–1963* (Washington, D.C.: Howard University Press, 1982), p. 136; Thomas Borstelmann, *Apartheid's Reluctant Uncle: The United States and Southern Africa in the Early Cold War* (New York: Oxford University Press, 1993), pp. 24–25.

2. George Padmore, "Hitler Makes British Drop Color Bar," *Crisis*, 48, no. 3 (1941): 72; C. L. R. James, *A History of Pan-African Revolt* (1938; Chicago: Charles H. Kerr, 1995); James, *The Black*

Jacobins: Toussaint L'Ouverture and the San Domingo Revolution (1938; London: Allen and Busby, 1980). On James, see Paul Buhle, ed., *C. L. R. James: His Life and Work* (London: Allison & Busby, 1986); W. E. B. Du Bois, *Black Reconstruction in America; an essay toward a history of the role black folk played in the attempt to reconstruct democracy in America, 1860–1880* (New York: Russell & Russell, [c1963]).

3. Paul Gordon Lauren, *Power and Prejudice: The Politics and Diplomacy of Racial Discrimination* (Boulder: Westview Press, 1988), pp. 200–201. See Christopher Thorne, *The Issue of War: States, Societies, and the Far Eastern Conflict of 1941–1945* (London: Hamish Hamilton, 1985), esp. pp. 106–7, for a discussion of Japanese victories. See also Cheah Boon Kheng, *Red Star over Malaya: Resistance and Social Conflict during and after the Japanese Occupation of Malaya, 1941–1946* (Singapore: Singapore University Press, 1983); and Benedict Anderson, *Java in a Time of Revolution: Occupation and Resistance, 1944–1946* (Ithaca: Cornell University Press, 1972).

4. George Padmore, "Race Issue Takes Spotlight in Great Britain," *Chicago Defender*, May 23, 1942, p. 1.

5. John Robert Badger, "World View: A Stroke of Irony," *Chicago Defender*, November 21, 1942, p. 15. Likewise, the *Pittsburgh Courier* editorial "Why Cripps Failed," April 18, 1942, argued that "when force remains in the hands of alien races there can be no real independence nor successful defense against foreign invaders, as recently demonstrated in Malaya, Burma and Java." This theme continued to be important throughout the war. See, e.g., "Holland and her Colonial Possessions," *Chicago Defender*, November 11, 1944, arguing that during the Japanese invasion the people of Java and Sumatra took the "attitude that one master was as good as another."

6. Walter White, "People and Places," *Chicago Defender*, March 6, 1943, p. 15.

7. Liu Liang-Mo, "China Speaks: Will India Be Another Burma? Colored Races Have Big Stake in War," *Pittsburgh Courier*, November 7, 1942, p. 7.

8. Editorial, *Pittsburgh Courier*, February 22, 1942.

9. Ellis A. Williams, "West Indians Unsympathetic to British War Effort," *Chicago Defender*, September 12, 1942, p. 4.

10. Editorial, *Pittsburgh Courier*, July 11, 1942.

11. Lauren, *Power and Prejudice*, pp. 138–39; M. S. Venkataramani and B. K. Shrivastava, *Roosevelt, Gandhi, Churchill: America and the Last Phase of India's Freedom Struggle* (New Delhi: Radiant, 1983), pp. 9–12.

12. A U.S. intelligence report of April 21, 1943, noted initial skepticism followed by growing hope among West Africans about the Atlantic Charter. See "A Strategic Survey of the Gold Coast," reel 7, frame 0890,OSS/State Department Intelligence and Research Reports, vol. 13, Africa (1941–1961), microfilm, Columbia University. On the responses of Africans and other colonized peoples to the Atlantic Charter, see Kenneth Robert Janken, *Rayford W. Logan and the Dilemma of the African-American Intellectual* (Amherst: University of Massachusetts Press, 1993), pp. 167–68; and Borstelmann, *Apartheid's Reluctant Uncle*, p. 13. See also Francis Meli, *South Africa Belongs to Us: A History of the ANC* (Bloomington: Indiana University Press, 1988), for analysis of responses among the nonwhite peoples of South Africa.

13. George Padmore, "Nigeria Questions Intent of Atlantic Charter," *Chicago Defender*, January 31, 1942, p. 12; "Twenty Million Africans Ask Churchill to Explain Atlantic Charter Meaning," *Pittsburgh Courier*, February 7, 1942, p. 12.

14. "Can't Grant India Dominion Status or End Color Bar Yet Says British," *Chicago Defender*, February 14, 1942, p. 9; "Churchill Still Not Specific in Replying to Nigerian Charter Inquiry," *Chicago Defender*, March 7, 1942, p. 12; "Britain's Reply to Africa," *Chicago Defender*, March 14, 1942. See also "What about an Atlantic Charter?" *Pittsburgh Courier*, April 25, 1942; "What

about a World Charter?" and "Asiatics Seeking Pacific Charter," *Pittsburgh Courier*, May 16, 1942.

15. American Committee on Africa, "The War and Peace Aims," in *The Atlantic Charter and Africa from an American Standpoint* (New York, 1942), p. 31; P. L. Prattis, "The Horizon: Churchill Singles Himself Out as the Defiant Exponent of Exploitation of Browns and Blacks and Yellows," *Pittsburgh Courier*, November 21, 1942, p. 13; Kumar Goshal, "As An Indian Sees It: Churchill's Speech Omits Mention of Colonial People and Their Fight for Freedom," *Pittsburgh Courier*, December 12, 1942, p. 12; Horace R. Cayton, "That Charter: We Seem To Be Reneging on the Principles of the Atlantic Charter," *Pittsburgh Courier*, November 28, 1942, p. 12.

16. Lauren, *Power and Prejudice*, pp. 140–41.

17. George S. Schuyler, in *Pittsburgh Courier*, March 14, 1942.

18. "Danger from Overseas," *Chicago Defender*, November 28, 1942.

19. *Pittsburgh Courier*, "In Defense of Churchill," December 5, 1942. See also P. L. Prattis, "Churchill Singles Himself Out"; and Goshal, "Churchill's Speech Omits Mention of Colonial People."

20. "Wanted: An African Charter," *Pittsburgh Courier*, December 19, 1942.

21. "'Atlantic Charter Applies To All' Says Roosevelt," *Pittsburgh Courier*, November 7, 1942, p. 7. See also "Adopts 8-Point Plan for Darker World Peoples," *Pittsburgh Courier*, November 21, 1948, p. 8, on the U.S. government position; and "Sumner Wells 'Extend Atlantic Charter to All People': His Pleas," *Pittsburgh Courier*, June 6, 1942, p. 1, on the undersecretary of state's assertion that "the Principles of the Atlantic Charter must be guaranteed to the world as a whole in all oceans and in all continents."

22. See, e.g., *New Africa* 4, nos. 4–9 (1945).

23. "Where Does Mr. Hull Stand?" and "The Four Freedoms," *Chicago Defender*, December 26, 1942.

24. L. D. Reddick, "Africa: Test of the Atlantic Charter," *Crisis* 50, no. 7 (1943): 202.

25. "India: England's Thorn," *Pittsburgh Courier*, November 18, 1939.

26. "India Justified in Freedom Fight, Readers Declare," *Pittsburgh Courier*, October 10, 1942, p. 1. In mid-August 1942 an American Institute of Public Opinion poll registered 43 percent of Americans favoring immediate independence for India. See Gary R. Hess, *America Encounters India, 1941–1947* (Baltimore: Johns Hopkins University Press, 1971), pp. 83–84. On U.S. relations with the Indian independence movement during the war, see also M. S. Venkataramani and B. K. Shrivastava, *Quit India: The American Response to the 1942 Struggle* (New Delhi: Vikas, 1979); Venkataramani and Shrivastava, *Roosevelt, Gandhi, Churchill*; Kenton J. Clymer, *Quest for Freedom: The United States and India's Independence* (New York: Columbia University Press, 1994).

27. Martin Bauml Duberman, *Paul Robeson* (New York: Knopf, 1988), pp. 225, 266.

28. "Rally for Cause of Free India," *Chicago Defender*, September 12, 1942, p. 3.

29. In *News of Africa* 1, no. 2 (1942): 1; Hollis R. Lynch, *Black American Radicals and the Liberation of Africa: The Council on African Affairs, 1937–1955* (Ithaca: Africana Studies and Research Center, Cornell University, 1978), p. 26. See also *News of Africa* 1, no. 3 (1942): 1, for a report on the rally.

30. Venkataramani and Shrivastava, *Quit India*, p. 295.

31. Venkataramani and Shrivastava, *Roosevelt, Gandhi, Churchill*, p. 52; Venkataramani and Shrivastava, *Quit India*, pp. 295–96; Hess, *America Encounters India*, pp. 63–64.

32. Venkataramani and Shrivastava, *Roosevelt, Gandhi, Churchill*, p. 255; Hess, *America Encounters India*, pp. 91–92.

33. Historians have tended to argue that the roots of black Americans' opposition to the war lay in feelings of racial solidarity with the Japanese, but the argument that "race, not class, was the distinguishing element" in African American reservations seriously misreads the complexity of the anticolonial position. See, e.g., Clayton R. Koppes and Gregory D. Black, "Blacks, Loyalty, and Motion-Picture Propaganda in World War II," *Journal of American History* 73, no. 2 (1986): 385.

34. "Imperialism Must End," *Chicago Defender*, January 9, 1943.

35. Denton J. Brooks Jr., "Gandhi's Stand May Cause Crisis in Allied Ranks," *Chicago Defender*, August 8, 1942, pp. 1–2. See also "Mr. Nehru Goes to Town," *Pittsburgh Courier*, March 14, 1942.

36. Howard Thurman, *With Head and Heart: The Autobiography of Howard Thurman* (New York: Harcourt Brace Jovanovich, 1979), pp. 130–35.

37. "Dr. Thurman Speaks on Indian Question: One of America's Great Mystics and Religious Leaders Gives Views," *Pittsburgh Courier*, August 29, 1942, p. 14.

38. George Padmore, "India Leaders Want British to Quit: Want Complete Independence as Price for War Support," *Pittsburgh Courier*, July 25, 1942, p. 2. See also "Mr. Nehru Goes to Town," *Pittsburgh Courier*, March 14, 1942; and J. A. Rogers, "Giving India Her Independence: The Only Weapon against Axis," *Pittsburgh Courier*, August 8, 1942, p. 8, for reports on Nehru.

39. "U.S. Mediation of Indian Crisis Sought by NAACP," and "Pandit Nehru Refused Air by Networks: Diplomacy Caused Speech Suppression Claim 3 Radio Chains," *Chicago Defender*, August 15, 1942; "Showdown in India," *Pittsburgh Courier*, August 15, 1942.

40. "Showdown in India," *Pittsburgh Courier*, July 25, 1942.

41. "Gandhi Tells Churchill: 'Free India and Africa and the Colored Races Will Help the United Nations Turn Japan out of the Countries She Has Conquered,'" *Pittsburgh Courier*, August 8, 1942, p. 20.

42. George Padmore, "Gandhi Urges Unity of All Dark Races," *Chicago Defender*, January 20, 1945.

43. "Gandhi Leery of U.S. Aid for India: Fears American Race Prejudice," *Chicago Defender*, May 23, 1942, p. 1. On the same day the *Pittsburgh Courier* carried an almost identical article. Neither had a byline, but both were "By our London correspondent," George Padmore. See "Britain and Gandhi," *Chicago Defender*, March 6, 1943, on Gandhi's imprisonment.

44. S. Chandrasekhar, "I Meet the Mahatma," *Crisis* 49, no. 10 (1942): 312, 313, 331. See also "Mahatma Gandhi Sent Message to American Negroes Five Years Ago," *Pittsburgh Courier*, September 12, 1942, p. 1, for report of an interview with Gandhi by Channing Tobias.

45. Denton J. Brooks Jr., "U.S. Ignores Atlantic Charter, India Fears," *Chicago Defender*, November 11, 1944, p. 16.

46. Richard Dalfiume, *Desegregation of the U.S. Armed Forces: Fighting on Two Fronts, 1939–1953* (Columbia: University of Missouri Press, 1969), pp. 44–104, 204–7.

47. Editorial, *Pittsburgh Courier*, June 8, 1940. See also Louis R. Lautier, "Europe Is on the March," *Pittsburgh Courier*, September 9, 1939, p. 4; and "Senegalese Fight War out of German Trap, Losses Heavy," *Pittsburgh Courier*, September 23, 1939, p. 1.

48. Editorial, *Pittsburgh Courier*, August 17, 1940.

49. Editorial, *Pittsburgh Courier*, September 14, 1940.

50. "The African Offensive," *Chicago Defender*, November 21, 1942. Padmore articles include "African Troops Go into Battle on Burmese Front," *Defender*, February 26, 1944; "Padmore Tells How Panzers' Invasion of Suez Was Checked," *Pittsburgh Courier*, September 12, 1942; "Padmore Finds Colorful Characters in Second AEF," *Pittsburgh Courier*, September 26, 1942, p. 1; "Padmore Visits Troops in Britain," *Pittsburgh Courier*, August 15, 1942; "Colored U.S. Troops May Defend African Life Line," *Pittsburgh Courier*, May 23, 1942; and "African Troops Lead Ad-

vance on Burma Japs," *Chicago Defender*, January 6, 1945. See also, *Pittsburgh Courier*, July 4, 1942, for reports on British military experts' recommendation that black American troops be used to drive the Germans out of Dakar, Senegal.

51. Editorial, *Chicago Defender*, July 11, 1942. Black American journalists also carefully followed Roosevelt's wartime alliance with Admiral Jean Darlan of the Vichy government in France. See John Robert Badger, "World View," *Chicago Defender*, December 12, 1942, p. 15.

52. "Allies Send Colonials to Firing Line Unarmed," *Chicago Defender*, April 11, 1942, p. 9.

53. Editorial, *Chicago Defender*, July 11, 1942.

54. "British Banish African Labor Chief to Exile: Wallace-Johnson, Man Who Organized Natives Sent to Sherboro," *Chicago Defender*, May 23, 1942, p. 2. See "West African Leader Freed by British," *Chicago Defender*, January 27, 1945, for Wallace-Johnson's release from prison.

55. See, e.g., Lee Finkle, "The Conservative Aims of Militant Rhetoric: Black Protest during World War II," *Journal of American History* 60 (December 1973): 692–93; and Finkle, *Forum for Protest: The Black Press during World War II* (Cranbury, N.J.: Associated University Presses, 1975).

56. "Lost Faith," *Pittsburgh Courier*, May 15, 1943.

57. Langston Hughes, "Brazenness of Empire: From Here to Yonder," *Chicago Defender*, January 27, 1945.

58. John Robert Badger, "World View," *Chicago Defender*, November 28, 1942, p. 15; Badger, "World View: A Stroke of Irony," *Chicago Defender*, November 21, 1942, p. 15. The CAA's *New Africa* consistently carried coverage of African troops: e.g., *New Africa* 3, no. 4 (1944): 1–3. "Africans at War," *New Africa* 2, no. 2 (1943): 2, covered troops from British East Africa, the Belgian Congo, British West Africa, Ethiopia, and the Union of South Africa. See also "Africans at War: Home Front Production," *New Africa* 2, no. 3 (1943): 2; "Review of 1943: Africa and the Fight for Freedom," *New Africa* 3, no. 1 (1944): 1–2; and "When the African Soldiers Come Marching Home?" *New Africa* 3 no. 9 (1944): 2.

59. "British Hypocrisy" and "The Atlantic Charter and India," *Chicago Defender*, August 22, 1942.

60. Reddick, "Africa: Test of the Atlantic Charter," p. 217.

61. Walter White, "Britain and the Color Problem: Pot and Kettle," *Chicago Defender*, February 17, 1945.

62. John Robert Badger, "World View," *Chicago Defender*, May 6, 1944, p. 13.

63. "Racial Differences Exist on Trinidad, but Islanders Opposed to Jim Crowism," *Pittsburgh Courier*, November 1, 1941, p. 12.

64. Ramona Lowe, "Rum and Coke Author Sings Woes of Trinidad after Invasion by GIs," *Chicago Defender*, March 31, 1945, p. 11. See Louis Nizer, *My Life in Court* (New York: Doubleday, 1961), pp. 265–328.

65. Alfred E. Smith, *Chicago Defender*, May 29, 1943, p. 3.

66. Randy Dixon, "Pawns of Empire Builders: Interest in Colonial Possessions on Upswing," *Pittsburgh Courier*, October 21, 1944, p. 3.

67. John Robert Badger, "World View: Prospects for Surinam," *Chicago Defender*, January 16, 1943, p. 16.

68. John Robert Badger, "World View: Caribbean Economics," *Chicago Defender*, May 13, 1944, p. 13; Badger, "World View," *Chicago Defender*, May 27, 1944, p. 13; Alfred E. Smith, "U.S. Hurts, Doesn't Help, Puerto Rico in Solving Island's Ills of Hunger, Disease," *Chicago Defender*, May 22, 1943, p. 9.

69. "Independence for Puerto Rico," *Pittsburgh Courier*, June 19, 1943.

70. Denton J. Brooks Jr., "Negro Fate in U.S. Tied to Puerto Rico Freedom," *Chicago Defender*, July 31, 1943, p. 7. Brooks also traced the history of opposition to U.S control from the begin-

ning of American occupation in 1898 and argued that until the Popular Party took control in 1940, Puerto Rican "legislation was ruled by the sugar trust."

71. Denton J. Brooks Jr., "Sugar Trust Gets Congress Aid to Enforce Puerto Rico Poverty," *Chicago Defender*, July 10, 1943; Brooks, "Congress Is Threat to Puerto Rico Reform," *Chicago Defender*, September 4, 1943, p. 13; Brooks, "Puerto Rico Up in Arms against Colonial Status," *Chicago Defender*, August 7, 1943, p. 13; Brooks, "Puerto Rico a Test Tube for Atlantic Charter," *Chicago Defender*, September 11, 1943.

72. "Free Puerto Rico," *Chicago Defender*, October 16, 1943.

73. Harold Preece, "Haiti Now a Weed Patch under Wall Street Rule," *Chicago Defender*, August 5, 1944, p. 1.

74. "Haiti to Supply U.S. with Needed Rubber," *Pittsburgh Courier*, August 9, 1941, p. 3; "Haiti Starts Vast Rubber Plantation," *Chicago Defender*, January 31, 1942, p. 3; "A New Day for Haiti," *Pittsburgh Courier*, October 30, 1943.

75. Preece, "Haiti Now a Weed Patch under Wall Street Rule." See also Harold Preece, "Whites Invade Haiti to Run Rubber Plantations for Wall Street," *Chicago Defender*, August 19, 1944, p. 1; Preece, "'Quadroon Quislings' Face Revolt in Haiti," *Chicago Defender*, September 2, 1944, p. 1. See "Misrepresented Haiti," *Baltimore Afro-American*, October 30, 1943, for earlier criticisms of the Elie Lescot government.

76. "May Set Up Naval Base at Monrovia," *Pittsburgh Courier*, October 5, 1940, p. 5; "U.S. May Build Air Bases in Liberia," *Pittsburgh Courier*, August 2, 1941, p. 1.

77. Ernest E. Johnson, "The Liberian State Visit," *Crisis* 50, no. 10 (1943): 296–98, 312–14.

78. George Padmore, "Padmore Sees Wall St. Invasion of Liberia," *Chicago Defender*, November 18, 1944, p. 2.

79. Arthur Ingram Hayman and Harold Preece, *Lighting Up Liberia* (New York: Creative Age Press, 1943). Hayman, a former engineer for the Firestone company in Liberia, and Preece charged Firestone, the first American big business in West Africa, with bringing the "worst forms of modern industrial exploitation to Liberia . . . at the expense of thousands of black peasants who were uprooted from their fields to make way for the rubber plantation." They also charged the U.S. government with propping up a clique headed by President Arthur Barclay and failing to realize "the importance of building democracy in Liberia" (p. 69). Hayman published an article in the January 1943 issue of the magazine *Tomorrow*, summarizing the main points of the book. In a classic defense of imperialism, Henry Villard, head of the African division of the State Department, attacked the article, calling Liberia "a most successful experiment in self-government by colored people," endorsing Barclay's relationship with the United States, and defending the Firestone company; see Harry McAlpin, "Engineer's Attack on Liberia Policy Draws Fire of U.S. State Department," *Chicago Defender*, January 23, 1943, p. 6.

80. Liberian diplomats sought assurance that Liberia's rubber production, expanded to help meet U.S. war needs, would not be supplanted by the synthetic rubber industry in the postwar period. See John P. Davis, "'Liberia in Need of Negro Technicians' Tubman Tells Courier," *Pittsburgh Courier*, June 5, 1943, p. 1; "Liberia's Chief of State Spikes Lend-Lease Talk: President Trippe of Pan-American Airways, Which Has Air Base for Clipper Ships at Site Near Monrovia, Confers With Barclay," *Pittsburgh Courier*, June 5, 1943, p. 4.

81. John Robert Badger, "World View: Mission to Firestone," *Chicago Defender*, June 19, 1943, p. 15; Badger, "World View: Liberia and Negro America," *Chicago Defender*, June 26, 1943, p. 15.

82. Horace R. Cayton, "An Awakening: The Negro Now Fights for Democratic Rights of All the World's Peoples," *Pittsburgh Courier*, February 27, 1943, p. 14. Cayton, a frequent *Courier* contributor, was a Chicago-based sociologist whose works included *Black Metropolis: A Study of Negro Life in a Northern City*, co-authored with St. Clair Drake (New York: Harcourt, Brace and

Company, 1945), and *Black Workers and the New Unions* (Chapel Hill: University of North Carolina Press, 1939), coauthored with George S. Mitchell.

83. Edgar T. Rouzeau, "Hitler Is Only a Symbol of World Exploitation: Colored Americans Need to Think in Terms of World Conditions Affecting Their Kind," *Pittsburgh Courier*, May 23, 1942, p. 12.

84. Edgar T. Rouzeau, "An Independent India Would Help Black America Get Rights: Fate of India Closely Related to Struggles of Negroes for Enjoyment of Democratic Rights in America," *Pittsburgh Courier*, April 4, 1942, p. 14.

85. "British Hypocrisy" and "The Atlantic Charter and India."

86. "Paul Robeson Speaks of the Negro's Desire for Freedom," *Pittsburgh Courier*, April 22, 1944, p. 5.

87. See Anthony Brewer, *Marxist Theories of Imperialism: A Critical Survey* (London: Routledge & Kegan Paul, 1990), for the major strands of thought and central debates about imperialism.

88. Ralph J. Bunche, *A World View of Race* (Washington, D.C.: Associates in Negro Folk Education, 1936), pp. 42–43, 92–93; Lawrence S. Finkelstein, "Bunche and the Colonial World: From Trusteeship to Decolonization," in *Ralph Bunche: The Man and His Times*, ed. Benjamin Rivlin (New York: Holmes & Meier, 1990), pp. 110–12; Walter A. Jackson, *Gunnar Myrdal and America's Conscience: Social Engineering and Racial Liberalism, 1938–1987* (Chapel Hill: University of North Carolina Press, 1990), pp. 103–4, 42–43.

89. John Robert Badger, "World View," *Chicago Defender*, November 28, 1942, p. 15.

90. "'Race Is an Invention,' Says George Schuyler," *Pittsburgh Courier*, March 28, 1942, p. 24.

91. See James L. Roark, "American Black Leaders: The Response to Colonialism and the Cold War, 1943–1953," *African Historical Studies* 4, no. 2 (1971): 258.

92. "The Result of Hate," *Chicago Defender*, March 26, 1938.

93. *Paul Robeson Speaks*, pp. 147–48.

94. Max Yergan, "Negro Sees His Future Linked to Independence for 400,000,000," *Pittsburgh Courier* magazine section, September 26, 1942. The same issue contained another in-depth article on India—V. V. Oak, "A Plea For India's Freedom"—and George Padmore, "The Atlantic Charter and the British Colonies."

95. George Padmore, "The Second World War and the Darker Races," *Crisis* 45, no. 11 (1939): 327–28. See also Padmore, "A New World War for Colonies," *Crisis* 44, no. 10 (1937): 302–4, 309–10, for an analysis of the economics of colonialism.

96. See Gerald Horne, *Black and Red: W. E. B. Du Bois and the Afro-American Response to the Cold War, 1944–1963* (Albany: State University of New York Press, 1986), pp. 20–24; Roark, "American Black Leaders," pp. 256–57.

97. "F.D.R., Churchill Asked to Consider Color Problems," *Baltimore Afro-American*, August 28, 1943, p. 9.

98. "Social and Political Forces in Dependent Areas of the Caribbean," December 1944, pp. 402–3, RG 59, 844.00/3-945, National Archives.

CHAPTER THREE   To Forge a Colonial International

1. "British Strangle Azikiwe Papers," *Baltimore Afro-American*, March 30, 1946, pp. 1, 17.

2. John Hope Franklin, *From Slavery to Freedom* (New York: McGraw-Hill Publishing Co., 1988), pp. 597–98; Herbert Shapiro, *White Violence and Black Response: From Reconstruction to Montgomery* (Amherst: University of Massachusetts Press, 1988), pp. 310–41; George Lipsitz, *Rainbow at Midnight: Labor and Culture in the 1940s* (Urbana: University of Illinois Press, 1994), pp. 69–71; Thomas Borstelmann, *Apartheid's Reluctant Uncle: The United States and*

Southern Africa in the Early Cold War (New York: Oxford University Press, 1993), p. 20; Dominic J. Capeci and Martha Wilkerson, *Layered Violence: The Detroit Rioters of 1943* (Jackson: University of Mississippi Press, 1991); Chester Himes, *If He Hollers Let Him Go* (New York: Signet Books, 1971).

3. On Amy Jacques Garvey, see Barbara Bair, "True Women, Real Men: Gender, Ideology, and Social Roles in the Garvey Movement," in *Gendered Domains: Rethinking Public and Private in Women's History*, ed. Dorothy O. Helly and Susan M. Reverby (Ithaca: Cornell University Press, 1992), pp. 162–63.

4. On the earlier Pan-African Congresses, see W. E. B. Du Bois, *The World and Africa: An Inquiry into the Part Which Africa Has Played in World History* (New York: International, 1987), pp. 7–12, 240–44; Manning Marable, *W. E. B. Du Bois: Black Radical Democrat* (Boston: Twayne, 1986), pp. 100–107; Paul Gordon Lauren, *Power and Prejudice: The Politics and Diplomacy of Racial Discrimination* (Boulder, Colo.: Westview Press, 1988), pp. 64, 77–79, 83–84, 106–7; George Padmore, *Pan-Africanism or Communism* (Garden City, N.Y.: Anchor Books, 1972), pp. 107–13, 117–22.

5. A. Jacques Garvey to Du Bois, January 31, 1944, W. E. B. Du Bois Papers, microfilm collection, Columbia University, reel 56, frame 104.

6. In addition to Garvey and Moody, he approached the West African Students' Union (WASU) and Robeson and Yergan for the CAA: Du Bois to Garvey, April 8, 1944, and Garvey to Du Bois, April 24, 1944, Du Bois Papers, reel 56, frames 110, 111. WASU was founded in 1925 by Lapido Solanke and Dr. Bankole-Bright, a Sierra Leonean medical practitioner and a member of the colony's Legislative Council; see G. O. Olusanya, *The West African Students' Union and the Politics of Decolonization, 1925–1958* (Ibadan, 1982), p. 4. See also in Du Bois Papers: Du Bois to Solanke, April 17, 1944, reel 56, frame 670; Du Bois to Robeson and Du Bois to Yergan, April 7, 1944, and Yergan to Du Bois, April 21, 1944, reel 55, frames 1130–31; Du Bois to Harold Moody, April 7, 1944, and Harold Moody to Du Bois, April 29, 1944, reel 56, frame 317–18.

7. Du Bois to Solanke, April 17, 1944, Du Bois Papers, reel 56, frame 670. Moody and Garvey, like Du Bois, argued for the necessity of the involvement of "Africans and persons of African descent" in the liberation of Africa. Garvey exemplified the emphasis on leadership from the diaspora when she appealed to Du Bois, "We are depending on you to help frame this African Charter of Freedom for *Africans at home and abroad*. . . . All people of African descent must be included": Garvey to Du Bois, January 31, 1944, Du Bois Papers, reel 56, frame 104.

8. Garvey to Du Bois, January 31, 1944. In the cultural argument about bonds between Africans and those of African descent in the diaspora, there were deep affinities between some Harlem Renaissance writers and the black organizations formed in Britain and the Caribbean in the 1920s. On the Harlem Renaissance, see Charles T. Davis, *Black Is the Color of the Cosmos: Essays on Afro-American Literature and Culture, 1942–1981*, ed. Henry Louis Gates Jr. (Washington, D.C.: Howard University Press, 1989), pp. 63–79.

The African American philosopher Alain Locke had argued in an address delivered to WASU and reprinted in its journal that "to-day the American Negro is culturally re-discovering Africa and many lines of thinking are trying to bridge the broken span between the Motherland and to make the racial background effective in our group life and culture." See Frederick Robb, "Negro in America: A Message to the Africans," *WASU*, August 1928, pp. 12–16; and Alain Locke, "Afro-Americans and West Africans: A New Understanding," *WASU*, January 1929, pp. 18–24, British Library, London.

A later article explained the politics of the organization in terms of the complex meaning of *wasu*, which in Yoruba, in one of the Gold Coast languages, in Efik, and in Ibo, meant respectively, "to preach," "self-help," "to wipe off disgrace or reproach," and "to speak first in one's own interests"—the last interpreted as a call for "acquiring and developing healthy national aspirations." See "The Philosophy of the Term 'Wasu,'" *WASU*, December 1932, pp. 1–2.

9. Padmore, *Pan-Africanism or Communism*, pp. 139, 142–48; James R. Hooker, *Black Revolutionary: George Padmore's Path from Communism to Pan-Africanism* (New York: Praeger, 1967), pp. 91–99; Imanuel Geiss, *The Pan-African Movement: A History of Pan-Africanism in America, Europe, and Africa* (New York: Africana, 1974), chap. 19; Lauren, *Power and Prejudice*, pp. 162–63.

Although leadership shifted to new organizations, the politics of earlier groups did not remain static. In WASU, for example, shifts during the war were similar to those in African American politics. In 1943 its journal explained "why we chose these critical days of war to ask for complete self-government." It stressed the Atlantic Charter, "which has been declared not to include us," and the "lessons of Malaya and Burma," as well as the "obvious need of giving the peoples of the Empire something to fight for": *WASU*, May 1943, pp. 7–8, CO 554/127/12: 143811; PRO, Kew Gardens. For the history of WASU and this particular shift, see Hakim Adi, "The West African Students Union" (Ph.D. diss., School of Oriental and African Studies, London).

10. "Jamaican Leader Seeks Pan-Africa Unity," *Chicago Defender*, January 5, 1946, p. 9.

11. Nelson Lichtenstein, "From Corporatism to Collective Bargaining: Organized Labor and the Eclipse of Social Democracy in the Postwar Era," in *The Rise and Fall of the New Deal Order, 1930–1980*, ed. Steve Fraser and Gary Gerstle (Princeton: Princeton University Press, 1989), p. 135.

12. On increases in the numbers of black workers employed as skilled craftsmen and semiskilled operatives and on the diversification of the black labor force during World War II, see William H. Harris, *The Harder We Run: Black Workers since the Civil War* (New York: Oxford University Press, 1982), pp. 113–22. On shifts in black employment and job diversification, see Neil A. Wynn, *The Afro-American and the Second World War* (New York: Holmes & Meier, 1975), pp. 55–59. On increases in the number of black workers in industrial and unionized jobs, see Nelson Lichtenstein, *Labor's War at Home: The CIO in World War II* (Cambridge: Cambridge University Press, 1982), pp. 124–26; August Meier and Elliott Rudwick, *Black Detroit and the Rise of the UAW* (New York: Oxford University Press, 1979).

13. Lipsitz, *Rainbow at Midnight*, p. 74.

14. On local and state FEPC initiatives, see Wynn, *Afro-American*, p. 55; *New York Age*, October 27, 1945; Martha Biondi, "The Early Civil Rights Movement in New York City, 1945–1954" (Ph.D. diss. in progress, Columbia University), chap. 1.

15. While endorsing the standards for labor adopted at the conference, Robeson and the CAA also criticized the refusal of the AFL leadership to share American representation at the ILO with the CIO. See "I.L.O. Standards Endorsed—Voice For Colonies Urged," *New Africa* 3, no. 4 (1944).

16. Thyra Edwards, "The ILO and Postwar Planning for the African Colonies," *Crisis* 51, no. 7 (1944): 218–20. The AME met in conference in Philadelphia at the same time as the ILO conference.

17. Patrick Renshaw, *American Labour and Consensus Capitalism, 1935–1990* (London: Macmillan, 1991), p. 121.

18. George Padmore, "World Parley of Labor Opens," *Chicago Defender*, February 3, 1945, p. 1; "World Labor and the Color Line," *Chicago Defender*, February 3, 1945.

19. "Amazing Jamaica Labor Boss Stages Blitz at Polls, Becomes Dictator," and George Padmore, "South Africans Win Two-Month Transit Strike," both in *Chicago Defender*, February 3, 1945.

20. George Padmore, "Labor Unites Colonials at WTU Confab," *Pittsburgh Courier*, February 17, 1945, p. 1; Padmore, "Two Colonials in WTU Group," *Pittsburgh Courier*, February 24, 1945,

p. 1. See also Padmore, "World Labor Parley Hears Colonial Plea," *Chicago Defender*, February 17, 1945, p. 1; and Padmore, "British Queen Worried over U.S. Race Riots: Unionists Told She Hopes for End of Violence: World Labor Parley Gives Full Rights to Colonials," *Chicago Defender*, February 24, 1945, p. 1.

21. See, e.g., George Padmore, "World Conference Hears Voice of Black Labor," *Crisis* 52, no. 4 (1945): pp. 105–6.

22. "Logan Wires Hillman," *Pittsburgh Courier*, February 17, 1945, p. 2.

23. Henry Lee Moon, "British Imperial Rule Defied by African Unionist at World Parley," *Chicago Defender*, April 14, 1945, p. 14. See also "World Aid for Colonial People Receives Attention at International Labor Congress in London," *New Africa* 4, no. 2 (1945); and "Hail African Delegates Role at the Labor Parley," *New Africa* 4, no. 3 (1945), for the role of African delegates at the conference.

24. Henry Lee Moon, "Negro Gets World Trade Union Congress Post," *Chicago Defender*, March 3, 1945, p. 1.

25. "Hillman Betrays Africans," *Pittsburgh Courier*, October 13, 1945. On Hillman and the WFTU Paris Conference, see Steven Fraser, *Labor Will Rule: Sidney Hillman and the Rise of American Labor* (New York: Free Press, 1991), pp. 547–49.

26. Editorial, *Pittsburgh Courier*, October 20, 1945.

27. The CAA, for example, urged the WFTU "to end the division between free and colonial peoples, as a guarantee to the security of all labor"; see "Colonial Freedom Urged at Paris Labor Parley," *New Africa* 4, no. 9 (1945): 6.

28. Henry Lee Moon, "Pan-African Conference Set for Paris in Fall," *Chicago Defender*, March 10, 1945, p. 2. See "World Aid for Colonial Peoples Receives Attention at International Labor Congress in London," *New Africa* 4, no. 2 (1945): 1, for the CAA's report on the meeting and Robeson's message to the conference.

29. George Padmore in *African Standard* 6, no. 23 (1944): 3 (official organ of the West African Youth League, Sierra Leone Section), Marx Memorial Library, London.

30. George Padmore, "Call for Pan-African Parley in Paris Drafted by British Colonial Leaders," *Chicago Defender*, March 17, 1945, p. 18; Padmore, "Pan-African Congress Plans Paris Meeting: Colonial Charter to Outline Peace Plans," *Pittsburgh Courier*, March 3, 1945, p. 1; Du Bois to Padmore, March 22, 1945, Du Bois Papers, reel 57, frame 1028. See Du Bois to Moody, March 22, 1945, reel 57, frame 520, in which Du Bois wrote that he had "heard through Negro American Newspapers a long report from Padmore saying that various organizations in London have called a Pan-African Congress. Is this authentic?" See also Marable, *W. E. B. Du Bois*, pp. 164–65. On the organization and significance of the conference, see Padmore, *Pan-Africanism or Communism*, pp. 132–48 (this 1956 account, however, contains inaccuracies in conference logistics).

31. Du Bois to Walter White, NAACP Memorandum, 1945, Du Bois Papers, reel 57, frame 1043.

32. Du Bois to Padmore, Du Bois Papers, reel 57, frame 1037.

33. Padmore to Du Bois, Du Bois Papers, reel 57, frame 1041.

34. Padmore to Du Bois, April 12, 1945, Du Bois Papers, reel 57, frame 1033. Padmore introduced himself as a nephew of the Pan-Africanist Sylvester Williams.

35. Henry Lee Moon to Du Bois, April 9, 1945, Du Bois Papers, reel 56, frame 1342.

36. Du Bois to Harold Moody, April 11, 1945, Du Bois Papers, reel 57, frame 522.

37. Du Bois to Hunton and Hunton to Du Bois, January 23, 1945, Du Bois Papers, reel 57, frames 387–88.

38. Du Bois to Harold Moody, April 11, 1945. Padmore invited Philip Murray, president of the CIO and an African American CIO delegate to the conference, and Moon discussed the confer-

ence proposals with Willard Townsend and George L. P. Weaver of the CIO: Padmore to Moon, cablegram, and Henry Moon to Philip Murray, August 22, 1945, Du Bois Papers, reel 56, frames 1343–44.

39. P. Olisanwuche Esedebe, *Pan-Africanism: The Idea and Movement, 1776–1963* (Washington, D.C.: Howard University Press, 1982), pp. 161, 163, also pp. 172–93 for a full report on the conference.

40. Geiss, *Pan-African Movement*, chap. 19; Geiss, "Some Remarks on the Development of African Trade Unions," *Journal of the Historical Society of Nigeria* 3, no. 2 (1965): 367.

41. Padmore in a *Defender* clipping, in Du Bois Papers, reel 57, frame 1071. West African coverage of the conference is beyond the scope of this book, but for an example, see the *Gold Coast Observer and Weekly Advertiser* 6, no. 35 (1945): 1.

42. Padmore in *Defender* clipping.

43. "Colonials Demand Full Independence," *Baltimore Afro-American*, October 22, 1945.

44. Padmore in *Defender* clipping, in Du Bois Papers, reel 57, frame 107.

45. In a December 30, 1946 letter Du Bois asked Padmore to "remember that the N.A.A.C.P. is not definitely committed to the Africa program. Against the desire of the secretary and several powerful members of the board, I was sent to the Fifth Pan-African Congress": Du Bois Papers, reel 59, frame 375. On his transportation problems, see Du Bois to Harold Laski, University of London, requesting help in obtaining a visa, September 15, 1945, reel 57, frame 513. See also Du Bois to Metz T. P. Lochard, editor, *Chicago Defender*, September 14, 1945, reel 56, and October 11, 1945, reel 56, frames 1294 and 1299.

46. Padmore to Du Bois, September 18, 1945, Du Bois Papers, reel 57, frame 1048. Later, Padmore would claim that he had invited the Council on African Affairs, "the Garvey organization," and the African Academy of Arts and Research directly, but that the CAA had never responded: Padmore to Du Bois, August 9, 1946, and Du Bois to Padmore, July 12, 1946, reel 59, frames 370 and 366.

47. See Chapter 1.

48. Du Bois to Padmore, July 12, 1946, and Padmore to Du Bois, August 9, 1946, Du Bois Papers, reel 59, frames 366 and 369. Padmore's attack was based on alleged reports by black South African doctors in England who claimed that Yergan identified with the white church community in South Africa and treated the Africans—even the intellectuals at Fort Hare, the students and Professor Jabavu—"with the greatest contempt" (these reports are not corroborated in the extensive correspondence of Yergan and other CAA members with South Africans).

49. Padmore to Du Bois, August 9, 1946, Du Bois Papers, reel 59, frame 369; *New Africa* 4, no. 9 (1945): 3. Hunton and Du Bois also discussed the federation's work, and Du Bois telegraphed Robeson, Hunton, and Yergan that "the London Office of the Pan African Congress has asked me to lay before your meeting June sixth a ten minute statement of the plans and objectives of the movement": Du Bois to Robeson, CAA, June 3, 1946, reel 58, frame 749.

50. Following the conference Du Bois spoke at public meetings in Britain, including a mass protest meeting sponsored by the Federation of Indian Organizations in Great Britain against the use of Indian troops to suppress the struggles of the natives of Java and Indochina. Padmore reported that Du Bois "told of the fight of thirteen million coloured Americans to become first class citizens and of the ever increasing interests among them in matters affecting the hundreds of millions of darker peoples throughout Asia and Africa": George Padmore, "American Negro Will Speak for African World: Dr. Du Bois Elected Official Leader of Pan-Africanism; Interviews G. H. Wells, Professor Laski, and Other British Intellectuals," *Gold Coast Observer and Weekly Advertiser* 6, no. 37 (1945): 240.

51. Pan-African Federation, Petition to the United Nations, September 1946, Du Bois Papers, reel 59, frames 40–41.

52. Du Bois Papers, reel 59, frame 348; see also frames 340–47. For participating African and Caribbean organizations, see frames 132, 149, 486, 610, and 703 re St. Kitts–Nevis Trades and Labour Union; Kwame Nkrumah, Secretary-General, the West African National Secretariat; Ken Hill, Trades Union Congress of Jamaica; the Nyasaland African Congress (affiliated with the Pan-African Congress through Dr. Banda); and the Non-European Unity Committee, South Africa.

53. As the historian William H. Harris has pointed out (*The Harder We Run*, p. 122), despite the doubling of black Americans employed as skilled craftsmen and semiskilled operatives 1940–44, in 1945 four-fifths of black workers were still unskilled laborers. For an occupational breakdown comparing the employment of black men for the years 1940 and 1950 (also 1960 and 1970), see William Julius Wilson, *The Declining Significance of Race: Blacks and Changing American Institutions* (Chicago: University of Chicago Press, 1980), p. 128. The most relevant figures by percentage of the work force are these: craftsmen, foremen, etc., 1940—4.5, 1950—7.8; operatives, 1940—12.7, 1950—21.3; service workers and laborers, 1940—37.1, 1950—38.1; farm workers, 1940—41.0, 1950—24.0.

54. Harris, *The Harder We Run*, p. 121.

55. On employment shifts, job diversification, and black workers in unions, see Harris, *The Harder We Run*, pp. 118–21; and Wynn, *Afro-American*, pp. 51–59.

56. Kevin K. Gaines, *Uplifting the Race: Black Leadership, Politics, and Culture since the Turn of the Century* (Chapel Hill: University of North Carolina Press, 1996), pp. 14–17.

57. Richard D. Ralston, "Colonial African Leadership: American and Afro-American Influences," *Ufahamu* 4, no. 2 (1973): 90–92. See also Ben N. Azikiwe, "Liberia Declares a Moratorium," *Southern Workman* 62, no. 6 (1933): 276–80.

58. Azikiwe remained the leading figure in Nigerian politics until he lost the 1951 interim election to Obafemi Awolowo. His changing politics with the approach of Nigerian independence and the onset of the Cold War and its effect on his relations with the CAA are covered in Chapter 6.

59. George Padmore, "African Labor," *Chicago Defender*, April 27, 1946, p. 15.

60. Harold Preece, "Africa Awakens," *Crisis* 52, no. 2 (1945): 348–50, 363.

61. "Nigerian Trade Unionists Urge Constructive Reforms: Seek Ties with U.S. Labor," *New Africa* 3, no. 9 (1944): 1; "Crisis Looms in Nigeria as Trade Unions Demand Government Act on Wages," *New Africa* 4, no. 7 (1945): 1.

62. On the Joint Emergency Committee on Nigeria, see British Embassy, Washington, D.C., to North American Department, Foreign Office (FO), London, August 13, 1945 (reference telegram no. 8087, FO to Washington, August 5, 1945), FO 371/44602:AN 2544; "Nigerian Strike Spotlights Exploitation of Labor in Colonies," *New Africa* 4, no. 8 (1945): 1; Hollis R. Lynch, *Black American Radicals and the Liberation of Africa: The Council on African Affairs, 1937–1955* (Ithaca: Africana Studies and Research Center, Cornell University, 1978), p. 47.

63. Kwame Nkrumah, "Africans in London Rally in Support of Nigerian Strikers: Africans in London Appeal to Workers of the World for Nigerian Strikers: Resolution Condemns Governor for Suppressing African Newspapers and Arresting Labor Leaders," *Gold Coast Observer and Weekly Advertiser* 6, no. 15 (1945): 114.

64. Nnamdi Azikiwe, *Suppression of the Press in West Africa*, pamphlet, in Du Bois Papers, reel 59, frame 358.

65. Charles Grannison, African Academy of Arts and Research, telegram to Halifax, July 17, 1945, requesting verification of news cables to the *Pittsburgh Courier* from George Padmore; Washington Chancery to North American Department in London, July 20, 1945, enclosing the

Grannison telegram and stating, "As matter is arousing certain amount of interest, requests information on the subject and whether Colonial Office wish any particular line to be taken in dealing with enquiries," FO 371/44602:AN 2335/95/45.

66. Walter White to Colonel Oliver Stanley, Colonial Office, July 17, 1945; R.J. Thomas to Oliver Stanley, Colonial Office (FO 371/44602:AN 2335/95/45).

67. Colonial Office, London, to British Embassy, Washington, August 8, 1945, FO 371/44602; North American Department, London, series of telegrams to the Chancery, British Embassy, Washington, August 13, 1945, requesting Embassy to respond on behalf of the Secretary of State for the Colonies, F0371/446020.

68. "British Keep Ban on African Press," *Baltimore Afro-American*, March 2, 1946, p. 7.

69. "British Strangle Azikiwe Papers: Essential Supplies, Services, Ads Denied," *Baltimore Afro-American*, March 30, 1946, p. 1.

70. "British Campaign to Smash Nigerian Papers," *Chicago Defender*, March 30, 1946, p. 7. See also "Azikiwe Charges Victimization of His Newspaper Chain by Nigerian Government," *New Africa* 5, no. 4 (1946): 1. "Rap British Gag on African Press: Demand Full Report from Colonial Office," *Chicago Defender*, April 6, 1946, p. 3.

71. Lipsitz, *Rainbow at Midnight*, pp. 120–21; Lichtenstein, "From Corporatism to Collective Bargaining," pp. 123–24; Patrick Renshaw, *American Labor and Consensus Capitalism, 1935–1990* (London: Macmillan, 1991), pp. 79–84.

72. *Baltimore Afro-American*, February 2, 1946: "Liberians Get Skilled Jobs on Harbor after Protests," p. 1; "5,000 Steel Workers Join in Demand for Higher Pay," p. 8; "Fifth of Jersey Strikers on Picket Lines Colored," p. 8; "Veterans at Picketing among General Electric Strikers," p. 8; "Trinidad Workers Ask New Union Contract," p. 8; "Jamaica Governor Halts R.R. Strike," p. 8; "Will Be Right There on the Picket Line with You Says Singer," p. 11; the same issue covered the CAA's campaign to aid famine victims in South Africa, in "$1000, Large Supply of Food Sent Starving South Africans."

73. Doxey Wilkerson attempted to recruit Hunton to serve as director of the CP-run Peoples School in Harlem and suggested working for the CAA as another option. Hunton accepted the CAA position as more in accord with his own concerns and interests. Author's interview with Doxey Wilkerson, September 8, 1991, Norwalk, Conn.

74. Dorothy Hunton, *Alphaeus Hunton: The Unsung Valiant* (Chesapeake, Va.: ECA Associates, 1986), pp. 55–57. See also Doxey A. Wilkerson, "William Alphaeus Hunton: A Life That Made a Difference," *Freedomways*, 3d quarter 1970, pp. 254–57; George B. Murphy Jr., "William Alphaeus Hunton: His Roots in Black America," *Freedomways*, 3d quarter 1970, pp. 249–52.

75. Addie W. Hunton, *William Alphaeus Hunton: A Pioneer Prophet of Young Men* (New York: Association Press, 1938), pp. 2–4; Nina Mjagkij, *Light in the Darkness: African Americans and the YMCA, 1852–1946* (Lexington: University Press of Kentucky, 1994), pp. 35–38.

76. A. Hunton, *William Alphaeus Hunton*, p. 167; D. Hunton, *Alphaeus Hunton*, pp. 1–5; Mjagkij, *Light in the Darkness*, pp. 35–38.

77. A. Hunton, *William Alphaeus Hunton*, p. 133.

78. D. Hunton, *Alphaeus Hunton*, pp. 5–13.

79. Ibid.

80. Paula Giddings, *When and Where I Enter: The Impact of Black Women on Race and Sex in America* (New York: William Morrow, 1984), pp. 166–70; Nancy F. Cott, *The Grounding of Modern Feminism* (New Haven: Yale University Press, 1987), pp. 69–70.

81. "Hunton, Addie Waite (1866–1943)," in *Black Women in America: An Historical Encyclopedia*, ed. Darlene Clark Hine, Elsa Barkley Brown, and Rosalyn Terborg-Penn, vol. 1 (Bloomington: University of Indiana Press, 1944), pp. 596–97.

82. D. Hunton, *Alphaeus Hunton*, p. 26.

83. Ibid., p. 29.

84. William Alphaeus Hunton Jr., manuscript on William Morris, p. 63, W. A. Hunton Papers, microfilm reel 2, Schomburg Library, New York.

85. D. Hunton, *Alphaeus Hunton*, pp. 46–49.

86. Ibid. In this biography of her husband, which is also a valuable political memoir for students of anticolonialism and the Cold War era, Dorothy Hunton does not supply the reader with her own family name.

87. See, e.g., "Organize Trade Unions among Africans: Urge More Benefits for All Workers," *Chicago Defender*, August 15, 1942, p. 5.

88. "British and British Africa—A Few Comparisons," *New Africa* 3, no. 3 (1944): 2.

89. Giddings, *When and Where I Enter*, pp. 199–230.

90. Kenneth Robert Janken, *Rayford W. Logan and the Dilemma of the African-American Intellectual* (Amherst: University of Massachusetts Press, 1993), p. 189; Lynch, *Black American Radicals*, pp. 21–23.

91. *New Africa* 2, no.1 (1943): 2.

92. Among its reports on conditions in South Africa, see "South Africa 'Justice': Six Africans Killed by Johannesburg Police," *New Africa* 4, no. 9 (1945): 1. "At Paynesville Springs, near Johannesburg in South Africa, police assaulted and opened fire upon a crowd of unarmed Africans." In response to riots in Johannesburg, in which the offices of the *Bantu World* were burned by white extremists, the CAA sent a letter of protest to S. F. N. Gie, minister of the Union of South Africa to the United States; see *New Africa* 3, no. 11 (1944).

93. *New Africa* 4, no. 7 (1945): 2; "African National Congress Strikes at Pass Laws," *New Africa* 3, no. 3 (1944): 1.

94. See, e.g., "Africa Revealed as Hotbed of Bias," *Baltimore Afro-American*, November 24, 1945, p. 12, on a speech at a CAA meeting by Wulf Sachs, editor of the *Democrat*, published in Johannesburg. "Laud Trade Union Gains in Africa," *Chicago Defender*, July 4, 1942, p. 5, reported that Max Yergan and the CAA had sent a letter to the South African minister of native affairs, praising the decision "to recognize African trade unions and relax the pass laws in urban areas." See also "South African Color Bar Condemned: Endangers Post War Security, Yergan Says" (citing a CAA news release), *African Standard* 6, no. 32 (1944): 2.

95. James Gilbert Coka, "Political Segregation in South Africa," *Crisis* 42, no. 9 (1935): 266; "Africans in Protest over Cop Brutality," *Pittsburgh Courier*, September 20, 1941, p. 3. "The South African Way," *Pittsburgh Courier*, August 21, 1943, compared "Attorney General Biddie's recommendation to the White House that the federal government limit, and possibly prohibit the further migration of African Americans to congested war production centers," to South African laws. Also covering conditions in Kenya and providing comparisons of the Kenyan and South African color bars that were rare in the wider press in the 1940s was "What about Kenya?" *New Africa* 3, no. 2 (1944): 2.

96. Coka, "Political Segregation in South Africa," p. 266.

97. "Africans in Protest over Cop Brutality," p. 3. Journalists in the early 1940s continued to cover protests against police brutality, trade union organizing, and protests against new forms of the color bar in South Africa: e.g., "South African Dutch Prove Treacherous," *Chicago Defender*, January 31, 1942, p. 7; "South Africans Hold Mass Meeting to Protest Factory Color Bar Bill," *Pittsburgh Courier*, May 24, 1941, p. 6.

98. George Padmore, "The Atlantic Charter and the British Colonies," *Pittsburgh Courier* magazine section, September 26, 1942; George Padmore, "New Jim-Crow Ban Brings Fresh Crisis to S. Africa," *Chicago Defender*, May 1, 1943, p. 9.

99. George Padmore, "Half Million Join Africa Bus Boycott," *Chicago Defender*, December 9, 1944, p. 2; Padmore, "South Africans Strike against Trolley Lines: Protest Native's Death in Johannesburg Race Riots," *Chicago Defender*, January 13, 1945, p. 1; George Padmore, "Fares Reduced: Africans Win Transit Fight," *Pittsburgh Courier*, February 3, 1945.

100. George Padmore, "Pan-African Confab Looms: White Settlers Initiate Their Plans," *Pittsburgh Courier*, June 12, 1943, p. 12; Padmore, "Mob Burns Newspaper Office in Africa Riot," *Chicago Defender*, November 11, 1944, p. 1.

101. L. D. Reddick, "South Africa: A Case for the United Nations," *Crisis* 50, no. 5 (1943): 137.

102. Rayford W. Logan, "Smuts Speaks of Africa, 1917–1942," *Crisis* 50, no. 9 (1943): 264–65.

103. "Gen. Smuts Plan for the Colonial Races," *Chicago Defender*, June 10, 1944. There was also coverage of Afrikaner challenges to Smuts. E.g., "Pro-Nazis in South Africa Heading Country toward Fascism and Chaos," *New Africa* 3, no. 9 (1944): 1, reported that the *Cape Times*, "the conservative European-published newspaper of Capetown," had warned of the turn toward fascism.

104. "Africans Paid 50 Cents per Day for Mine Work: Economic Pressure by Smuts's Regime Forces Workers to Accept or Starve," *Baltimore Afro-American*, March 16, 1946, p. 10.

105. Tom Lodge, *Black Politics in South Africa since 1945* (Johannesburg: Raven Press, 1983), pp. 19–20.

106. "Colour Bar Is Slavery," *Inkululeko*, June 1946 (first issue), p. 1, William Cullen Library, University of Witwatersrand, Johannesburg.

107. Lodge, *Black Politics in South Africa*, p. 20; Borstelmann, *Apartheid's Reluctant Uncle*, p. 71; Dan O'Meara, "The 1946 African Mine Workers' Strike and the Political Economy of South Africa," *Journal of Commonwealth and Comparative Politics* 13, no. 2 (1975): 146; Jon Lewis, *Industrialization and Trade Union Organization in South Africa, 1924–1955: The Rise and Fall of the South African Trades and Labour Council* (Cambridge: Cambridge University Press, 1984), pp. 71–74. See "African Mine Workers Stage Greatest Strike in South African History; Police Shoot Down Strikers, Force Them Back to Work at 40c a Day Wages," *New Africa* 5, no. 8 (1946): 1, for the CAA's detailed report on the strike.

108. Paul Robeson, letter to the editor, *New York Times*, September 6, 1946; in SAB, BNY, box 14, papers of South African Consulate General, Pretoria.

109. "South African Freedom Fight Calls for American Support," *Chicago Defender*, October 19, 1946, p. 3.

110. Ibid. See "African Mine Workers Stage Greatest Strike in South African History," and "All-Out Attack on South African Democratic Forces Is Government's Answer to Mine Workers' Strike," *New Africa* 5, no. 9 (1946): 1, for CAA coverage of the strike. See also, D. Hunton, *Alphaeus Hunton*, pp. 76–77.

111. "African Miners Voice Plea for WFTU Aid," *Chicago Defender*, October 26, 1946, p. 13. The article further hoped that the "Congress of Industrial Relations, an affiliate of the WFTU, may mobilize a demonstration or send a direct appeal to the UN Assembly in behalf of the African mine workers."

112. CAA press release, May 31, 1946, in *PM*, June 4, 1946, Hunton Papers, microfilm reel 2. The rally is covered in Chapter 4. For the speeches on the South African famine, see "Transcriptions by Miss O'Connor of Speeches made at the Madison Square Garden Rally of the Council on African Affairs, 6th June, 1946," SAB, BNY, box 14. On the CAA campaign see Bernard Makhosezwe Magubane, *The Ties That Bind: African-American Consciousness of Africa* (Trenton, N.J.: Africa World Press, 1989), p. 174.

113. Author's interview with Govan Mbeki, March 31, 1992, Port Elizabeth, R.S.A.; "Drought Continues, Save the Remaining Cattle," November 29, 1945, p. 5, and "African Food Fund Re-

port," December 6, 1945, pp. 1–3, *Guardian*, William Cullen Library, University of the Witwatersgrand, Johannesburg. The Food Fund was covered extensively in the *Guardian* throughout late 1945 and 1946.

114. Yergan to Du Bois, January 17, 1946, Du Bois Papers, reel 58, frame 735.

115. "Overflow Meeting Launches Famine Relief for Africans: Money, Canned Food Being Collected for Starvation Victims," *New Africa* 5, no.1 (1946); D. Hunton, *Alphaeus Hunton*, pp. 74–75.

116. "American Aid Is Now on the Way across Atlantic to Relieve Starvation Victims in South Africa," *New Africa* 5, no. 2 (1946): 1.

117. "Facts about Starvation in the Union of South Africa," issued May 1946 by the Council on African Affairs, SAB, BNY, box 14. See also, " 'Abhorrent' to All Democrats: U.S. Meeting Condemns S.A.'s Native Policy," *Guardian*, February 14, 1946, p. 3.

118. "Council Explains African Famine: Blames Food Scarcity on British Policies," *Baltimore Afro-American*, March 16, 1946, p. 3.

119. John Robert Badger, "World View: Hoover and African Hunger," *Chicago Defender*, March 27, 1946, p. 15.

120. "Robeson Urges U.S. Aid for Africa's Starving Millions," *Chicago Defender*, March 23, 1946, p. 7.

121. CAA press release, May 31, 1946, Hunton Papers, microfilm reel 2.

122. Badger, "World View: Hoover and African Hunger," p. 15.

123. "U.S.A. Helps African Food Fund," *Guardian*, April 25, 1946, p. 5.

124. S. A. Haynes, "The Battle for Freedom," *Baltimore Afro-American*, March 2, 1946, p. 7.

125. "Robeson Urges U.S. Aid for Africa's Starving Millions," p. 7; "Nation-Wide 'HELP AFRICA' Day, March 31, to Climax Campaign for Famine Relief," *New Africa* 5, no.3 (1946): 1.

126. See "Statement on the Council's Campaign to Aid African Famine Victims: Report of Campaign Jan. 7–May 17, 1946," *New Africa* 5, no. 5 (1946): 3, for a full list of contributors; *New Africa* 5, no. 2 (1946): 3, for a picture of Hunton's visit to PS 3 in Brooklyn; and *New Africa* 5, no. 3 (1946), for a picture of food collection by Brooklyn community organizations.

127. "U.S.A. Helps African Food Fund," *Guardian*, April 25, 1946, p. 5.

128. Michael Carter, "Murder of a Race Primed in South Africa: 8,000,000 Natives Slowly Starving to Death on a Pound of Meal a Day," *Baltimore Afro-American*, February 9, 1946, pp. 1, 19. See also "American Donations Bolster Morale of Starving Africans," *Chicago Defender*, February 23, 1946, p. 5, which discussed the grain imported to save European cattle.

129. Badger, "World View: Hoover and African Hunger," p. 15.

130. "Paul Robeson Speaks: Harlem Meeting Answers Ciskei Appeal," *Guardian*, February 7, 1946, p. 1.

131. "Council on African Affairs Inc., 4,500 Denounce South African Fascism: Wide Support Given Famine Relief," *Gold Coast Observer and Weekly Advertiser* 6, no. 43 (1946); "Council on African Affairs Receives Thanks, Endorsements of Africans," *Gold Coast Observer* 21, no. 7 (1946).

132. "Robeson 'Almost Deity' to African People, Council Learns," *Gold Coast Observer and Weekly Advertiser* 7, no. 7 (1946): 51.

133. *Gold Coast Observer* 7, no. 10 (1946); and "African Food Fund Appeal Spreading," *Guardian*, May 23, 1946.

134. See Legation of the Union of South Africa to the Consul General for the Union of South Africa, May 6, 1946, re correspondence with the CAA on the campaign; also Legation to Consul, April 30, 1946, re report on the CAA prepared by Ronald Sinclair, British Consul, New York, and enclosed report by Sinclair, SAB, BNY, box 14, 30/5. Correspondence between the South

African legation in Washington and the consul general state that they had been corresponding about the CAA in 1943 and 1944: Consul General to South African Legation, May 1, 1946, re African Famine Relief Campaign, SAB, BNY, box 14.

The South African consul and legation discussed the CAA with the British consulate as well. In addition to reports on the CAA received from Ronald Sinclair (above), see F. B. A. Rundall, British Consulate-General, to T. Hewitson, South African Consulate, January 29, 1946, and South African Legation to South African Consul General, February 15, 1946, re *New York Amsterdam News*, SAB, BNY, Box 14.

CHAPTER FOUR   The Diaspora Moment

1. Victor C. Gaspar, General Secretary-Treasurer, National Joint Conference Committee, The New Harlem Tenants League, to Mayor William O'Dwyer, May 15, 1946; O'Dwyer Papers, box 37, folder "Discrimination 1946," Municipal Archives, New York City. I thank Martha Biondi for bringing this document to my attention.
2. See Christopher Thorne, *Allies of a Kind: The United States, Britain and the War against Japan, 1941–1945* (London: Hamish Hamilton, 1978), pp. 214–18, for a discussion of different positions within the U.S. government on colonial policy.
3. William Roger Louis and Ronald Robinson, "The United States and the Liquidation of British Empire in Tropical Africa, 1941–1951," in *The Transfer of Power in Africa: Decolonization, 1940–1960* (New Haven: Yale University Press, 1982), p. 37. William Roger Louis, *Imperialism at Bay: The United States and the Decolonization of the British Empire, 1941–1945* (New York: Oxford University Press, 1978), p. 341. See also Christopher Thorne, *The Issue of War: States, Societies, and the Far Eastern Conflict of 1941–1945* (London: Hamish Hamilton, 1985), p. 195; Thorne, *Allies of a Kind*, pp. 664–67, 490–91.
4. "For a New Africa: Proceedings: Conference on Africa," New York, April 14, 1944, p. 17, W. A. Hunton Papers (CAA, organizational, to 1944), MG 237, Schomburg Library, New York.
5. "Canada Told of Africa's Needs," *Chicago Defender*, February 12, 1944, p. 11.
6. "For a New Africa: Proceedings, Conference on Africa," p. 16.
7. John Robert Badger, "World View: Correct Policy for Africa," *Chicago Defender*, July 29, 1944, p. 13.
8. See Thorne, *Allies of a Kind*, pp. 100, 340–41, for the differences and Henry Wallace's criticism of the position of Bernard Baruch.
9. See Richard M. Freeland, *The Truman Doctrine and the Origins of McCarthyism: Foreign Policy, Domestic Politics, and Internal Security, 1946–1948* (1972; New York: New York University Press, 1985), chap.1, "Origins of the Foreign Aid Program," pp. 13–69, for a summary of postwar economic restructuring.
10. Kumar Goshal, "As an Indian Sees It: Collaboration Not Rivalry, Key To Post-War World," *Pittsburgh Courier*, July 1, 1944.
11. Timothy Sander Oberst, "Cost of Living and Strikes in British Africa c.1939–1948: Imperial Policy and the Impact of the Second World War" (Ph.D. diss., Columbia University, 1991), p. 101.
12. Ibid., p. 169.
13. "Protest Unfair Control of Cocoa Marketing," *New Africa* 3, no. 11 (1944): 2.
14. The CAA was informed that its letter had been referred to the commodities division, which explained that the State Department's previous communication with the British government had expressed "the views of the members of both the cocoa trade and chocolate industry" in the United States and that "it does not appear to us appropriate for the Department to facilitate the

holding of a conference between representatives of the Farmers Committee of British West Africa and representatives of our Embassy in London." In response, Yergan reiterated his hope that "the interests of the African producers" receive consideration "in the exchange of views between our own government and the British government with regard to the cocoa control policy." See Max Yergan to Henry S. Villard, Chief Division of African Affairs, Department of State, January 31, 1945. RG 59, 848K.61334/1-3145 CS/EG; Edward G. Cale, Acting Chief, Commodities Division to Yergan, February 14, 1945, RG 59 848K.6661334/1-3134; and Yergan to Cale, February 21, 1945, RG59 848K.41334/1-3145, National Archives.

15. "U.S. Policy in Africa Outlined by Henry S. Villard, State Department Official," *New Africa* 2, no. 2 (1943): 1.

16. "Conference on Africa Planned," *Pittsburgh Courier*, April 1, 1944, p. 3; Hollis R. Lynch, *Black American Radicals and the Liberation of Africa: The Council on African Affairs, 1937–1955* (Ithaca: Africana Studies and Research Center, Cornell University, 1978), pp. 26–27; Dorothy Hunton, *Alphaeus Hunton: The Unsung Valiant* (Chesapeake, Va.: ECA Associates, 1986), p. 58; John Robert Badger, "World View: Post War Jobs in Africa," *Chicago Defender*, April 29, 1944. See also, "Roosevelt Leads Way in Making Atlantic Charter a Living Reality for Dependent Peoples," *New Africa* 2, no. 3 (1943): 1.

17. Robeson to Du Bois, March 31, 1944, W. E. B. Du Bois Papers, microfilm collection, Columbia University, reel 55, frame 1130.

18. Nkrumah to Robeson and Yergan, March 26, 1944, W. A. Hunton Papers, box 1, folder 16 (CAA Correspondence).

19. "Africa and Post-War Security Plans: Outstanding American Citizens Join in Endorsing Recommendations to the Government of the United States," letter forwarded by the Council on African Affairs, December 15, 1944, published in *New Africa* 3, no. 11 (1944).

20. Ibid.

21. Ibid.

22. Viscount Halifax to Anthony Eden, May 11, 1944, FO 371/38639 188471:AN 1837/397/45.

23. For an example of the cover letter, see Du Bois Papers, reel 55, frame 1133.

24. "Africa and Post-War Security Plans."

25. Lynch, *Black American Radicals*, p. 28.

26. Endorsements are listed with letter "Africa and Post-War Security Plans," and further endorsements in *New Africa* 4, no. 1 (1945). Robeson's letter seeking endorsements further encouraged "independent action" in "voicing the state of colonial peoples in the post-war security plans" by "the Church, the trade unions, fraternal bodies, women's and youth groups."

27. In addition to conference coverage, the work of Robeson, Yergan, and Hunton received much publicity. John Robert Badger, "World View: A Survey of African Events," *Chicago Defender*, February 17, 1945, reported that "*New Africa*, organ of the Council on African Affairs, contains in its January issue a summary of African events during 1944 which is the best I have seen." The CAA's work on postwar colonial policy also received attention in the West African press. Wallace-Johnson's *African Standard* carried news from the CAA's *New Africa* via Azikiwe's *West African Pilot*: "American Institutions Demand Economic and Political Freedom for All Colonies," *African Standard* 6, no. 22 (1944): 10–11, Marx Memorial Library, London.

28. The text of this letter is reprinted in "FDR Asked to Fight Colonial Exploitation," *Chicago Defender*, September 23, 1944, p. 18. For a reply to the letter from the Department of State to Walter White, October 4, 1944, see Du Bois Papers, reel 56, frame 433.

29. See Chapters 1 and 2.

30. From *The Autobiography of W. E. B. Du Bois: A Soliloquy on Viewing My Life from the Last Decade of Its First Century*, quoted in Robert L. Harris Jr., "Racial Equality and the United Na-

tions Charter," in *New Directions in Civil Rights Studies*, ed. Armstead L. Robinson and Patricia Sullivan (Charlottesville: University of Virginia Press, 1991), p. 128.

31. Harris, "Racial Equality and the United Nations Charter," p. 128.

32. Ibid., p. 130.

33. Paul Gordon Lauren, *Power and Prejudice: The Politics of Diplomacy and Racial Discrimination* (Boulder: Westview Press, 1988), pp. 147–50.

34. Harris, "Racial Equality and the United Nations Charter," pp. 131–32.

35. A. N. Fields, "Today's Talk," *Pittsburgh Courier*, December 2, 1944, p. 7.

36. "Dumbarton Oaks Proposals Exclude Colonies—Du Bois," *Baltimore Afro-American*, October 28, 1944, p. 3; "Dr. Du Bois 'Depressed' Colonial Questions Ignored at Dumbarton Oaks Peace Session," *Pittsburgh Courier*, October 28, 1944, p. 4.

37. "'Gate Open for Another War,' Warns Dr. Du Bois," *Chicago Defender*, March 3, 1945.

38. "Control of the Colonies," *Pittsburgh Courier*, December 16, 1944.

39. Kenneth Robert Janken, *Rayford W. Logan and the Dilemma of the African-American Intellectual* (Amherst: University of Massachusetts Press, 1993), pp. 169–73.

40. Rayford W. Logan, "Dumbarton Oaks Proposals Ignore Colonial Problem Says Dr. Logan," *Chicago Defender*, December 9, 1944, p. 2. Logan continued to write extensively on the issue. Identified as "Adviser on Foreign Affairs for the *Pittsburgh Courier*," he reported Assistant Secretary of the Treasury Harry White's "admission"—in a response to a question posed by Du Bois at a roundtable discussion—that "the Bretton Woods Agreement did not concern itself with the problems of colonies and other dependent areas" ("U.S. Admits: Colonies Ignored," *Pittsburgh Courier*, March 10, 1945, p. 1). Logan also addressed the National Council of Negro Women on the results of Dumbarton Oaks in October 1944 (Janken, *Rayford W. Logan*, p. 175).

41. Nkrumah to Du Bois, January 28, 1945; Kumar Goshal to Du Bois, February 26, 1945; and Amy Ashwood Garvey to Du Bois, February 1, 1945, Du Bois Papers, reel 57, frames 727, 240, 228. See also Janken, *Rayford W. Logan*, pp. 175–76.

42. Du Bois to Hunton, and Hunton to Du Bois, January 23, 1945, Du Bois Papers, reel 57, frame 388. Hunton suggested the names of Amy Ashwood Garvey; H. P. Osbourne, West Indian National Council; Jesus Colon, Puerto Rican Cervantes Society; Nkrumah; and Kumar Goshal. See also Du Bois to Hunton, February 26, 1945, reel 57, frames 388–94.

43. Du Bois to Villard, March 7, 1945, and Villard to Du Bois, March 17, 1945, Du Bois Papers, reel 58, frame 12 and 17; Bunche to Du Bois, January 31, 1945, reel 56, frame 1252; Du Bois to Bunche, March 7, 1945, reel 56, frame 56; Bunche to Du Bois, March 17, 1945, reel 56, frame 1253.

44. P. Bernard Young Jr., editor, "Dr. Ralph Bunche Advanced in State Dept. on Rare Merit," *Journal and Guide*, 1945, in Ralph Bunche Papers, box 144, University of California, Los Angeles.

45. Essie Robeson to Bunche, March 24, 1945; and Walter White to Bunche, June 25, 1946, both in Bunche Papers, box 1.

46. Janken, *Rayford W. Logan*, pp. 206–7.

47. Quoted in ibid., p. 176.

48. Ibid., pp. 173–74.

49. For an assessment of the Colonial Conference looking ahead to the founding conference of the United Nations, see "The San Francisco Conference," *Pittsburgh Courier*, April 14, 1945.

50. "Randolph Warns Negroes of After the War Fascism," *Chicago Defender*, January 6, 1945.

51. "Stettinius Takes Over," *Pittsburgh Courier*, December 16, 1944.

52. John Robert Badger, "World View: The Specter of Hooverism," *Chicago Defender*, August 26, 1944, p. 13. See also Harry Paxton Howard, "Chiang Kai-shek Resists Imperialism: Would

Not Accept U.S. Dictatorship," *Pittsburgh Courier*, November 18, 1944, p. 9, for a critique of Western interests in China.

53. Metz T. P. Lochard, "Parley May Skip Over Hot Issue of Colonies," *Chicago Defender*, May 5, 1945, p. 2. See also three front-page articles that day under the heading "Delegates Juggle Colonial Question; White, Du Bois Ask Equality of Races," in which Lochard discussed the "ducking" of the colonial issue; Richard Durham, the lobbying on the part of White and Du Bois; and John Robert Badger, the differences between the positions of the State and the Navy Departments. See also Harris, "Racial Equality and the United Nations Charter," p. 126; and Thomas Borstelmann, *Apartheid's Reluctant Uncle: The United States and Southern Africa in the Early Cold War* (New York: Oxford University Press, 1993), p. 65.

54. Quoted in Lauren, *Power and Prejudice*, pp. 151–52.

55. Ibid., pp. 154–55.

56. Alphaeus Hunton, "Upsurge in Africa," *Masses and Mainstreams* 3, no. 2 (1950): 18.

57. Barbara Bair, "True Women, Real Men: Gender, Ideology, and Social Roles in the Garvey Movement," in *Politics and Policies of the Truman Administration* (Chicago: Quandrangle Books, 1970), pp. 154–66.

58. Paula Giddings, *When and Where I Enter: The Impact of Black Women on Race and Sex in America* (New York: William Morrow, 1984), pp. 235–38.

59. John Robert Badger, "San Francisco Parley: Race Problem to Confront United Nations Parley," *Chicago Defender*, April 14, 1945, p. 1.

60. Quoted in Lauren, *Power and Prejudice*, p. 157. See W. E. B. Du Bois, "Color Line Absent at Frisco, Du Bois Finds," *Chicago Defender*, May 5, 1945, p. 1, for Du Bois's assessment of the opening of the conference.

61. W. E. B. Du Bois, "Du Bois Says Many at Parley Don't Know What It's About," *Chicago Defender*, May 19, 1945, p. 1.

62. Harris, "Racial Equality and the United Nations Charter," p. 136; "Statement on San Francisco Issued: Max Yergan Observer at Conference," *New Africa* 4, no. 4 (1945); Lauren, *Power and Prejudice*, p. 153.

63. Du Bois, "Du Bois Says Many at Parley Don't Know What It's About." On the role of Du Bois and the NAACP, see also Janken, *Rayford W. Logan*, p. 180.

64. George Padmore, "Colonial Issue on Frisco Agenda," *Pittsburgh Courier*, March 24, 1945, p. 1.

65. John Robert Badger, "San Francisco Parley: Race Problem to Confront United Nations Parley," *Chicago Defender*, April 14, 1945, p. 1.

66. Ibid. For earlier discussion of the Soviet Union, see George Padmore, "Soviets to Demand Equality at Peace Table," *Chicago Defender*, January 20, 1945, p. 1. For postwar French colonial policy, see Thyra Edwards and Murray Gitlin, "25 Million Negroes Getting New Deal in French Africa," *Chicago Defender*, January 13, 1945, p. 1.

67. Kumar Goshal, "As an Indian Sees It: Doubts Colonial Powers Will Want to Yield Control at San Francisco," *Pittsburgh Courier*, March 31, 1945, p. 7.

68. George Padmore, "Gandhi Urges Justice for Colored Peoples: Indian Leader Lashes Imperialist Rule over Colonies," *Chicago Defender*, April 28, 1945, p. 1.

69. W. E. B. Du Bois, "Du Bois, White Run from Photo with Indian Stooges," *Chicago Defender*, May 12, 1945, p. 5.

70. Lauren, *Power and Prejudice*, p. 155.

71. Ibid., pp. 155–56.

72. Louis, *Imperialism at Bay*, p. 354; Thorne, *The Issue of War*, p. 190.

73. Badger, "Delegates Juggle Colonial Question."

74. Rayford Logan, "U.S. Favors Two Forms of Trusteeship for Colonies," *Pittsburgh Courier*, May 12, 1945, p. 10. See also Janken, *Rayford W. Logan*, p. 180.

75. Rayford Logan, "Colonial Powers May Oppose International Trusteeship," *Pittsburgh Courier*, April 28, 1945, pp. 1, 9.

76. "Hits U.S. Opposition to Colonial Independence," *Chicago Defender*, May 26, 1945, p. 5.

77. "Words! Words! Words!" *Pittsburgh Courier*, May 26, 1945.

78. "No Hope for the Powerless," *Pittsburgh Courier*, May 12, 1945.

79. "Demand U.N. Help Africans: Conferences Ask Political Rights," *Chicago Defender*, October 12, 1946, p. 4.

80. "6-Point Plan for Africa's Independence Suggested," *Baltimore Afro-American*, September 22, 1945, p. 7.

81. Paul Robeson to R. Webster, Consul General of the Union of South Africa, September 20, 1945, and enclosure, "Text and Analysis of the Colonial Provisions of the United Nations Charter" (8 pages), SAB, BNY, box 14, Papers of South African Consulate General, Pretoria.

82. Borstelmann, *Apartheid's Reluctant Uncle*, p. 79.

83. The origins of the CAA-ANC relationship are covered in Chapter 1.

84. Earl Conrad, "Color Issue Dominates U.N.: India, South Africa Cases High on Agenda; Protest of American Negroes against Oppression Listed," *Chicago Defender*, November 2, 1946, p. 1.

85. "South African Strife on Racial Issue Seen," *New York Times*, Tuesday, July 30, 1946; SAB, BNY, box 13; Borstelmann, *Apartheid's Reluctant Uncle*, p. 69.

86. The campaign continued into 1948, when the new Malan government arrested its leaders and closed down its newspaper, the *Passive Resister*. I owe special thanks to A. M. Kathrada of the African National Congress for alerting me to this paper's existence and its attention to the CAA, as well as for sharing his perceptions of the period and his memories of Hunton, Robeson, and Du Bois from the standpoint of his involvement with the South African Indian Youth Congress and the Young Communist League.

87. *Passive Resister*, August 20, 1948, p. 3, William Cullen Library, University of the Witwatersrand, Johannesburg.

88. "We Have Not Forgotten South African Indians," *Passive Resister*, June 11, 1948.

89. See Lauren, *Power and Prejudice*, pp. 166–71, for the role of India in the early United Nations.

90. "India and the U.N.," *New York Times*, June 25, 1946; SAB, BNY, box 14; Borstelmann, *Apartheid's Reluctant Uncle*, p. 75; Lauren, *Power and Prejudice*, p. 159.

91. Lauren, *Power and Prejudice*, p. 159.

92. Papers of the South African Indian Congress, Acc 105, 6.43, Unisa Documentation Centre for African Studies, Pretoria.

93. Ibid.

94. "India and the U.N."

95. "American Condemns S.A. Racial Policy," *Guardian*, April 25, 1946, p. 8, William Cullen Library, University of the Witwatersrand, Johannesburg.

96. "South African Freedom Fight Calls for American Support," *Chicago Defender*, October 19, 1946, p. 3.

97. Borstelmann, *Apartheid's Reluctant Uncle*, pp. 49–50.

98. Ibid., pp. 75–76.

99. "U.N. Approval of Indian Resolution Is Blow to Racialism throughout World," *New Africa* 5, no. 11 (1946): 1; Lauren, *Power and Prejudice*, p. 171. See *Passive Resister*, December 6, 1946, p. 4, on the interim proposal of the UN Joint Political and Legal Committee in November 1946.

100. Lauren, *Power and Prejudice*, p. 171. For continuing tensions at the UN over treatment of people of Indian descent in South Africa, see Borstelmann, *Apartheid's Reluctant Uncle*, p. 142.

101. A. M. Wendell Malliet, foreign editor, *New York Amsterdam News*, to Sir Francis Evans, British Consulate General, October 28, 1946; and South African Delegation to the United Nations to R. Webster, Consul General for the Union of South Africa, November 11, 1946, both in SAB, BNY, box 14.

102. Ronald Sinclair, British Consulate General, New York, to Robert Webster, South African Consulate General, New York, August 7, 1946; SAB, BNY, box 14.

103. "Gen. Smuts Plan for the Colonial Races," *Chicago Defender*, June 10, 1944. For an example of Afrikaner challenges to Smuts, see "Pro-Nazis in South Africa Heading Country toward Fascism and Chaos," *New Africa* 3, no. 9 (1944): 1.

104. William Minter, *King Solomon's Mines Revisited: Western Interests and the Burdened History of Southern Africa* (New York: Basic Books, 1986), pp. 124–25; Borstelmann, *Apartheid's Reluctant Uncle*, pp. 76–77.

105. Richard Durham, "South African Plot Aims at Grabbing More Colonies," *Chicago Defender*, May 19, 1945, p. 1.

106. *New Africa* 4, no. 9 (1945): 4.

107. George Padmore, "UNO Gets South African Appeal," *Chicago Defender*, February 16, 1946, p. 5. See also Padmore, "Starvation and Sadism: Famine Grows in South Africa," *Chicago Defender*, February 23, 1946, p. 5; "South Africa, France Balk on Giving Up Colonies to UNO," *Chicago Defender*, January 19, 1946, p. 4.

108. R. T. Bokwe to Chief Tshekedi Khama, May 20, 1946, papers of South African Institute of Race Relations, AD843 B21:2, Historical Papers Library, University of the Witwatersrand, Johannesburg.

109. Jas. A. Calata, Secretary General of the ANC, wrote, "Although you have gone to America for treatment and recuperation your people in South Africa will expect to hear from you when you return that you did represent them at the U.N.O. somehow": see Calata to A. B. Xuma, All Saints Day 1946, ABX 461101; Working Committee to Xuma, ABX 461025; R. V. Selope Thema, on behalf of Working Committee African National Congress, to Xuma, November 18, 1946, ABX 461118, all in A. B. Xuma Papers, Historical Papers Library, University of the Witwatersrand, Johannesburg.

110. Alphaeus Hunton to A. B. Xuma, October 4, 1946, Xuma Papers, ABX 46004.

111. Records of this work survive in the Xuma Papers. See ABX 470928 for the CAA's "Memorandum on the Issue of South-West Africa under Consideration by Committee 4 of the General Assembly," September 28, 1947; ABX 47002b, 471029d, and 471029e for CAA press releases. See also "Colonial Empires Assailed in Rally: Communist-Controlled Council Says U.S. Aids Others in 'Plundering Africa,'" *New York Times*, June 7, 1946, on the CAA's South Africa resolutions at the June 6 rally (also covered in Chapter 2).

112. See "Facts about South-West Africa—Annexation or Trusteeship," issued October 1946 by the CAA, Xuma Papers, 461031.

113. Edgar D. Draper to Walter White, June 3, 1948, Du Bois Papers, reel 61, frame 907.

114. "Facts about South-West Africa—Annexation or Trusteeship," pp. 1–2. The report also covered education and health care.

115. "Colonial Empires Assailed in Rally."

116. H. T. Andrews, Secretary for External Affairs, memorandum, June 13, 1946, SAB, BNY, box 14.

117. R. Webster, Consul General, New York to H. T. Andrews, June 11, 1946, SAB, BNY, box 14. Webster forwarded his report, transcriptions of speeches taken by a Miss O'Connor, a summary

of the resolutions from the *New York Times*, and four CAA pamphlets distributed at the rally: "Facts about Starvation in the Union of South Africa"; "Facts about the Union of South Africa: South Africa's Aggressive Imperialism"; "What Do the People of Africa Want?" by Paul Robeson; and *The Job to Be Done*. Transcripts of speeches included those of Ferdinand Smith, National Maritime Union; Etukah Okala (Nigerian citizen), Columbia University; William S. Gaelmor, radio commentator, WHN, New York; Mary McCloud [*sic*] Bethune, president, National Council of Negro Women; Benjamin J. Davis, New York City Council; Adam Clayton Powell, U.S. congressman from New York and pastor, Abyssinian Baptist Church; W. E. B. Du Bois, director of special research, NAACP; William P. Hayes, president, New England Baptist Missionary Convention; Paul Robeson, president, CAA.

118. Webster to Andrews, June 11, 1946.

119. Council on African Affairs, Notes on the Meeting at Madison Square Garden, on June 6, 1946, SAB, BNY, box 14.

120. "S.A. People's Spokesmen Welcomed in New York," *Guardian*, November 14, 1946, p. 1; "Smuts' Annexation Demand Is Boomerang; Delegates Expose South African Misrule," *New Africa* 5, no. 10 (1946): 1–2.

121. Major Robinson, "Money behind Smuts Plea for S.W. Africa," *Chicago Defender*, November 2, 1946, p. 13; "On Smuts," *Chicago Defender*, November 2, 1946.

122. Major Robinson, "Africa Issue Perils UN: Dictator Smuts Demands Rule of New Territory," *Chicago Defender*, November 23, 1946, p. 1.

123. "On Smuts."

124. *New Africa* 5, no. 10 (1946): 3.

125. Caption: "A New York Demonstration: Demonstration outside S.A. Embassy in New York, organized by the Council on African Affairs," *Passive Resister*, December 20, 1946, p. 1, *Passive Resister*, December 13, 1946, p. 1, and July 31, 1947, p. 1.

126. Borstelmann, *Apartheid's Reluctant Uncle*, p. 77.

127. Ibid.

128. "South African Freedom Fight Calls for American Support," *Chicago Defender*, October 19, 1946, p. 3. See "Annexing of S.W.A. Opposed: Council on African Affairs Resolution," *Guardian*, November 14, 1946, p. 8, for South African reporting on these CAA resolutions.

129. "Probe of Racism in Africa Asked: UN Unit Gets Data from African Council," *Baltimore Afro-American*, May 25, 1946, p. 10; "Africa—Continent in Bondage: Pleads for Subject Colonial Peoples on Eve of Mass Meeting," *New York Herald Tribune*, June 5, 1945.

130. "Council Urges United Nations Human Rights Commission to Act on Discrimination in South Africa and All Colonies," *New Africa* 5, no. 6 (1946): 2. "S.A. Exposed in U.S.A.: Council's Charge of Racialism," *Guardian*, June 13, 1946, p. 1.

131. *Guardian*, December 5, 1946, p. 1; and "Smuts' Annexation Demand Is Boomerang."

132. *Guardian*, December 5, 1946, p. 1.

133. Borstelmann, *Apartheid's Reluctant Uncle*, p. 77.

134. John Foster Dulles, United States Delegation to the General Assembly of the United Nations to Paul Robeson, Chairman, Council on African Affairs, Inc., December 7, 1946, Hunton Papers, box 1, folder 16 (CAA 1945–55), MG 237.

135. CAA, "Memorandum on the Issue of South-West Africa under Consideration by Committee 4 of the General Assembly."

136. "Vindictive Attitude of U.S. Government: Stand at U.N.O. Condemned," *Passive Resister*, October 16, 1947, p. 7.

137. CAA, "Analysis of the Government of the Union of South Africa on the Administration of South West Africa for the Year 1946," December 10, 1947, Xuma Papers, ABX 471210.

138. CAA Press Release, April 9, 1947, Hunton Papers, microfilm reel 2. Flyers and other publicity for the rally are in the papers of Lloyd Brown, in author's possession.

139. *Passive Resister*, November 20, 1947, p. 4. See also *New Africa* 6, no. 8 (1947): 1.

140. "Messages to Paul Robeson," *Passive Resister*, April 25, 1947, p. 3; "UNO Rally Unites Non-Europeans: Biggest Meeting Ever," *Passive Resister*, May 9, 1947, p. 1.

141. CAA news release, "Council on Africa Urges U.S. Take Strong Stand on South West Africa," October 29, 1947, Xuma Papers, ABX 471029e. See "U.S. Afraid to Hurt Smuts," *Passive Resister*, November 13, 1947, for the South African Indian Congress coverage of the Sayre meeting.

142. CAA news release, "U.N. Assembly Reverses Committee Decisions on S.W. Africa and Colonies—Viewpoint of Colonial Powers Prevails," November 4, 1947, Xuma Papers, ABX 471104c.

143. Lauren, *Power and Prejudice*, p. 262.

CHAPTER FIVE Domesticating Anticolonialism

1. Robert L. Zangrando, *The NAACP Crusade against Lynching, 1909–1950* (Philadelphia: Temple University Press, 1980), p. 6. For the text of Dean Acheson's speech, see Joseph M. Jones, *The Fifteen Weeks (February 21–June 5, 1947)* (New York: Viking Press, 1955), p. 281. I thank Eric Foner for drawing my attention to the speech.

2. Herbert Shapiro, *White Violence and Black Response: From Reconstruction to Montgomery* (Amherst: University of Massachusetts Press, 1988), pp. 355–77; Zangrando, *NAACP Crusade*, pp. 172–73; Thomas Borstelmann, *Apartheid's Reluctant Uncle: The United States and Southern Africa in the Early Cold War* (New York: Oxford, 1993), pp. 62–65; Nelson Peery, *Black Fire: The Making of an American Revolutionary* (New York: New Press, 1994), p. 339.

3. Patrick Renshaw, *American Labor and Consensus Capitalism, 1935–1990* (London: Macmillan, 1991), p. 76. On the precarious economic situation for black workers and the expansion of black poverty and unemployment following the war, see Robin D. G. Kelley, *Race Rebels: Culture, Politics, and the Black Working Class* (New York: Free Press, 1994), pp. 78–79.

4. On the Truman Doctrine, see Melvyn P. Leffler, *A Preponderance of Power: National Security, the Truman Administration, and the Cold War* (Stanford, Calif.: Stanford University Press, 1992), pp. 144–46; Michael H. Hunt, *Ideology and U.S. Foreign Policy* (New Haven: Yale University Press, 1987), p. 158; and David Caute, *The Great Fear: The Anti-Communist Purge under Truman and Eisenhower* (New York: Simon & Schuster, 1978), p. 29. On the impact of the announcement of the Truman Doctrine on race relations within the United States and in the international sphere, see Borstelmann, *Apartheid's Reluctant Uncle*, pp. 61–68; and Paul Gordon Lauren, *Power and Prejudice: The Politics and Diplomacy of Racial Discrimination* (Boulder, Colo.: Westview Press, 1988), pp. 186–87.

5. Leffler, *A Preponderance of Power*, p. 109. Leffler adds that although Americans reacted negatively to Churchill's call for a military alliance, the speech accelerated widespread hostility towards the Soviet Union. On negative reaction to the speech, see also Richard M. Freeland, *The Truman Doctrine and the Origins of McCarthyism: Foreign Policy, Domestic Politics, and Internal Security, 1946–1948* (New York: New York University Press, 1985), p. 64.

6. Martin Bauml Duberman, *Paul Robeson* (New York: Knopf, 1988), pp. 303–4.

7. "Paul Robeson Flays Churchill Plan for Anglo-Saxon World," *Chicago Defender*, March 30, 1946, p. 5.

8. "Churchill's Speech Shatters Colonials' Hopes for Freedom," *Chicago Defender*, March 16, 1946, p. 12.

9. Quoted in S. A. Haynes, "The Battle for Freedom," *Baltimore Afro-American,* June 22, 1946, p. 14, and April 27, 1946.

10. James L. Roark, "American Black Leaders: The Response to Colonialism and the Cold War," *African Historical Studies* 4, no. 2 (1971): 262; Mark Solomon, "Black Critics of Colonialism and the Cold War," in *Cold War Critics: Alternatives to American Foreign Policy in the Truman Years,* ed. Thomas G. Paterson (Chicago: Quandrangle Books, 1971), pp. 217–18.

11. "Churchill and Colonials," *Baltimore Afro-American,* March 16, 1946.

12. "Imperialism vs. Peace," *Chicago Defender,* March 30, 1946.

13. "What Churchill Wants," *Chicago Defender,* March 16, 1946. See also Ollie Stewart, "Colossal Colonial Flop: U.S. Dollars Go down British African Drain," *Baltimore Afro-American,* December 24, 1949, p. 6, for a discussion of U.S. policy ties to the interest of the colonial powers.

14. Editorial, *Chicago Defender,* October 12, 1946. See also George Padmore, "British Fight Russ Threat to Imperialism: Bevin Asks Foreign Ministers to Okay Abyssinian Grab," *Chicago Defender,* May 11, 1946, p. 1; "Robeson Hails Russia as Symbol of Progress," *Chicago Defender,* May 11, 1946, p. 5; George Padmore, "Colonials in Temporary UNO Setback Despite Soviet Aid," *Chicago Defender,* February 23, 1946, p. 5; Padmore, "Soviet Envoy Tells Stand to UNO Assembly: Gromyko Warns Colored Peoples Eye United Nations," *Chicago Defender,* February 2, 1946, p. 1; Padmore, "Trusteeship: The New Imperialism," *Crisis* 53, no. 10 (1946): 302–5, 318.

15. "Imperialism vs. Peace," *Chicago Defender,* March 30, 1946.

16. John Robert Badger, "World View: An Anglo-American Axis," *Chicago Defender,* March 16, 1946, p. 15.

17. "FDR Aired Colonial Evils in 1944," *Baltimore Afro-American,* September 14, 1946, p. 1. In "Colonial Policy and War," September 21, 1946, the *Afro-American* added, "It was the elder Roosevelt's view that British, French, and Dutch imperialism will start World War III."

18. Quoted in Leffler, *A Preponderance of Power,* pp. 79–80.

19. David S. Painter, *Oil and the American Century: The Political Economy of U.S. Foreign Oil Policy, 1941–1954* (Baltimore: Johns Hopkins University Press, 1986), p. 1.

20. Kumar Goshal, "As an Indian Sees It: Imperialism in Oil? Britain and America Control Three-Fourths of Known Oil Reserves," *Pittsburgh Courier,* January 25, 1947, p. 8. See also Goshal, "United States Seems to Have Become World Conscious with a Vengeance," *Pittsburgh Courier,* February 1, 1947, p. 6; and Goshal, "America Holds Most Important Instrument for World Peace, but Is Misusing It," *Pittsburgh Courier,* May 17, 1947, p. 7.

21. "The Ethiopian Oil Deal," *Baltimore Afro-American,* September 15, 1945, p. 4.

22. Leffler, *A Preponderance of Power,* pp. 79–80, 110–11; Painter, *Oil and the American Century,* pp. 111–13.

23. Walter White, "Russo-Iranian Dispute: People, Politics, and Places," *Chicago Defender,* April 20, 1946, p. 15. See also John Robert Badger, "The Persian Question," *Chicago Defender,* April 20, 1946, p. 15.

24. "Iran and American Business," *Chicago Defender,* May 4, 1946.

25. "Madison Square Garden Rally, June 6, Will Voice American People's Demand for U.S. Anti-Imperialist Policy and a Free Africa!" *New Africa* 5, no. 5 (1946).

26. "Africa—Continent in Bondage: Pleads for Subject Colonial Peoples on Eve of Mass Meeting," *New York Herald Tribune,* June 5, 1945.

27. CAA Press Release, May 31, 1946, W. A. Hunton Papers, microfilm reel 2, Schomburg Library, New York.

28. "The Stakes for Peace and Freedom in Africa: What Role Will the United States Play?" *New Africa* 5, no. 6 (1946): 3; Paul Robeson, "Anti-Imperialists Must Defend Africa," address at

Madison Square Garden rally sponsored by CAA, June 6, 1946, in *Paul Robeson Speaks: Writings, Speeches, Interviews, 1918–1974,* ed. Philip S. Foner (New York: Citadel Press, 1978), p. 169.

29. "African Council Meeting Asks End to Imperialism," *Chicago Defender,* June 22, 1946, p. 8.

30. "Transcriptions by Miss O'Connor of Speeches made at the Madison Square Garden Rally of the Council on African Affairs, 6th June, 1946," SAB, BNY, box 14, Papers of South African Consulate General, Pretoria.

31. "Robeson Assails British and U.S. Roles in Africa: Tells Rally Imperialism is Stifling Development," *New York Herald Tribune,* June 7, 1946.

32. "Colonial Empires Assailed in Rally: Communist-Controlled Council Says U.S. Aids Others in 'Plundering Africa,'" *New York Times,* June 7, 1946.

33. "African Council Gets 'Holiday' for Xmas Benefit Performance," *People's Voice,* December 14, 1946, p. 22; Edward Kennedy Ellington, *Music Is My Mistress* (Garden City, N. Y.: Doubleday, 1973), p. 185.

34. George Padmore, "U.S. Stalls on Colonies at UNO, Haunted by Threat of World Revolt," *Chicago Defender,* February 9, 1946, p. 7.

35. "Navy 'Democracy' on Guam," *Crisis* 53, no. 10 (1946); Earl Conrad, "Spy Ring in Cuba: American Imperialists Accused," *Chicago Defender,* November 16, 1946, p. 13. See Ralph Izzard, "Jim Crow Wails—and India Hears," *Chicago Defender,* November 16, 1946, p. 13; and Izzard, "Eyes on America, India Links British, U.S. Bias," *Chicago Defender,* October 5, 1946, p. 13, on India's suspicions of U.S. imperialism. See George Padmore, "From Indo-China: U.S. Lynchings Called Barbarism," *Chicago Defender,* September 28, 1946, p. 13, for a fascinating interview with Ho Chi Minh.

36. See Chapter 2, for black journalists' wartime coverage of U.S. government and corporate activity in Haiti and Liberia.

37. George Padmore, "Padmore Sees Wall St. Invasion of Liberia," *Chicago Defender,* November 18, 1944, p. 2; Padmore, "American Mission Plans to Modernize Liberian Republic," *Pittsburgh Courier,* February 17, 1945, p. 5.

38. "State Department Denies Crisis Threatens Liberia," *Baltimore Afro-American,* January 12, 1946, p. 1. Demands by the striking workers included higher wages, a reduction of the eighty-four-hour work week, canteen privileges (then limited to white employees), equal pay for foreign and Liberian employees, and an end to harsh treatment. See "Long List of Grievances against U.S. Company Given by Striking Liberians," *Baltimore Afro-American,* January 19, 1946, p. 1.

39. James L. Hicks, "State Department Denies Hand in Liberia Strike Crisis," *Chicago Defender,* January 12, 1946, p. 1; "State Department Denies Crisis Threatens Liberia," *Baltimore Afro-American,* January 12, 1946, p. 1.

40. "Huge Concession Granted in Liberia as Ships Stand By," *Baltimore Afro-American,* January 26, 1946, p. 1.

41. "Liberian Judges Who Opposed U.S. Land Grab Disciplined," *Baltimore Afro-American,* February 9, 1946, p. 1; "State Department Denies Coercion in Getting Liberia Mine Concession," *Chicago Defender,* February 9, 1946, p. 5; "Unrest in Liberia, Greatly Exaggerated, Walton Says," *Baltimore Afro-American,* March 16, 1946, p. 1; "Necessities Denied Native Laborers at U.S. Rubber Plantations in Liberia: Engineers, Highest Paid, Earn Only 50 Cents; Manager Blamed for Conditions at Firestone," *Baltimore Afro-American,* May 26, 1946, p. 16; "Firestone Gives Liberia $250,000 Medical Center," *Afro-American,* September 28, 1946, p. 15; and "Firestone Workers in Liberia Get First Raise in 20 Years," *Chicago Defender,* March 23, 1946, p. 13.

42. Max L. Hudicourt, "Jim Crow Menaces Haiti," *Crisis* 51, no. 11 (1944): 354, 356; "Haitian Color Bar," *Chicago Defender,* January 19, 1944; Fred Atwater, "'White Cabinet' Imposes Rigid Haiti Color Line," *Chicago Defender,* February 26, 1944, p. 1. See also Chapter 1.

43. Ralph Matthews, "Washington Shocked by News of Haitian Revolt," and "Regime Collapse Stuns Ambassador," *Baltimore Afro-American,* January 19, 1946, p. 1. See also headline "Revolt Grips Haiti," lead article "People Back Military Junta; Lescot Hiding: 15 to 25 Killed, 100 Wounded; 4 U.S. Destroyers, 'on Maneuvers,' Drop In," and Venice T. Spraggs, "Revolt in Black Republic, 25 Killed," all in *Chicago Defender,* January 19, 1946, p. 1. See Harold Preece, "'Quadroon Quislings' Face Revolt in Haiti," *Chicago Defender,* September 2, 1944, p. 1, on political divisions in Haiti. On the ousting of Lescot and the views of the U.S. State Department, see Brenda Gayle Plummer, *Haiti and the United States: The Psychological Moment* (Athens: University of Georgia Press, 1992), p. 148.

44. Enoc P. Waters, "U.S. Intervention, Economic Muddle Seen Causes of Haitian Revolt," *Chicago Defender,* February 9, 1946, p. 6. See also Waters, "No Admittance, Haitian at State Depart. Door," *Chicago Defender,* April 13, 1946, p. 5, for analysis of the post-coup government.

45. Rayford W. Logan, "Haiti's Plea for More Aid Ignored," *Pittsburgh Courier,* March 15, 1947, p. 1; "Haiti's Sovereignty Dearer Than Dollars," *Chicago Defender,* April 19, 1947.

46. The *Defender* reported a Haitian debt of $6 million to private American bondholders and another $3.2 million to the U.S. government through the Export-Import Bank: "Haiti Seeks to Ease Economic Ties to the U.S.," *Chicago Defender,* September 28, 1946, p. 9. The *Afro-American* reported a Haitian debt of $23 million in 1922, $5 million in 1940, and $5 million during the war: Ollie Stewart, "End of Political, Financial Control by U.S. Sought by Haitian Mission: Renewal of Loan, More Equitable Relationship Requested as Island Republic Plans Expansion of Export Market," *Baltimore Afro-American,* January 18, 1947, p. 1. See also Helen Stone, "It's Almost Impossible to Make a Living in Haiti," *Baltimore Afro-American,* June 1, 1946, p. 8.

Similarly, "Haiti Raps U.S. Debt Deal: Black Republic Enslaved by Financial Tie: Export-Import Bank Denies Relief from Heavy Obligation," *Chicago Defender,* April 5, 1947, p. 1, reported, "Under an agreement made in 1941, the United States exercises such control over Haitian finances that Haiti cannot prepare its own budget, amend its budget law, or increase its public debt without the previous consent of this country."

47. "Plenty for Other Countries but Nothing to Lend Haiti: U.S. Government Refuses Aid to Island Republic Whose Fields American Machines Destroyed," *Baltimore Afro-American,* April 12, 1947, p. 1. See also John A. Diaz, "Refused in Effort to Wipe Out Debt," *Pittsburgh Courier,* March 29, 1947, p. 1, which also discussed the destruction of Haitian agriculture through the failed U.S. rubber scheme.

48. Solomon, "Black Critics," pp. 219–20.

49. Rayford W. Logan, "Haiti's Plea for More Aid Ignored," *Pittsburgh Courier,* March 15, 1947, p. 1.

50. "Haiti's Sovereignty Dearer Than Dollars," *Chicago Defender,* April 19, 1947.

51. Leffler, *A Preponderance of Power,* pp. 144–45; Borstelmann, *Apartheid's Reluctant Uncle,* pp. 61–62; Freeland, *The Truman Doctrine,* pp. 8, 135.

52. Hunt, *Ideology and U.S. Foreign Policy,* p. 158.

53. Caute, *The Great Fear,* p. 30; Leffler, *A Preponderance of Power,* pp. 144–46; Hunt, *Ideology and U.S. Foreign Policy,* p. 158.

54. Norman D. Markowitz, *The Rise and Fall of the People's Century: Henry A. Wallace and American Liberalism, 1941–1948* (New York: Free Press, 1973), pp. 220, 232, 234.

55. On the Marshall Plan, see Michael J. Hogan, *The Marshall Plan: America, Britain, and the Reconstruction of Western Europe, 1947–1953* (Cambridge: Cambridge University Press, 1987); Leffler, *A Preponderance of Power,* pp. 157–65; Stephen E. Ambrose, *Rise to Globalism: American Foreign Policy since 1938* (New York: Penguin Books, 1986), pp. 87–95; Thomas J. McCormick, *America's Half-Century: United States Foreign Policy in the Cold War* (Baltimore: Johns Hopkins

University Press, 1989), pp. 78–86; Freeland, *The Truman Doctrine,* pp. 151–200. On the positions of the ADA and the PCA, see Markowitz, *The Rise and Fall of the People's Century,* pp. 246–47; Donald R. McCoy and Richard T. Ruetten, *Quest and Response: Minority Rights and the Truman Administration* (Lawrence: University Press of Kansas, 1973), pp. 72–73.

56. On labor's support of the Marshall Plan, see Nelson Lichtenstein, "From Corporatism to Collective Bargaining: Organized Labor and the Eclipse of Social Democracy in the Postwar Era," in *The Rise and Fall of the New Deal Order,* ed. Steve Frazer and Gary Gerstle (Princeton: Princeton University Press, 1989), pp. 138–39; and George Lipsitz, *Rainbow at Midnight: Labor and Culture in the 1940s* (Urbana: University of Illinois Press, 1994), pp. 190–91.

57. *Paul Robeson Speaks,* p. 207.

58. P. L. Prattis, "Methods Used by United States to Check Communism Set Stage for Next War," *Pittsburgh Courier,* March 15, 1947, p. 7; O. E. M'Kaine, "Marshall Plan Awarded Cool Reception in Europe," *Baltimore Afro-American,* December 20, 1947, p. 1.

59. See Lichtenstein, "From Corporatism to Collective Bargaining," pp. 138–39; and Lipsitz, *Rainbow at Midnight,* pp. 190–91.

60. Zangrando, *NAACP Crusade,* p. 191; "Walter White Warns That Bias in U.S. Is Hurting Program," *Pittsburgh Courier,* February 7, 1948, p. 3. Manning Marable, *W. E. B. Du Bois: Black Radical Democrat* (Boston: Twayne Publishers, 1986), p. 173.

61. "Defender Publisher Aids in Forming Liberal Group," *Chicago Defender,* April 5, 1947, p. 1.

62. Marable, *W. E. B. Du Bois,* p. 173.

63. On Walter White's anti-Communism in the 1930s, see Robin D. G. Kelley, *Hammer and Hoe: Alabama Communists during the Great Depression* (Chapel Hill: University of North Carolina Press, 1990), p. 228; and Mark Naison, *Communists in Harlem during the Great Depression* (New York: Grove Press, 1983), pp. 180–82.

64. The development of this position over the late 1940s and early 1950s is detailed in Chapter 7.

65. Harvard Sitkoff's discussion of the ADA-led revolt in the northern Democratic Party in 1947 and 1948 argues that for ADA, civil rights became the moral justification for anti-Communist liberalism, as well as a lever against southern Democrats and northern Communist appeals to black Americans; see "Harry Truman and the Election of 1948: The Coming of Age of Civil Rights in American Politics," *Journal of Southern History* 37, no. 4 (1971): 606.

66. "Walter White Warns That Bias in U.S. Is Hurting Program." See Borstelmann, *Apartheid's Reluctant Uncle,* pp. 66–67, on the separation of civil rights issues in the United States from racial and colonial problems abroad.

67. Shapiro, *White Violence and Black Response,* pp. 355–77; Zangrando, *NAACP Crusade,* pp. 172–73; Borstelmann, *Apartheid's Reluctant Uncle,* pp. 62–65.

68. Walter White, *A Man Called White: The Autobiography of Walter White* (New York: Viking Press, 1948), pp. 329–33; Henry Lee Moon, *Balance of Power: The Negro Vote* (New York: Doubleday, 1948), pp. 200–201; McCoy and Ruetten, *Quest and Response,* pp. 47–53; Borstelmann, *Apartheid's Reluctant Uncle,* p. 66.

69. White, *A Man Called White,* pp. 329–33; McCoy and Ruetten, *Quest and Response,* pp. 47–48; Duberman, *Paul Robeson,* p. 307.

70. *Paul Robeson Speaks,* p. 204.

71. McCoy and Ruetten, *Quest and Response,* pp. 47–48; Duberman, *Paul Robeson,* p. 307.

72. McCoy and Ruetten, *Quest and Response,* p. 48; Duberman, *Paul Robeson,* p. 307.

73. Duberman, *Paul Robeson,* pp. 306–7.

74. White, *A Man Called White,* pp. 347–48.

75. Barton J. Bernstein, "The Ambiguous Legacy: The Truman Administration and Civil Rights," in *Politics and Policies of the Truman Administration,* ed. Barton J. Bernstein (Chicago:

Quadrangle Books, 1970), pp. 278–80; Alexander Deconde, *Ethnicity, Race, and American Foreign Policy: A History* (Boston: Northeastern University Press, 1992), p. 130; Sitkoff, "Harry Truman and the Election of 1948"; Borstelmann, *Apartheid's Reluctant Uncle*, pp. 66–67; United States, President's Committee on Civil Rights, *To Secure These Rights: The Report of the President's Committee on Civil Rights* (Washington: U. S. Government Printing Office, 1947).

76. Quoted in Duberman, *Paul Robeson*, p. 343. For another example of this argument, see Moon, *Balance of Power*, pp. 202–4. Moon's position is particularly important since he was involved in the 1945 Manchester Pan-African Congress (Chapter 3).

77. White participated in the tour while on leave from the NAACP. See NAACP, "Memorandum to the Press," September 22, 1949; and "Mr. White Returns," *News Digest*, Sept. 1–29, 1949, both in NAACP Paper, part 17, National Staff Files 1940–55; microfilm, reel 23, Princeton University.

78. On African American support of the Wallace campaign, and specifically Du Bois' support and its contribution to growing strains between Du Bois and White, see Marable, *W. E. B. Du Bois*, pp. 173–74; Gerald Horne, *Black and Red: W. E. B. Du Bois and the Afro-American Response to the Cold War, 1944–1963* (Albany: State University of New York Press, 1986), pp. 86–89.

79. Robert A. Divine, "The Cold War and the Election of 1948," *Journal of American History* 59, no. 1 (1972): 91–93; Duberman, *Paul Robeson*, p. 316; Leffler, *A Preponderance of Power*, pp. 138–39; Freeland, *The Truman Doctrine*, pp. 139–40.

80. Duberman, *Paul Robeson*, p. 324.

81. *New Africa* 6, no. 8 (1947): 1.

82. McCoy and Ruetten, *Quest and Response*, pp. 144–45; Divine, "The Cold War and the Election of 1948," p. 93; Freeland, *The Truman Doctrine*, pp. 304–5; Duberman, *Paul Robeson*, p. 335.

83. Sitkoff, "Harry Truman and the Election of 1948," pp. 606, 612. The orders were intended to forbid discrimination in the armed services and in federal employment but did not mention segregation. The initiatives were widely praised in the black press. The *Crisis*, for example, argued that "the orders represent a spirit and a courage on these issues refreshing as they are rare." See "President Truman's Orders," *Crisis* 55, no. 9 (1948); "President Truman Bans Segregation in Military: 2nd Order Sets Up FEPC in All Government Jobs," *Chicago Defender*, July 31, 1948, p. 1; "Mr. Truman Makes History," *Chicago Defender*, August 7, 1948; and "The Order Mr. Truman Did Not Issue," *Pittsburgh Courier*, August 7, 1948.

84. Alonzo L. Hamby, "The Clash of Perspectives and the Need for New Syntheses," in *The Truman Period as a Research Field: A Reappraisal*, ed. Richard S. Kirkendall (Columbia: University of Missouri Press, 1974), p. 136; David W. Southern, *Gunnar Myrdal and Black-White Relations: The Use and Abuse of an American Dilemma* (Baton Rouge: Louisiana State University Press, 1987), pp. 101–2.

85. For a breakdown of the black American vote in the 1948 election, see McCoy and Ruetten, *Quest and Response*, pp. 143–44. See also Sitkoff, "Harry Truman and the Election of 1948," p. 613.

86. See e.g., Sitkoff, "Harry Truman and the Election of 1948," p. 615.

87. Zangrando, *The NAACP Crusade*, p. 201.

88. E.g., Robert Korstad and Nelson Lichtenstein, "Opportunities Found and Lost: Labor, Radicals, and the Early Civil Rights Movement," *Journal of American History* 75, no. 3 (1988): 811, have argued that the mid-1940s saw the growth of "an autonomous, labor-oriented civil rights movement" that was diffused and defeated in the early Cold War era as "the rise of anti-communism shattered the Popular Front coalition on civil rights, while the retreat and containment of the union movement deprived black activists of the political and social space necessary to

carry on an independent struggle." Martha Biondi, "The Early Civil Rights Movement in New York City, 1945–1954" (Ph.D. diss. in progress, Columbia University), emphasizes that there was a proliferation of antidiscrimination legislation on the local and state levels in the 1940s that dissipated with the Cold War. See also Richard M. Dalfiume, "The Forgotten Years of the Negro Revolution," in *The Negro in Depression and War: Prelude to Revolution, 1930–1945*, ed. Bernard Sternsher (Chicago: Quadrangle Books, 1969), pp. 298–316.

89. Lipsitz, *Rainbow at Midnight*, pp. 190–92; Lichtenstein, "From Corporatism to Collective Bargaining," pp. 122–23; Barbara S. Griffith, *The Crisis of American Labor: Operation Dixie and the Defeat of the CIO* (Philadelphia: Temple University Press, 1988); Michael K. Honey, *Southern Labor and Black Civil Rights: Organizing Memphis Workers* (Urbana: University of Illinois Press, 1993). See also Steve Rosswurm, ed., *The CIO's Left-Led Unions* (New Brunswick, N. J.: Rutgers University Press, 1992).

90. Renshaw, *American Labour and Consensus Capitalism*, pp. 123–24. See also Jay Lovestone Papers, box 259, folder "1949 AFL International Labor Relations Committee"; box 258, "Free Trade Union Committee A.F. of L., Report for Audit Year 1951"; and "Report for Audit Year 1952," Hoover Institution on War, Revolution, and Peace, Stanford University.

91. See, for examples, Lovestone Papers, box 398, folder "Africa Trade Unions," and box 399, folder "African-American Labor Center"; Renshaw, *American Labour and Consensus Capitalism*, p. 123; and Tiyambe Zeleza, "Colonialism and Internationalism: The Case of the British and Kenyan Labour Movement," *UFAHAMU* 14, no. 1 (1984): 9–28.

92. Freeland, *The Truman Doctrine*, pp. 305, 131, 210–16; Caute, *The Great Fear*, p. 32.

93. On the rise of bipartisan foreign policy during the 1948 election, and the stifling of objections to Truman's policy both by liberal critics such as Wallace and by isolationist Republicans, see Divine, "The Cold War and the Election of 1948," pp. 99–107.

94. Caute, *The Great Fear*, p. 32; Ellen Schrecker, "McCarthyism and the Decline of American Communism, 1945–1960," in *New Studies in the Politics and Culture of U.S. Communism*, ed. Michael E. Brown et al. (New York: Monthly Review Press, 1993), pp. 123–40.

95. Caute, *The Great Fear*, p. 177.

96. David H. Anthony, "Max Yergan and South Africa: A Transatlantic Interaction," in *Imagining Home: Class, Culture, and Nationalism in the African Diaspora*, ed. Sidney Lemelle and Robin D. G. Kelley (New York: Verso, 1994), pp. 192–94. Anthony is working on a biography of Yergan that in its extensive use of FBI sources dating surveillance to the 1930s, promises a critical analysis not only of Yergan but of the relationship between the left, government surveillance, and popular politics in the 1930s and 1940s.

97. Duberman, *Paul Robeson*, p. 258. Nevertheless, surveillance continued: CAA meetings were bugged and phone conversations regularly tapped in 1945 and 1946 (pp. 298, 303).

98. See, e.g., "The Belgian Congo and Uranium Politics," *New Africa* 6, no. 10 (1947): 3; "International Finance Looks to Undeveloped African Resources: Anglo-Saxon Scheme of Super-Exploitation Expected to Save Bankrupt Europe," and "U.S. Big Business in Africa," *New Africa* 6, no. 11 (1947): 1 and 3; "A U.S. Loan for South Africa?" *New Africa* 7, no. 3 (1948): 1; "U.S.A.— New Boss in Africa," *New Africa* 7, no. 2 (1948): 1. On growing U.S. economic interests in Africa, see William Minter, *King Solomon's Mines Revisited: Western Interests and the Burdened History of Southern Africa* (New York: Basic Books, 1986); Borstelmann, *Apartheid's Reluctant Uncle;* and William Alphaeus Hunton, *Decision in Africa: Sources of Current Conflict* (New York: International, 1957).

99. Duberman, *Paul Robeson*, pp. 330–33; author's interview with Doxey Wilkerson, September 8, 1990, Norwalk, Conn.; Anthony, "Max Yergan and South Africa," pp. 194–96. For CAA accounts of the 1948 dispute and split, see Hunton Papers, box 1, folders 16 (CAA Correspon-

dence) and 17 (CAA Administrative), MG 237. See also Horne, *Black and Red,* pp.115–19; Hollis R. Lynch, *Black American Radicals and the Liberation of Africa: The Council on African Affairs, 1937–1955* (Ithaca: Africana Studies and Research Center, Cornell University, 1978), pp. 35–37; and D. Hunton, *Alphaeus Hunton,* p. 78.

100. Anthony, "Max Yergan and South Africa," p. 199.

101. Quoted in Duberman, *Paul Robeson,* p. 331; "Council on African Affairs Faces Split on Policies," *Chicago Defender,* February 28, 1948, p. 13.

102. Quoted in Duberman, *Paul Robeson,* p. 331; Hunton Papers, box 1, folders 16 (CAA Correspondence) and 17 (CAA Administrative), MG 237.

103. Duberman, *Paul Robeson,* p. 392; Anthony M. Platt, *E. Franklin Frazier Reconsidered* (New Brunswick, N. J.: Rutgers University Press, 1991), pp. 193–94.

104. See W. E. B. Du Bois Papers, University of Massachusetts, Amherst, CAA FBI files, box 376, folder 31, for nomination of Channing H. Tobias to be U. S. alternate at sixth General Assembly of the United Nations, October 18, 1951, U. S. Senate Committee on Foreign Relations; A. H. Belmont from F. J. Baumgardner, re CAA, Inc., Internal Security, June 28, 1954; Director FBI (100-69266) from SAC, Cincinnati (100-11431), July 20, 1954. See also Duberman, *Paul Robeson,* pp. 332–33, 441; Louis Lautier, "Max Yergan, Ex–Y Official, Once Pal, Now Foe of Reds," *Chicago Defender,* May 24, 1952, p. 1. Kenneth Robert Janken, *Rayford W. Logan and the Dilemma of the African-American Intellectual* (Amherst: University of Massachusetts Press, 1993), pp. 191–92.

105. Hugh H. Smythe (NAACP Department of Special Research), "Afro-Americans Petition the United Nations for Equal Rights," W. E. B. Du Bois Papers, microfilm collection, Columbia University, reel 60, frames 708–9. See also Lauren, *Power and Prejudice,* pp. 172–73; Marable, *W. E. B. Du Bois,* p. 169; and Horne, *Black and Red,* pp. 76–82.

106. "Statement for U. N. Cites Denial of Freedom: NAACP Research Group Cites Hypocrisy in U. S.; Statement Charges Failure to Live Up to Ideals Is Biggest Threat to Democracy," *Baltimore Afro-American,* October 25, 1947, p. 3.

107. Smythe, "Afro-Americans Petition the United Nations for Equal Rights."

108. Ibid. In 1946 the National Negro Congress also presented a petition appealing to the United Nations Security Council "to intervene in United States affairs in order to halt the oppression of Negro-Americans"; see John Robert Badger, "Is the UN Worth Saving," *Chicago Defender,* June 15, 1946, p. 15.

109. Smythe, "Afro-Americans Petition the United Nations for Equal Rights." The journal established by the 1945 Pan-African Congress in Manchester, *Pan-Africa: A Monthly Journal of African Life, History, and Thought,* reprinted the NAACP petition to the U.N. as a special issue. For correspondence regarding publication of this document, see Du Bois Papers: T. R. Makonnen, editor and publisher, *Pan-Africa,* to Lillian Murphy, October 21, 1947, reel 60, frames 699–700; Hugh H. Smythe to Makonnen, October 27, 1947, reel 60, frame 702; and Makonnen to Smythe, July 9, 1948, reel 62, frame 1029.

110. Du Bois, memorandum to White, 14 November 1946, Du Bois Papers, reel 59, frame 257.

111. Memorandum to: Secretary and Board of Directors, NAACP, from: Du Bois, re the United Nations and the NAACP, September 7, 1948, in *The Correspondence of W. E. B. Du Bois,* vol. 3, ed. Herbert Aptheker (Amherst: University of Massachusetts Press, 1978), pp. 243–45. The NAACP's increasingly anti-Communist internal policies were also important to this rift. As political pressure from the right mounted, and some members lost their jobs or were denied government positions because of their "pinkist tendencies" in 1947 and 1948, parts of the NAACP began internal purging of Communists, and the *Crisis* "assumed an anti-communist tone" (Marable, *W. E. B. Du Bois,* p. 173).

112. Marable, *W. E. B. Du Bois*, pp. 174–75; Duberman, *Paul Robeson*, p. 334; Horne, *Black and Red*, pp. 102–4.

113. T. R. Makonnen, to W. E. B. Du Bois, February 2, 1949; Du Bois Papers, reel 64, frames 203–5.

114. In 1948 Makonnen of the Pan-African Federation wrote to Smythe at the NAACP, expressing concern that there be direct and continuous contact between the organizations: Makonnen to Smythe, July 9, 1948, Du Bois Papers, reel 62, frame 1029. For a proposed petition on U.S. human rights violations in Cold War repression, see "To: The General Assembly of the United Nations and the Commission of Human Rights," n.d., Du Bois Papers, reel 60, frame 983.

115. "U.S. Should Show Interest in Africa," *Baltimore Afro-American*, September 1, 1956. In the intervening years, West Africans such as Nkrumah had solicited the help of the NAACP in gaining U.S. economic aid. See Kwame Nkrumah to Walter White, July 7, 1951, and Nkrumah to Henry Lee Moon, n.d., NAACP Papers, part 14, Race Relations in the International Arena, microfilm reel 2, frames 162 and 179.

116. Examination of the papers of Metz T. P. Lochard, executive editor of the *Chicago Defender* throughout the 1940s and 1950s (Howard University); the papers of P. L. Prattis, executive director of the *Pittsburgh Courier* through the same period (Howard University); and the papers of Claude Barnett and the Associated Negro Press (microfilm, Center for Research Libraries) suggests that this will not be an easy task. Correspondence and business records reveal no records of this important shift. It seems highly plausible that in the anti-Communist fervor of the late 1940s, many of these records were "cleaned." One indication is that although George Padmore wrote almost weekly for both papers from the early 1940s through 1947, there is no record of the editors' correspondence with him until the late 1950s, *after* he had become an adviser to the newly independent state of Ghana. Patrick S. Washburn, *A Question of Sedition: The Federal Government's Investigation of the Black Press during World War II* (New York: Oxford University Press, 1986), does not deal with the period beyond 1945.

117. Caute, *The Great Fear*, pp. 447, 449.

118. In November 1948, Walter White expressed dismay at the "increasing tendency on the part of the government agencies to associate activities on interracial matters with disloyalty": McCoy and Ruetten, *Quest and Response*, p. 264. On circulation, see Roland E. Wolseley, *The Black Press, U.S.A.* (Ames: Iowa State University Press, 1971), p. 56. See also Andrew Buni, *Robert L. Vann of the "Pittsburgh Courier"* (Pittsburgh: University of Pittsburgh Press, 1974), p. 325.

119. "Isolationism Is Dead," *Chicago Defender*, March 22, 1947.

120. "Segregation in the Armed Services," *Pittsburgh Courier*, April 10, 1948; Jervis Anderson, *A. Philip Randolph: A Biographical Portrait* (New York: Harcourt Brace Jovanovich, 1972), pp. 275–82. On Randolph's campaign, see also Lem Graves Jr., "Civil Disobedience Movement Urged," *Pittsburgh Courier*, April 10, 1948, p. 1; Theodore Stanford, "Randolph Invites Arrest: Violates Provision of Pending Draft Law," *Pittsburgh Courier*, July 24, 1948; and "A. Philip Randolph," *Pittsburgh Courier*, August 28, 1948.

121. "Financing Imperialism," *Pittsburgh Courier*, June 7, 1947 (emphasis added).

122. "The Marshall Plan," *Chicago Defender*, March 13, 1948.

123. Editorial, *Pittsburgh Courier*, May 21, 1949.

124. Robert J. McMahon, *Colonialism and Cold War: The United States and the Struggle for Indonesian Independence, 1945–1949* (Ithaca: Cornell University Press, 1981), p. 260, and see also pp. 253–80; William Roger Louis and Ronald Robinson, "The United States and the Liquidation of British Empire in Tropical Africa, 1941–1951," in *The Transfer of Power in Africa: Decolonization, 1940–1960,* ed. Prosser Gifford and William Roger Louis (New Haven: Yale University

Press, 1982), p. 46; Leffler, *A Preponderance of Power*, pp. 259, 302; Borstelmann, *Apartheid's Reluctant Uncle*, pp. 58–59.

125. As noted earlier, attention to the Dutch East Indies was an important component in the growth of black American anticolonialism. For earlier African American coverage of the Indonesian struggle for independence, see Kumar Goshal, "Dutch Promise of Dominion Status to Malaya Only Cloak for More Dominance," *Pittsburgh Courier*, March 13, 1943; "Indonesians and the Dutch," *Baltimore Afro-American*, November 10, 1945, p. 4; "Dutch Truce Hailed as Victory for Indonesians," *Baltimore Afro-American*, November 10, 1945, p. 6; "Indonesians Slaughtered to Halt Asiatic Revolt," *Baltimore Afro-American*, November 17, 1945, p. 18; S. A. Haynes, "The Battle for Freedom," *Afro-American*, April 13, 1946, p. 7; "The Rape of Indonesia," *Chicago Defender*, August 2, 1947; and "American Dollars Back Dutch Imperialism," *Chicago Defender*, August 30, 1947.

126. "India Takes the Lead," *Chicago Defender*, January 22, 1949; J. A. Rogers, "The Rape of Indonesia, South Africa, Only Bodes Ill for the Oppressors," *Pittsburgh Courier*, January 22, 1949, p. 15; Trezzvant W. Anderson, "Rape of Indonesia Stirs Colored Races," *Pittsburgh Courier*, January 1, 1949, p. 1; Anderson, "War between Races Can Spring from Indonesia," *Pittsburgh Courier*, January 8, 1949, p. 2; "Darker Races Give UN Mandate Calling for Indonesian Showdown," *Pittsburgh Courier*, January 29, 1949, p. 7.

127. Walter White, "Dutch Lying Has Been Incredible and Contemptible," *Chicago Defender*, January 8, 1949, p. 7.

128. "Bloody Dutch Go to War," *Chicago Defender*, January 1, 1949.

129. W. E. B. Du Bois, *The World and Africa: An Inquiry into the Part Which Africa Has Played in World History* (New York: International, 1987), p. 265.

CHAPTER SIX Hearts and Mines

1. See, e.g., W. E. B. Du Bois, "to the House Committee on Foreign Relations on Aug. 8, testifying on behalf of the Council on African Affairs and the American Continental Congress for Peace, in opposition to the Congressional Military Assistance Bill," and the "Statement to the President of the United States, signed by 55 Negro churchmen," which argued in behalf of colonial independence: *New Africa* 8, no. 8 (1949). Before a Harlem rally of five thousand in June 1949, Robeson argued that "the Big Money Rulers of America have taken on the role of bankers and overlords of all Western Europe and its colonial holdings": *New Africa* 8, no. 7 (1949).

2. A $200 check for assistance to the families of Nigerian workers was sent in January 1950 via Nnamdi Azikiwe following his visit to the United States. "African Aid Committee Sends Help to Nigerian Strike Victims," *New Africa* 9, no. 1 (1950): 1; W. A. Hunton Papers, box 1, folder 18 (CAA Financial Records), MG 237, Schomburg Library, New York; "African Aid Unit Gives Miners $200," *Baltimore Afro-American*, January 21, 1950, p. 19; Hollis R. Lynch, *Black American Radicals and the Liberation of Africa: The Council on African Affairs, 1937–1955* (Ithaca: Africana Studies and Research Center, Cornell University, 1978), pp. 47–48; Gerald Horne, *Black and Red: W. E. B. Du Bois and the Afro-American Response to the Cold War, 1944–1963* (Albany: State University of New York Press, 1986), p. 184.

Another $200 check was sent in March 1950 from Du Bois to M. A. O. Imodu, president, and Nauka Eze, secretary general of the Nigerian National Federation of Labor. Du Bois to Mr. Nduka Eze, Secretary General, Nigerian National Federation of Labor, March 28, 1950, Hunton Papers, box 1, folder 18, MG 237. See "Azikiwe Questions U.S. Policy in Africa; Urges Support for Africans' Freedom," *New Africa* 9, no. 1 (1950): 2.

3. See *New Africa* 8, no. 2 (1949) and 7, no. 11 (1948) for reports of deportation from Liberia of journalists who had criticized the company (organized by Stettinius) and U.S. plans to establish a military base at the Port of Monrovia. See also, William Alphaeus Hunton, "Liberia's Open Door," chap. 9 in his *Decision in Africa: Sources of Current Conflict* (New York: International, 1957), pp. 110–14.

4. On the banning, W. E. B. Du Bois reflected that "every once in a while something happens that makes us realize how dangerous the truth is even when spoken by oppressed people, and how men fear the truth or any discussion of the evils of which they are the authors": "Repression Madness Rules South Africa," *New Africa* 9, no. 4 (1950).

5. Sterling Stuckey, *Slave Culture: Nationalist Theory and the Foundations of Black America* (New York: Oxford University Press, 1987), pp. 356–58.

6. *Paul Robeson Speaks: Writings, Speeches, Interviews, 1918–1974*, ed. Philip Foner (New York: Citadel Press, 1978), p. 207.

7. Ibid.

8. Thomas Borstelmann, *Apartheid's Reluctant Uncle: The United States and Southern Africa in the Early Cold War* (New York: Oxford University Press, 1993), p. 195.

9. Excerpted in *New Africa* 10, no. 2 (1951): 1. The Truman statement that the West African Youth League refers to is from Truman's State of the Union Address, January 8, 1951, and is also quoted in Borstelmann, *Apartheid's Reluctant Uncle,* pp. 162–63.

10. Martin Bauml Duberman, *Paul Robeson* (New York: Knopf, 1988), pp. 342–50.

11. Ibid., pp. 342–43.

12. *Paul Robeson Speaks*, p. 203.

13. Hunton Papers, box 1, folder 19 (CAA Organizational, 1945–55), MG 237.

14. Ibid.; Duberman, *Paul Robeson*, p. 434.

15. Ibid. On the revocation of Robeson's passport, see Duberman, *Paul Robeson,* pp. 388–90. See also Warren Olney III, Assistant Attorney General, Criminal Division, to Director FBI, (146-28-376), 1953, in W. E. B. Du Bois Papers, University of Massachusetts, Amherst, box 379, folder 60, pp. 1–3.

16. Borstelmann, *Apartheid's Reluctant Uncle,* p. 139; William Roger Louis and Ronald Robinson, "The United States and the Liquidation of the British Empire in Tropical Africa, 1941–1951," in *The Transfer of Power in Africa: Decolonization, 1940–1960,* ed. Prosser Gifford and William Roger Louis (New Haven: Yale University Press, 1982), pp. 45–46.

17. E. H. Bourgerie, director, Office of African Affairs, to A. W. Childs, American Consul General, Lagos, Nigeria, April 23, 1951, RG 59, 745H.00/4-2351, National Archives.

18. William Minter, *King Solomon's Mines Revisited: Western Interests and the Burdened History of Southern Africa* (New York: Basic Books, 1986), pp. 116–17.

19. Borstelmann, *Apartheid's Reluctant Uncle,* pp. 44–46, 181, 198–99.

20. Minter, *King Solomon's Mines Revisited,* pp. 116–17; Borstelmann, *Apartheid's Reluctant Uncle,* pp. 96–99. Minter explains that U.S. planners gave particular attention to the mineral-rich south, from the Congo's cobalt, essential for jet engines, to the range of minerals—manganese, chrome, asbestos, copper, platinum, and uranium—from farther south. The CIA was instructed to provide covert surveillance and protection for Union Minière in the Congo, as well as for manganese and chrome complexes in South Africa, Southern Rhodesia, and Mozambique. See also Thomas Borstelmann, "Apartheid, Colonialism and the Cold War: The United States and Southern Africa, 1945–1952" (Ph.D. diss., Duke University, 1990), p. 252. See A. W. Childs, American Consul General, Lagos, to Department of State, Washington, April 23, 1951, RG 59, 745H.00/6-951, for an example of regular reports assessing the availability of minerals and other raw materials and industrial capacity "from a war potential standpoint."

Minter and Borstelmann are important correctives to scholars who have argued that in the period immediately following the 1945 United Nations Organization conference in San Francisco, the U.S. government was willing to take a back seat to European colonial powers on issues relating to Africa, and who suggest that U.S. concern about Africa dated only from the post-1953 period and can be best understood as a reaction to the new Soviet interest in the continent. See, e.g., Peter Duignan and L. H. Gann, *The United States and Africa: A History* (New York: Cambridge University Press, 1989), pp. 285–86.

21. Borstelmann, *Apartheid's Reluctant Uncle,* pp. 143, 161. Melvyn P. Leffler, *A Preponderance of Power: National Security, the Truman Administration, and the Cold War* (Stanford, Calif.: Stanford University Press, 1992), pp. 506–9.

22. Bourgerie to Childs, April 23, 1951.

23. George F. Kennan, "Notes for Essays," Spring 1952, George F. Kennan Papers, box 26, Seely G. Mudd Library, Princeton University. I thank Anders Stephanson for this document.

24. Paul Gordon Lauren, *Power and Prejudice: The Politics and Diplomacy of Racial Discrimination* (Boulder, Colo.: Westview Press, 1988), pp. 164, 192–95; Borstelmann, *Apartheid's Reluctant Uncle,* pp. 64–65, 141–42.

25. Borstelmann, *Apartheid's Reluctant Uncle,* p. 161.

26. See, e.g., Taylor Branch, *Parting the Waters: America in the King Years, 1954–1963* (New York: Simon & Schuster, 1988), p. 807: "Intelligence reports noted that the Soviet Union broadcast 1,420 anti-U.S. commentaries about the Birmingham crisis. . . . When President Kennedy sent a message on May 21 to a summit conference of independent African nations, stressing the importance of unity in the free world, Prime Minister Milton Obote of Uganda replied with an official protest against the fire hoses and 'snarling dogs' of Birmingham."

27. Telegram from Crowley, Lagos, to Secretary of State, April 5, 1951; and Acheson to American Consul, Lagos, April 6, 1951 ("Cleared in substance by phone with Foley, Justice Department") RG 59, 745H.011/4-551 and 745H.111/4-551; Department of State, Intelligence Report no. 6307, June 12, 1953, reel 7, frame 1055, microfilm, Columbia University.

28. On criticism in India see Carl T. Rowan, *The Pitiful and the Proud* (New York: Random House, 1956), pp. 21, 162–63.

29. From American Consul, Lagos, to Department of State, August 8, 1950, RG 59, 511.45H/8-850.

30. Roger P. Ross, Public Affairs Officer, American Consulate Accra, to Department of State, January 9, 1951, RG 59, 511.45K21/1-951.

31. Ibid.

32. Ibid.

33. Robert Alan, "Paul Robeson—The Lost Shepherd," *Crisis* 58, no. 11 (1951). On the publication of this article and other attacks on Robeson (including Walter White's "The Strange Case of Paul Robeson," published in *Ebony*, February 1951), see Duberman, *Paul Robeson,* p. 395. See also "Paul Robeson, Right or Wrong: Right, says W.E.B. Du Bois; Wrong, says Walter White," *Negro Digest,* March 1950, pp. 8–18.

34. Dwight D. Eisenhower had been "one of the earliest champions and most consistent supporters of America's unique brand of psychological warfare" from the time of the North African campaign in World War Two. See Blanche Wiesen Cook, *The Declassified Eisenhower: A Divided Legacy* (New York: Doubleday, 1981), pp. 14–15.

35. See, e.g., Thomas C. Sorenson, *The Word War: The Story of American Propaganda* (New York: Harper & Row, 1968), p. 165. See also John W. Henderson, *The United States Information Agency* (New York: Praeger, 1969); and Robert E. Elder, *The Information Machine: The United States Information Agency and American Foreign Policy* (Syracuse, N.Y.: Syracuse University

Press, 1968). These works, based on the USIA records, have little on Africa in the 1950s except a few project files on education and leadership programs in Nigeria and the Belgian Congo. One partial explanation is that the USIA was not independent from the State Department until 1953. Even after this date, the agency's close coordination with the State Department means that much of its work was still recorded in the Department of State General Files, National Archives, RG 59, sec. 5: Cultural Affairs, Propaganda, and Psychological Warfare. There are substantial records of USIS work in East Africa, West Africa, and South Africa.

36. Before 1953, when the USIA was established as a separate agency, USIS activities were directly under the auspices of the State Department. These records too are held in the department's General Files, RG 59, class 500: Culture Affairs, Propaganda and Psychological Warfare. Department of State records for the pre-1940 period were classified differently, and the specifically cultural categories were not saved; however, I have recovered some of this work by cross-referencing State Department political files with the separate embassy files.

37. E.g., Willard Quincy Stanton, American Consul General, Lagos, to Department of State, April 27, 1950, re "Political and Economic Events in Nigeria for the two weeks ending April 22, 1950," RG 59, 745H.00/4-2750.

38. Hyman Bloom, American Consul, Accra, to Department of State, April 2, 1951, RG 59, 511.45K5/4-251. The following year William E. Cole Jr., American consul in Accra, complained to Washington that his task was complicated by the fact that Gold Coast Africans "feel a community of interest with their fellow black men both in the United States and in the Union of South Africa": "Semi-Annual evaluation reports for periods ending May 31, 1951, and November 30, 1951," RG 59, 511.45G/2-1552, p. 6.

39. Robert Ross, American Vice Consul, Lagos, to Department of State, Washington, July 30, 1952:, re "Major Releases from the USIS Office, Lagos, published in the Local Press during the period June 1–30, 1952," RG 59, 511.45H21/7-3052.

40. The scripts were written by Noon and translated into Swahili by Symons W. Onyango, the translator for the information office. Edmund J. Dorsz, American Consul General, Nairobi, to Department of State, August 5, 1953, enclosing John A. Noon, Regional Public Affairs Officer, *IIA Nairobi Introduces Family Serial Program for African Audience*, RG 59, 511.45R5/8-553.

41. Gunnar Myrdal, Richard Stern, and Arnold Rose, *An American Dilemma: The Negro Problem and Modern Democracy* (New York: Harper, 1944); Dorsz to Department of State, August 5, 1953; enclosure, Noon, *IIA Nairobi Introduces Family Serial.* Programs focused on the following themes: ethnic accommodation as the American way; democracy in action; education opportunities and getting ahead; projections of American life; and advantages of scientific farming.

42. Department of State from Lagos, February 15, 1951, re "Press Misstatements on American Foreign Policy and USIS Replies," RG 59, 511.45H/2-1551.

43. Department of State from Lagos, April 25, 1950, re "Left-Wing *Labour Champion* Attacks United States Information Service," RG 59, 511.45R/4-2550.

44. American Consulate General, Accra, to Department of State, January 31, 1957, re "Current Developments in the Gold Coast," January 16–31, 1957, RG 59, 745K.00/1–3157.

45. Department of State from Lagos, November 24, 1950, re "Out of Context Use by Zik's Press of USIS Broadcast Material," RG 59, 511.45H21/11-2450.

46. American Consulate General, Johannesburg to Department of State, March 24, 1952 (reference Department's Confidential Airgram, February 6, 1952), re "Radio Programs Dealing with the American Negro," RG 59, 511.45A4/3-2452; W. J. Gallman, American Embassy, Cape Town to Department of State, April 3, 1952 (reference February 6, airgram), re "Projected Transcribed Radio and Television Series," RG 59, 511.45A4/4-352.

47. See Verus, "The Life and Times of Benjamin Franklin," and Verus, "True Tales—Abraham Lincoln," in the *World* (Johannesburg), June 2 and 23, 1956. For Voice of America jazz broadcasts, see *World,* November 17, 1956. "The Globe-trotters Spread Goodwill," *Bantu World,* July 2, 1955, supp. pp. 13–15, and "Althea Gibson—First Negro Lady of U.S. Tennis," *World,* January 28, 1956, p. 11, reported on tours of black American athletes.

48. A. W. Childs, American Consul General, Lagos, to Department of State, December 13, 1951, RG 59, 511.45H21/1-352. Typical among articles released by USIS and successfully reprinted in local papers were "Primary Elections in the U.S." and "Political Experience and Leadership Essential: The Choice of a U.S. President," both in the *Daily Times* (Lagos) in 1952. See Ross to Department of State, September 10, 1952.

49. Memorandum from the Representative at the Trusteeship Council (Sears) to the Secretary of State, February 15, 1956, Department of State IO/ODA Files, lot 62 D, 225, *Foreign Relations* 18 (1955–1957): 37–40.

50. Fitzhugh Green, *American Propaganda Abroad* (New York: Hippocrene Books, 1988), p. 22.

51. George M. Atkinson, American Consul, Accra, April 9, 1948, file 800 4/9/48, no. 21, RG 84, box 32: Foreign Service Posts of the Department of State, Gold Coast. The Gold Coast Advisory Committee was set up along with CASNA (Committee for African Students in North America) to oversee the activities of the students. Members included Chairman Emory Ross, secretary of the Foreign Missions Conference of North America as chairman; Academic Counselor Edgar J. Fisher, associate director of the Institute of International Education; and Personal Counselor Channing H. Tobias, director of the Phelps-Stokes Fund. For a later example of cooperation between USIE and CASNA, see Cole's report to the Department of State, for periods ending May 31 and November 30, 1951.

52. Robert W. Stookey, American Vice-Consul, Nairobi, to Department of State, November 22, 1950: re "Publicizing USIE Film Acquisitions, Enclosure: Specimen copy of the November 24 issue of the ISIE Nairobi Newsletter, p. 3," RG 59, 511.45R5/11-2250.

53. For example, between August and October 1950, *President Truman Reports on Korea* was seen in 20 theaters by 12,677 people; the 35-mm *United Nations in Korea* was seen by 36,158 people in 28 theaters and a 16-mm version by 1,745 people in 19 theaters. See Angus Ward, American Consul General, Nairobi, to Department of State, January 5, 1951, RG 59 511.45R5/1-55-1.

54. Robert Ross, American Vice-Consul, Lagos, to Department of State, June 2, 1952, re "Major Releases from the USIS Office, Lagos, published in the Local Press during the period April 1–30, 1952," RG 511.45H21/6-252.

55. Mombasa to Department of State, January 29, 1951, RG 59, 511.45T21/1-2951.

56. Willard Quincy Stanton, American Consul General, Lagos, to Department of State, November 13, 1950, RG 59, 511.45H/10-3050.

57. Willard Quincy Stanton, American Consul General, Lagos, to Department of State, January 17, 1951, re "Major Releases from the USIS Office, published in the local press during the period November 30–December 31, 1950," RG 511.45H21/1-1751; Childs to Department of State, December 13, 1951.

While trying to promote fear of Soviet imperialism, USIS attempted to project the United States as a champion of independence from colonial rule: e.g., "U.S. Grants Self Government to the Territory of Puerto Rico" was reprinted in the *Daily Success* (Lagos). Other attempts at portraying Soviet imperialism included the USIS article "Colonial Affairs Specialist Is Expected Today from Accra: Story of Communist Acts Told," reprinted in *New Africa* (Onitsha, Nigeria). See Ross to Department of State, September 10, 1952.

58. E.g., the USIS release "U.S. Labor *versus* Communist Aggression," was reprinted in the *West African Examiner* and the *Nigerian Observer* (Port Hartcourt) and "Trade Unionism in Amer-

ica" in the *Nigerian Catholic Herald* (Lagos) in December 1950. See Stanton to Department of State, January 17, 1951.

59. See Lauren, *Power and Prejudice*, pp. 166–74, for the role of India at the UN in 1946–47.

60. Robert J. McMahon, "United States Cold War Strategy in South Asia: Making a Military Commitment to Pakistan, 1947–1954," *Journal of American History* 75, no. 3 (1988): 819–20. See also Dennis Merrill, "Indo-American Relations, 1947–1950: A Missed Opportunity in Asia," *Diplomatic History* 11 (Summer 1987): 203–26.

61. Robert W. Stookey, American Vice-Consul, Nairobi, to Department of State, August 14, 1950, re "IE motion pictures filmed on Nehru's visit to the U.S.," RG 59, 511.45R5/8-1450.

62. Ross to Department of State, July 30, 1952.

63. McMahon, "United States Cold War Strategy in South Asia," pp. 820–22.

64. Department of State, Acheson, to American Consul, Nairobi, Kenya, A-34, January 15, 1951, RG 59, 511-45R5/1-1551; and Angus Ward, American Consul General, Nairobi, to Department of State, February 6, 1951, RG 59, 511.45R5/2-651. USIS in East Africa was especially concerned about the African-Asian bloc, both in Kenya and internationally. Noon called India another "source of outside influence on the subversive nationalist elements in Kenya. . . . It appears that the premise motivating the Republic of India . . . is the belief that the interest of the Asian community would be best served by creating an Asian-African front": John A. Noon, Regional Public Affairs Officer, Consulate General, Nairobi, to Department of State, January 8, 1953, re "Semi-Annual evaluation report for the period ending December 31, 1952," RG 59, 511.45S/1-853. See also Chapter 7.

65. Memorandum from the consul general at Leopoldville (McGregor), December 28, 1955, *Foreign Relations* 18 (1955–57): 25.

66. Borstelmann, *Apartheid's Reluctant Uncle*, pp. 143–44. Borstelmann's work is an important corrective to scholars such as William Roger Louis and Ronald Robinson, who have argued that in the immediate postwar period the U.S. role in the de-colonization of Africa came from top-down U.S. pressure on the British and had little to do with pressure from African anticolonial movements ("The United States and the Liquidation of the British Empire," pp. 45–46). Even if one accepts their emphasis on the role of U.S. pressure in colonial reform and independence, their conclusion that nationalist movements were relatively insignificant begs the question of what animated the "instability" in the colonies that so concerned the United States.

67. Bourgerie to Childs, April 23, 1951. An example of the earliest intelligence on nationalist movements in Africa is the 1942 OSS report "Native Morale in West and Equatorial Africa," discussing differences in "tribal," "racial," and "national" patriotism. See also the 1943 report "A Strategic Survey of the Gold Coast," stating that the West African National Congress and the West African Students Union whose "ideology is nationalistic and based on a pan-Africanism, . . . command a considerable following among the natives": OSS/State Department Intelligence and Research Reports, vol. 13, Africa (1941–61), reel 1, frames 36–39, and reel 7, frames 874 and 875, microfilm, Columbia University.

68. Mombasa 187 to Department of State, January 23, 1951, RG 59, 511.45T2/1-2351.

69. Noon to Department of State, January 8, 1953.

70. In the recent tendency to get away from a bipolar fixation on U.S.-Soviet relations, scholars of the Cold War have begun to look at the interplay of local politics and bipolar relations, and have argued that local forces (classes, elites, parties, and individuals) played active and in some cases crucial roles in unfolding events. See, e.g., Bruce Cumings, *The Origins of the Korean War* (Princeton: Princeton University Press, 1981); and Robert J. McMahon, "The Cold War in Asia: Toward a New Synthesis?" *Diplomatic History* 12 (Summer 1988). See also Robert J. McMahon,

Colonialism and the Cold War: The United States and the Struggle for Indonesian Independence,
1945–49 (Ithaca: Cornell University Press, 1981), p. 319; and Richard H. Immerman, *The CIA*
in Guatemala: The Foreign Policy of Intervention (Austin: University of Texas Press, 1982), pp.
82–100.

71. Noon to Department of State, January 8, 1953.

72. A. W. Childs, Consul General, Lagos, to Department of State, January 28, 1952, re "Fortnightly Newsletter—January 14–January 26, 1952," RG 59, 745.00/1-2852. See also Erwin P.
Keeler, American Consul General, Lagos, to Department of State, September 11, 1953, re "Conference on Nigerian Constitution," RG 59, 745H.03/9-853 and Keeler to Department of State,
September 15, 1953, re "Rupture of Alliance between NCNC and Action Group," RG 59,
745H.03/11-2853.

73. Erwin P. Keeler, American Consul General, Lagos, to Department of State, September 9,
1953, re "Communism in Nigeria today," RG 59, 745H.001/8-1453.

74. FBI report (NY 100-19377), June 3, 1952, in Du Bois Papers, box 377, folder 136. See also
Horne, *Black and Red,* pp. 187–88; and Lynch, *Black American Radicals,* p. 50.

75. W. A. Hunton, "Outline of Proposed Testimony," October 23, 1953, Hunton Papers, box 1,
folder 19, MG 237.

76. Herbert Brownell Jr., Attorney General of the United States, Petitioner; Council on African
Affairs, Inc., Respondent: "On Petition for an order requiring the Council on African Affairs,
Inc. to register with the Attorney General as required by Section 7(b), (c) and (d) of the Internal Security Act of 1950," in Du Bois Papers, microfilm collection, Columbia University, reel 69,
frames 692–93.

77. FBI report (NY 100-19377), June 3, 1952.

78. Hunton, "Outline of Proposed Testimony."

79. Herbert Brownell Jr., Attorney General of the United States, Petitioner; Council on African
Affairs, Inc., Respondent: "On Petition for an order."

80. In each case, the CAA's response was deemed "not responsive to the allegations of the petition, redundant, argumentative, and impertinent" by Justice Department attorneys David B.
Irons, Troy B. Conner, Max. H. Goldschein, and Francis E. Jordan. See Herbert Brownell Jr., Attorney General of the United States, Petitioner, vs. Council on African Affairs, Inc., Respondent:
"Petitioner's Motion to Strike Certain Allegations in the Respondent's Answer to the First Petition," Du Bois Papers, reel 69, frames 734–35.

81. Anthony M. Platt, *E. Franklin Frazier Reconsidered* (New Brunswick, N.J.: Rutgers University Press, 1991), p. 196.

82. Dorothy Hunton, *Alphaeus Hunton: The Unsung Valiant* (Chesapeake, Va.: ECA Associates,
1986), p. 82; Gerald Horne, *Communist Front? The Civil Rights Congress, 1946–1956* (London:
Associated University Presses, 1988), p. 241; David Caute, *The Great Fear: The Anti-Communist*
Purge under Truman and Eisenhower (New York: Simon & Schuster, 1978), p. 179.

83. D. Hunton, *Alphaeus Hunton,* p. 86.

84. Hunton to Du Bois, April 2, 1952, Du Bois Papers, reel 68, frame 187; Hunton, "Emergency
Conference on the Present Crisis in South Africa," reel 68, frame 197.

85. For summation of activities and money raised for CAA defense, see Du Bois fund-raising
letter, June 18, 1953, Du Bois Papers, reel 69, frame 697. For financial records of disbursements sent through the Corn Exchange Trust Bank, see Hunton Papers, box 1, folder 18, MG
237. On CAA support of the Defiance Campaign, see Lynch, *Black American Radicals,* pp.
44–45; Bernard Makhosezwe Magubane, *The Ties That Bind: African-American Consciousness*
of Africa (Trenton, New Jersey: Africa World Press Inc., 1989), pp. 211–12; Horne, *Black and*
Red, p. 185.

86. Ellen Schrecker, "McCarthyism and the Decline of American Communism, 1945–1960," in Michael E. Brown et al., ed., *New Studies in the Politics and Culture of U.S. Communism* (New York: Monthly Review Press, 1993), pp. 123–40.

87. R. T. Bokwe (Middledrift, Cape Province, South Africa) to Hunton, February 11, 1953, Hunton Papers, box 1, folder 16, acknowledging receipt of $900. Later that year, W. M. Sisulu, secretary general of the ANC, wrote to Robeson, CAA chairman, expressing "gratitude for the assistance you have given us in our Campaign for the Defiance of Unjust Laws": Sisulu to Robeson, June 9, 1953, Hunton Papers, box 1, folder 16, MG 23. See also O. R. Tambo, for Secretariat, ANC, to Du Bois, November 9, 1954, Du Bois Papers, reel 70, frame 389. Tambo continued to seek support for the treason trial: e.g., Tambo to Du Bois, November 1957, reel 72, frame 342. CAA leaders also corresponded with Yusuf Cachalia of the South African Indian Congress. See Yusuf Cachalia, South African Indian Congress, to Hunton, April 15, 1954, Hunton Papers, box 1, folder 16, MG 237.

Coverage of the CAA and Robeson in South African progressive papers included "Salute from Paul Robeson: Messages to Natal Indian Conference," *Advance,* February 11, 1954; "World Wide Campaign to Free Paul Robeson," *Advance,* June 10, 1954; and Walter Sisulu, "Let Us Work Together," *Fighting Talk,* June 1954, p. 9. On South African support and acknowledgment of the CAA, see also Horne, *Black and Red,* pp. 185–86.

88. Author's interview with Walter Sisulu, February 10, 1992, Johannesburg; author's interview with Henry Mohothe, April 24, 1992, Johannesburg. Azikiwe's *West African Pilot* was available in Johannesburg at the public reading room of the South African Institute of Race Relations. A collection from this period is held in the William Cullen Library, University of the Witwatersrand, Johannesburg.

89. Sisulu interview. See Walter M. Sisulu, "The Development of African Nationalism," *India Quarterly* 10, no. 3 (1954), for analysis of the Pan-African tradition of Du Bois and Azikiwe.

90. W. M. Sisulu, secretary general, ANC, to Du Bois, March 23, 1953, Du Bois Papers, reel 69, frame 438.

91. Ibid.

92. Du Bois to Sisulu, April 9, 1953; and Du Bois to Padmore, April 9, 1953, Du Bois Papers, reel 69, frames 439 and 1179.

93. He also forwarded a copy to Du Bois along with the list of addresses: Sisulu to Du Bois, May 6, 1953, Du Bois Papers, reel 69, frame 440. See frame 441 for Sisulu's call for a Pan-African Congress (sample copy addressed to the President General, N. Rh. African National Congress, Lusaka, N. Rhodesia).

94. John Edgar Hoover, Director, FBI to CIA director (Attention: Deputy Director Pleas), April 13, 1954, in Du Bois Papers, box 60A, folder 379. For U.S. intelligence on Pan-Africanism, see also Horne, *Black and Red,* p. 187. *Spotlight on Africa* was provided by George A. VanNoy, FBI Heidelberg, Germany, to John Edgar Hoover, Director, FBI, July 22, 1953, with a note reading "The attached material was made available by the assistant Chief of Staff, G-2, Headquarters, United States Army, Europe": Du Bois Papers, box 379, folder 60.

95. William E. Cole Jr., American Consul, to Department of State, May 5, 1953, re "Conference of West African Nationalists," RG 59, 745G.00/5-2253; Cole to Secretary of State, November 27, 1953, on meeting of West African nationalists at Kumasi, RG 59, 745.00/11-2753; and Cole to Secretary of State, December 8, 1953, RG 59, 745F.00/12–853.

96. This is true of the party in Moscow, the American Communist Party, and, in a somewhat more complex fashion, the South African Communist Party.

97. "In Quotation Marks," *Spotlight on Africa,* June 22, 1954, p. 5; in Hunton Papers, box 2, folder 5, MG 237.

98. "McCarthyism Threatens Nigeria and the Gold Coast," *Spotlight on Africa*, September 15, 1954, p. 3, in Hunton Papers, box 2, folder 5.

99. Hunton, for example, wrote to Du Bois in late 1954, "I received recently a long letter from Azikiwe which was sharply critical of things the *Newsletter* [*Spotlight on Africa*] has had to say about him and others": Hunton to Du Bois, September 27, 1954, Du Bois Papers, reel 70, frame 547. Both Du Bois and Hunton would eventually work in Ghana on the *African Encyclopedia;* see Chapter 7.

100. Advertisement for "A Working Conference in Support of African Liberation," April 24, 1954, and "Proposals for Kenya Aid Program, Conference in Support of African Liberation," Du Bois Papers, reel 70, frames 537, 533. See also L. O'Brien, Joint Secretary, Kenya Committee for Democratic Rights for Kenya Africans, to Du Bois, American Peace Crusade, May 17, 1954, reel 70, frame 738.

101. Director, FBI (100-69266), from SAC [Subversive Activities Control], New York (100-19377), re Council on African Affairs, IS-C. ISA of 1950, May 6 1954; and Assistant Attorney General Warren Olney III from Director, FBI (100-69266-397), May 17, 1954, in Du Bois Papers, box 372, folder 42. See also FBI internal memo, New York (100-19377) July 18, 1955, box 376, folder 33.

102. *Spotlight on Africa*, June 22, 1954, p. 3, Hunton Papers, box 2, folder 5, MG 237. On CAA work on Kenya, see also Lynch, *Black American Radicals,* p. 45; and Horne, *Black and Red,* pp. 189–90.

103. In 1952 J. A. Z. Murumbi, acting general secretary for the Kenya Africa Union, requested financial assistance for legal aid for KAU leaders who had been arrested and were on trial at Kapenguria, Kenya: Murumbi to Council on African Affairs, December 29, 1952, Hunton Papers, box 1, folder 16, MG 237. In response, Hunton forwarded a check for $100 to Murumbi in March 1953, and another $500 to the Kenyatta Defense Fund in London in September 1954: Corn Exchange Bank Trust Company, March 20, 1953, remittance of $100 to Mr. J. A. Z. Murumbi from Dr. W. A. Hunton; F. L. Tonge, Secretary Treasurer, Kenyatta Defense Fund, to Dr. W. A. Hunton, Secretary, Council on African Affairs, September 22, 1954, acknowledges receipt of check for $500 and notes that he will pass on "message of solidarity and friendship" to the Kenya Committee, Hunton Papers, box 1, folder 16, MG 237. See also box 1, folder 18 for records of this exchange.

104. Sisulu interview.

105. W. M. Sisulu, ANC, to Alphaeus Hunton, June 6, 1954, Hunton Papers, box 1, folder 16, MG 237.

106. Warren Olney III, Assistant Attorney General, to Director, FBI (146–28–376), 1953, Du Bois Papers, box 379, folder 60, pp. 1–3.

107. Olney to Director, FBI, 1953. Although I have found no evidence of communication between the FBI and the State Department on the CAA support of Nigerian mineworkers, there is extensive U.S. intelligence on the 1950 strikes at the Enugu Mines and the organizations that the CAA was supporting. See Willard Quincy Stanton, American Consul, Lagos to Secretary of State, July 2, 1950, RG 59, 745F.00/7-150; Stanton to Secretary of State, June 15, 1950, RG 59, 745F.00/6-1750; and on the "Fitzgerald Report on Enugu Riots" of the British government, Stanton to Department of State, June 12, 1950, RG 59, 745H.00/6-1550.

108. Olney to Director, FBI, 1953.

109. Hunton Papers, box 1, folder 19 (CAA Organizational, Legal 1945–1955), MG 237.

110. For example, there were new inquiries about the establishment and activities of the Kenya Aid Committee and the FBI reported throughout 1954–55 on the CAA's support of the Kenya African Union and Kenyatta, covering for example, the CAA's "Conference in Support of

African Liberation" at Friendship Baptist Church in Harlem in April 1954: SAC NY (100-19377) from Director, FBI (100-69266), July 19, 1954, Du Bois Papers, box 376, folder 31; "Proposals for Kenya Aid Program, Conference in Support of African Liberation," Du Bois Papers, reel 70, frame 537; and to Director, FBI (100-69266) from SAC, May 6, 1954.

111. Sisulu, June 9, 1953, Hunton Papers, box 1, folder 16, MG 237. On the Suppression of Communism Act in the Union of South Africa, see Borstelmann, *Apartheid's Reluctant Uncle*, pp. 160, 171.

In 1954, commenting on the case against Robeson, Sisulu thanked Hunton for the CAA support of the ANC and noted that on his trip to China and Europe he had been impressed by the impact of the CAA and Robeson: Sisulu to Hunton, June 6, 1954, Hunton Papers, box 1, folder 16, MG 237. On Robeson's continuing battle to regain his passport, see Duberman, *Paul Robeson*, pp. 434–37.

112. Du Bois to Hunton, September 26, 1952, Du Bois Papers, reel 68, frame 200.

113. Hunton to Du Bois, October 29, 1952, Du Bois Papers, reel 68, frame 201.

114. See Du Bois's letter of June 18, 1953, outlining the CAA's need of defense funds and the prosecution of individual CAA leaders, Du Bois Papers, reel 69, frame 697. On the disbanding of the CAA, see Lynch, *Black American Radicals*, p. 52; Duberman, *Paul Robeson*, p. 437; Hunton, *Alphaeus Hunton*, pp. 90–91.

115. The Department of State followed the repercussions in Africa of the CAA's dissolution. D. W. Lamm, American consul general in Accra, that the *Ashanti Sentinel* had "featured a very biased story on the dissolution of the Council on African Affairs, due to the fact that the U.S. has harassed them and obstructed their work": Lamm to Department of State, August 15, 1955, re "Current Developments in the Gold Coast," RG 59, 745.00/9-155. See also, Lamm to Department of State, July 31, 1956, re "Current Developments in the Gold Coast: July 15–31, 1956," RG 59, 745K.00/7-3156.

116. On the formation of the American Committee on Africa, see George Houser, *No One Can Stop the Rain: Glimpses of Africa's Liberation Struggle* (New York: Pilgrim Press, 1989), pp. 63–66.

117. Ibid., pp. 63, 81–90.

118. Hunton to Rev. Donald Harrington, March 21, 1952; George M. Houser to Hunton, March 28, 1952; and clippings from *New York Amsterdam News*, March 22, 1952, all in Hunton Papers, box 1, folder 16 (CAA, 1945–1955), MG 237.

119. Du Bois to Florence H. Luscomb, October 22, 1956, Du Bois Papers, reel 72, frame 68.

CHAPTER SEVEN Remapping Africa, Rewriting Race

1. W. E. B. Du Bois, "Africa and the American Negro Intelligentsia," in *W. E. B. Du Bois: A Reader,* ed. Meyer Weinberg (New York: Harper & Row, 1970), p. 401.

2. Mary L. Dudziak, "Desegregation as a Cold War Imperative," *Stanford Law Review* 41 (November 1988): 61–120.

3. On the impact of the Korean War on U.S. relations with Africa, see Thomas Borstelmann, *Apartheid's Reluctant Uncle: The United States and Southern Africa in the Early Cold War* (New York: Oxford University Press, 1993), pp. 138–44.

4. "Final Argument against Segregation," *Pittsburgh Courier,* September 30, 1950. See picture and caption, "Combat Radio Officer," and "First Canal Zone Soldier Dies in Korea," *Chicago Defender,* April 25, 1953, p. 6.

5. Richard Dalfiume, *Desegregation of the U.S. Armed Forces: Fighting on Two Fronts, 1939–1953* (Columbia: University of Missouri Press, 1969), pp. 204–7.

6. "Mobilization for What?" *Pittsburgh Courier,* December 23, 1950.

7. Joseph D. Bibb, "War and Peace: War May Bring More Freedom to the Darker Peoples of the Globe," *Pittsburgh Courier,* December 16, 1950, p. 7.

8. "Hoover Right, as Usual," *Pittsburgh Courier,* December 30, 1950. Two years later an editorial criticized the U.N. for abandoning Korea and leaving it "to the mercies of the aggressor" ("Korea, UN, and Africa," *Pittsburgh Courier,* July 4, 1953).

9. "World's Political Fate Rests with Dark Races: Dr. Mordecai Johnson Says They Hold Balance in Capitalist, Communist Fight," *Baltimore Afro-American,* March 18, 1950, p. 20.

10. "Crushing Soviet Lies," *Pittsburgh Courier,* April 29, 1950. The *Courier* continued to promote this argument aggressively over the next several years. Its new "Negro Press Creed" (January 9, 1954, p. 7) declared, "The Negro Press believes that America can best lead the world away from racial and national antagonisms when it accords to every man, regardless of race, color or creed, his human and equal rights."

11. "Courier's 4-Point Program for New Secretary of State," *Pittsburgh Courier,* December 6, 1952, pp. 1, 5.

12. Dunbar S. McLaurin, "India Would Welcome Negro Ambassador," *Pittsburgh Courier,* March 4, 1950, p. 1. See also "How to Win Friends in Asia," *Pittsburgh Courier,* March 11, 1950, p. 1: "We can win the friendship of the Asiatic peoples despite the blandishments of the Russians . . . but our State Department must first drop its arrogant jim crow policy."

13. Chatwood Hall, "U.S. Missing Propaganda Bus in the Colored World: Respect for This Country Not Increased by Its Failure to Mix Diplomatic Corps," *Baltimore Afro-American,* May 27, 1950, p. 11.

14. William Gardner Smith, "U.S. Told to Hire Negroes for Asia; Query White Envoy on Race Views, Asks AFL's Phil Randolph," *Pittsburgh Courier,* May 31, 1952, p. 1.

15. "Ready to Appoint Tan Diplomats: Intention Is Revealed by Powell," *Baltimore Afro-American,* May 21, 1955, p. 1. See also Ollie Stewart, *Baltimore Afro-American,* April 21, 1956, p. 13; and "Let's Have More Evidence," *Pittsburgh Courier,* October 3, 1953, on the failure of the U.S. State Department to appoint a black American Ambassador to Haiti.

16. Saunders Redding, *An American in India: A Personal Report on the Indian Dilemma and the Nature of Her Conflicts* (Indianapolis: Bobbs-Merrill, 1954); Carl T. Rowan, *The Pitiful and the Proud* (New York: Random House, 1956). See also Borstelmann, *Apartheid's Reluctant Uncle,* p. 141.

17. Kenneth Robert Janken, *Rayford W. Logan and the Dilemma of the African-American Intellectual* (Amherst: University of Massachusetts Press, 1993), pp. 183–84.

18. Rayford W. Logan, "Courier Urges Review of Employment Policy of State Department," *Pittsburgh Courier,* April 15, 1950, p. 1; Logan, "Our State Department: Negroes in Foreign Service Assigned to 'Colored' Countries," *Pittsburgh Courier,* April 22, 1950, p. 1; Logan, "President Shows Signs of Ending Government Bias," *Pittsburgh Courier,* April 29, 1950, p. 1; and Logan, "Our State Department: It Employs Few Negroes but Deserves Credit for Opening Some Doors to Us," *Pittsburgh Courier,* May 6, 1950, p. 1.

19. Janken, *Rayford W. Logan,* pp. 192–93.

20. Ibid., p. 196.

21. Walter White, minutes of Conference on Democracy in Housing, New York City, June 15, 1950, New York State Committee on Discrimination in Housing, "SCAD" folder, Papers at the Mayor's Committee on Unity, 1615, Municipal Archives, New York City.

22. Ibid.

23. E. Franklin Frazier, *Black Bourgeoisie* (New York: Macmillan, 1962), p. 159. The book was originally published in 1955 in France; first English edition 1957.

24. Ibid., p. 160.

25. Ibid., p. 159; Anthony M. Platt, *E. Franklin Frazier Reconsidered* (New Brunswick, N.J.: Rutgers University Press, 1991), pp. 154–55, 199–212, 220.

26. Frazier, *Black Bourgeoisie*, p. 97.

27. E. Franklin Frazier, "The Failure of the Negro Intellectual," in *The Death of White Sociology*, ed. Joyce A. Ladner (New York: Vintage Books, 1973), p. 64.

28. Frazier, *Black Bourgeoisie*, p. 91. Frazier would continue to write about "the absence of intellectual freedom in regard to national and international issues"; see his "Failure of the Negro Intellectual," p. 60. If Frazier thoroughly implicated the black middle-class leadership, he also indicted the state, noting that the FBI harassed black Americans who challenged government policy.

29. Frazier, *Black Bourgeoisie*, p. 146. See esp. chap. 8, "The Negro Press and Wish-Fulfillment."

30. Marjorie McKenzie, "Pursuit of Democracy: Rayford Logan Thinks Freedom for U.S. Negroes Rests upon a Free Africa," *Pittsburgh Courier*, February 28, 1953, p. 7.

31. Marjorie McKenzie, "Pursuit of Democracy: Recalls Rayford Logan's Linking of U.S. Blacks with Africa's Liberation," *Pittsburgh Courier*, May 16, 1953.

32. A. N. Fields, "Africa's Redemption Is Our Burden, Too," *Chicago Defender*, October 23, 1948, p. 7.

33. "Let's Get Acquainted," *Pittsburgh Courier*, March 10, 1956, p. 10.

34. William Gardner Smith, "European Colonials Feel Superior to U.S. Negroes," *Pittsburgh Courier*, February 9, 1952, p. 13; John Walcott, "Doesn't Like Emigrants from Caribbean Areas," letter to the editor, *Pittsburgh Courier*, February 18, 1950, p. 18. For critical responses, see *Courier* letters to the editor, March 11, 1950, p. 18.

35. "More Aid for Africa," *Pittsburgh Courier*, October 17, 1953.

36. Horace Cayton, "Africa: The Soft Under-Belly of American Defense; Russia Could Turn Africa into Another Korea," *Pittsburgh Courier*, November 29, 1952, pp. 1, 5.

37. Horace Cayton (UN correspondent for the *Courier*), "East and West Locked in Death Struggle to Control Africa's Black Armies," *Pittsburgh Courier*, December 6, 1952, p. 1.

38. Horace Cayton, "Pakistanian Uses Strong Language on Race Issue," *Pittsburgh Courier*, November 22, 1952, p. 13. The following week, in "Africa: The Soft Under-Belly of American Defense," Cayton pointed to Korea as a lesson that "the national aspiration of the peoples being denied by European powers can be aided and encouraged by the Russians."

39. Quoted in Clarence Mitchell, "Sobering Prediction Made about Africa," *Baltimore Afro-American*, March 19, 1955, p. 14. For an earlier example of this argument, see Mary McLeod Bethune, "The Only Real Answer to Communism Is Opportunities Offered Masses," *Chicago Defender*, January 27, 1951.

40. "Let's Bury Colonialism," *Chicago Defender*, August 7, 1954. See also "America in Dilemma on African Aid," *Chicago Defender*, September 11, 1954.

41. "Africa's Underground Riches Target of Reds," *Chicago Defender*, July 24, 1954.

42. "Negroes Hit Gestapo Tactics of Alabama Cops," *Pittsburgh Courier*, November 30, 1957, p. 6.

43. "Warning Now," *Chicago Defender*, February 19, 1949. See also "South Africa Steps Backwards," *Chicago Defender*, June 12, 1948; "All That's Needed Are Concentration Camps: South Africa Is a Reprint of Hitler," *Pittsburgh Courier*, May 3, 1952, p. 7.

44. Alan Paton, *Cry, the Beloved Country* (New York: Scribner, 1948). For an example of representation in the black press, see Paton, "A Letter from South Africa," *Negro Digest*, January 1950, pp. 60–63 (reprinted from *Harper's Bazaar*).

45. Rob Nixon, *Homelands, Harlem, and Hollywood: South African Culture and the World Beyond* (New York: Routledge, 1994), pp. 25–28; Cedric J. Robinson makes similar points in "The Utopian Break: South Africa as Other," unpublished manuscript in possession of author.

46. Quoted in Chatwood Hall, "S. African Racial Policy Termed 'Stupid, Idiotic'; 'Most Traveled Woman' Predicts Future Revolt: New Yorker Considers Natives 'Charming,' Says Treatment like Dogs Helping 'Reds,' " *Baltimore Afro-American,* February 11, 1950, p. 9.

47. Ibid.

48. "Warning Now," *Chicago Defender,* February 19, 1949. See also "Natives Getting Ideas from Reds: Fear Grips Whites in South Africa," *Pittsburgh Courier,* November 20, 1948, p. 2, on fear of Communist gains in South Africa.

49. The *Chicago Defender,* for example, reported the arrest of 130 persons for "violating Jim Crow restrictions" in "South Africans Flout Jim Crow: Say Campaign against Bias Will Flood Jails," July 5, 1952, p. 23. See also "Africans Open Campaign of Disobedience," *Chicago Defender,* July 5, 1952, p. 2; "10 Million in Africa Ready to Defy White Supremacy," *Pittsburgh Courier,* June 14, 1952, p. 3; "Protest White Domination, Picket S. African Embassy in D.C.: Marchers Carry Signs Denouncing '300 Years of Racial Discrimination,' " *Pittsburgh Courier,* April 19, 1952, p. 1; "1,783 Placed in Jail: 'Non-Violence' Grows in Union," *Pittsburgh Courier,* August 16, 1952, p. 20; "Africans Spur Campaign on Disobedience," *Chicago Defender,* July 19, 1952, p. 9; "Gandhi's Son Aids Cause: Whites Joining South Africans in Resistance: Seven Jailed in Johannesburg in Protest of Race Laws; Ex-Governor's Son in Group," *Pittsburgh Courier,* December 27, 1952, p. 3.

50. On political disorganization, see Chapter 6.

51. "10 Million in Africa Ready to Defy White Supremacy" and "S. African Race Laws Help Reds Gain Ground," *Chicago Defender,* January 16, 1954, p. 7.

52. "Americans Contribute to South African Drive," in *CORE-LATOR* (published by the Congress of Racial Equality), January 1953. On campaign in Port Elizabeth, see Tom Lodge, *Black Politics in South Africa since 1945* (Johannesburg: Raven Press, 1983), pp. 51–54.

53. Walter A. Jackson, *Gunnar Myrdal and America's Conscience: Social Engineering and Racial Liberalism, 1938–1987* (Chapel Hill: University of North Carolina Press, 1990), p. 285. See also Christopher Lasch, *The True and Only Heaven: Progress and Its Critics* (New York: Norton, 1991), p. 446.

54. See Gunnar Myrdal, "The American Paradox," *Crisis,* 55, no. 9 (1948): 167; Myrdal, *An American Dilemma: The Negro Problem and Modern Democracy* (New York: Harper, 1944).

55. Marjorie McKenzie, "Pursuit of Democracy: Racial Injustice in U.S. Imperils Nation's Bid to Lead Move for World Peace," *Pittsburgh Courier,* May 31, 1952.

56. See Irene L. Gendzier, *Managing Political Change: Social Science and the Third World* (Boulder, Colo.: Westview Press, 1985), p. 171, on how the exploitation of psychological and psychoanalytic language contributed to the depoliticization of political analysis in development studies.

57. Editorial, "Curing the Disease," *Chicago Defender,* April 16, 1949. See also Mary Jane Ward, "Does Prejudice Cause Mental Illness?" *Negro Digest,* April 1949, pp. 4–7.

58. Albert Barnett, "World Leaders Fight the 'Virus of Prejudice,'" *Chicago Defender,* April 16, 1949, p. 8; "Back in the Dog House," *Chicago Defender,* October 2, 1948.

59. "The Color Bar," *Chicago Defender,* February 4, 1956.

60. "Prejudice . . . Not Easy to Eradicate," *Pittsburgh Courier,* May 17, 1947.

61. "Outmoded, So Outlawed," *Pittsburgh Courier,* May 29, 1954.

62. For a contemporary discussion of a functionalist modernization approach to politics, see Gabriel A. Almond and James E. Coleman, eds., *The Politics of Developing Areas* (Princeton: Princeton University Press, 1960), esp. the introductory essay, "A Functional Approach to Comparative Politics," pp. 3–64. For a critique of this paradigm, and its roots in the conservative trend of political thought in America in the late 1940s and 1950s, see Irene Gendzier, *Managing Political Change,* pp. 80–87, 124–47.

63. "So. African Race Laws Dry Up Labor Market, Hit U.S. Uranium Sources," *Chicago Defender,* February 21, 1953, p. 5.

64. Horace Cayton, "It Is Clear That Malan's Government Is Out of Step with Rest of World," *Pittsburgh Courier,* January 23, 1954, p. 7.

65. "Liberals Win in Rhodesia," *Pittsburgh Courier,* February 13, 1954.

66. William Minter, *King Solomon's Mines Revisited: Western Interests and the Burdened History of Southern Africa* (New York: Basic Books, 1986), p. 132, has pointed out that Britain's exile of Seretse Khama was one of the major issues around which criticism of the South African government arose in the U.S. mainstream. Minter cites *Time* magazine's criticism of "the racist Malan government of South Africa" in 1950 on "South Africa's incorporation of South West Africa, Britain's exile of Seretse Khama, and religious protests against the Mixed Marriages Act."

67. One exception did discuss the dispute over resources underlying the conflict: "Rich Coal Mines Believed Motive for Seretse Exile: Disclosure of British Plans to Work Mines Surprises Banished Tribal Chief," *Baltimore Afro-American,* May 13, 1950, p. 12.

68. "African Tribe OK's Prince's White Wife," *Chicago Defender,* July 2, 1949, p. 2; "British Get Hotfoot," *Chicago Defender,* April 29, 1950. In "The Blockheads in Britain," March 18, 1950, the *Defender* argued that the United States was morally obligated to crack down on the Union of South Africa and Britain "for this inhuman attack upon the natives of Africa which is now climaxed by the exile of Prince Seretse Khama and his wife." See also Eric Robins, "White Queen in Darkest Africa," *Negro Digest,* December 1949, pp. 60–69 (reprinted from *New York Daily Times*); "Cause of African Chief Stirs World: Fight Plot To Exile White Queen's Mate," *Chicago Defender,* March 18, 1950, p. 1; and "The Case of Seretse Khama," *Chicago Defender,* April 5, 1952.

69. "Seretse's Backers Plan Boycott against British," *Baltimore Afro-American,* March 25, 1950, p. 1. "Britain's Hot Potato," *Pittsburgh Courier,* March 18, 1950; "Is Seretse a Menace to His People?" *Pittsburgh Courier,* April 1, 1950. See also George S. Schuyler, "Views and Reviews: Legally, It Was None of England's Business Whom Seretse Married," *Pittsburgh Courier,* March 25, p. 15; and Marjorie McKenzie, "Pursuit of Democracy: The Bamangwatos Have Behaved in a Politically Wise and Sophisticated Fashion," *Pittsburgh Courier,* March 25, 1950, p. 15. The *Courier* also publicized Churchill's criticism of the Labor government for their handling of the issue: "Exiled Prince Bares Bribery Offer: Doublecrossed, Seretse Charges," March 18, 1950, p. 1.

70. See "England Bows: Seretse Returns to White Wife," *Pittsburgh Courier,* March 25, 1950, p. 1; "Socialist Surrender," *Pittsburgh Courier,* March 25, 1950; "African Chief Tricks British: Refuses to Rule without White Wife," *Baltimore Afro-American,* February 25, 1950, p. 1. For later repercussions, see "British Labor Leader Admits Government Made Mistake in Exiling Seretse Khama," *Baltimore Afro-American,* February 19, 1955, p. 19.

71. Harold L. Keith, "Facts about Africa," *Pittsburgh Courier,* January 9, 1954, p. 7; February 27, 1954, p. 10; September 25, 1954, p. 7; and March 26, 1955, editorial page.

72. See *Chicago Defender,* February 14, 1953, for the new organization of "Foreign News."

73. Marjorie McKenzie, "Myrdal, Paton Contrasted," *Pittsburgh Courier,* October 16, 1954.

74. "Turmoil in Africa," *Chicago Defender,* January 24, 1953.

75. Claude A. Barnett, "Tells of Trip to West Africa: ANP Director in Sierra Leone," *Chicago Defender,* May 3, 1947, p. 4.

76. "Chief Imprisoned, He Beat War Drums," *Chicago Defender,* March 25, 1950, p. 5. "Inflation: Hike Price of Brides in Nigeria," *Pittsburgh Courier,* February 4, 1950, p. 6.

77. "Ex-African Chief, 90, Asks UN to Restore Faith; Threatens Suicide," *Chicago Defender,* September 13, 1952, p. 5.

78. Malcolm Johnson, "Turmoil in Africa," *Chicago Defender,* January 17, 1953, p. 1; January 24, 1953, p. 15; January 31, 1953, p. 15; and February 7, 1953, p. 15.

79. *Chicago Defender,* February 29, 1951.

80. Charles P. Davis, *Black Is the Color of the Cosmos: Essays on Afro-American Literature and Culture, 1942–1981* (Washington D.C.: Howard University Press, 1989), pp. 42–43. See Marianna Torgovnick, *Gone Primitive: Savage Intellects, Modern Lives* (Chicago: University of Chicago Press, 1990), for a discussion of Western images of the primitive.

81. Padmore himself sometimes used this language.

82. See Gendzier, *Managing Political Change,* pp. 129–31.

83. William Townsend, *Chicago Defender,* December 18, 1948, p. 7.

84. "Turmoil and Progress," *Pittsburgh Courier,* editorial, April 18, 1953.

85. "The Tropical Frontier: The Congo Progressing Slowly without Bias," *Chicago Defender,* January 15, 1955. See also Patsy Payne, "Farm Community Flourished in French West Africa: The French Sudan Is Moving Ahead in Developing Arable Land in the Dry Inland Delta of the Niger River; The Secret: Cooperation," *Pittsburgh Courier,* September 25, 1954, magazine section, p. 7. Payne cited cooperation between the French government and "local inhabitants" as the key to the development of new arable lands through irrigation.

86. "Lessons of the Belgian Congo: Here Is a Story of Racial Co-Existence in Seething Africa," *Pittsburgh Courier,* December 4, 1954, magazine section, p. 4. See also Marguerite Cartwright, "A New Day in the Belgian Congo?" *Pittsburgh Courier,* January 2, 1954, magazine section, p. 4. Cartwright called the Belgian system "the world's shrewdest and most successful colonial administration."

87. Allen R. Dodd Jr., "The Tropical Frontier: Belgium Congo Rules Natives without Whip," *Chicago Defender,* January 8, 1955, p. 4.

88. "The Truth about Moral Rearmament: Where Does the Money Come From," *Advance,* November 19, 1953, p. 5 (William Cullen Library, University of the Witwatersrand, Johannesburg).

89. "The Truth about Moral Rearmament," *Advance,* November 12, 1953. For sympathetic coverage of MRA in South Africa, see "New Way to Fight for Freedom," *Bantu World,* August 30, 1952, p. 3; "A Shrine of Faith and Hope," *Bantu World,* May 3, 1952, p. 11; and "Moral Rearmament Group Welcomed in City," *World,* February 18, 1956, p. 2. See Kathleen Vundla, *PQ: The Story of Philip Vundla of South Africa* (Lansdowne: Citadel Press, MRA, 1973), for the story of a South African political leader's conversion to MRA.

90. Robert G. Nixon, "For Communists: Africa Seen Next Major World Target," *Pittsburgh Courier,* January 1, 1955, p. 1; see, also, "MRA Is Projected as Africa's Hope," *Pittsburgh Courier,* January 8, 1955, p. 1; "Says MRA Is Answer to Mau Mau," *Pittsburgh Courier,* January 15, 1955; "Just What Is It: Moral Re-Armament?" *Baltimore Afro-American,* magazine section, January 22, 1955; "Azikiwe, Ita Join Hands: MRA Testimonial Unites Nigerians," April 2, 1955, p. 3; "Afro-Asia Dilemma: Us or Reds," *Chicago Defender,* February 5, 1955, p. 4.

91. Consulate General, Nairobi, to Department of State, February 4, 1955, re "Moral Rearmament Program at Athi River," RG 59, 745R.00/2-455.

92. Barrow further noted that the British army's chief of staff and the deputy governor supported MRA: Consulate General, Nairobi, to Department of State, February 4, 1955, re "Moral Rearmament Drive in Nairobi," RG 59, 745R.00/7-1955; Consulate General, Nairobi, to Department of State, August 11, 1955, RG 59, 745.00/8-1155.

93. See Chapter 2.

94. Frank E. Bolden, "India Loses Its Apostle of Peace," *Pittsburgh Courier,* February 7, 1948, p. 1.

95. "Mohandas K. Gandhi," *Pittsburgh Courier*, February 7, 1948.

96. See also, "The Mahatma," *Chicago Defender*, February 14, 1948. The rare exception, discussing Gandhi in terms of the struggle against British imperialism, was written by an Indian: Sirdar J. J. Singh, "Mahatma Gandhi—India's Bapu," *Crisis* 55, no. 3 (1948).

97. George Daniels, "Nkrumah and Gandhi: The Differences, Similarities of Two Great Leaders," *Chicago Defender*, July 10, 1954, p. 6.

98. I. J. K. Wells, "Haiti on Doorstep of Mighty Growth," *Pittsburgh Courier*, February 4, 1950, p. 24. Brenda Gayle Plummer, *Haiti and the United States: The Psychological Moment* (Athens: University of Georgia Press, 1992), pp. 131–38, has argued that the years 1949–56 were Haiti's golden age of tourism, when its popularity with the black American intelligentsia was unmitigated by a critique of its politics.

99. Mary McLeod Bethune, "Calls Haiti Symbol of Attainable Freedom for Thousands of Blacks," *Chicago Defender*, July 23, 1949, p. 4.

100. "Live like A Millionaire: Haiti, the Paradise of the Greater Antilles," *Chicago Defender*, June 4, 1949, magazine section.

101. Claude A. Barnett, "Haiti Fair Entertaining: It'll Be Dream Come True for Lucky Girls," *Chicago Defender*, April 8, 1950, p. 2.

102. Ibid. See Constance Curtis, "Haiti! Contrasts! Must See Again," *New York Amsterdam News*, May 10, 1952, p. 1, on the premiere, hosted by 20th Century Fox and the Haitian government, of *Lydia Bailey* (based on the Kenneth Roberts novel about Haitian revolt against the French in the 1800s), the first American movie to open outside the United States. See also "New Horizons," *Chicago Defender*, March 31, 1951.

103. Roy Garvin, "Haiti Making Progress, Still a Long Way to Go," *Baltimore Afro-American*, April 29, 1950, p. 20. See also "Haitians Learn American Farm Tricks to Help Native Economy," *Chicago Defender*, May 20, 1950, p. 14.

104. Philippa Schuyler, "President Tells Plans for Haiti," *Pittsburgh Courier*, December 23, 1950, p. 2.

105. "Haiti Needs Stability to Finish All Reforms," *Chicago Defender*, April 4, 1953, p. 6. See also Barnett, "Haiti Fair Entertaining," for a celebration of the presence of the United States military.

106. Plummer, *Haiti and the United States*, pp. 166–68. According to "How She Carved Out Her Own Magnificent Progress," *Chicago Defender*, special magazine supplement, February 12, 1955, Haiti's stress on "self-reliance" had attracted the "admiring aid" of the United States; in Haiti's "new forward look," U.S. "technical aid" had been a "big helping hand." Albert Barnett reported that the visit of Magloire to the United States had "focused the international spotlight on that fabulous tropical republic, familiar to tourists as the iridescent gem of the Caribbean sea." According to Barnett, President Paul Magloire's "five-year plan of economic development has the tourist trade as the featured attraction on the agenda"; see "Hail the Republic of Haiti, 'Gem of the Caribbean Sea,'" *Chicago Defender*, February 12, 1955, p. 4. A *Pittsburgh Courier* editorial advocated tourism as "one of the most effective ways in which we can honor Haiti" ("Distinguished Visitor," February 5, 1955).

107. "Haiti, Troubled Island," *Pittsburgh Courier*, December 22, 1956.

108. "Haiti, a Lovely Land of Woe," *Pittsburgh Courier*, April 27, 1957, magazine section, p. 4.

109. Claude A. Barnett, "Liberia's Inauguration an Expensive Spectacle," *New York Amsterdam News*, January 5, 1952, p. 5.

110. "Liberia to Inaugurate Tubman January 7," and "USS Monrovia Sets Courtesy Trip to Liberia," *Chicago Defender*, January 5, 1952, p. 4, 1. See also Claude A. Barnett, "Liberia Inaugurates President Tubman: Top Diplomats Witness Impressive Ceremonies," *Chicago Defender*, January 12, 1952, p. 1.

111. Mary McLeod Bethune, "Trip to Africa Stirs Memory of the Future of Liberia in 1822," *Chicago Defender,* January 5, 1952; Mary McLeod Bethune, "Mrs. Bethune Describes Liberia as a Land of Opportunity for All," *Chicago Defender,* February 2, 1952, pp. 1–2.

112. Bethune continued, "But I got the real feel of Africa as I stood in line with other official delegates to the inauguration at the reception for the native chiefs," where she was "privileged to personally greet 126 tribal chiefs all clad in their native robes" ("Mrs. Bethune Describes Liberia as a 'Land of Opportunity For All'"). On Bethune, see Paula Giddings, *When and Where I Enter: The Impact of Black Women on Race and Sex in America* (New York: William Morrow, 1984), pp. 199–230.

113. David Maughan-Brown, *Land, Freedom, and Fiction: History and Ideology in Kenya* (London: Zed Books, 1985); Donald L. Barnett and Karari Njama, *Mau Mau from Within: An Analysis of Kenya's Peasant Revolt* (New York: Monthly Review Press, 1966).

114. "50 Die in New Mau Mau Raids," *Chicago Defender,* March 7, 1953, p. 6; "Terror Reign Growing," *Pittsburgh Courier,* March 7, 1953, p. 1.

115. "Rush White Troops to Fight Mau Maus: Officials Blame Revolt on Sex, Missionaries," *Pittsburgh Courier,* November 8, 1952, p. 1; "Says Key to Mau Mau Peace Is Word of God," *Chicago Defender,* November 8, 1954, p. 6. See also "Gable, Ava Ain't Scared of Mau Maus," *Pittsburgh Courier,* November 22, 1952, p. 17; "Mau Mau Burn Elizabeth's Treetop Lodge; Cross Tanganyika Border," *Chicago Defender,* June 5, 1954, p. 21; "Queen Visits Uganda despite Mau Mau; Opens Huge Dam," *Chicago Defender,* May 8, 1954, p. 6; Horace Cayton, "Mau Mau Organization in Africa Still Retains Most of Its Original Mystery," *Pittsburgh Courier,* May 29, 1954, p. 7; and "Kenya Settlers Spin Tall Tales to Bolster Courage against Feared Mau Mau," *Baltimore Afro-American,* September 18, 1954, for some of the more sensational and trivializing coverage.

116. Cayton, "Africa: The Soft Underbelly of American Defense," p. 5.

117. Sam Morris, "Kenyans Demand Return of Land, Self-Government," *Pittsburgh Courier,* February 28, 1952, p. 20.

118. "Mau Mau War Spreads despite Huge Killings," *Chicago Defender,* May 29, 1954, p. 6. On land policy, see also "Africans Say Settling Land Feud Could End Present Row in Kenya," *Chicago Defender,* January 16, 1954, p. 6; "Commission Studies Kenya Land Problem," *Chicago Defender,* March 14, 1953, p. 6; "British Pushing Last Big Anti–Mau Mau Drive," *Chicago Defender,* March 5, 1955, p. 4; and Nat Turner, "The Mau Mau Story," *Baltimore Afro-American,* April 16, 1955, p. 6. A four-part series by Tom Mboya, "Truth and Untruth about Mau Mau: Kenya—The Africa Case," ran in the *Pittsburgh Courier* magazine, December 1–22, 1956.

119. George Houser, *No One Can Stop the Rain: Glimpses of Africa's Liberation Struggle* (New York: The Pilgrim Press, 1989), p. 75.

CHAPTER EIGHT No Exit: From Bandung to Ghana

1. The signatories of the treaty were the United States, Britain, France, Australia, New Zealand, the Philippines, Pakistan, and Thailand.

2. Paul Gordon Lauren, *Power and Prejudice: The Politics of Diplomacy and Racial Discrimination* (Boulder, Colo.: Westview Press, 1988), pp. 209, 340 n. 55.

3. "Neutrality Issue at Asian-African Parley," *Baltimore Afro-American,* April 9, 1955, p. 8.

4. "Asian-African Parley Hopes to Allay Fears," *Baltimore Afro-American,* March 12, 1955.

5. "Afro-Asian Conference," *Baltimore Afro-American,* April 9, 1955.

6. Ibid.

7. "Recipe for Peace," *Baltimore Afro-American,* April 30, 1955.

8. "Dark Nations Call Conference," *Pittsburgh Courier,* January 8, 1955, p. 1.

9. See "Asian-African Meet Threat to Colonialism," *Chicago Defender,* March 26, 1955, p. 4. See also "What Other Newspapers Say: Afro-Asian Conference" (from the *New York Herald Tribune*), *Chicago Defender,* January 15, 1955; Louis Lautier, "Neutrality Issue at Asian-African Parley," *Baltimore Afro-American,* April 9, 1955, p. 8; and "Nehru Tells Afro-Asian Confab Aim," *Pittsburgh Courier,* February 5, 1955, p. 9.

10. Richard Wright, *The Color Curtain* (Cleveland: World, 1956), p. 207.

11. Ibid., pp. 158–59.

12. "Will Visit Capitals, Asia Europe," *Chicago Defender,* April 16, 1955, p. 1.

13. Ethel L. Payne, "Afro-Asia Meet First Conference of World's Darker Peoples," and "Ceylon Envoy Says Reds Won't Dominate the A-A Meet," *Chicago Defender,* April 16, 1955, p. 12; and Ethel L. Payne, "Africa-Asia Conference Rocked by Freedom Fever," and "Philippines Seek Power at Bandung," *Chicago Defender,* April 30, 1955, p. 12.

14. Lauren, *Power and Prejudice,* p. 214; Martin Bauml Duberman, *Paul Robeson* (New York: Knopf, 1988), p. 431.

15. Wright, *The Color Curtain,* pp. 87–88.

16. American Consul General, Accra, to Department of State, January 3, 1955, RG 59, 745K.00/1-355; American Consul General, Accra, to Department of State, re "Current Developments in Gold Coast, March 15–31, 1955," RG 59, 745.K.00/3-3155; American Consul General, Accra, to Department of State, April 15, 1955, RG 59, 745K.00/4-1555.

17. Adam Clayton Powell Jr., *Adam by Adam: The Autobiography of Adam Clayton Powell, Jr.* (New York: Dial Press, 1971), p. 103.

18. "Powell Will Attend Asian-African Meet," *Baltimore Afro-American,* March 12, 1955, p. 2; "Powell to Attend Afro Asia Meet Despite Ban," *Chicago Defender,* April 2, 1955, p. 4; "Powell Tells Why He'll Defy Afro-Asian Meet Ban," *Chicago Defender,* April 9, 1955. p. 2; "Powell Paints Grim Picture for America," *Baltimore Afro-American,* April 9, 1955, p. 6; Alice A. Dunnigan, "Powell Off to Afro-Asia Parley as Good Will Envoy," *Baltimore Afro-American,* April 16, 1955, p. 2; Charles Hamilton, *Adam Clayton Powell, Jr.: The Political Biography of an American Dilemma* (New York: Macmillan, 1991), pp. 237–42; Powell, *Adam by Adam,* p. 103.

19. Powell, *Adam by Adam,* p. 103.

20. Payne, "Africa-Asia Conference Rocked by Freedom Fever"; Powell, *Adam by Adam,* pp. 107–17.

21. Quoted in "Lauds Powell's Role in Asia: Upset Strategy of Red Envoys," *Chicago Defender,* May 7, 1955, p. 1; Duberman, *Paul Robeson,* p. 431.

22. James L. Hicks, "'Nehru Through'—Powell: Suggests Colombo Powers' Conference," *Baltimore Afro-American,* May 7, 1955, p. 1; Powell, *Adam by Adam,* pp. 108–11.

23. "Lauds Powell's Role in Asia."

24. "Diplomat Powell," *Chicago Defender,* May 14, 1955.

25. "Mr. Powell at Bandung," *Baltimore Afro-American,* April 30, 1955.

26. "The New Cong. Powell," *Pittsburgh Courier,* June 4, 1955.

27. P. L. Prattis, "Horizon, Letter to Adam Powell," *Pittsburgh Courier,* May 21, 1955.

28. Hicks quoted in *Spotlight on Africa* 14 (April 1955): 20, in W. A. Hunton Papers, box 2, folder 5, MG 257, Schomburg Library, New York. The April and May 1955 issues are devoted to coverage of the conference.

29. "Asian-African Conference Is Acclaimed by Du Bois, Robeson," *Baltimore Afro-American,* April 30, 1955, p. 8; W. E. B. Du Bois, "Memorandum on the Bandung Conference," April 1955, and Du Bois, "To the Peoples of Asia and Africa Meeting at Bandung, April 1955," April 6, 1955, both in Du Bois Papers, microfilm collection, Columbia University, reel 71, frames 935, 936;

Duberman, *Paul Robeson,* pp. 431 and 434. See also W. E. B. Du Bois, "Pan-Colored," *Spotlight on Africa* 14 (January 1955): Hunton Papers, box 2, folder 5, MG 237.

30. Duberman, *Paul Robeson,* p. 434. For the full text of Robeson's message to Bandung, see *Spotlight on Africa* 14 (May 1955), in Hunton Papers, box 2, folder 5, MG 237.

31. *Spotlight on Africa* 14 (April 1955) and 14 (May 1955).

32. Du Bois, "Pan-Colored."

33. Reprint of President Sukarno's keynote address, *Spotlight on Africa* 14 (May 1955): 4.

34. *Spotlight on Africa* 14 (May 1955): 6. For a more extended analysis of Bandung, see W. Alphaeus Hunton, "New Horizons: The Worlds of Bandung and Socialism," chap. 16 in his *Decision in Africa: Sources of Current Conflict* (New York: International, 1957), pp. 218–29.

35. "African Representation at Bandung and the Question of African Freedom," *Spotlight on Africa* 14 (May 1955): 12. The Gold Coast was represented by Minister of State Kojo Botsio. According to George Padmore, Nkrumah did not attend because he did not want to leave his country until he was able to represent it as a full sovereign state: Padmore to Du Bois, June 21, 1955, Du Bois Papers, reel 79, frame 1079.

On the issue of South Africa at Bandung, see Brian Bunting, *Moses Kotane: South African Revolutionary,* chap. 12, "The Bandung Conference," pp. 206–13 (London: Inkululeko Publications, 1973). See also Louis Lautier, "Explosion Certain in South Africa: Delegates at Bandung Get Prediction," *Baltimore Afro-American,* April 30, 1955, p. 1; Payne, "Africa-Asia Conference Rocked by Freedom Fever." Kotane and Cachalia had left the Union of South Africa without passports but met Pandit Nehru and Krishna Menon in London and were given Indian travel documents (Bunting, *Moses Kotane,* p. 206).

36. American Consul, Lagos, to Department of State, July 29, 1952, RG 59, 745H.00/7-2952; "Max Yergan in Africa," *Chicago Defender,* August 2, 1952, p. 3. On Yergan's trip to South Africa, see Thomas Borstelmann, *Apartheid's Reluctant Uncle: The United States and Southern Africa in the Early Cold War* (New York: Oxford University Press, 1993), p. 129.

37. Quoted in Duberman, *Paul Robeson,* p. 333.

38. Department of External Affairs, Pretoria, to South African Embassy, Washington, October 30 and November 8, 1957, BWA 102 1952:58, Papers of South African Consulate General, Pretoria.

39. Max Yergan, "Yergan Predicts Conflict," *Pittsburgh Courier,* April 23, 1955, p. 1; Max Yergan, "Claims Nehru Lost Face: Africans Not among Bandung Sponsors," *Pittsburgh Courier,* June 11, 1955, p. 2; and "African-Asian Conference: Max Yergan to Bandung for Courier," *Pittsburgh Courier,* April 16, 1955, p. 1.

40. Max Yergan, "Purposes of Confab Outlined: Why the Bandung Parley?" and "Correction of Max Yergan Report on Bandung Conference," *Pittsburgh Courier,* May 28, 1955, p. 1; Max Yergan, "Claims Nehru Lost Face: Max Yergan, Africans Not among Bandung Sponsors," *Pittsburgh Courier,* June 11, 1955, p. 2.

41. Max Yergan, "Pigment Fades in World Affairs Says Yergan, Bandung Conference Marked by a Major Factor: Color," June 4, 1955, p. 2; Max Yergan, "Bandung Nations Need West's $$$," *Pittsburgh Courier,* May 7, 1955, p. 7. See also the accounting of the conference in Carl T. Rowan, *The Pitiful and the Proud* (New York: Random House, 1956), pp. 381–414. Rowan attended the conference as part of a one-year tour through India, Pakistan, and Southeast Asia under the auspices of the U.S. State Department.

42. James L. Hicks, "Dark Nations Assert Power," *Baltimore Afro-American,* October 8, 1955, p. 1. See also "The Algerian Vote," an editorial in the same issue.

43. James L. Hicks, "Says Battle to End Colonialism Won at Bandung Conference," *Baltimore Afro-American,* October 15, 1955, p. 18.

44. Ferruccio Gambino, "Transgression of a Laborer: Malcolm X in the Wilderness of America," *Radical History Review* 55 (Winter 1993): 22–24. Gambino's fascinating account is based largely on FBI documents. See also Clayborn Carson, *Malcolm X: The FBI File* (New York: One World Books, 1991).

45. Gambino, "Transgression of a Laborer," pp. 7–9, 13–16, 22–25.

46. Ibid., pp. 14–16.

47. Ibid.; Jan Carew, *Ghosts in Our Blood: With Malcolm X in Africa, England, and the Caribbean* (Chicago: Lawrence Hill Books, 1994), p. 42. See Leon Forrest's essay "Elijah," on the Nation of Islam and his own experiences working with Richard Durham on *Muhammad Speaks,* in *The Furious Voice for Freedom: Essays on Life* (Wakefield, R.I.: Asphodel Press, Moyer Bell, 1994), pp. 67–116. See also C. Eric Lincoln, *The Black Muslims in America* (Trenton, N.J.: Africa World Press, 1994), pp. 127–28; E. U. Essien-Udom, *Black Nationalism: A Search for an Identity in America* (Chicago: University of Chicago Press, 1962).

48. Ollie Stewart, "Artists, Writers in Paris; Du Bois Sends Message," *Baltimore Afro-American,* October 6, 1956, p. 7.

49. Ibid.

50. James Baldwin, "Princes and Powers," in *Nobody Knows My Name* (New York: Dell, 1962), p. 21.

51. Ibid., pp. 17–20. Richard Wright's *Black Power: A Record of Reactions in a Land of Pathos* (New York: Harper, 1954), while presenting what he describes as a "Marxist analysis of historic events to explain what has happened in this world for the past five hundred years or more" (p. xiii), opens by confronting a psychological abstraction: "Africa! I repeated the word to myself, then paused as if something strange and disturbing stirred slowly in the depths of me. I am African! I am of African descent. What would my feelings be when I looked into the face of an African, feeling that maybe his great-great-great-grandfather has sold my great-great-great-grandfather into slavery? Was there something in Africa that my feelings could latch onto to make all this dark past clear and meaningful?" (pp. 3–4).

52. See E. Franklin Frazier's sharp criticism of black American participation at the Paris Congress of 1956 and the subsequent meeting in Rome in 1959: "The Failure of the Negro Intellectual,"in *The Death of White Sociolgy,* ed. Joyce A. Ladner (New York: Vintage Books, 1973), p. 55.

53. Wayne F. Urban, *Black Scholar: Horace Mann Bond, 1904–1972* (Athens: University of Georgia Press, 1992), pp. 158–64.

54. Ibid., pp. 162–63. On the Congress for Cultural Freedom and its impact on the interpretation of Third World politics, see Irene L. Gendzier, *Managing Political Change: Social Scientists and the Third World* (Boulder, Colo.: Westview Press, 1985), pp. 87–97.

55. *Africa Seen by American Negro Scholars* (New York: American Society of African Culture, 1963).

56. St. Clair Drake, "The Black Diaspora in Pan-African Perspective," *Black Scholar* 7 (September 1975): 2–14; Drake, "Diaspora Studies and Pan-Africanism," in *Global Dimensions of the African Diaspora,* ed. Joseph E. Harris (Washington, D.C.: Howard University Press, 1982), pp. 341–402.

57. Whereas Horace Mann Bond saw no conflict between African emancipation and the interest of the United States government, Martin Kilson accused AMSAC of imperialism and of putting the interest of the United States over that of Africans (Urban, *Black Scholar,* p. 163).

58. St. Clair Drake, "The International Implications of Race and Race Relations," *Journal of Negro Education* 20, no. 3 (1951): 261–78.

59. Ibid., p. 264.

60. Ibid., pp. 275–76.

61. Ibid., p. 277.

62. Drake, "Diaspora Studies and Pan-Africanism," pp. 451–514.

63. "Gil Cruter, Ex-High Jump Ace, Big Hit on West African Tour," *Baltimore Afro-American,* March 3, 1956, p. 15.

64. Dave Zinkoff with Edgar Williams, *Around the World with the Harlem Globetrotters* (Philadelphia: Macrae Smith, 1953), pp. 109, 169; "U.S. Basketball Team See World: The Globetrotters Spread Goodwill," *Bantu World,* July 2, 1955, supplement.

65. Quoted in "U.S. Basketball Team See World."

66. Dizzy Gillespie with Al Fraser, *Dizzy: To Be or Not to Bop* (New York, 1982), p. 413.

67. "Jazz Wins U.S. Friends," *Baltimore Afro-American,* July 21, 1956.

68. "Indians Dizzy over Gillespie's Jazz," *Pittsburgh Courier,* June 2 and 9, 1956.

69. "Diz Set for Tour of South America," *Pittsburgh Courier,* July 21, 1956, p. 23.

70. "Dizzy Urges Ike to Back Jazz Tours," *Pittsburgh Courier,* August 4, 1956, p. 21. On the tours see Frank Kofsky, *Black Nationalism and the Revolution in Music* (New York: Pathfinder Press, 1970), pp. 109–11, 119–21.

71. Gillespie, *To Be or Not to Bop,* p. 414.

72. Ibid., p. 415–18; "Indians Dizzy over Gillespie's Jazz"; Andrew Ross, *No Respect: Intellectuals and Popular Culture* (New York: Routledge, 1989), p. 242.

73. *Pittsburgh Courier,* July 21, 1956, p. 23.

74. "Modern Jazz Is Here to Stay," *World* (Johannesburg), January 28, 1956, p. 5. See also four-part series on Louis Armstrong—"Satchmo's Own Story: The Modern Pied Piper," April 1956; "The Louis Armstrong Story: Satchmo on the Streets," May 1956, p. 71; "Satchmo's Big Break," June 1956, p. 67; and "Satchmo Blows Up the World," August 1956, p. 40—in *Drum.*

75. The programs were very popular in South Africa, and information and publicity was carried by local papers. "Enjoys Jazz Program," *World,* November 17, 1956, p. 4; "Jazz Corner," *World,* February 1, 1958, p. 6.

76. "100,000 Dig the King: Armstrong 'Axe' Gasses Ghanese Fans," *Pittsburgh Courier,* June 2, 1956; "Modern Jazz Is Here to Stay," *World,* January 28, 1956, p. 5; "Satchmo Blows Up the World"; Gary Giddins, *Satchmo* (New York: Doubleday, 1988), pp. 159–60.

77. American Consulate General, Accra, to Department of State, June 4, 1956; RG 59, 745K.00/6-456.

78. "Armstrong to Tour Russia, S. America," *Pittsburgh Courier,* August 10, 1957, p. 22. See also "Satchmo Blows for Hungary," *Chicago Defender,* December 22, 1956, on Armstrong's benefit concert with the Royal Philharmonic in London, for Hungarian refugees.

79. "Brightest Lights," *Pittsburgh Courier,* December 29, 1956, magazine section, p. 4.

80. On Duke Ellington's extensive State Department tours, see Edward Kennedy Ellington, *Music is My Mistress* (Garden City, N.Y.: Doubleday, 1973), pp. 301–89. On the 1960s, see also Ronald M. Radano's discussion of an African-inspired cultural nationalism in the Chicago-based Association for the Advancement of Creative Musicians in *New Musical Figurations: Anthony Braxton's Cultural Critique* (Chicago: University of Chicago Press, 1993), pp. 95–103.

81. On Gillespie's South American tour, see the chapter on samba music in Gillespie, *To Be or Not to Bop,* pp. 428–33 (quotation, p. 428).

82. Giddins, *Satchmo,* p. 159.

83. Horace R. Cayton, "World at Large," *Pittsburgh Courier,* June 9, 1956, p. 9.

84. Ibid.

85. "Louis Armstrong, Barring Soviet Tour, Denounces Eisenhower and Gov. Faubus," *New York Times,* September 19, 1957, p. 23; "Satchmo Tells Off Ike, U.S.," *Pittsburgh Courier,* September 28, 1957; Giddins, *Satchmo,* pp. 160–65.

86. Giddins, *Satchmo*, p. 163.

87. Carl T. Rowan, "Has Paul Robeson Betrayed the Negro?" *Ebony* 12 (October 1957): 31–42. See also Rowan's reflections on the piece some three decades later in Carl T. Rowan, *Breaking Barriers: A Memoir* (New York: Harper Perennial, 1991). Paul Robeson, *Here I Stand* (Boston: Beacon Press, 1988), originally published 1958, pp. 70–72, 82.

88. Rowan, "Has Paul Robeson Betrayed the Negro?" p. 33.

89. Ibid., p. 42.

90. Musicians continued to relate the State Department tours to the U.S. South. In 1962, Miles Davis said of Armstrong: "People really dig Pops like I do myself. He does a good job overseas with his personality. But they ought to send him down South for goodwill. They need goodwill worse in Georgia and Alabama and Mississippi than they do in Europe": Miles Davis interviewed by Alex Haley, September 1962, in *The Playboy Interview*, ed. G. Barry Golson (New York: Playboy Press, 1981), p. 10.

91. Although they avoided discussions of political controversies—such as the splits in the Convention People's Party (CPP)—that would have touched on Cold War taboos, black American newspapers did follow the transitions to independence in Ghana and Nigeria. See, e.g., "Nkrumah Prime Minister," *Pittsburgh Courier*, March 15, 1952, p. 1; "Africa's First Black Premier," *Pittsburgh Courier*, March 15, 1952; "Dr. Azikiwe Is Defeated: Nigerians Complete National Elections," *Pittsburgh Courier*, February 16, 1952, p. 2; Paul D. Davis, "Nkrumah Backed; Azikiwe Follows: Gold Coast Endorses Bid for Independence," *Pittsburgh Courier*, August 1, 1952, p. 1; "Progress in Africa," *Chicago Defender*, July 3, 1954; "Foreign News," *Chicago Defender*, July 3, 1954, p. 6; "Gold Coast Becomes a Self-Governing Colony," *Chicago Defender*, June 26, 1954, p. 6; and "Dawn of Independence," *Chicago Defender*, August 11, 1956. For a rare exception to this sparse coverage, see George Padmore, "Bloodless Revolution in the Gold Coast," *Crisis* 59, no. 3 (1952): 172.

92. "Salute to Ghana: New African Nation Born," "The Courier Salutes Ghana," and "Pertinent Facts on Ghana," *Pittsburgh Courier*, March 9, 1957, p. 1; "Courier Sees Birth of Ghana," *Pittsburgh Courier*, March 16, 1957, p. 2; "Celebrate Birth of Ghana Here," *Chicago Defender*, March 2, 1957, p. 1; John Farquharson, "African Drama Helps Americans Learn Lesson of Real Freedom," *Chicago Defender*, February 9, 1957, p. 12.

93. Taylor Branch, *Parting the Waters: America in the King Years, 1954–1963* (New York: Simon & Schuster, 1988), p. 214; Ethel L. Payne, "World's Notables See Ghana Become Nation," *Chicago Defender*, March 9, 1957, p. 1; Maida Springer, "West Africa's Fight for Freedom Should Inspire U.S. Negroes," *Pittsburgh Courier*, April 13, 1957, p. 5.

94. "Ghana—It Is a New Black African Nation That May Influence World Affairs," *Chicago Defender*, March 2, 1957, p. 4; Ethyl L. Payne, "Ghana—Its Independence Has Great Impact in Africa," *Chicago Defender*, March 16, 1957, p. 12.

95. Manning Marable, *African and Caribbean Politics: From Kwame Nkrumah to Maurice Bishop* (London: Verso, 1987), p. 110.

96. Ibid.; George Padmore, *Pan-Africanism or Communism* (Garden City, N.Y.: Anchor Books, Doubleday, 1972).

97. Representation was by parties rather than governments; the conference was attended by some three hundred delegates representing sixty-five organizations and parties. Participants included Tom Mboya, whom Nkrumah had chosen to chair the conference, and the then unknown Patrice Lumumba, representing the recently formed National Congolese Movement. Despite the political fragility of African nonalignment (for example, a permanent rift developed between Nkrumah and Mboya over Mboya's support of the pro-West ICFTU, and Nkrumah increasingly turned to the Soviet Union as he failed to get American backing and funds), the lead-

ership of Nkrumah and Ghana in a politics of African nonalignment had tremendous appeal to a broad spectrum of African Americans. See George Houser, *No One Can Stop the Rain: Glimpses of Africa's Liberation Struggle* (New York: Pilgrim Press, 1989), pp. 69–73. For a Padmore obituary, see "Internationally Known Scribe George Padmore Dies in London," *Pittsburgh Courier,* October, 3, 1959, p. 9.

98. "Ghana in the United Nations," *Chicago Defender,* March 23, 1957.

99. "Will Ghana Accept Russian Aid?" *Pittsburgh Courier,* December 7, 1957, p. 2.

100. Payne, "Ghana—Its Independence Has Great Impact In Africa."

101. "Aid for Africa," *Pittsburgh Courier,* March 30, 1957; "Who Gets African Posts?" *Pittsburgh Courier,* March 23, 1957.

102. "Investment Opportunities: American Team of Business Experts Issues Report on Ghana's Economy," *Pittsburgh Courier,* March 9, 1957, p. 22; Marguerite Cartwright, "Nigeria" (third in a series), *Pittsburgh Courier,* March 30, 1957, p. 3.

103. "African Nationalism and U.S. Policy," *Chicago Defender,* April 6, 1957.

104. Albert G. Barnett, "Ghanians Ignore Politics, Concentrate on Raising Their Economic Level," *Chicago Defender,* October 26, 1957.

105. "Ghana's Independence, Africa's Biggest Event," *Chicago Defender,* February 16, 1957, p. 3; "Textile Mill Opens New Industry in West Africa," *Chicago Defender,* December 21, 1957, p. 4; "Future Bright for Gold Coast," *Chicago Defender,* January 5, 1957, p. 10.

106. See Robert G. Weisbord, *Ebony Kinship: Africa, Africans, and the Afro-American* (Westport, Conn: Greenwood Press, 1973), chap. 6, "Afro-America's African Renaissance"; Bernard Makhosezwe Magubane, *The Ties That Bind: African-American Consciousness of Africa* (Trenton, N.J.: Africa World Press, 1987), chap. 8, "Afro-American Response to Africa's Independence." See also St. Clair Drake's introduction to Hollis R. Lynch, *Black American Radicals and the Liberation of Africa: The Council on African Affairs, 1937–1955* (Ithaca: Africana Studies and Research Center, Cornell University, 1978), pp. 10–12, on the differences between the CAA and African American organizations interested in Africa that arose in the 1950s and 1960s.

107. Two days before Ghana's independence ceremonies, Nkrumah wrote to Du Bois that "it was a great and bitter disappointment to us all here that you were prevented from being here during our independence ceremonies": Nkrumah to Du Bois, April 4, 1957, Du Bois Papers, reel 72, frame 592. See also Du Bois to Immanuel Wallerstein, May 3, 1961, reel 75, frame 724.

108. Alex Rivera, "M. L. King Meets Nixon in Ghana," *Pittsburgh Courier,* March 16, 1957, p. 2; Branch, *Parting the Waters,* p. 214.

109. Payne, "World's Notables See Ghana Become Nation," *Chicago Defender,* March 9, 1957, p. 1.

110. "U.S. and Africa: Here's What Nixon Feels U.S. Should Do for Africa He Saw," *Chicago Defender,* March 30, 1957, p. 2.

111. "Sees Link between U.S. Race Relations and Africa," *Chicago Defender,* March 23, 1957, p. 2; Ethyl L. Payne, "Nixon Calls Bias Peril to U.S.; Lauds Africa," *Chicago Defender,* April 12, 1957, p. 13.

112. Duberman, *Paul Robeson,* p. 463.

113. Manning Marable, *W. E. B. Du Bois: Black Radical Democrat* (Boston: Twayne, 1986), p. 203; Anthony M. Platt, *E. Franklin Frazier Reconsidered* (New Brunswick, N.J.: Rutgers University Press, 1991), pp. 198–99. Platt notes that while Frazier, a member of the CAA since 1941 and a consistent ally of Robeson and Du Bois, did not, like Du Bois, leave the United States or join the CP, "he expressed his solidarity with Du Bois's 'example of courage' and with Nkrumah's revolutionary nationalism by bequeathing his vast library to Ghana."

114. Marable, *W. E. B. Du Bois,* p. 213.

115. Rowan, "Has Paul Robeson Betrayed the Negro?" p. 41.
116. Certainly Harold Cruse's influential 1967 *Crisis of the Negro Intellectual: A Historical Analysis of the Failure of Black Leadership* (New York: Quill, 1984), portraying Robeson as an integrationist duped by the Communists, did much to contribute to his continuing obscurity.
117. Duberman, *Paul Robeson,* pp. 446–47, 534.
118. Author's interview with Ray Simons, March 18, 1992, Cape Town (the South African historians and activists Ray and Jack Simons were in Zambia with the Huntons); Dorothy Hunton, *Alphaeus Hunton: The Unsung Valiant* (Chesapeake, Va.: ECA Associates, 1986), pp. 163–77. On Hunton's years in Ghana, see also June Milne, ed., *Kwame Nkrumah, the Conakry Years: His Life and Letters* (London: Panaf, 1990), pp. 93, 167, 235, 359–60, 364.
119. See the tribute to Hunton in *Freedomways,* 3d quarter 1970, including Doxey A. Wilkerson, "William Alphaeus Hunton: A Life That Made a Difference," pp. 254–57; George B. Murphy Jr., "William Alphaeus Hunton: His Roots in Black America," pp. 249–52; and a selection of Hunton's writings on Africa.

Conclusion

1. See, as examples, "President Sekou Toure of Guinea," *Chicago Defender,* November 21, 1959; "Toure Blames UN for the Chaos in the Congo," *Chicago Defender,* October 22–28, 1960, p. 12; "Toure Claims Snub by Ike," *Pittsburgh Courier,* May 16, 1959, p. 4; "Lumumba's Still in Congo Saddle with Strong Horses," *Pittsburgh Courier,* September 17, 1960; "Group Denounces U.S. Race Stand in Africa," *Chicago Defender,* December 31, 1960–January 6, 1961.
2. William Blum, *Killing Hope: U.S. Military and CIA Intervention Since World War II* (Monroe, Maine: Common Courage Press, 1995), pp. 156–62.
3. Jan Carew, *Ghosts in Our Blood: With Malcolm X in Africa, England, and the Caribbean* (Chicago: Lawrence Hill Books, 1994); *Malcolm X Speaks: Selected Speeches and Statements,* ed. George Breitman (New York: Merit, 1965).
4. Quoted in Taylor Branch, *Parting the Waters: America in the King Years, 1954–1963* (New York: Simon & Schuster, 1988), p. 791. See Mary L. Dudziak, "Desegregation as a Cold War Imperative," *Stanford Law Review* 41, no. 61 (November 1988): 61–120, for an analysis of the role of foreign policy concerns in *Brown v. Board of Education.*
5. Quoted in Harold R. Isaacs, *The New World of Negro Americans: The Impact of World Affairs on the Race Problem in the United States and Particularly on the Negro, His View of Himself, His Country, and of Africa* (Cambridge: MIT Press, 1963), p. 228.
6. Clayborne Carson, *Malcolm X: The FBI File* (New York: One World Books, 1991); David Garrow, *The FBI and Martin Luther King, Jr.: From 'Solo' to Memphis* (New York: Norton, 1981); Ward Churchill and Jim Vander Wall, *The COINTELPRO Papers: Documents from the FBI's Secret War against Domestic Dissent* (Boston: South End Press, 1990).
7. Blum, *Killing Hope,* pp. 156–62, 249–62, 370–83; Henry F. Jackson, *From the Congo to Soweto: U.S. Foreign Policy toward Africa since 1960* (New York: William Morrow, 1982).
8. Tribute to Du Bois by Martin Luther King Jr., in *W. E. B. Du Bois Speaks: Speeches and Addresses, 1890–1919,* ed. Philip Foner (New York: Pathfinder Press, 1970), pp. 14, 19.

INDEX

Bethune, Mary McLeod (*cont.*)
    and Haiti, 163; and Liberia, 165; and
    women's leadership, 79
Bibb, Joseph D., 147
Bishop, Maurice, 187
black troops: and anticolonialism, 32–34; and
    Jim Crow, 33–35; violence against, 96–97,
    110–11
Bloom, Hyman, 128
Bokwe, R. T., 66, 88, 137
Bolden, Frank E., 162
Bond, Horace Mann, 174, 176, 181
Bowman, Isaiah, 82
Briggs, Cyril, 10
Brockway, Fenner, 139–40
Brooks, Denton J., 31, 32, 38
Browder, Earl, 74
Brown, Ethelred, 76
Brownell, Herbert Jr., 135–36, 141–42
Buchman, Frank N. D., 161
Buell, Raymond L., 19
Bunche, Ralph, 17–19, 41, 55, 76–77, 155, 181
Burgum, Edwin Berry, 59
Bustamante, Alexander, 48
Byrnes, James, 66, 83, 97, 100

Cachalia, Maulvi, 172
campaigns for jobs and housing, 44, 47, 54, 69,
    96, 149
Caribbean: impact of World War II, 24, 36–39;
    labor relations, 7, 14–15, 47–48, 57
Carter, Michael, 67
Cayton, Horace R., 26, 40, 152, 157, 166, 179
Central Intelligence Agency, 114, 175
Chandrasekhar, S., 32
Chiang Kai-shek, 30, 106
Chicago Defender, 8, 74, 87, 118–20, 157–59
Childs, A. W., 130
Choudree, Ashwin, 93
Chou En-lai, 169–70, 173
Churchill, Winston, 62, 69, 88, 101, 104; and At-
    lantic Charter, 7, 25–28; Iron Curtain speech,
    97–100; lobbied by Walter White, 42
Citizenship: and anticolonial, antidiscrimina-
    tion strategies, 63, 69, 78–79, 186; contest
    over meanings of, 4; redefined during Cold
    War, 151–52; and United Nations, 78–79
Civil rights: and anticolonialism, 2, 5, 30–31,
    33–34, 40–41, 69–70, 74–85; and anti-Com-
    munism, 109–14, 120–21, 126, 186
Clark, Thomas C., 115

Cold War: challenges to, 168–73; and civil
    rights argument, 3, 109–14, 126, 146–49,
    153–58; and destruction of anticolonial al-
    liances, 3, 96–121, 134–44; and U.S. re-
    sponses to Asian and African nationalism,
    124–33
Communist Party, USA: and CAA, 20–21, 53,
    139–40; and Pan-Africanism, 9–10, 139–40
Congress for Cultural Freedom, 175
Congress of Colored Writers and Artists, Paris
    (1956), 167, 174–76
Congress of Industrial Organizations (CIO),
    47–50, 52–53, 60, 114
Congress of Racial Equality (CORE), 155
Council for Non-European Trade Unions
    (CNETU), 63
Council on African Affairs (CAA): African sup-
    port work, 122, 137–43, 154; analysis of post-
    war economic prospects, 71–72; anticolonial
    strategies, 73–74, 76, 83–84; and Bandung
    Conference, 171–73; Big Three Unity Rally,
    103–4; and black leadership, 20; and
    Churchill's Iron Curtain speech, 97, 100;
    Ciskei famine relief campaign, 65–68; dis-
    banding of, 142–43; founding of, 17–21; gov-
    ernment prosecution of, 1, 6, 115–16,
    123–24, 134–37, 141–43; and Indian chal-
    lenge to British rule, 28–30; and labor, 48, 52;
    lobbying U.S. government, 63–64, 69, 71–74,
    86–87, 98; and Nigerian strike, 55; 1948 split
    in organization,115–17; and Pan-African
    Federation, 53; and protests to the Union of
    South Africa, 63–64; relationship to Commu-
    nist Party, 20, 53, 139–40; reorganization of,
    60–61; shift to militant diaspora conscious-
    ness, 20; South African mine worker support
    campaign, 61–64; and United Nations,
    69–70, 80, 83–96; and Henry Wallace cam-
    paign, 113–14
Crisis, 8–9, 42–43
Crummell, Alexander, 9
Cullen, Countee, 74

Dana, Peter, 31
Davis, John A., 174
Davis, John P., 59–60
Delany, Hubert T., 18, 66, 116
Delany, Martin R., 9, 58, 79
democracy: anticolonialism as precondition for,
    2, 11, 22–23, 30–31, 40, 43, 99, 104; contests
    over meanings of, 4